Chinese Immigration

Also from Westphalia Press
westphaliapress.org

The Idea of the Digital University

Masonic Tombstones and Masonic Secrets

Eight Decades in Syria

Avant-Garde Politician

L'Enfant and the Freemasons

Baronial Bedrooms

Conflicts in Health Policy

Material History and Ritual Objects

Paddle Your Own Canoe

Opportunity and Horatio Alger

Careers in the Face of Challenge

Bookplates of the Kings

Collecting American Presidential Autographs

Misunderstood Children

Original Cables from the Pearl Harbor Attack

Social Satire and the Modern Novel

The Amenities of Book Collecting

The Genius of Freemasonry

A Definitive Commentary on Bookplates

James Martineau and Rebuilding Theology

No Bird Lacks Feathers

The Young Vigilantes

The Man Who Killed President Garfield

Anti-Masonry and the Murder of Morgan

Understanding Art

Homeopathy

Ancient Masonic Mysteries

Collecting Old Books

The Boy Chums Cruising in Florida Waters

The Thomas Starr King Dispute

Ivanhoe Masonic Quartettes

Lariats and Lassos

Mr. Garfield of Ohio

The Wisdom of Thomas Starr King

The French Foreign Legion

War in Syria

Naturism Comes to the United States

New Sources on Women and Freemasonry

Designing, Adapting, Strategizing in Online Education

Gunboat and Gun-runner

Meeting Minutes of Naval Lodge No. 4 F.A.A.M

Chinese Immigration
Turn of the Century Views

by Mary Roberts Coolidge, Ph.D.

WESTPHALIA PRESS
An imprint of Policy Studies Organization

Chinese Immigration: Turn of the Century Views
All Rights Reserved © 2015 by Policy Studies Organization

Westphalia Press
An imprint of Policy Studies Organization
1527 New Hampshire Ave., NW
Washington, D.C. 20036
info@ipsonet.org

ISBN-13: 978-1-63391-229-8
ISBN-10: 1633912299

Cover design by Taillefer Long at Illuminated Stories:
www.illuminatedstories.com

Daniel Gutierrez-Sandoval, Executive Director
PSO and Westphalia Press

Updated material and comments on this edition
can be found at the Westphalia Press website:
www.westphaliapress.org

American Public Problems

CHINESE IMMIGRATION

BY
MARY ROBERTS COOLIDGE, Ph.D.
Formerly Associate Professor of Sociology, Stanford University

> "Abide here all the rest of you, my dear companions; I will go with mine own ship and my ship's company, and make proof of these men, what manner of folk they are, whether froward, and wild and unjust, or hospitable and of a god-fearing mind."
> —The Odyssey, Book II.

TO MY FATHER
Isaac Phillips Roberts,
PROFESSOR EMERITUS,
FOR THIRTY YEARS PROFESSOR AND DEAN
OF THE COLLEGE OF AGRICULTURE,
CORNELL UNIVERSITY

PREFACE

THIS study was begun during the excitement incident to the passage and enforcement of the Geary law in 1892 and 1893; continued as part of a course in Race Problems given at Stanford University; and completed with the assistance of the Carnegie Institution of Washington. The historical portion ends with the fire of April eighteenth, 1906, in which the Chinese quarter and most of the city libraries in San Francisco were destroyed. It now appears that this date also marked the close of a natural historical period; for since that time important changes have been made both in the regulations and the official personnel of the Chinese immigration and consular service, which may result in even more important modifications of policy.

In the original plan a chapter on the Chinese in other Pacific states was contemplated, but since, up to 1882, over 70 per cent. of the Chinese were in California, it was thought best for the sake of space to omit it. However, many of the illustrations in the chapters on administration, competition and assimilation, have been drawn from this unused material and it is believed that no factor essential to a just presentation of the subject has been neglected.

It is a difficult matter to acknowledge obligations when one is indebted to hundreds of individuals, all of whom cannot be mentioned. Yet out of many I must formally name, Colonel John P. Irish, Naval Officer of Customs at San Francisco, and Mr. Ng Poon Chew, Editor of *Chung Sai Yat Po,* who have read the manuscript critically; Mr. Max J. Kohler of New York City, Mr. Oliver P. Stidger of San Francisco and Mr. F. H. Lysons of Seattle,

Washington, who have contributed legal information on the operation of the exclusion laws; President Kendric C. Babcock of the University of Arizona, Professor John C. Fryer and Professor Carl C. Plehn of the University of California. But to Professor Walter F. Willcox of Cornell University and to the Honorable Chester Holcombe, formerly Secretary of Legation at Peking, I have been under constant obligation, not only for critical, scholarly assistance but for the friendly encouragement which it is the joy of such scholars to bestow. Nor can I omit a word of thanks to those many nameless Chinamen whose courtesy has made it possible for a foreigner and a woman to understand and reproduce something of their life in this country.

DWIGHT WAY END,
   BERKELEY, CALIFORNIA,
      August, 1909.

CONTENTS

PART I

FREE IMMIGRATION, 1848-1882

CHAPTER	PAGE
INTRODUCTION—THE CHINAMAN AT HOME	3
I. THE PERIOD OF FAVOR	15
II. CALIFORNIA FOR AMERICANS	26
III. THE COOLIE FICTION	41
IV. THE DEVELOPMENT OF ANTI-CHINESE POLITICS	55
V. ANTI-CHINESE LEGISLATION IN CALIFORNIA	69
VI. THE CALIFORNIA SENATE ADDRESS AND MEMORIAL	83
VII. THE CONGRESSIONAL COMMITTEE ON CHINESE IMMIGRATION	96
VIII. THE CHINESE MUST GO	109
IX. THE CHINESE QUESTION IN CONGRESS	127

PART II

RESTRICTION AND EXCLUSION

X. TREATY RELATIONS BEFORE 1882	145
XI. THE RESTRICTION LAW OF 1882	168
XII. THE SCOTT ACT AND THE ABORTIVE TREATY OF 1888	183
XIII. THE GEARY LAW AND THE MCCREARY AMENDMENT	209
XIV. THE BEGINNING OF REACTION	234
XV. THE TREATMENT OF THE CHINESE IN THE UNITED STATES	254
XVI. THE CHINESE PROTEST	278
XVII. THE ADMINISTRATION OF THE CHINESE EXCLUSION LAWS	302

PART III

COMPETITION AND ASSIMILATION

CHAPTER	PAGE
XVIII. Labor in California Before the Kearney Period.	337
XIX. The Chinese in Manufacture	357
XX. Labor and Chinese Competition	378
XXI. The Chinese in San Francisco	401
XXII. The Menace of Numbers and Non-Assimilation	423
XXIII. The Effect of Unfriendly Exclusion upon China.	459
XXIV. Conclusion	486

APPENDIX

Statistical Tables	497
Selected Bibliography	505
Index	519

PART I
FREE IMMIGRATION, 1848-1882

INTRODUCTION [1]

THE CHINAMAN AT HOME

For half a century the curious customs and behavior of the Chinese in this country have been a mystery, subject to many explanations, distorted by ignorance and colored by prejudice, and never fully understood. Half a century ago China was an unknown country, the Chinese a strange, weird, incredible people; but with the opening of Chinese ports to the establishment of international relations, and the publication of a mass of information acquired by missionaries and travelers, the "dummy" Chinaman of 1850 has gradually become human to the western imagination, and it is discovered to the world's astonishment that he behaves much as other men do.

Yet in the average mind, the traditional Chinaman—a left-handed, cunning, industrious, stolid, cruel and inhuman creature—is still the typical Chinaman, in spite of a long acquaintance which has proved him as human as ourselves. But, fully to understand the Chinese in the United States, it is necessary to know the immigrant Chinaman as he was at home.

In China, there is no caste as there is India, nor feudal classes as there were formerly in Japan, but, instead, a division of classes by occupations which is not to any great extent dependent on birth. The classes are rated

[1] This section relating to the Chinese in China, is the briefest possible digest of recent authorities on Chinese life and Characteristics with reference to the traits which they have shown in this country. The principal authorities used are: Williams, *The Middle Kingdom*; Smith, *Chinese Characteristics* and *Village Life in China*; Colquhoun, *China in Transformation*; Medhurst, *The Chinese as Colonists* in the Nineteenth Century, vol. 4; and most valuable of all for this purpose, Holcombe's *Real Chinaman*.

3

in the following order: scholars, farmers, laborers, but even a laborer may by his own exertions and by the sacrifices of his family, become a scholar and a high official. Holcombe says that every boy in the Empire is a possible prime minister, that China is second only to the United States in its opportunities for a poor man to become distinguished.

The bulk of the population in China is engaged in agriculture and fisheries—and these classes, as producers, are more highly valued than manufacturers and merchants—but only small farmers, laborers and merchants have emigrated in any considerable numbers. Laborers —coolies—formerly went under contract to Cuba and South America; the merchants in small numbers have gone over the whole world; but the greater part of the emigration to British Columbia, Australia and the United States, has been from the small farmer class. The very poorest of these immigrants lived in a one-story house, seldom of more than one room, in a village alley, and obtained the money to come to California by borrowing from his relatives or from a passage broker. But the better portion came from the small farms on which their families had lived for generations, and were sent to America to make the fortune of the family, just as other sons might be destined for the literary examinations and official life at home.

The young farmer-emigrant had not lived in isolation as farmers do in this country but in a village composed of his relations and connections. In such a village the family, not the individual, was the unit of society; groups of families made up the villages, groups of towns and villages the districts, and several districts, the province. The villages are self-governing, having the right to elect their own headmen, who are the links with the officials of the superior governments appointed by the Emperor. In local affairs the villagers are most democratic and independent; but in public affairs as we conceive them, they have no share. If the Chinese government be regarded from the top, it appears to be a centralized autocracy; if from the bottom, a pure democracy. While self-government is characteristic of the village, the general control is a form of paternalism which has grown out of the patriarchal family. Officials have large discretionary powers and often consult the wishes of their people, for the test of competence in a governor is that his people shall be contented. The right of appeal, though hedged about with strict etiquette, is not infrequently exercised by the community, and invariably discredits an official, sometimes to the extent of causing his removal. The greatest freedom of speech prevails and popular discontent is expressed by means of anonymous placards denouncing unpopular measures and men. Williams declares that the Chinese race has perhaps risen as high as is possible in the two great objects of human government—security of life and property to the governed, and freedom of action under the individual restraints of the law.

The Chinese village farmer, having the fundamental rights—possession of land, freedom of trade and industry, local self-government, appeal against official misgovernment, and the opportunity to rise to any social or political station—is remarkably free from political interference. In some respects he is accustomed to a greater degree of actual civic freedom than the similar class in the United States. Whatever tyranny he suffers is due to the excessive discipline of family and social custom, a social rather than a political despotism. Even in such a matter as taxation, the Chinese village pays what it has been accustomed to pay and refuses to pay much above that. The sum will be the actual taxes plus the "squeeze," that is, the additional amount added by each official for his own benefit and that of his superiors. This system of "farming out" the taxes is bad—as bad as possible—and yet works better in China than elsewhere because of the independent character of the villagers. Nobody expects an official to live on his salary from the government; the villagers recognize his right to a living salary and so long as the official does not raise the tax beyond the rate established in part by custom, in part by the consensus of the villagers themselves, his people will contentedly pay it.

The government may deal arbitrarily with individuals, but it places no unnecessary and vexatious restrictions upon the masses of the people. To the Western mind the thing most difficult to comprehend is the number of things the government does not do and with which the individual appears to have no concern. All land belongs to the people and is minutely subdivided among families, even the land which in any western country would be appropriated to streets, parks, reserves and other public purposes. No such thing as a public right of way, in the occidental sense, exists; and the villagers have no idea that it is their business to improve the streets, lay sewers, provide a common water supply, organize a police, a fire department or a park system. If a bridge, a railway, or a public building is to be built the government officials may take over the family rights involved and do the work, but no family or village would dream of agitating or promoting such an improvement.

This lack of public spirit is incomprehensible to the foreigner and seems not only to produce friction and discomfort but to be the chief check upon progress. But just because the family is the social unit and no individual controls or owns anything wholly, the villages need no police and almost no governmental machinery. "In point of fact," says Holcombe, "the Chinese are governed less than almost any nation in the world. So long as they pay their taxes and violate none of the requirements of the moral code, they are not disturbed by the authorities. A thousand and one official inspections,

The Chinaman at Home

exactions and interferences, common enough everywhere in America and Europe, are quite unknown in China."

Leaving out of consideration the appointment of higher officials by the Emperor, there is a remarkable similarity between the workings of the governmental system in China and in the United States. The result is a general spirit of democracy among the Chinese very puzzling to those accustomed to the tradition that China is a despotism and the Chinese, slaves. Even more incomprehensible in the light of a democratic spirit so like our own, is the total lack of what we call patriotism—loyalty to the country and its principles as a whole. Its place is taken by what Colquhoun calls the "village spirit," a clannishness composed of race loyalty and true piety,—a devotion to family and locality which makes it difficult for the Chinaman ever to feel at home anywhere else in the world. The development of national feeling has been greatly retarded by the immense variety of dialects and the slow and inadequate methods of travel and communication.

Nevertheless, within their own limited sphere of sympathies the Chinese people are wonderfully organized: secret societies serve the purpose of political agitation and social reform; trade-guilds control industrial activity, the family rule provides for morals and religion. No Chinaman acts alone; always he expects to act and live subject to the limitation and coöperation of his family, his village relations, his society and his guild. As a citizen he has great freedom; as an individual he is entangled in a thousand customs, rules and relations which, though voluntary, he regards as absolutely binding.

Relying for protection on this network of relations the villager expects to settle all minor difficulties by arbitration and rarely goes to law, except under extreme provocation. The Chinese code of law is wise, moderate and humane, and their legal procedure is simple and just, with the exception of certain methods of torture used until recently to coerce witnesses. There are no juries and no lawyers, the judges deciding all cases by the obvious intention of the parties and by precedent. This gives occupation to a class of searchers who are open to bribery and who often levy blackmail on the contestants. An oath is seldom administered and never relied upon, for the Chinese act upon the theory that if a man will lie no oath will make him truthful. As formerly in England, prisons are merely places of detention, not of punishment; and the punishments consist of fines, the stocks, the bastinado and execution. In short, the administration of law, like everything else in China, is based upon the patriarchal idea. The Judge, like the Viceroy, is a discretionary father to his people; but unlike the patriarchs of other lands, he may be disavowed by his people and removed by the Emperor, if the people complain too much of his rule.

The business man in China rarely goes to law, but defends himself against fraud by dealing with people of known probity and by exacting bargain money rather than a written contract. The debts of an individual are an obligation upon his family and kindred, and thus the family solidarity gives security in business and property relations as it does in public order.

As to morals, the Chinese have an almost ideal standard; but, like their Christian neighbors, they fall far short of it in practice. Their high integrity in financial transactions is contrasted with as great a degree of unreliability in speech, which produces an extraordinary inconsistency of behavior. Every Chinaman pays his debts once a year at least, and the suicide of a man who is unable to meet his obligations is not uncommon.

Indeed, among the trading and mercantile classes there is probably more honor than is to be found among similar classes in any other country, and Chinese laboring men

The Chinaman at Home

are certainly not less reliable than others of their kind in other parts of the world.

Yet the Chinese appear to be indifferent to truth as such. A lie is no disgrace; it is only disgraceful not to put a good face upon things. Lying is regarded as a necessary talent in business operations and an essential of good breeding. Smith says that they are by far the most truthful of all Asiatic peoples, and yet that disingenuousness is to them second nature. The arbitrary power vested in the higher officials appears to render falsehood necessary on the part of the people in order to escape oppressive burdens and punishments; while the necessity that all officials are under of getting as much "squeeze" as possible invites peculation. Minister Low wrote to Secretary Fish in 1871 that he was "inclined to doubt the efficacy of Christianity when exposed to the temptations that Chinese officials are." The result of this untruthfulness is mutual distrust; nobody trusts anybody else for the excellent reason that he is aware that in similar circumstances it might not be safe to trust himself.

As to vices, the Chinese differ in kind rather than in degree from the rest of the civilized world. The opium habit, notwithstanding its expense, prevails among the poor as well as the rich, but it is difficult to say to what extent. Among Caucasians the taking of opium is the synonym of ruin; but if we should judge of the extent of the use of opium by the number of Chinese who are incapacitated by it, it would certainly be very small. The immigrant farmers and laborers that are found in the United States have as a class none of the characteristic symptoms of the habitual opium taker. Either they use opium in moderation, much as the American uses tobacco, or they are less affected by it than Caucasians are. In some parts of China alcoholic stimulants are used freely by all classes but drunkenness is almost unknown.

Sexual morality in the villages is very high, prostitution and illegitimacy occurring only rarely. The restraints upon women, the very early and almost universal marriage, the strength of the family ties and, among the middle and higher classes, the system of concubinage, all combine to produce a very high standard of moral restraint. Prostitution exists in all the cities and especially in the river and sea-board towns where single men congregate, but its extent is small as compared with the great cities of Europe and America. Married women are universally chaste, but as wives always remain at home to care for the husbands' parents, married men when traveling live much as men of western nations do. Marriage is regarded as a duty, not based on affection or undertaken for the sake of happiness, though affection and happiness often follow. But the wife who bears a son is highly respected, and if she is not the fortunate mother of sons she expects that her husband will take a second wife. Concubinage is very uncommon among the poorer classes but, when resorted to, the children of the second wife are legitimate. Arthur Smith declares that "Chinese morality at its best is fully equal to that of any western land;" and if other modern writers may be believed, he might have said with truth, that at its worst, it is no worse.

Divorce is rare and desertion by the husband still more so; indeed, the strength of the family tie is beyond anything western civilization can show. The responsibility of members of the family for each other to remote degrees, the sacrifices and obligations which they will undertake, the kindness of men to their wives and the extravagant pride and affection which they have for their children, forms a striking contrast to the narrow limits of the family and the looseness of the ties in Occidental nations.

The treatment of women is the darkest blot upon the civilization of China. Daughters are unwelcome in the family because, when married, they are lost by absorp-

The Chinaman at Home

tion into the husband's family. The young wife is subordinate to her mother-in-law and, until she bears a son, is of slight account except as a servant. As the mother of sons alone can she rise to anything like individuality. For this reason infanticide of female children prevails to some extent. The more recent writers agree that reports of it have been exaggerated because of the curious custom of exposing the dying, and they report it to be more common in southern than in northern China.

The enormous extent and the predominance of the Chinese Empire in the Orient and the isolation of its population for many centuries has bred an extraordinary and—to the Westerner—insufferable pride in the behavior of the Chinese toward foreigners. The less they know of foreigners, the more contempt and the less curiosity they have; and although in proportion as they come in contact with Western peoples these qualities may vary in degree, the Chinaman never loses his pride of nationality. The Chinese lay so much more stress upon etiquette and politeness than any Western people that the mere superficial coarseness of newer civilizations has intensified their sense of superiority. Good breeding among them demands a dignified impassivity in social intercourse, but the inference that they are stolid is entirely erroneous. All foreigners who have intimate knowledge of them testify to their extreme sensitiveness of feeling, especially in personal matters; to their capacity for cruelty and revenge when they are injured, and an equal capacity for loyalty and generosity when they are well-treated. Owing to the distinctly agricultural character of the population, and to ages of predominance in the international relations of Asia, the Chinese have had no occasion to emphasize military life. They still regard military men with much the same dislike as they do pugilists and butchers. Among themselves minor difficulties are settled by arbitration and although independent and determined in maintaining their rights, they are nevertheless cautious, conservative and accommodating. Their universal habit of settling disputes by discussion and mutual concession results in an unusual degree of toleration and patience in religion, in politics, and in all the ordinary frictions of life. In spite of hardships and in spite of occasional outbursts of violent temper to which they are liable, the Chinese are an unusually happy-natured, contented and even-tempered people.

Schools, supported by subscription fees, abound in China and public sentiment in favor of education is universal. Even the lowest classes have a limited knowledge of the written characters in daily use. Students, who become the government officials, come from the middle classes chiefly and furnish a striking proof of the high average of intellectual ability possessed by the race.

The most conspicuous characteristic of the Chinese is their industry; indeed, the Chinese have almost a passion for labor. And this is true not only of workingmen but of all classes, including even the high government officials. The common laborer combines with this habitual industry patience, docility, accuracy, and temperance. Though he lacks inventiveness and initiative, he has remarkable powers of imitation. He will take low wages and contrive always to live within them; but never any lower than is necessary to keep in work, and at the first opportunity he will demand higher. In fact, he is remarkably keen in bargaining for his labor and always ambitious to rise from the laboring or " coolie " class into the farming or merchant class.

The industrial adaptability of the Chinese laborer is greater than that of the European peasant; although chiefly engaged at home in farming, fishing and rude labor, the Chinese immigrants to the United States have become laundrymen, cooks, miners, operatives and merchants with almost incredible facility. Intense competition and a strongly democratic spirit long ago produced a highly organized guild system whose aims

The Chinaman at Home

correspond quite closely to those of western trade unions and whose regulations are even more stringent. The control of these guilds over the minutest subdivisions of trades enables them to distribute workmen to the best markets, to hold up wages, to coerce employers and to adapt themselves to industrial changes. The members of a guild are bound to help each other in case of sickness, accident or death, and to prevent "scabs" from coming into the business.

These conspicuous characteristics of the common people of China scarcely suffice as an outline of so thorough-bred, varied and complex a nation. Many other peculiarities overlay the picture and make it almost impossible to fathom their motives and conduct. Their gregarious habits of life, the absence of privacy and the prevalence of a noisy hubbub; the habit of bodily cleanliness and the lack of any sanitary system; extreme poverty and yet universal—almost humorous—cheerfulness; their superior mental ability combined with the crudest forms of superstition; a universal habit of lying and yet a national habit of paying their debts; an extreme love of gambling and theatrical amusements combined with the highest capacity for industry of any people in the world—all these have produced a race truly most complicated and wonderful and yet, as exhibited in the individual, most humanly contradictory.

Though the Chinaman, when measured by the more elastic standards of the West, may be difficult to understand in his native country, yet it should be easy to guess what he would do when transplanted to foreign soil. Being a thorough-bred he will remain true to his type much longer than the mixed European peasantry and his greater social prepotency would inevitably make him seem incapable of change. He would try to reproduce the village government and the system of arbitration, and would have little use for Courts of Law; he would expect to pay the squeeze in addition to his taxes; he might have no use for plumbing and yet be as cleanly as ever in person; he would leave his wife in China for a lifetime and yet support her and his parents and children faithfully and return at last to lay his bones in his native soil; he could gamble and smoke opium and yet be industrious and temperate while at work; he might be a decent, law-abiding fellow and yet pay his regular blackmail to the hatchet societies and the city police in order to avoid trouble; he might refuse to strike for more wages and an eight-hour day along with the Irishman and the Swede and yet he would at the same time be a member of a union far more highly organized than theirs. In short, he would still be democratic and docile, cunning and loyal, deceitful and honorable, superstitious and intelligent, law-abiding and self-governing, clean and dirty, good and bad, all at the same time just as he had always been—and as the rest of the world's inhabitants are. But being ambitious and having a certain intellectual keenness he would weigh our American habits and character, our government and society, against his own and with the in-born pride of an older race his conservatism would at first declare it all unworthy of imitation. Nevertheless, as the years spent here compelled him to a certain readjustment he might change a very little and if he went back to China he might—like other immigrants—see it with other eyes and, reasoning, from that moment he would begin to be assimilated.

CHAPTER I

THE PERIOD OF FAVOR

" The marvellous exodus of the Chinese from their country is one of the most remarkable ethnological circumstances in modern history and is producing and will produce extraordinary and lasting results."—SIR JOHN BOWRING, British Consul, Plenipotentiary, Governor of Hong Kong, 1847-1860.

" When the Emperor rules over so many millions, what does he care for the few waifs that have drifted away to a foreign land? The Emperor's wealth is beyond computation; why should he care for those of his subjects who have left their home or for the sands they have scraped together?"—CHINESE VICEROY to CAPTAIN DUPONT, 1858.

" Quite a large number of the Celestials have arrived among us of late, enticed thither by the golden romance that has filled the world. Scarcely a ship arrives that does not bring an increase to this worthy integer of our population. The China boys will yet vote at the same polls, study at the same schools and bow at the same altar as our own countrymen."
—*Daily Alta California*, May 12, 1852.

ALTHOUGH regarded as a menace to Western civilization and subjected to discriminating legislation by the United States, the Chinese are not, as compared with European peoples, an emigrating nation. The inhabitants of the two southeastern provinces of China— Kwang Tung and Fuh Kien—have, it is true, always been somewhat more adventurous and more ambitious to better their economic condition than their inland countrymen, and from an early period have emigrated in small numbers to Cochin China, Cambodia and Siam, the islands of the Indian Archipelago, Java, the Philippines and the Malayan peninsula, Formosa and Hainan.[1] But in spite of a dense population and great poverty the united restraints of law, religion and family ties hold them to the land of their birth; and only the greatest stress of war

[1] Poole. *Life of Parkes*, v. 1, pp. 177, 318. Boulger, *Hist. of China*, v. 8, p. 316. Williams, *Social Sci. Assoc.*, 1879, pp. 6-7.

and devastation at home, coincident with the lure of gold and marvelous industrial opportunity in California, served to uproot the three hundred thousand who came to the Pacific Coast during thirty-three years of free immigration.

Chinese emigrants were, indeed, regarded by their conservative countrymen as rash or desperate; and their departure was long ignored by the Imperial Government either because the officials were preoccupied with civil rebellions and with struggles against foreign powers or, perhaps, because of its relative insignificance.[2] Their exile was, nominally at least, temporary, for the laws of the Empire forbade expatriation, and in the earlier centuries the punishment of disobedience was death.[3] But contact with their immediate neighbors in the seventeenth and eighteenth centuries, and with Western nations in the early nineteenth century, modified this policy so that the law had become a dead letter when they began to emigrate to the Pacific Coast. Yet even at this late time, pride of country, strong sectional sympathies and family ties prevented the peasantry from coming in large numbers, while social prejudices almost wholly checked the emigration of the upper classes and of women.[4]

The first effective contact of China with Western nations was through the Opium War of 1840, which resulted in an increase of Chinese taxes, a general disturbance of the laboring classes, and the penetration of some slight knowledge of European ideas into the maritime provinces.[5] Although this prepared the way for the emigration to the West, its precipitating cause lay in " the Golden Romance " that had filled the world. The news

---

[2] Martin, *Cycle of Cathay*, p. 160.
[3] Chinese *Repository*, v. 2, p. 101 (July, 1853).
[4] Williams, *Soc. Sci. Assoc.*, 1879; *Middle Kingdom*, v. 2, p. 278. Poole, *Life of Parkes*, v. 1, p. 176. Boulger, *Hist. of China*, v. 2, 318. *Parl. Rept.*, Parkes to Bowring, Oct. 1, 1852.
[5] Williams, *Soc. Sci. Assoc.*, 1879, p. 7. *Blackwood's*, v. 72, p. 101-2, (1852).

of the discovery of gold in the Sacramento Valley in January, 1848, reached Hong Kong in the spring and created much excitement there as well as at the seaports on the Atlantic ocean.[6] There began at once to be a demand for ready-made clothing, goods and provisions and houses shipped in frame, all of which could be obtained from Hong Kong and Honolulu more quickly than from the eastern United States.[7] The news of the high wages paid to laborers spread gradually among the farming peasantry about Canton and drew them to the Coast quite as effectively as the tales of golden marvels.

Masters of foreign vessels afforded every facility to emigration, distributing placards, maps and pamphlets with highly colored accounts of the Golden Hills, and reaping enormous profits as the demand for passages and freight increased.[8] In 1850 forty-four vessels left Hong Kong for California with nearly 500 passengers and by the end of 1851 it was estimated that there were 25,000 Chinese in California engaged either in placer mining or in domestic and manual labor.

But behind the opportunity afforded by foreign shipping and the enticement of the discovery of gold lay deeper causes for emigration—the poverty and ruin in which the inhabitants of Southeastern China were involved by the great Taiping rebellion which began in the summer of 1850.[9] The terrors of war, famine and plundering paralyzed all industry and trade and the agricultural classes of the maritime districts especially, were driven to Hong Kong and Macao. Owing to the multitudes out of employment, the contract coolie trade to the Isthmus of Panama, Cuba and South America, and voluntary emigration to California and Australia, flourished.

[6] Helms, *Pioneering in the Far East*, p. 74.
[7] Eitel, *Europe in China*, p. 273; *Parl. Rept.*, White to Governor Barkley, (1851).
[8] Williams, *Soc. Sci. Assoc.*, 1879. Speer, *The Oldest Empire*, p. 486.
[9] Marquis Tseng, *Asiatic Monthly Review*, 1887. *Blackwood's*, v. 72, pp. 101-2.

Those who had no money and could give no security, shipped as contract coolies to Cuba and the Spanish countries and so escaped the evils everywhere about them;[10] while those embarking for San Francisco in 1852, alone are said to have paid in passage money not less than a million and a half dollars.[11] Before 1852 no record was kept of the Chinese passengers returning from San Francisco to China, but that many did soon return, having made their stake, and spread the news of the Golden Hills among their countrymen, is the testimony of Englishmen and Americans resident in China at that period.[12]

There were in China at this time numbers of single men connected with various *hongs* or corporations that gave them employment, besides a large population of coolie laborers and vagabonds in the English colony of Hong Kong, and a boat population of about 27,000 about Canton.[13] Such as these emigrated, if at all, from Macao and Whampoa as contract laborers to Cuba and South America. Those who were able to pay their own passage sailed from the British city of Hong Kong to America or Australia. After the passage of the British Passengers Act in 1855, Hong Kong became the sole port from which the Chinese sailed to America.

Of the Chinese who came to California at least one-half were married and expected not merely to make their personal fortune but to support a family at home; for no man in China over twenty remains unmarried unless he is a wanderer or very poor. At this period there was so strong a sentiment in China against any respectable woman leaving home even with her husband that very few went

---

[10] Williams, Letter from Canton, July 20, 1850. Parker, *Cong. Docs.* s. n. 824, Oct. 16, 1854.

[11] See appendix for a careful résumé of all trustworthy figures.

[12] Parker to Webster, *Cong. Docs.*, s. n. 824, Doc. 99, 1852. Bowring, *Philippine Islands*, p. 344. Speer, *The Oldest Empire*, p. 486. Williams, *Soc. Sci. Assoc.*, p 11. *Parl. Rept.*, Elmslie to Bowring, Aug. 25, 1852. *Blackwood's*, v. 72, p. 102.

[13] Coltman, *The Chinese*, etc., p. 109. Dennys, *Treaty Ports*, p. 19 ff. (1854). Holcombe, *The Real Chinese Question*, p. 5.

The Period of Favor 19

to America or Australia. The few who went to California were for the most part large-footed women of the working class or women of disreputable character. But since 1880 public opinion in China has changed appreciably on this point and in recent years the merchant class have brought their small-footed wives to this country.[14]

Only six prefectures, lying along the two provinces of Kwang Tung and Fuh Kien from Hing-Kwa near Fuchau to Shan-King west of Canton, have furnished all the emigrants from China to foreign countries.[15] The coolie emigration to Cuba and South America in the hands of the Portuguese and the Spaniards, was largely from the province of Fuh Kien, while the emigration to California has been almost exclusively from the agricultural districts of Kwang Tung. In this rich and fertile territory European trade centered, and the Cantonese have therefore had far more contact with foreigners than the inland population, and are, moreover, distinguished from the Chinese farther inland and northward by superior energy and ambition.

Much misconception of the character of the American Chinese has arisen from the erroneous idea that they were mostly drawn from the homeless, idle classes or from the boat population about Canton. But these classes had no security to offer for their passage money and were the material from which the contract coolie trade to Cuba and South America was recruited. In a society so closely bound together by ties of kinship and with a tradition which makes the payment of debts only second to filial duty, the inefficient, the helpless and the vicious had

---

[14] Of the 28 Chinamen murdered at Rock Springs in 1885, fifteen had wives and children in China. *Cong. Docs.* s. n. 2460, p. 109 ff. By the Census of 1900, 38 per cent of Chinese males over fifteen years of age were married, although there was only one Chinese female to each 26 males in the United States.

[15] Kerr, *The Chinese Question*, p. 13. Speer, *The Oldest Empire*, p. 489. Williams, *Soc. Sci. Assoc.*, p. 7.

no means of getting away without the aid and security of their families; nor when they arrived at San Francisco would they have been able to obtain the assistance of their countrymen necessary to obtain a foothold in this country.[16]

The emigrants to the United States were, in fact, free agricultural peasantry from the country districts and villages—young, thrifty and industrious; and, coming from a country where the land is divided into small holdings and where agriculture is a highly respected occupation, they possessed unusual independence of character.[17] Medhurst says:

> "The emigrants who hailed from these particular districts . . . to this day constitute the most respectable type of the emigrating class, and are, perhaps, as little open to the charge of being the scum of the population as any emigrants in the world. . . . Whilst the refuse of the Chinese population does to a great extent foul the stream of emigration going on from Chinese shores, there is nevertheless a vast, if not a preponderating element of the class who form the backbone of trade, and have as much interest in leading a quiet, well-ordered life as any colonist who leaves the shores of Great Britain for the purpose of bettering his prospects."[18]

Nor were they, as was often asserted during the time of the exclusion agitation, paupers, lepers and criminals. This is, perhaps, sufficiently disproved by their exasperating thrift and universal industry after their arrival here; for among the Chinese, as well as among Anglo-Saxons, industry is the antithesis of weakness, disease and vice. During fifty years of residence here they have proved themselves quite as decent, industrious and honest as the majority of the foreign born immigrants to the Coast.[19]

---

[16] For full discussion of Coolie question see Ch. III.
[17] Poole, *Life of Parkes*, v. I., p. 318. Speer, *The Oldest Empire*, 489. Holt, *Pac. Mo.*, v. 4-5, p. 284. Wen Chang, *Chinese Crisis from Within*, p. 31.
[18] Medhurst, *Nineteenth Century*, v. 4, p. 518.
[19] Holcombe, *The Real Chinese Question*, p. 5. Speer, *The Oldest Empire*, p. 489. See Ch. XXII, for discussion of character and assimilation.

The Period of Favor 21

During the first thirty-three years—the period of free immigration—the Chinese, despite their racial peculiarities, were of much the same age and class as the German and Irish agricultural immigrants of the same period at the port of New York. Like them, they sold their little property or borrowed on family security the necessary passage money. But they differed from the European peasantry in that a large proportion were married men—though unaccompanied by their families; in having smaller financial resources on arrival, but a greater solidarity and protective organization among their own race; and in a universal capacity for self-support.[20]

The early Chinese were, indeed, very like the Irish in that economic rather than political and religious forces drove them hither, and in that the prospect of highly paid work lured them from their native country to the land of work and gold. One marked difference is distinguished: the stronger family ties at home and the entire absence of a political motive, made it inevitable that the Chinaman should return when he had paid his debts and gained a competence; yet even in this he differed only in degree from the Italian and Austro-Hungarian immigrant of a later period.

In the first few years the Chinaman was welcomed, praised and considered almost indispensable; for in those days race antipathy was subordinated to industrial necessity, and in a heterogeneous community where every Caucasian expected to be a miner or a speculator, the reticent, industrious, adaptable Chinese could find room and something more than toleration. They were highly valued as general laborers, carpenters and cooks; the restaurants established by them in San Francisco and in the mines were well kept and extensively patronized; they took to pieces the old vessels that lay abandoned in the channel of the Golden Gate; they cleared and drained the rich tule

[20] The Chinese in the fall of 1849 chose Selim Woodworth to act as arbiter and adviser; and the Four Companies were organized in 1852.

lands, which the white miners were too busy to undertake. Governor McDougal recommended in 1852 a system of land grants to induce the further immigration and settlement of the Chinese—" one of the most worthy of our newly adopted citizens." [21] The editor of the Pacific News remarked upon their industry, quietness, cheerfulness and the cleanliness of their personal habits. Whatever the white man scorned to do the Chinaman took up; whatever white men did, the Chinese could learn to do; he was a gap-filler, doing what no one else would do, or what remained undone, adapting himself to the white man's tastes, and slipping away, unprotestingly, to other tasks when the white man wanted his job.

But the Chinese were not merely desired because of their invaluable services at this period, but respected for the picturesque and dignified element which they added to society.[22] On August twenty-eight, 1850, Mayor Geary, and a committee of citizens assembled on a platform in Portsmouth Square, San Francisco, to present the Chinese residents with certain religious tracts, papers and books printed in Chinese characters. The "China Boys" were clothed richly in their native costume and made a fine appearance. The Mayor invited them to take part the next day in the funeral services commemorative of the death of President Taylor, in which all citizens participated, and they were assigned a prominent position.[23] At the celebration of the admission of California into the Union the Chinese turned out in large numbers and formed a striking feature in the ceremonies of the day. Justice Nathaniel Bennett, in welcoming the Chinese with other foreigners, said:

[21] Lang, *Hist. of Tuolumne County*, p. 5. Borthwick, *Three Years in California*, p. 330-1. Shaw, *Golden Dreams*, p. 42. Frost, *Pictorial Hist. of Cal.* Helms, *Pioneering in the Far East.* Bancroft, *Hist. of Cal.* v. 6, p. 189. *Sen. Jo.*, 1852, p. 15.
[22] Tuthill, *Hist. of Cal.* (1866), p. 368.
[23] *Annals of San Francisco*, pp. 287–8.

The Period of Favor

"Born and reared under different Governments and speaking different tongues, we nevertheless meet here to-day as brothers.... You stand among us in all respects as equals. ... Henceforth we have one country, one hope, one destiny." [24]

"A Philadephian settled at San Francisco," thus described the celebration of Washington's Birthday in 1852:

"All countries and ages were represented in the ceremonies of the day. Scarcely had the French, Spanish and Hebrew Societies passed from view before some two hundred Celestials, or, as their banner termed them 'China Boys of San Francisco,' came before the admiring gazer. * * * Preceded by their mandarins and a band of music, straggling and evidently amused with their position, came this large delegation of our most orderly and industrious citizens." [25]

On the following Fourth of July large bands of foreigners, particularly of the French and Chinese, attracted much attention and were praised for their patriotism.[26] The barbaric feature they contributed was a source of pride to the people.[27] The principal Daily of the City remarked optimistically: "The China Boys will yet vote at the same polls, study at the same schools, and bow at the same altar as our own countrymen." [28]

The cleanliness, unobtrusiveness and industry of the Chinese was often commented upon. As cooks and laundrymen they supplied the places of women domestics.[29] The few women in California at that period wer ot of a class to fill these needs, and on the basis of the virtues a permanent place in society was predicted for the Chinamen. James A. Carson, a pioneer, declared that they were the best immigrants in California—sober, industrious and inoffensive. He thought that thousands of them were ready to become citizens if protection was afforded them,

[24] *Alta*, Oct. 31, 1850.
[25] *Blackwood's* vol. 72, p. 105.
[26] *Annals of San Francisco*, p. 397.
[27] Tuthill, *Hist. of Cal.* (1866), p. 368.
[28] *Daily Alta California*, May 12, 1852.
[29] Frost, *Pictorial Hist. of Cal.*, p. 100. Helms says that in the summer of 1851 washing cost six dollars per dozen pieces in San Francisco, and Ryan that the price was twelve dollars in the mines; washing was sometimes sent to Honolulu to be done at eight dollars per dozen.

and that no better class of men could be chosen to develop the agricultural resources of the country.[30]

At this time even in the mining districts they were often tolerated because of their unaggressive character, or welcomed because they did not preempt new grounds, but bought up worked-out claims thus giving the white miners an opportunity to re-locate. Their rivalry was not feared, for they were said to handle tools like women and to expend a vast deal of labor in their method of working. They were systematic and steady, however, and by degrees learned to use tools and to undertake more extensive works.[31] Their curiously timid and unaggressive character was shown in every line of industry. Huntley remarked that they "were the most quiet, inoffensive people ever maltreated by a stronger power; no sooner have they found out good diggings than they are dispossessed of them by the American miners, who though an appeal to law may eject the latter, yet then they so harass and annoy the timid Chinese that he is glad to remove and content himself with some poorer location."[32]

Not the least of their good qualities appeared to be this tendency to mind their own business and to slip away before the more aggressive Anglo-Saxon. In this early time, the contrast was often drawn in their favor between them and the South and Central Americans, the Mexicans and the Kanakas. Capron thought them "much less objectionable though American prejudice was stronger against them."[33] Several early observers and pioneers praised their spirit of subordination to the law in comparison with other and more lawless immigrants, and a few thought their intelligence promised good citizenship, if they were given the right of suf-

[30] Carson, *Life in Cal.*, p. 55. Capron, *Hist. of Cal.*, p. 277. Kelly, *Stroll through the Diggings*, p. 181-2.
[31] Haskins, *Argonauts of Cal.*, pp. 188-190. Tuthill, *Hist. of Cal.*, p. 368. Borthwick, *Three Years in Cal.*, pp. 100, 143-4, 264-5.
[32] Sir Henry Huntley, *California*, etc. (1852), v. 2, p. 33.
[33] Schaeffer, *Sketches of Travels in . . . California* (1852), p. 60. Capron, *Hist. of Cal.*, p. 277 ff. Carson, *Life in Cal.*, p. 55.

frage.[34] In 1856, when the lawlessness of some elements of the white population in San Francisco became unendurable and the better citizens formed a Vigilance Committee to suppress them, the Chinese merchants contributed liberally and received a vote of thanks.[35]

In the light of the fifty years of intolerance that followed, the cordiality with which the Chinese were welcomed by the first pioneers is almost incredible. It finds explanation in the necessities and contradictions of the time. In San Francisco the services of the Chinese were indispensable to decent living, and there were few other immigrants who would condescend to menial services or even to manual labor. The city itself had not yet become the prey of politicians and of so-called labor parties; and though the " Sydney Ducks " and other criminal adventurers took their toll from Chinamen as from the other inhabitants, the predatory hoodlum had not yet been evolved.

But while the citizens of San Francisco were presenting the Chinese with religious tracts in the public square and calling them brothers and equals, the race prejudice and jealousy of the miners was gathering force in the mountains. Already white adventurers of all nationalities were driving their colored competitors from the mines with the cry of " California for Americans "; and when, within a few years, the Frenchman, the Mexican and the Chileno had been driven out, the full weight of anti-foreign prejudice fell upon the Chinaman. Even at a time when the praises of the Chinese virtues—so conspicuous in a community built up on speculation rather than labor—were still in the mouths of the public officials of San Francisco, the Governor of the State was writing a violent anti-Chinese message to satisfy his constituents in the mines.

[34] Capron, *Hist. of Cal.*, p. 277 ff. Carson, *Life in Cal.* (1852), p. 55.
[35] Hittell, *Hist. of Cal.*, v. 3, p. 627, quoted from the Vigilance Committee records. Bancroft, *Works*, v. 37, (Popular Tribunals, v. 2) p. 662.

CHAPTER II
CALIFORNIA FOR AMERICANS

"The feeling against the colored races rose to a pitch of exasperation .... The mines becoming more thickly populated, the Americans, relying on their numerical strength, commenced acts of hostility and aggression on any placer inhabited by colored people if it were worth appropriating; .... Ejectments constantly occurred and, driven from the placers, thousands left the country while others penetrated farther into the hill ranges. These conflicts were often serious in their results; retaliations were made and where might was right, retributions upon unoffending individuals often took place, which were nigh producing a war of race against race."—WILLIAM SHAW, *Golden Dreams*, (1851-2).

"Chinese rank with the most successful foreigners in the mines. .... It is asserted that as a class they are hirelings sent from China by wealthy men to work on low wages, that the gold which they obtain is carried out of the country .... It is, however, equally true that very few miners of any class settle in the state and all the gold acquired by those who do not is taken or sent out of it. Many Americans, Mexicans and Europeans dig gold here under contracts with other parties at home, who furnish capital and these miners receive a return for their labor, very little better than the wages of ordinary laborers. The justice of the discrimination is not therefore clearly perceptible even if the right of the state to impose restrictions .... is conceded."—CAPRON, *History of California*, (1854).

IN the spring of 1849, streams of adventurous men set out for the gold fields of California; from the middle and south-west across the Plains; from Honolulu, Sydney and Hong Kong; from New York and New Orleans and South America via the Isthmus of Panama. Upon arriving at Panama the Americans were disgusted to find that many foreigners had taken passage and were going "to steal the gold" of the United States. General P. F. Smith, on his way to take charge of the military forces in California, proclaimed at Panama that he would exclude from the mines as trespassers, all who were not citizens of the United States.[1] T. Butler King, special agent of the United States government, reported that during the season of 1849 more than 15,000 foreigners, mostly Mexi-

[1] *Panama Star*, Feb. 24, 1849. Royce, *California*, pp. 233-9. Bancroft, *Hist. of Cal.*, v. 6, p. 273. *Cong. Docs.* s. n. 573, pp. 704-8, 716.

cans and Chilenos, came in armed bands into the mining district and carried away some twenty millions of gold dust. He protested that no nation should thus permit its treasure to be carried away and proposed an elaborate scheme of mining regulations.

Congress, however, declined to pass any laws restricting the working of the placers. Governor Riley, in sympathy with this policy, would not countenance any class of men in the attempt to monopolize the mines and left all questions of the temporary rights of those in actual possession, to the local judicial authorities. After a visit to the mines in 1849, he reported that the hostilities between Americans and foreigners had been greatly exaggerated, but that some of the English, Irish and German immigrants had exerted themselves much more than the Americans to create a prejudice against the Mexicans, Peruvians and Chilenos.

While the first Constitution of California provided that foreigners who were bona fide residents should enjoy the same rights of property as native-born citizens, race antipathy was nevertheless intensifying the competition and the hatred of the Americans and foreigners in contact in the mines. The contempt of the American for the dark and undersized Mexican—aggravated by the border war and conquest of 1846—was not lessened by his superior skill and success in gold mining. Greed and jealousy intensified the race feeling towards the Indians, South Americans and Hawaiians as well and even the French were as bitterly persecuted as the Chinese came to be in subsequent years.[2]

As the number of the gold-seekers increased in the second and third seasons, the competition for good placers became more intense and the difficulty of keeping order

---

[2] Smith, S., *Settler's New Home*, (1849), London. Bancroft, *Hist. of Cal.*, v. 3, p. 233. Hittell, *Hist. of Cal.*, v. 3, pp. 262-5. Taylor, *Eldorado*, v. 1, pp. 87, 102, (1850). Auger, *Voyage En Californie*, pp. 161-2, (1854). Sonora *Herald*, June, 1850. Frost, *Pictorial Hist. of Cal.*, p. 101. Shinn, *Mining Camps*, p. 212. Ryan, *Adventures*, v. 2, pp. 296-8.

among such a miscellaneous population became constantly greater. Many camps passed resolutions forbidding foreigners to mine. At Sonora in July, 1850, after a riot and attempted lynching, all foreigners were ordered to leave the country within fifteen days and "good citizens" were given the power to disarm any foreigner.[8] The resolutions recite that the lives and property of American citizens were in danger from the lawless marauders of every clime, class and creed under heaven and that they had in their midst, the *peons* of Mexico, the renegades of South America, and the convicts of the British Empire. William Shaw, an English sailor and gold-seeker, describes his own company, composed of several Americans, two Chilians, a Frenchman, two Germans, two Cornishmen and two servants—a Chinese and a Malay—as having been attacked by other Americans on the pretense that they were keeping the Chinaman and the Malay in servitude.

"Shirley"[4] writing from Columbia, Tuolumne County, described the gradually increasing state of bad feeling, the crimes committed, and the violence of the rowdies who formed themselves into companies and paraded the streets all night, howling, breaking into houses, taking miners out of their beds and throwing them into the river. Many other eyewitnesses comment upon the hatred engendered by these aggressions and the resulting collisions, robberies and murders. Retaliation on the part of the foreigners was to be expected since a majority of them were of Spanish blood.

The disorders in the mines of California in the first years were due to many and complex causes. The doctrine that California was for Americans alone, and that all

---

[8] For descriptions of disorders in the mines see: Royce, *California*, Lambertie, *Voyage*, etc.; Woods, *Sixteen Months in the Gold Diggings*; Shinn, *Mining Camps*; Shaw, *Golden Dreams*; Bancroft, *Hist. of Cal.*; Eaves, *Labor Legislation in California*; Hittell, *Hist. of Cal.*, v, 3; Bates, *Four Years on the Pacific Coast*; Shirley's Letters, in *Pioneer Magazine*, v. 4.

[4] *Pioneer Mag.*, v. 4.

California for Americans

foreigners were trespassers, was acted upon under the impetus of greed and jealousy, although not justified by law. Race antipathy was mixed with the political doctrines of Know-Nothingism which shortly afterward rolled in a wave across the country from East to West. In the West, the so-called Americans—native, naturalized and unnaturalized—of whom a considerable proportion were Irish Roman Catholics, combined against the brown, black and yellow foreigners in the mines.[5]

The anti-foreign feeling in California was unquestionably intensified by the presence of Southerners, who comprised nearly one-third of her population in the first decade. Of these a minority were educated, pure-American stock who brought, in some cases, their slaves with them and a profound conviction that this should be a white man's country. But this class was greatly outnumbered by immigrants from the border states of the Pike county Missourian type, whose ignorance and extreme race antipathies classed all persons, other than European whites, together. South Americans, South Europeans, Kanakas, Malays, or Chinese—all were colored; even the French, partly because they were of a darker skin and partly because they, like the Spanish Americans, were too high spirited, were attacked as foreigners. The Germans, Irish and Englishmen alone were excepted although many of them were not naturalized, and had far less right in the country than the native Indians and Spaniards.

The doctrine of trespass early found legislative expression in the Foreign Miners License tax law. The bill, as passed in 1850, provided that all persons not native-born citizens of the United States (California Indians excepted), or who had not become citizens under the treaty of Guadelupe Hidalgo, must take out a license to mine at twenty dollars per month. The collector received three dollars and the law was to be printed in English and

[5] Davis, *Political Conventions*, pp. 216-7.

Spanish for circulation among the miners.⁶ Although the Committee on Mines, which had framed the law, had counted upon its bringing in at least two hundred thousand dollars a month, the principal result was the almost immediate depopulation of certain camps and the serious injury of all. At Sonora, the Mexicans refused to pay; in the surrounding camps the miners defied the collectors and armed themselves; many moved to new diggings, some became highwaymen, others drifted into dependent positions or were assisted to return home. Sonora lost four-fifths of its population while Columbia was reduced from a camp of ten thousand persons to nine or ten. The city of San Francisco was crowded with penniless foreigners and the Chilian Consul prepaid the homeward passages of eight hundred miners. The State Controller reported that the tax was a failure as a revenue measure and, having become inoperative, it was repealed in 1851.⁷

For the purpose of this work the significant fact in this violent, pro-American movement, is the absence of specific anti-Chinese feeling before 1852. Such attacks as the Chinese suffered seem to have been merely incidental to their employment where all foreigners were at a disadvantage. Being relatively few in number and un-aggressive, they were probably let alone chiefly because the mobs and rowdies were preoccupied with the more conspicuous elements of society. Between 1849 and 1852 there are only occasional instances where the Chinese were driven from the mines. The Foreign Miners License tax was directed against the Spanish Americans principally, and although in the debate in the Legislature there was a strong anti-Chinese minority report, the law was enforced upon the Latin races.⁸ But by the end of 1852, the Spaniards had been driven out, and the Chinese

---

⁶ App. *Sen. Jo.* 1850, p. 496. California *Statutes*, 1850, pp. 221–3. Shinn and Royce erroneously say the tax was $30 per month.
⁷ *Rept. State Controller*, 1852. Only $33,147.47 was received. *Statutes*, 1851, p. 424.
⁸ *Legisl. Jos.* 1850, Doc. 28.

numbered, according to Custom House figures 20,025, and, according to general estimate, 25,000. By the time the Legislature met they constituted the largest single body of unnaturalized foreigners in the State.[9]

Attention was suddenly drawn to them by the introduction of Senator Tingley's Coolie bill, the purport of which was to enforce in the courts the contracts made in China to perform work in California for a term of years. Although lost, it was the occasion of a vigorous minority report by Senator Roach, who rehearsed many of the anti-Chinese arguments used by public men from this time onward. He stigmatized it as an attempt to introduce cheap labor and to perpetuate the feudal rights of capital. The Chinese, he said, had at least 500,000 criminals who would come over as contract laborers and thus expose our people to a pestilence as foul as leprosy and the plague; the only reason they had not come already was because their families were held as hostages.[10]

Not long afterward, the Committee on Mines and Mining Interests called the attention of the Legislature to the danger from the vast numbers of Asiatics, who were the absolute slaves of foreign masters and predicted that it would soon be necessary to shut them out.[11] This report was immediately followed by a special message from the Governor on the subject of Chinese immigration. Governor Bigler charged them with being Contract coolies, avaricious, ignorant of moral obligations, incapable of being assimilated and dangerous to the welfare of the state. The committee to which the report was referred reiterated these charges, recommended that all contracts of servitude be declared void and that the Chinese be immediately excluded from the mines. The committee did not wish, however, to suggest a policy which would disturb commercial relations with China and they thought

[9] App. *Sen. Jo.* 1853, Doc. 14.
[10] *Sen. Jo.* 1852, pp. 67-8, 192, 217, 306-7, 669-675.
[11] App. *Legisl. Jos.* 1852, p. 829.

that the example of California might become the means of Christianizing other nations.[12]

The Chinese in San Francisco were greatly disturbed by these attacks and replied in an open letter denying the charges.[13] Although the bill did not pass and the Governor's message was generally disapproved as an offensive campaign measure, the agitation bore immediate fruit in the mining districts where the deep-seated objection to foreigners was ready to take shape against the Chinese. Early in May the Chinese miners were driven from many districts, generally peaceably, because they made no resistance. At Columbia, the resolutions passed at the miners' mass meeting were worthy of the sand-lotters of a later time in the vehemence of their expressions against capitalists as well as against the Chinese.[14] The miners at Jamestown demanded from the Legislature a hospital tax of five hundred dollars on each immigrant and a prohibition of naturalization to the Chinese.

In response to the demands of the mining constituency the Legislature renewed the Miners' License, but in more reasonable terms. The law of 1852 required all persons (California Indians excepted), not citizens of the United States to take out a mining license at three dollars per month; collectors were to receive ten per cent and the net revenue to be equally divided between State and County. Any person hiring foreigners to work in the mines was liable for the tax and the law was to be enforced by the county courts. Still, there was no direct mention of the Chinese in the law, for the preamble only recited the disorders arising from foreigners in the diggings who had the privileges and yet performed none of the duties of citizens.[15]

[12] *Sen. Jo.* 1852, pp. 731–7.
[13] *Annals of San Francisco*, April 29, 1852, p. 381. Hittell, *Hist. of Cal.*, v. 4, p. 108.
[14] Marysville *Herald*, May 4, 1852. Sacramento *Union*, May 2, 1852. Daily *Alta California*, May 12, 14, 1852. See for other illustrations, Shinn, *Land Laws of Mining Districts*, Index.
[15] *Legisl. Jos.* 1852, pp. 668–9. California *Statutes*, 1852, p. 84.

California for Americans

At the session of 1853, the majority report of the committee on Mines and Mining Interests was against the discouragement of Chinese immigration and merely suggested some slight amendments to the law. But the tax was raised to four dollars per month, the collectors' percentage to fifteen per cent, and they were given power to seize and sell the property of the debtor at one hour's notice. All foreigners in the mining districts, unless engaged in some other lawful business, were miners under the act. Then for the first time, the law was printed not only in Spanish and French but also in Chinese.

Despite the decline of Chinese immigration from 20,000 in 1852 to only 4,470 in 1853, and the departure for China of 4,000 more, due in part to the license tax and in part to the discovery of gold in Australia, the income from the tax nearly doubled in the following year. In 1855 Governor Bigler repeated for a third time and more emphatically, his objections to the Chinese; the miners of Shasta County presented a strong anti-Chinese memorial and many anti-Chinese bills were offered in the Legislature.[16] The Select Committee appointed to consider them made five separate reports differing widely in their recommendations. The majority report, signed by six members, recited that the direct issue was between the American laborer on the one side and the Capitalist and the Chinese laborer on the other. Two of the minority reports recommended exclusion, but pointed out that it must not be accomplished too suddenly because the counties could not live without the income from the taxes paid by the Chinese and their patronage of business. Two others were distinctly favorable to the Chinese, pointing to the money value of their consumption, to the future value of Oriental trade and the impracticability of deportation.[17]

It was evident that there was no unanimity of sentiment

[16] *Sen. Jo.* 1855, pp. 50-4.
[17] App. *Ass. Jo.* 1855, Doc. 19; Doc. 16; *Sen. Jo.* 413.

either in the Committee or throughout the State, but since the miners comprised the one solid body of working men, mining was the most important industry, and the almost evenly balanced parties were dependent on the mining vote, it was inevitable that the measure reported should be strongly anti-Chinese. The foreign miners license tax was again raised to the prohibitive point; it was to continue four dollars per month until October first, 1855, and then to be increased two dollars per month each succeeding year.[18]

The immediate effect of the law was similar to that of the law of 1850. Many Chinese miners, unwilling and perhaps unable to pay what they regarded as an unjust tax, went into other occupations. The revenues of the mining counties rapidly dwindled. Merchants and mechanics who had relied upon the Chinese for much of their business suffered serious loss. Chinese merchants wrote to China to stop the forwarding of merchandise and as many Chinese went back as came in. Business men in the mining districts discovered to their loss, that the Chinese were a profitable element of the population.[19]

As a result, numerous petitions were presented to the Legislature of 1856, praying for a reduction of the "tax on the Chinese." Although the Assembly Committee on Mines continued to support Governor Bigler theoretically, they made a practical concession to the demands of the petitioners and of the newspapers of the mining districts which were loud in condemnation of the exclusion-by-taxation policy.[20]

In spite of a strong sentiment in the Assembly and of Governor Bigler's protest against any modification of the law, the majority report of the Senate Committee recom-

[18] California *Statutes*, 1855, p. 194, 216 declared unconstitutional, *Peoples* vs. *Downer*, 7 Cal. 169; Attorney-General of Cal., July 2, 1856.
[19] Cleveland to J. Ross Browne, *Cong. Docs.* s. n. 1374 (1868). *State Journal* (Democratic) Oct. 26, 1855, which quotes a number of Mountain papers. The amount of income from the license tax declined considerably in Calaveras, El Dorado, Mariposa and Sierra counties.
[20] App. *Ass. Jo.* 1856, Doc. no.

California for Americans 35

mended the repeal of the law of 1855 and the return to the four dollar tax of 1853. They pointed out the fact that the total amount of the license tax—a large part of which had been paid by the Chinese—had amounted to $850,000, one-half which went to the State and the other half to the Counties and that the Counties at least were not in a condition to do without this income. They condemned the law as "a hasty, imprudent, and mischievous piece of legislation unauthorized by the existence of any evil then in view or demanded by any fair expression of public opinion." The mines were not crowded nor exhausted and the Chinese worked only abandoned placers. Most of the gold produced by them was left in the State; and the Chinese unlike other foreigners were not found in almshouses nor begging nor seen in the Courts. They urged that the Chinese should be decently treated.[21]

For some years after this the Miners' License Law was untouched. The discovery of gold on the Fraser river in 1858 drew off a large number of the white miners and the Chinese miners increased in number, taking possession of deserted cabins, claims and tools.[22] In 1861 the State Controller called attention to the decline of income from this source from one hundred and eighty-five thousand in 1856 to one hundred and seventeen thousand in 1860, and the necessity for devising more efficient means of collection.[23] The Legislature, thereupon, raised the Collector's percentage to twenty per cent and defined foreign miners as "all foreigners not eligible to become citizens of the United States residing in the mining district."[24]

The revenue from the tax rose to one hundred and eighty-seven thousand dollars in 1863, but again gradually declined to about eighty thousand dollars in 1867, which the State Controller attributed to other causes

[21] *Sen. Jo.* 1856, pp. 398-401.
[22] Hittell, J. S., *Mining* (ed. 1861), p. 32.
[23] He remarks: "It is surmised that large frauds are perpetrated in connection with these taxes and thousands of dollars diverted from the Treasury."
[24] Cal. *Statutes*, 1861, p. 447 ff.

than dereliction on the part of the collectors. He said that this tax had for several years been exacted exclusively from Chinese miners, who, because of the law and the opening of other industries, had gradually left the mines for other employments on railroads and in the mines of Idaho and Montana.[25] In 1868, the law was slightly amended to give the whole income to the counties, and in 1870, it was declared void by the amendments to the Federal Constitution.[26]

It had long been known that it was unconstitutional, but the Chinese had no standing in the courts and State officials ignored the fact because the income was so necessary to the government of both State and counties. By this time the mining counties were willing to acknowledge the debt the community owed to the Chinese, for Chinese trade and labor had literally kept them alive in some seasons. The full extent of the contribution in the shape of license taxes was never realized, perhaps, except by those officials whose difficult task it was in the first two decades of California's statehood, to raise the money for the support of government in a state which had only two or three persons per square mile.

The income from the Foreign Miners' licenses in the decade from 1854 to 1865, amounted to one-eighth, and for the whole period from 1850 to 1870, to one-half, of the total income of the State from all sources. From 1855 onward, it is conceded by all authorities that the Chinese paid practically the whole of these taxes—a sum amounting altogether to nearly five million dollars paid into State and County treasuries. The following table, condensed from the details of the Controller's reports, with the cost of collection added, shows to what extent the mining counties profited by this law which was known, and afterwards declared to be, unconstitutional.

---

[25] Controller's reports; McClellan, *The Golden State*; Hittell, *Mining* (ed. 1861), p. 179–80.
[26] California *Statutes*, 1868; *Laws of the U. S.*, CXIV, Sec. 16.

TABLE I.

FOREIGN MINERS' LICENSE TAXES, 1850–1870.

Paid into State and County Treasuries of California.
(Controllers' Reports.)

COUNTIES.	1850–1854.	1854–1870.	
Amador...		$137,019.35	
Butte.....		151,444.26	
Calaveras........		130,873.59	
El Dorado.........		375,227.35	
Fresno.............		44,705.95	
Klamath...........		33,038.58	
Mariposa..........		109,543.82	
Nevada............		103,250.02	
Placer		210,011.74	
Plumas		59,596.23	
Sacramento........		53,145.84	
Siskiyou		96,374.02	
Sierra		59,496.49	
Shasta.............		79,521.00	
Tuolumne.........		116,135.89	
Trinity		89,157.17	
Yuba..............		89,916.00	
Ten other mining....		30,357.40	including $325.9 taxes in arrears paid in 1872.
Paid to State........	$ 87,271.01	$1,967,814.70	one-half of net proceeds...............
" " Counties.....	85,525.59	1,967,814.70	" " "
" " Collectors[27]..	1,745.42	983,907.00	20% of total collections.............
Total Paid..........	$174,542.02	$4,919,536.40	by foreigners of all races.... ....
Paid by Chinese.....	87,271.01		50% of total collections...............
" " "		4,821,145.28	" 98% " "
Total: paid by Chinese			$4,908,416.29

[27] In 1852–4, Collector was only allowed 10 per cent of total collections; in 1854–61, Collector was allowed 15%, Sheriff 3%, Recorder, 3%; in 1861–69, Collector was allowed 20%.

Free Immigration

Aside from the financial advantage to the State, the most conspicuous result of the Foreign Miners' License tax, was to drive many foreigners—French, Mexicans, Spanish-Americans, Pacific Islanders—from the State and to drive the Chinese from mining into other industries. In 1860 sixty per cent of the Chinese were in eleven mining counties engaged in mining and in domestic occupations; but, by 1870, only forty-five per cent remained in these counties, while thirty-eight per cent were now settled in and about the cities of San Jose, Sacramento and San Francisco.

Although the movement toward cities and into agriculture would have taken place to some extent if there had been no miners' license tax, or other checks on mining, it was precipitated and greatly accelerated by the tax.[28] Thus many of the Chinese, whose competition in abandoned and low-grade placers was infinitesimal, and whose services to the mining districts in domestic occupations were invaluable, were driven into other employments and into cities where their presence in manual labor and incipient manufacture was much more likely to be injurious,[29] and where they became the target of race prejudice and the bug-a-boo of the workingman and the politician.

The decline of placer and the development of quartz mining in the sixties gradually divided the Chinese miners into two classes, those who continued to work old placers for themselves and those who were hired out to work for mining companies in the quartz mills. A number of companies made attempts to introduce them into the mines but not with great success, sometimes owing to the hostility of other miners, more often because the white foremen did not know how to manage them. Yet

---

[28] Hittell, J., *Resources of Cal.*, (1874). Rept. Cal. *Bureau of Labor*, 188-34; App. Legisl. Jos. v. 4, p. 205. In 1900 there were forty to fifty mines leased and operated by Chinamen, employing only about 500 men.

[29] Hittell, *Hist. of Cal.* v. 3, p. 264.

California for Americans 39

the cost of white labor was so high that the Chinese continued to be in great demand. The special report on mining made by R. W. Raymond, United States Commissioner of Mining Statistics, in 1871, summed up fairly the conditions of Chinese and white labor in the mines. He found that it was universally acknowledged that the Chinese worked with greater economy than the whites, and that in most cases they bought up abandoned placers and re-opened them with profit. The result of conflicts between the whites and Chinese in 1869, had been a reduction of wages, which the condition of mining enterprises imperatively demanded and the cheapness of clothing and provisions rendered reasonable. He explained that political and race jealousies caused each party to deal in wholesale assertion without any basis of acknowledged facts; that both parties appeared to be equally afraid to speak the truth on the Chinese question; and that they had settled on the convenient fiction that the Chinese were contract coolies. He concluded that the Chinese would maintain their hold—if they maintained it at all—not by the cheapness but by the excellence of their labor, and that the question of wages was likely to settle itself " by a rise in the demands of Chinamen and a fall in the price of Christians." [30]

The natural human tendency to monopolize any good thing, has had an extreme demonstration in California. Beginning with the attempt to keep the treasure of the State for the white Americans—that is, white Americans of North European birth or extraction—it developed into a systematic exploitation of the colored immigrants for the purpose of revenue. Anti-foreign prejudice joined hands with race antipathy and was intensified by the lawless greed of a community composed primarily of adventurers rather than settlers. At the end of the first decade, the Census—which though defective as to numbers, is

[30] *Mining Statistics West of the Rocky Mountains, Cong. Docs.* s. n. 1470, *Exc. Doc.* 10.

probably substantially correct as to racial proportions—showed that forty-two per cent of the total white population was foreign-born; and that this foreign element was chiefly composed of Irish, British, German, Spanish-Americans, French and Italians. From among these very early the Irish—who were one-fourth of the foreign-born whites—and the Missourians, had singled themselves out by their stronger racial antipathies which had been as fully reciprocated by the Spanish-Americans. Between 1860 and 1870, the Chinese—who also constituted about one-fourth of the foreign-born males—became the inheritors of this anti-foreign and anti-color feeling. From 1870 onward, the North European whites, and especially the Irish immigrants, increasingly objected to sharing the rich opportunities and the high wages of California with the Chinamen; and as they became naturalized they were able to express it by their ballots and through their political representatives, with greater and greater effectiveness. The race disorders of the mining camps were repeated in the towns and cities. Yet as in all the early mining camps, there was a solid substratum of intelligent, law-abiding American citizens—rarely a majority—so the whole history of California has been a history of the efforts of this minority to establish order and justice in the midst of a fluctuating population swayed in varying degree, by greed, jealousy, ignorance and race prejudice, and the primitive spirit of monopoly.

CHAPTER III

THE COOLIE FICTION

"Being from a race of dwellers upon the sea-coast, they [Chinese laborers] have desired to go thither and have regarded California as a land of abundance and as furnishing great opportunities. They have also rejoiced in the freedom of the United States. Hence they have not gone there as a result of deceit, or by being kidnapped, nor under contract as coolies, but have flown thither as the wild geese fly."—PAO CHUN and LI HUNG TSAO, Treaty Commissioners, 1880.

"There are no coolies in the state and never have been. They are as much free agents as our own people."—DANIEL CLEVELAND, 1868.

"The only slavery among them is an honest compliance with their contracts entered into freely."—JOHN S. HITTELL, Historian and Statistician, 1874.

"By the unalterable structure of their being, voluntary slaves."—Memorial of California Senate to Congress, 1878.

"Chinese immigration involves sordid wages, no public schools, the absence of families, and a constant outflow of persons who have worked out specified years of service."—Senator A. A. SARGENT of California, 1877.

"The Chinese are slaves and their labor practically for the benefit of those who own them."—Senator JAMES T. FARLEY of California, 1882.

"It is well known that they are in practical slavery."—Senator GEORGE C. PERKINS, of California, 1906.

FOR more than fifty years the word "coolie" has been used in the United States to designate a Chinese laborer, the term from long misuse having taken on the color of vague discredit or opprobrium. In its larger sense it is employed to designate some sort of contract laborer, but it is oftener used to convey the idea of servitude, slavery or peonage. Yet the history of the term gives no sanction for such usage, and the manner in which these laborers came to America shows that they were all perfectly free immigrants, at the very worst coming on money borrowed at a high rate of interest.

In China, the term "coolie" is in constant use as a

phrase but never as a single word.[1] It describes the nature of a man's occupation, tells what he can do, but has nothing whatever to do with the wages, terms, or contract, or any sort of conditions under which he will do it. It is, in fact, two words—not one. Although there is nothing among the Chinese even remotely approaching caste, the people divide the entire range of humanity into four classes, reckoned more or less honorable in the following order, beginning with the highest: *shih, nung, kung, shang;* or in English, scholar, farmer, laborer, merchant. In regard to the *kung* or laboring classes, two phrases are used: the first is " tso kung chi," which may be translated " to do work " or " a workingman," and the second is " koo-lee." " Koo " is a verb and in the loose grammatical structure of the Chinese language may be either active or passive, meaning to hire, to rent, or to be hired or to be rented, or again, to be hired out. It is extremely general in its application and has no reference whatever to the terms of agreement—in fact, it corresponds precisely to the English word hire.

The second word *" lee "* means " strength " or more liberally, " muscle," and the phrase " koo-lee " means " to rent muscle." Thus it becomes an idiomatic expression for hiring out to do any form of unskilled labor—the man has nothing to offer in exchange for wages but his muscle. The two phrases " tso kung " and " koo-lee," in common use in China have come to refer to two kinds of labor; the first is used to mean skilled labor while the second always refers to unskilled labor. Either sort is perfectly free and would rank higher in China than the grades of men who spend their lives in making money in business.[2]

[1] This careful explanation of the phrase " Koo-lee " is given by the Honorable Chester Holcombe, who was for thirty years Secretary to the United States Legation at Peking and who is the author of several scholarly books on China.
[2] Corroborated by many authorities as: S. Wells Williams, Soc. Sci. Assoc. (1879), p. 7; *Middle Kingdom*, v. 2, p. 631; Speer, *The Oldest Empire*, p. 475; Gibson, *Chinese in America*, pp. 30-1. 268-70, 333-6; *Cong. Docs.* s. n. 1052, (1858) Minister Reed to Secretary Cass.

The Coolie Fiction 43

About the middle of the nineteenth century the phrase "koo-lee,"[3] which meant merely unskilled laborer, was loosely applied by foreigners to the laboring classes at the open ports of China; and when the pseudo-slave trade in contract laborers arose, it was naturally used to describe the common laborers who went for a term of service to Cuba, South America or British Guiana. It was also sometimes carelessly applied as a generic word to the voluntary emigrants to California and Australia. Thus it happened that many foreigners who were ignorant of the Oriental use of the phrase made no distinction between contract laborers to the Spanish countries and voluntary emigrants to America, calling them all coolies, indiscriminately; and the word itself, as the horrors of the contract-trade became known, took on an odious meaning of semi-slavery.

The misapprehension of the phrase was probably furthered by the fact that the free emigrants upon arriving in San Francisco used the term to mean that they desired to rent their strength, that is, to obtain unskilled labor; and still more by the fact that these emigrants were of two classes. Some had paid their own passage with money obtained from the sale of property or borrowed from relatives; while others had borrowed from the passage brokers at Canton and Hong Kong, either without security at an exorbitant interest or upon the security of their relatives.

In order to understand fully how it came to be currently supposed in the West that the Chinese who came to the United States were coolies under contract for a term of service, it is necessary here to mention briefly the contract coolie emigration in China with which the voluntary emigration was confused. The coolie trade was the direct result of the discontinuance of slavery throughout the English-speaking world. White men could not and free

---
[3] The word coolie is Anglo-Indian from the original Bengalese or Tamil word *kuli* meaning burden-bearer; supposed to have been introduced into China by Englishmen.

negroes would not work in the tropical plantations of the West Indies and South America. The British colony of Guiana in 1844, arranged to import laborers for a term of service under a specified contract; shortly afterward Cuba, Peru and a few other tropical countries entered into the business. The Chinese were known to have emigrated satisfactorily for short periods to the neighboring countries and efforts were therefore made to induce them to emigrate under this form of contract. Each coolie was bound for seven or eight years at a fixed rate of wages—about four dollars per month—plus clothing, provisions, etc., of a certain kind. After a few years, when some thousands had gone to these plantations, ugly reports began to come out of the abuse and hardship to which they had been subjected. The stories of kidnapping, overcrowding and abuse on the coolie transportation ships repeated the horrors of the " Middle Passage " and roused the English Government especially to interfere. The ghastly details of the cruelties perpetrated on the Chinese who went to the Chincha Islands, compelled the English Governor of Hong Kong to issue a proclamation regulating coolie emigration in ships sailing under the British flag.[4] In 1855 the English Passengers Act was passed, providing that the term " Chinese passenger ship " should include every ship carrying from any port of Hong Kong, and every British ship carrying from any port in China. The emigration officer must satisfy himself that the ship complied with the regulations as to food, water, and cubic air space, and must ascertain from the passengers that they understood whither they were going and the nature of any contracts of service which they had made. Emigration under contract of service was prohibited altogether from the Colony of Hong Kong unless the ship was proceeding to a British colony.[5]

[4] Dennys, *Treaty Ports*, p. 66.
[5] British Passengers Act may be found in 18 and 19 Vict. c. 104, or in *Cong. Docs.* s. n. 1913 (1879).

The Coolie Fiction 45

The immediate result of these stringent regulations was to drive the contract coolie trade to other ports beyond the reach of the English Government, and it was shortly concentrated in the Portuguese city of Macao and carried on in shipping not British. After the Chinese War of 1856–7 it again crept into Whampoa and Canton, but in 1859 the mercantile community of Canton rose against it and it was again confined to Macao, where it was only nominally controlled by the Portuguese Government.[6]

Meanwhile, all the other foreign powers, led by England, regulated the contract coolie trade more and more strictly. Emigrants from Canton and Hong Kong were inspected and registered by English officers, and passage brokers paid a heavy license. In 1862 the United States forbade the coolie trade in American vessels and at American ports; in 1866, France, England and China drew up joint regulations with which the West Indies refused to comply, thus bringing the legalized trade to an end. Although it still continued at the port of Macao, and occasionally from Cumsingmoon and other illegal ports, it shortly afterward died out altogether at the Treaty Ports.[7]

It is easy to see that, when the newspapers were full of references to the cruelties of this contract coolie trade and the difficulty of suppressing it, the casual reader might readily infer that the Chinese laborers who came to California were of the same class. The peculiar behavior of the Chinese upon their arrival in the United States looked to the outsider as if they were under some mysterious control, and it was, therefore, most natural for careless persons to infer that the coolie trade was being insidiously transplanted to American soil. Such appears to be the only way of accounting for the general

---

[6] *Parl. Repts.* Bowring to Molesworth, Oct. 6, 1855; Corresp. relating to Emig. from Canton, 1860, p. 168. Speer, *The Oldest Empire*, p. 483; Ency. Brit. vol. 6, art. *Coolie.*

[7] *U. S. Stats.*, 37 Cong. 3ess. 11, Ch. 27 (1862). Eitel, *Europe in China*, p. 505.

46 Free Immigration

and persistent belief that the Chinese immigrants were under a contract to serve somebody, somewhere, for a term of years at starvation wages.

It is only necessary to turn to the reports of English officials at Oriental ports to obtain convincing proof that this was an entire error. The British agent sent out in 1852, to obtain contract labor for the West Indian colonies described one class of emigrants as coolies, the other "those who pay their own expenses to California." Interpreter Parkes reported to his superior, in 1852, that the emigration to California was an exception to the general mode, and he thought these should be called passengers, rather than coolies. In his frequent dispatches to the Home Government, Dr. John Bowring, English Consul and Plenipotentiary for many years at Hong Kong, always distinguished, as a matter of course, between contract coolies and the free emigrants to California and Australia.[8]

These English officers were men of distinguished ability, who understood the Chinese language or had competent interpreters and were perfectly familiar with the forms of the Coolie contract and the horrors of the barracoons. It can scarcely be supposed that men of such training and such experience could be mistaken as to the facts of Chinese emigration from the ports where they were employed for so many years.

No authority, either in China or the United States, has disputed the fact that the Chinese who went to California after 1855, sailed from the British port of Hong Kong and must, therefore, have been under the inspection of both English and American emigration officers; nor that the center of the contract coolie trade was at the Portuguese port of Macao and the Chinese non-treaty port of

---

[8] *Parl. Repts.* Bowring to Malmesbury, May 17, 1852. Consul Alcock to Bowring, Sept. 1., 1852. Parkes to Bowring, Oct. 1, 1853. Bowring to the Earl of Clarendon, Nov. 28, 1854. Bowring to Molesworth, Oct. 6, 1855. See also Eitel, *Europe in China*, p. 344; 387.

The Coolie Fiction 47

Whampoa. The two most scholarly Americans living in China for a whole generation, have repeatedly stated these facts and declared that only a very few of the earliest emigrants to California could possibly have been contract coolies.[9]

If further proof is needed it is found in the fact that the British Agents could not obtain ships to transport contract coolies to the British Colonies in 1853 and 1854, because shipmasters obtained much higher rates by carrying tea, silk and manufactured articles and passengers to California. The number of voluntary emigrants was so great at one time that they waited by hundreds for weeks to obtain passage, and even then were left behind after having paid from fifty to sixty dollars passage money.[10]

It would be surprising, however, if in the years before the Passengers Act took effect and when voluntary emigration was not yet wholly confined to the port of Hong Kong, some attempts had not been made to ship contract coolies to the United States. A few such instances did occur, of which the most important was the affair of the *Robert Bowne*, sailing from Amoy in 1852, which was reported to the State Department by Minister Parker. Four hundred Chinese emigrants had been enticed on the vessel nominally bound for San Francisco; when they discovered that they had been deceived and were being carried into contract service, they mutinied and killed the officers; and afterwards testified in court that they had been promised four dollars a month in the United States as hired laborers and not as contract coolies.[11]

If we turn from the Chinese to the American end of

---

[9] Dr. S. Wells Williams and Honorable Chester Holcombe.
[10] *Parl. Repts.* Agent White, Dec. 10, 1853; Gov. Bonham, Jan. 6, 1854. *Cong. Docs.* s. n. 982, Dec. 22, 1854. *China Mail*, April 16 and 24, 1854.
[11] Details of the affair of the Robert Bowne are given in *Cong. Docs.* s. n. 824, Sen. Doc. 99. (1852); *Parl. Repts.* Consul Alcock to Bowring, Sept. 1, 1852, gives what is probably another instance.

the story there is abundant refutation of this mistake in both official and private documents. President Lincoln's Message in 1861, the voluminous report on the Coolie Trade in the House in 1862, and the correspondence between Minister Burlingame and Secretary of State Seward in 1866, all show clearly that the State Department, as well as the Commissioners, Ministers and Consuls of the United States in China, was engaged in preventing the shipment of Chinese laborers under contract to Cuba, the West Indies and South America. Nowhere in these papers is there even a suggestion that contract coolies had been shipped to this country.[12] Moreover, almost every intelligent American who has studied Chinese life or written upon it, all the missionaries among them, the better educated immigration officials in this country and many employers of Chinese, unite in declaring that they came just as freely as the immigrants at Atlantic ports.

To this testimony may be added that of the Chinese of all classes, perfectly unanimous throughout fifty years that only a few contract coolies were ever brought here and those before 1853. No Chinaman has ever been known to acknowledge that he was under a coolie contract in California; nobody has ever produced in evidence such a labor contract in the State; and the Six Companies, as spokesmen for their countrymen, have always asserted that Chinese laborers came as voluntary immigrants, either paying their own passage or borrowing the money to pay it, and that this payment did not involve any term of service either by written or verbal contract.

Even in California the coolie error has been occasionally, if not adequately, refuted. In 1852, when the term "Celestials" was superseded—probably as a result of Senator Tingley's much-debated "Cooley Bill"—by the

[12] *Cong. Docs.* s. n. 1069, H. Rept. 443, (1860); s. n. 1057. no, 88, (1860); s. n. 1127, no. 16 (1861); s. n. 1281, pp. 492-4, 506-7 (1866); see also U. S. *Stats.* 1862, sess. 11, Ch. 27; 1864, sess. 1, Ch. 246; *Cong. Docs.* 1913 (1879); Williams, Soc. Sci. Assoc. 1879, p. 5; Fisher, *Personal Narrative*, p. 260.

The Coolie Fiction 49

word coolie, the *Daily Alta California* described the Contract Trade accurately and said that the conditions under which the Chinese took up their residence in the State were very different. In 1862 and 1868, the charge was authoritatively denied by the San Francisco Protection Society, by a Committee of the State Legislature and again by the leading newspapers: Such men as Daniel Cleveland, the Reverend William Speer and the Reverend Otis Gibson, who were intimately acquainted with the life of the Chinese in this country, repeatedly explained that all were voluntary immigrants; and John S. Hittell and Theodore Hittell, the foremost historians of the State, corroborated them. Senator Stanford, from the experience of the Pacific Railroads in employing them; Senator Horace Davis from a thorough study of their history and institutions, Ministers Low, John Russell Young and Charles Denby from their residence in China—all were perfectly convinced that the Chinese in the United States were free immigrants.

In spite of such incontrovertible witnesses, Congressmen, Senators from the Pacific states and many of the Coast newspapers have continuously declared and still say whenever an anti-Chinese agitation occurs, that the Chinese laborers in this country came here under a servile contract. Some say that they are in slavery to the Six Companies, some to capitalists in China, some to employers in this country—but, however vague and contradictory as to details, the lack of freedom is stoutly asserted as a fact. Such assertions would appear at this day to be a wilful misrepresentation, were it not that there is a certain official authority for the error in the statements of Consul D. H. Bailey who was stationed at Hong Kong from 1871 to 1879. His reports on the Coolie Trade and on Slavery in China have been more often quoted by Congressmen than any other authority, partly because he was the first consul to discuss the subject and partly, no doubt, because of their sensational character.

In the light of Consul Bailey's subsequent history [13] and of the later and fuller knowledge of China, his reports are seen to be a mosaic of falsehood and misrepresentation. He understood neither the Chinese language nor people apparently and it was necessary for him to cover up mal-administration in office by an appearance of zeal. In his dispatches he generally made no distinction between free and contract emigration, and his vague and false implications suggested that the essentials of the terrible coolie trade were being perpetrated in American ships and at American ports.[14] This elaborate misinformation would have been of small account if it had not become the chief source of American authority.

The first effect of it was seen in President Grant's Message of 1874, in which he called the attention of Congress to the fact that the Chinese immigrants to the United States did not come voluntarily. The question of Chinese exclusion was just beginning to be discussed seriously in Congress, and nearly the whole of Bailey's report on the Coolie Trade was quoted there, reprinted in the *Globe* and accepted at the time as authoritative. In 1876 a Committee of the California Legislature investigated the subject of Chinese immigration and following Consul Bailey, concluded that the Chinese in California were in a condition of servitude. Yet a careful examination of the testimony shows that, of ten witnesses on this point, nine said positively that they were not contract coolies and the tenth knew nothing about it.

Immediately afterward a Congressional Committee declared that the Chinese immigrants who went home had "worked out specified years of servitude." Yet of the

---

[13] During the nine years of his service he added to a salary of $3,500 per year between $35,000 and $40,000 by the embezzlement of consular fees.

[14] In 1880 his report on *Expatriation and Slavery in China* was transmitted to the House by the President. It stated positively that one-sixth of the population of China consisted of slaves to the number of 50 millions; and pictured the dangers of Chinese slavery and concubinage in the United States. *Cong. Docs.* s. n. 1925.

The Coolie Fiction

fourteen witnesses who testified on the subject, nine believed them free immigrants and three were sure they were not under any servile contract. But a certain Captain King, who had been one of Consul Bailey's assistants in the embezzlement of consular fees—and of whom Consul Mosby said that he had the reputation of being the greatest pirate that ever sailed the Chinese coast—described at length the shipment of contract coolies, said he had seen hundreds of contracts and testified that all who came to the United States were under such contracts.[15] It was on the unsupported statements of such a man that Senator Sargent, the Acting-Chairman of the committee, wrote the statement in the report. This statement was contradicted by the posthumous report of Senator Morton, the original chairman of the committee, who drew from the same testimony the conclusion that the Chinese in California were absolutely free.[16]

The vitality of the Coolie Fiction was partly due to the prejudices of an unintelligent class who wished to believe it and partly, no doubt, to the behavior of the Chinese immigrants, which seemed to make it plausible. The laborers who arrived in San Francisco had very little money, yet their passages had been prepaid; they were met at the wharves, went directly to the rooms of the Six Companies, and often to employment which seemed to await them; they appeared to make no individual bargains, but to be guided by some Chinese agent and when working in gangs often received their money through such an agent. It was naturally inferred by casual observers that the Six Companies had imported them and were holding them in control until the cost of immigration was repaid; though these circumstances, as we shall see, have a very simple explanation and do not indicate any degree of servitude on the part of the immigrant.[17]

[15] *Cong. Docs.* s. n. 1834.
[16] *Cong. Docs.* s. n. 1785, Doc. 20 (1878).
[17] The curious mixture of ideas among Californians is well shown in Lloyd, *Lights and Shades*, pp. 12–13 (1876).

A farther lease of life was undoubtedly given to the coolie error by the importation of several thousand Chinese laborers by the Pacific Railroads in 1868 and 1869. In order to complete the roads in the time required by Congress, a very large force of laborers was needed; since very few white men were to be had at any price the Central Pacific sent an agent to China, who engaged several thousand Chinamen there and prepaid their passages and other expenses. Each Chinaman signed a promissory note for $75 in gold coin, payable on demand, secured by the endorsement of friends in China and agreed to repay it in regular instalments for seven months, from a guaranteed wage of $35 per month. Every laborer was free to go home as soon as his debt was paid.[18]

Since 1870, no person who has understood the Chinese language, no one who has had any considerable firsthand knowledge of the Chinese at home or in this country, but has denied that they were in any kind of slavery. The Chinese merchants have explained again and again that they acted as agents to furnish labor but that they received no pay for this service except the profit which they make on provisions and merchandise sold to the laborer. Nevertheless, in the face of a mass of incontrovertible testimony the representatives of California in Congress continued to defend the exclusion laws on the ground that the Chinese do not come as free agents.[19] As recently as 1906 Senator George C. Perkins declared that they were in practical slavery and quoted Consul Bailey as final authority; endeavoring by this means to convince the Eastern public, not merely on the floor of Congress for political purposes but through the pages of a reputable magazine, that the opposition to the Chinese is not merely an unreasoning prejudice.[20]

---

[18] *Alta*, June 24, 1869, statement of foreman of construction; similar instance in Sacramento *Union*, Feb. 26, 1878.
[19] Additional authorities: Foster, *American Diplomacy*; O'Meara, *Overland Mo.*, v. 3, p. 481; Willis, *Report*, s. n. 1822, H. R. 240; Tuan Kai, California Labor Com., App. *Legisl. Jos.* (1886), p. 429.
[20] *N. A. Review*, July, 1906.

The Coolie Fiction 53

The coolie superstition is an example of the principle that an error has only to be repeated to be believed. The apparent control of the Chinese Six Companies over their immigrant countrymen, the mobility of Chinese labor, and the custom of Chinese merchants to act as employment agents, gave color to the inference that they were not free agents; while the horrors of the coolie contract trade, the confusing use of the word " coolie " in several different senses and the anti-slavery agitation throughout the English-speaking world made public opinion unusually sensitive to the possibility of such conditions in the United States. The rapidly growing objection to contract labor and the still more rapidly growing power of labor interests over the press and over politicians combined with all these causes to make those who were opposed to Chinese immigration for any reason ready to believe and to spread the belief in coolie slavery wherever it would influence the public and the legislator against them.

The history of the Chinese immigration debates in Congress through more than thirty years—given in other chapters—shows the unfortunate effect of these combined interests and influences. Few men who wished to continue in office in any Coast state dared to contradict the misstatement of the anti-Chinese representatives. Many eastern Congressmen were sufficiently well-educated in the history of China and the Coolie Trade to dispute it, but the majority of legislators knew nothing about the matter and naturally supposed that the continuous repetition of it on the Coast and by nearly all the Coast Congressmen was sufficient evidence of its truth. When to all this is added the fact that California has always been a doubtful state in national elections and that something had always to be conceded to her just preceding elections, it is easy to see why even those legislators who knew better should pass over such an error or pander to it.

The mischievous effect of such a misunderstanding,

current through so long a period, handed down as a tradition to the younger generation who could not know of its truth or falsehood, and repeated by the newspapers for purely political interests, can never be calculated. It has embittered the Chinese with a sense of injustice; it has led the conscientious citizen and legislator to vote for measures that were repugnant to their American sense of fair-play; and it has intensified the worst aspects of race prejudice. Even to this day the principal newspapers in California repeat the same fiction to arouse race feeling against the Japanese. Yet whichever way we turn, to negative, positive, direct or indirect testimony of first-hand witnesses, the proof of error is indisputable. The persons who now assert that the Chinese came here as contract coolies, bound to a term of service, as slaves or peons, either have no personal knowledge of the subject of coolie emigration or are deliberately repeating a false tradition in order to cater to anti-Chinese feeling.

CHAPTER IV
THE DEVELOPMENT OF ANTI-CHINESE POLITICS

"It must be conceded that the extraordinary wants of this State will demand novel if not extraordinary legislation."—Governor JOHN BIGLER, 1852.

If this wail for relief from Chinese immigration . . . . was an expression of agony wrung from poor laboring men and women . . . by the oppressive yoke the heathen has laid upon them, then would we say, let us arise and shake it off. But in the cadence we can plainly distinguish the assumed lamentations of weak but aspiring politicians who lead in this dismal concert, hoping they will be caught up . . . by the wave that follows after and borne on its crest to political glory."—LLOYD, *Lights and Shades of San Francisco.*

"If the privileges of your laws are open to us, some of us will doubtless acquire your habits, your language, your ideas, your feelings, your morals, your forms and become citizens of your country. Many have already adopted your religion as their own, and will be good citizens. There are very good Chinamen now in the country; and a better class will, if allowed, come hereafter—men of learning and of wealth, bringing their families with them."—Open Letter of the Chinese, 1852.

THE rapid increase of the Chinese between 1850 and 1852 and the expulsion from the mines of the Spanish Americans and the French, combined to turn attention suddenly upon Asiatic immigration. As the winter of 1852-3 came on the miners came into the settlements, particularly San Francisco, and it doubtless appeared to them—especially to those who had been unsuccessful—that they had got rid of their Latin competitors only to be overwhelmed by worse. From this time on the Chinese were marked for the convenient attack of the discontented classes; but the organized antagonism might have been long postponed but for the violent race prejudices and political ambition of Governor Bigler.[1]

[1] John Bigler was a Pennsylvanian of German antecedents; a printer, lawyer, editor and Broderick Democrat; he served two terms. J. S. Hittell says of him: "a man who had neither the capacity, the educa-

In the State campaign of 1852 he was a candidate for re-election and, although only a few months before he had publicly expressed his friendship for the Chinese, he now seized upon the question of immigration as an effective campaign appeal to the mining vote. In a special message he stated that vast numbers of the Chinese were coming in, actuated by cupidity rather than by a desire to share the blessings of a free government. They were migratory and unassimilable and if, as was supposed, they were ignorant of the solemnity of an oath, it would be unwise to admit them to citizenship. He described the coolie trade to Spanish countries, implying that the Chinese in the United States were brought on similar terms; yet in the same document he said he had "no official information" on this point, but if it were so, it ought to be discouraged. After making other equally equivocal and misleading charges, he recommended heavy taxation and an appeal to Congress to prohibit contract coolies from working in the mines.[2]

The message was looked upon as merely a strategic move in the coming campaign and failed to carry public opinion. Although Governor Bigler was re-elected, no anti-Chinese legislation except the Miners' License tax—not then specifically aimed at the Chinese—was enacted. The more intelligent Chinese appealed from Bigler to the judgment of the public in an open letter, reasonable in tone and admirably stated.[3] Various meetings were held in San Francisco at which lectures were given by the Reverend William Speer, a returned missionary from China, and pro-Chinese resolutions were passed which

---

tion or the manners to grace the position . . . the better Democrats were ashamed of him." (*Hist. of San Francisco*, p. 281.) Theodore Hittell says; "He was generally regarded as a mere politician and by no means a strong or high-minded one. His administration has always been looked upon as signalized by many abuses and very great extravagance.—" (*Hist. of Cal.*, v. 4, p. 180.)

[2] *Sen. Jo.* 1852, p. 373.

[3] *Annals of San Francisco*, p. 381, (1854). Hittell, *Hist. of Cal.*, v. 4, 108.

were favorably noticed by the newspapers.[4] The reaction was registered in the Legislature where the Committee on Mines and Mining Interests reported that the fear of overwhelming numbers of the Chinese was unfounded and that Chinese trade should be encouraged.[5]

At the session of 1853 the legal adviser of the Six Companies appeared before this committee and stated that the number of the Chinese had declined four thousand in the year because of the Governor's message. He explained that all the Chinese in this country were members of one of several companies representing their different dialects and localities in China. Each immigrant paid ten dollars registration fee; but if he was very poor, the company advanced him money to pay his mining license tax and to buy tools. The companies acted as arbiters to settle petty differences; and the company buildings were used as hotels, hospitals and post-offices. The Six Companies assured the Committee that although the Chinese had at one time been hired by other Chinese and by foreign capitalists to work under contract, it had not been profitable and was no longer done. Most of the immigrants came with their own means, borrowing on property or labor or family security. The companies complained that their testimony was excluded from the courts and that they were taxed for the privilege of working in the mines while at the same time the State did not afford them protection. They recommended an increase of the License tax and asked that some settled policy be pursued towards them so that they might in fact as well as in law occupy the same position as other foreigners.

Just at this time the *Daily Alta California*, the most influential paper in the State, which had been warmly pro-Chinese, went over to the Bigler party owing to a

[4] *Alta*, Apr. 29, 1852. Speer, *China and California*, (pamphlet, 1853.) Gibson, *The Chinese in America*, p. 225.
[5] App. *Ass. Jo.* 1853, Doc. 28, pp. 7–12.

change of editors. The series of anti-Chinese editorials published in the spring of 1853 did much to inflame the people. They charged the Chinese with being debased and servile coolies, inferior to the negroes morally and mentally—more clannish, dangerous, deceitful and vicious—and immeasurably lower than the Indians; with living upon rats and lizards and shell-fish where flour, beef and bacon abounded. The editor even declared that they made neither good servants nor laborers, though he did acknowledge that there were many who made intelligent citizens and that much of the prejudice against them was due to the jealous greed of the miners.[6]

Although the Governor reiterated his objections to the Chinese, the Legislature of 1854 declined to make the question of immigration the principal issue. A few radical propositions were lost or buried in Committee and the only record of note was the curious report of the Committee on Vice and Immorality, in which anti-Chinese sentiment was coupled with a decrease of gambling, an increase of Temperance, Sunday-School attendance and refined society, as signs of moral growth.[7]

The rise of the Know-nothing party whose purpose was to exclude all foreign-born citizens from office and to discourage immigration, gave a new impetus to the anti-Chinese movement in California. While on the Atlantic Coast the Know-nothings clamored against the Irish Catholic immigration, the Irish Catholic and the other European aliens on the Pacific Coast, under the leadership of the Chivalry faction of the Democrats, vented their foreign prejudices on the still newer alien Chinese.

The feeling against them was still further aggravated by hard times and industrial discontent. The pursuit of mining had dwarfed every other legitimate business;

[6] *Daily Alta*, 1853, May 21, June 4 and 15, July 29. The *Alta* was pro-Chinese till toward the end of 1852, then anti-Chinese till 1855, then again moderately pro-Chinese. In later years it recommended Federal exclusion measures and remained conservative and capitalistic as compared with other papers.
[7] *Sen. Jo.* 1854, pp. 623-4.

Development of Anti-Chinese Politics 59

real estate, building and importation of goods were on a purely speculative basis. Profits were enormous and three times in as many years the market was overstocked with merchandize. The yield of the placers began to decline in 1853-4 and with the discovery of gold in Australia white immigration also declined. Prices, rents and values fell rapidly in 1854 and throughout that and the next year many serious failures of business houses occurred and foreign investors became alarmed and withdrew their capital.[8] As a result, there were strikes for higher wages among laborers and mechanics although the current wages of skilled labor was ten dollars per day, and of unskilled, three and a half to five dollars per day.

In addition to the small floating supply of labor, many small speculators and even miners were driven back to their original professions and to farming and manual labor. San Francisco was full of men out of work and of men whose ideas of wages and profits had been raised to an exorbitant standard by speculative conditions. Such as these were extravagant, disappointed and unwilling to accept either the wages or the labor that they had been accustomed to in the states from which they came. To such men, the presence of thousands of un-American, thrifty, industrious " cheap " Chinese laborers was the perfectly obvious cause of their condition. Doubtless, the Chinese suffered, too, in the general disaster, but not so seriously because they had been more thrifty and less dissipated, their occupations were on a less speculative basis and their ambitions had not been so high.

From the general confusion and readjustment of values and of social stations, there emerged a few rich and shrewd capitalists comparatively unharmed. They alone could give employment to the unemployed and they

[8] Seyd, *California and its Resources*, (1849–1853) e. c. *Annals of San Francisco* (1853-4), pp. 459, 519–20. Bancroft, *Hist. of California*, v. 6, p. 781. Hittell, J. S., *Hist. of San Francisco* (1854-7), p. 196.

chose to employ the cheapest labor available—the Chinese —who took whatever they could get to do at whatever wage, while white men walked the streets.

The average man is not an economist when he is poor and hungry. He might scorn the decent work and fair wage which the Chinese accepted, but he was nevertheless sure that if no Chinese were in the labor market there would be agreeable work at high wages for himself. Most of all he hated the rich man who had been successful and who now, overlooking his unsuccessful white competitor, preferred an alien inferior. From this time on, therefore, the violence of class as well as of race prejudice, increased and the cry against the Chinese is in part, at least, to be explained by the deeper agitation against the class made rich by speculation.

When for a third time Governor Bigler reiterated his objections to the Chinese he was listened to with sympathy, for the Legislature reflected inevitably the general economic discontent. Every imaginable charge was now brought against them except that of laziness and extravagance; they were "cheap," they bought nothing and sent their savings back to China, they were "contract coolies," they were corrupt, filthy and vicious, selling their children into slavery; their quarters were unsanitary and made the neighborhood uninhabitable; though they could neither be naturalized nor testify in the courts in white cases, yet—strangely enough—they did not intend to make the United States their permanent home and preferred the secret government of the Six Companies to that of enlightened San Francisco.[9] To such representations of the workingmen, the Legislature responded with a prohibitive Miners License tax and a high capitation tax which was shortly afterward declared unconstitutional.

In San Francisco the general fall in values and the

[9] *App. Sen. Jo.* 1855, Doc. 16, Minority Report of Crenshaw and Norman. *App. Sen. Jo.* 1855, Doc. 19, Majority Report of Select Committee; J. E. Clayton, speech in Assembly, Apr. 18, 1855.

Development of Anti-Chinese Politics 61

flocking in of the unemployed and discontented was coincident with conspicuous corruption in City affairs and culminated in a kind of terrorism for white citizens and Chinamen alike. The Chinese became the scape-goats for the evils of the time; they were stoned, robbed, maltreated in the streets with impunity by the idler and the hoodlum, who suffered no restraint.[10]

In a city so corrupt and intimidated by the adventurers of all nations, it was inevitable that race antipathy and the spirit of bullying on one side and fear and lack of political power on the other, should make a dark-skinned and peculiarly unintelligible race the victims of the situation. Yet even then the Chinese had many friends among the more orderly population, and, joining in the uprising for the restoration of order represented by the Vigilance Committee of 1856, they ranged themselves on the side of decency by a handsome contribution, in return for which they received some measure of protection and a vote of thanks.

When California with the whole nation became absorbed in the dissensions preceding the Civil War, local issues were almost forgotten in the splitting up of the great parties on the question of slavery. The discovery of the Comstock Lode in 1859 still further diverted the adventurous and unemployed to the mines; the settlement of many land titles gave encouragement to the development of agriculture and all these influences united to give greater stability to business and to population than California had known before.

The agitation against the Chinese was somewhat allayed also by the fact that immigration had not reached the number predicted. Although in the year 1852, 20,000 had arrived, the average gain per year between 1852 and 1855 had been only 3,500.

[10] On causes of the Vigilance Committee of 1856 see: Hittell, *Hist. of Cal.*, v. 3, p. 627 ff. Bancroft, *Works*, v. 37 (*Popular Tribunals*, v. 2) p. 662. Hittell, J. S. *Hist. of San Francisco.*

In 1862 the State went Republican, though by the narrowest margin, and State politics thus passed from the control of Southern Democrats to the party whose interest was engaged for the slave and whose race prejudices were, therefore, relatively less active. This more temperate attitude was expressed in Governor Stanford's inaugural address in which he said that since the Chinese could not vote or testify in the courts, they would necessarily be oppressed. On this account as well as for the benefit of the white workingman, immigration should not be encouraged. They should be protected while here but he would concur with the Legislature in any constitutional action to check their coming.[11]

A joint committee of the Legislature appointed to confer with the Chinese merchants, made a most favorable report. They stated that there were about 50,000 Chinese in the State who had contributed not less than fourteen millions of dollars in Customs duties, fares, freights, taxes and purchase of American products and property, toward the business of the community. They pointed out that many lines of industry carried on by white men were indebted to Chinese patronage for their recompense and that the Chinese had received in exchange little more than the privilege of mining placers and doing work which white men scorned. They found no competition except with European servants in a few cities, and they denied that the Chinese were Contract Coolies and inordinately immoral and criminal. They stated in plain terms that there had been a wholesale system of wrong and outrage practised upon them; and urged the wisdom of preserving friendly trade relations with China and the unwisdom of driving from the State a class of foreigners so peaceful, industrious and useful.[12]

During the Civil War there was little legislation and agitation concerning the Chinese, for California, though

[11] *Sen. Jo.* 1862, p. 61.
[12] App. *Legisl. Jos.*, 1862, v. 3.

Development of Anti-Chinese Politics 63

so isolated, was nevertheless deeply stirred by the Civil Struggle. There were many causes of industrial discontent, the panic of 1862, the droughts, the insecurity of capital and high rates of interest, the lack of coal, iron and cotton which delayed the beginnings of manufacture—which must inevitably have broken out as before in anti-Chinese demonstrations but for the construction of the Pacific railroads.[13]

In 1864, the working force on the Central Pacific railroad was raised to 4000 men of whom only 1000 were white laborers—all that could be obtained.[14] In 1865 the railroads called for 5000 more men and 600 teams with offers of high wages, steady employment and sure pay; but white men were unwilling to leave the more congenial and profitable work of mining and farming. When the Central Pacific was finished in 1869 the railroads were employing nearly ten thousand men, nine-tenths of whom were Chinese. Mr. Stanford reported that without them it would have been impossible to complete the western portion of this great enterprise within the time required by law; and that they were peaceable, industrious and economical, apt to learn and quite as efficient as white laborers.[15]

With the absorption of all manual labor—white and Chinese—in railroad building, with the decline of immigration and the preoccupation of politicians in war and reconstruction, there was neither motive nor inclination for anti-Chinese agitation. But with the return of peace and an era of extraordinary prosperity due to an abundance of rain and new silver discoveries, the diverse elements of which the Union party was composed, under the pressure of the slavery question, began to break apart. The conservative Republican faction reappeared as an independent party and the Democrats of California,

[13] Hittell, J. S., *Resources of California* (ed. 1863) pp. 304–5, 346–7.
[14] Rept. of Leland Stanford to the Legislature, 1865.
[15] Rept. of S. S. Montague, Chief Engineer, 1865. Stanford, *Progress of Work*, Oct. 10, 1865. Hittell, *Hist. of Cal.*, v. 4, pp. 478–480.

so long split into segments by the war issues, were welded anew into a homogeneous party by the rising local issue of labor.

The immigration of white Europeans increased rapidly during this decade until in 1870 the Irish alone constituted one-fourth of the 210,000 foreign-born persons in the State.[16] This element naturally affiliated with the Democrats and as naturally emphasized labor issues. In the campaign of 1867 all parties were occupied with race and labor questions. As in many subsequent campaigns the bitterness of class and color prejudice was invoked to win the unstable workingmen and alien voters. Before the nominations, anti-Chinese associations, formed chiefly of workingmen, invited the four Union candidates for the governorship to express their opinions on the Chinese question. Their somewhat guarded and moderate statements did not please the laboring men as was proved by an overwhelming Democratic victory.[17] On taking office, Governor Haight urged the discouragement of Chinese immigration and thought that the decline of white immigration and the lack of white labor would cease upon the completion of the Pacific railroads.[18] Although strongly opposed to negro suffrage, he believed that if suffrage was given to the negro, it should be given to the Chinaman also.

It had been supposed that the completion of the transcontinental railway would usher in an era of unprecedented prosperity; but it was, on the contrary, the occasion of widespread disappointment on the Pacific Coast. Lands did not continue to rise in value, the change from steamship to railway transportation threw many men out of employment, freights remained inordinately high, and ten thousand white and Chinese laborers were discharged

[16] The total population of California in 1870 was 560,247.
[17] Davis, *Political Conventions*.
[18] Governor Haight had been favorable to the Chinese and a Straight Republican until after 1860; but having changed his political opinions, he was elected Governor in 1867 on the Democratic ticket.

upon the California labor market. The working classes centered their ill-feeling upon railroads, corporations and the Chinese—for to the prejudices of race was now added the most bitter feeling against the capitalists of the railways. The State Democratic platform of 1869 championed the rights of the workingmen and was violently anti-negro, anti-railway, anti-corporation and anti-Chinese. Article Six of that document declared:

"We are opposed to the adoption of the proposed Fifteenth Amendment of the United States Constitution, believing the same to be designed, and if adopted, certain to degrade the right of suffrage; to ruin the white laboring men, by bringing untold hordes of pagan slaves (in all but name) into direct competition with his efforts to earn a livelihood; to build up an aristocratic class of oligarchs in our midst created and maintained by Chinese votes; to give the negro and the Chinaman the right to vote and to hold office; and that its passage would be inimical to the best interests of the country." [19]

The Republican party was becoming identified in the West not only with conservative and capitalistic interests, but with the demand for cheaper labor in agriculture, manufacture and large construction enterprises. It deprecated the further agitation of questions of race and suffrage, and although it, too, found it necessary—and safe—to be nominally anti-Chinese for political purposes, it posed as their protector and urged restriction of immigration by constitutional and Congressional measures only.

In a State so nearly divided between the two parties the whole body of workingmen must be won over by either, in order to carry a campaign. The rapid development of labor organizations during this period, and their entrance into politics, placed labor issues among all party questions. A rising tide of popular discontent, intensified by panic and unemployment, expressed itself in attacks upon railway subsidies, monopoly and cheap labor. The cam-

[19] Davis, *Political Conventions*, p. 289 ff.

paign of 1871, waged upon these issues, resulted in a Republican victory. At once the tone of public utterances upon the Chinese question became more moderate.

Governor Booth in his inaugural address, emphasized the fact that the Federal government had sole control of immigration. His paragraph on the persecution of the Chinese is memorable among the public statements of officials in California, for its uncompromising quality. In urging that they should be protected, he said:

> "Mob violence is the most dangerous form in which law can be violated not merely in the immediate outrage committed but in the results which often follow—communities debauched, jurors intimidated and courts controlled by the political influence of the number that are guilty; and when to all this, banded ruffianism selects for its victims a race notoriously defenseless, when pillage are its exploits, the race from which such wretches are recruited, the community which suffers such deeds to be enacted, the officials who stand supinely by without an effort to prevent the crime, are sharers in a common disgrace and the statute which prevents the victim from testifying, becomes party to the offense." [20]

The Eastern panic of 1873 resulted in a sudden increase of overland emigration to California which was accelerated by the silver discoveries, the development of new industries and the greater ease of transportation. Unfortunately Eastern capitalists had been frightened by the violent fluctuations of markets in California, and, in spite of a current rate of interest of ten per cent, money was not invested in sound industrial enterprises as rapidly as the laborers to man them arrived. Many other adverse conditions increased the popular unrest. The per capita tax was $18.75, twice that of many Eastern states and higher than any other; gigantic frauds in public offices increased the burden; farming lands were held by speculators in large parcels at prices practically prohibitive to the Colonist, while the high wages of farm labor and the cost of transportation, made even the profits of bonanza farming extremely precarious. A temporary

[20] *Sen. Jo.* 1871-2, pp. 115-16.

prosperity in 1874 and 1875 absorbed the surplus immigrant labor and diverted the discontented classes, but the political and social upheaval, which found its outlet ultimately in Kearneyism and the Workingmen's party, was now inevitable.

From this time onward the question of Chinese immigration was the test of political advancement. That it may be understood how little Chinese character and behavior had to do with this result, the steps by which the Chinese question became a foremost one in party politics, have been traced. It has been shown that Governor Bigler, an unscrupulous politician, desirous of re-election, invited the allegiance of the miners by a message full of unwarranted assumptions. The dominant political party, recruited by white immigration and pledged against the colored races, met with no opposition from the Chinese, who could neither vote nor testify in the courts. The party out of power, in their turn, hastened to put themselves right with the miners and workingmen, by adopting an anti-Chinese plank. The labor element, newly organized and encouraged by its success in obtaining an eight-hour law, was spurred on by panic-stricken recruits from the East; and, while ignorantly confusing the causes of their discontent, which were fundamentally industrial, with their race and class prejudices, came to hold the balance of power.

With all this the Chinaman had nothing to do. He was not responsible for mining and real estate booms and slumps, for criminal waves requiring Vigilance Committees; for corruption, extravagance and profligacy in State and City government; nor for land and railway monopoly. He was, meanwhile, doing the work which white men refused to do, taking the placers the white man left, wearing his queer clothes, eating his strange food, paying his debts and taxes, and unconsciously drawing upon himself by that very strangeness and docility, an organized antagonism.

That antagonism, arising in part from race antipathy and in part from industrial turmoil, was expressed at first in a variety of curious and almost inhuman legislative measures; and for twenty years was the convenient method by which the California aspirant in politics endeavored to put himself right with that most important constituency, the workingmen.

CHAPTER V

ANTI-CHINESE LEGISLATION IN CALIFORNIA[1]

"If this attempt to force Africans, Chinese and Diggers into our white schools is persisted in, it must result in the ruin of our schools. The great mass of our citizens will not associate on terms of equality with these inferior races, nor will they consent that their children should do so."—A. J. MOULDER, State Superintendent of Public Instruction, 1859.

"That the evidence of all Asiatics ought by law to be excluded, is generally admitted, I believe. The same reasons of a political character which exist for the exclusion of negroes and Indians as witnesses apply with equal force to such Asiatics as usually immigrate to this State; while in veracity and other moral qualities they are beneath either of those races."—J. R. McCONNELL, Attorney-General of California, 1854.

"If all classes pay taxes for the support of schools there is no reason why the children of all classes, whether white, black, tawny or copper-colored, should not be educated."—JOHN SWETT, State Superintendent of Public Instruction, 1865.

"There is not a county government in the mining counties that could live but for the taxes paid by the Chinese . . . . In the upper end of Sacramento and the lower end of Placer county scarcely any but Chinese buy water of the ditch companies."—JOHN E. BENTON, State Assemblyman, 1862.

"Nor was the ground taken by California in opposing foreign immigration reasonable or tenable;—she made war alone on an individual class, on a single nationality, not by any means the one that was doing or had done or was likely to do, the greatest injury to the Commonwealth; indeed it was the most harmless class of all, its chief offense being the only one that was never mentioned, the fact that it could not vote."—BANCROFT, *History of California*.

The Foreign Miners' License tax, originally intended to exclude the Spanish-Americans, the French and other foreigners from the mines, was finally directed specific-

[1] This whole subject will be covered in great detail in a chapter on "The Struggle to Exclude Oriental Labor from California" in Eaves' *History of Labor Legislation in California*, now in press.

ally against the Chinese. The State officials discovered that many of the counties could not exist without the income from this tax and the amount was therefore reduced to a point where the thrifty Chinese would just bear it without leaving the district. In this way it was made to yield an income of more than five million dollars between 1850 and 1870, of which not less than ninety-five per cent was paid by them. At the same time, the strong anti-foreign feeling, intensified by race antipathy, was seized upon by State politicians as the most effective means of appeal to the miners who constituted the largest body of voters outside of San Francisco. Thus, two contradictory motives, thrift and anti-Chinese prejudice, found expression in legislation of two general classes: taxation—on the one hand for revenue, on the other for exclusion—and the denial of privileges enjoyed by other foreigners.

The attempts at taxation invited by the thrift and docility of the Chinese, though made under a variety of titles, were generally in the form of head-taxes or licenses. In 1852, the California Legislature passed a bill requiring the masters of vessels to give a per capita bond of five hundred dollars as indemnity against the costs of medical and other relief of alien passengers; or to commute such bond by the payment of not less than five and not more than ten dollars per passenger. The income arising from this tax was to be apportioned among the principal hospitals of the State.[2] The tax was collected until rendered unconstitutional by the Federal statute enforcing the Fifteenth Amendment;[3] and the whole amount paid into the State Treasury was $433,654.94, of which the Chinese never paid less than 45 per cent and, in 1869, were paying 85 per cent. During the whole of this period they were excluded from the city hospital in San Francisco, and the only ones to which they

---

[2] *Stats. of Cal.* 1852, Ch. 36, p. 79 ff.
[3] U. S. 114, sec. 16, 1870. *People* v. *Constitution*, 42 Cal. 578.

were ever freely admitted were the insane asylums and the pest-house.[4]

The Capitation tax levied in 1855 required the master, owner or consignee of any vessel, having on board persons ineligible to become citizens, to pay fifty dollars per person.[5] E. C. McGowan, the Commissioner of Immigration at San Francisco, reported in 1856 that ninety-six Chinese had arrived since September, 1855, but he had not collected the head tax because "everybody knew" it was unconstitutional. He was removed from office ostensibly for this offense;[6] whereupon seventy-eight merchant firms of San Francisco memorialized the Legislature on his behalf. The memorial objected to the statute because it placed a positive restriction on Chinese immigration, which would be detrimental to the interests of the state, depriving it of consumers and revenue, and because it was unenforceable.

The committee on Mines and Mining Interests to which the memorial was referred, reported that unrestricted immigration would be a temporary benefit to a small class of citizens in San Francisco, but "would prove suicidal to the great mining interests of the state." They assumed a lofty attitude referring to the signers as "extremely disloyal" and to the memorial as "an insult to the Legislature."[7] An attempt having been made to collect from the owners of the ship *Stephen Baldwin*, the Supreme Court declared the tax unconstitutional.[8]

[4] If the 139,000 who arrived before 1870 had paid five dollars each, the full amount would have been $695,000, i. e. $262,000 more than was paid into the treasury. It is probable that this discrepancy is accounted for by one or two embezzlements which are known to have occurred in the history of this fund.
[5] *Cal. Stats.* 1855, p. 194. A Senate Resolution was passed in 1864 urging Congress to permit California to impose a capitation tax on the Chinese. *Sen. Jo.* 1854, p. 600, 617.
[6] Hittell, *Hist. of Cal.*, vol. 4, p. 388–9.
[7] Appendix *Ass. Jo.* 1856, Doc. no. (blank).
[8] People vs. Downer, Cal. 169; under the authority of the passenger cases, 7 How. 122, as "an attempt to regulate Commerce." Report of Attorney-General, July 2, 1856, *Ass. Jo.*

Another form of Capitation Tax was the so-called "Police Tax. The one passed in 1862 taxed all Mongolians over eighteen years of age who were not engaged in the production of rice, sugar, tea or coffee, or who had not already paid the Miners' License Tax, two dollars and a half per month.[9] This was declared unconstitutional in the following year by the Supreme Court of California.[10] Governor Stanford pronounced this statute "stringent and oppressive," but trusted that the Legislature might find it possible to avoid these constitutional objections by a substitute which might reach "the object desired, the discouragement of Chinese immigration and not its total prohibition."[11]

Another measure, similar in character, was proposed in 1870, but failed. It levied special taxes on the Chinese to provide a special Police force to watch the Six Companies, to break up female and coolie slavery, and to provide for the support of sick and indigent Chinese. The bill is mentioned only because of the report accompanying it in which the Special Committee purports to have discovered that the increase of the Chinese was fifty per cent faster than the whites; that nine-tenths were Coolie slaves, and that their 3000 women were nearly all prostitutes. The committee said these were disgraceful facts which they challenged any one to controvert.[12]

The success of the Foreign Miners' License Tax led to other attempts to tax the occupations chiefly undertaken by the Chinese. The Fishing license was suggested by the predominance of the Chinese in certain kinds of fishing, particularly the catching of the *abalone,* a shell-fish which was an important article of consumption among their countrymen and of export to China.[13] In 1860 a tax

---

[9] *Cal. Stats.* 1862, 462-3.
[10] *Ling Sing* v. Washburn, 20 *Cal.* 534-586.
[11] Annual Message, *Sen Jo.* 1863, p. 30.
[12] App. to *Jos. of Ass. and Sen.*, v. 2, 1870.
[13] *Hutching's Mag.* v. 1, p. 347. *Alta,* Mar. 5, Apr. 24, May 20, 1853, Bancroft, *Works,* v. 38, p. 348.

Anti-Chinese Legislation in California

was laid of four dollars per month on all Chinese engaged in fishing, to be enforced by the seizure of fish, boat or other property.[14] Only a small revenue was obtained from this source and the law was repealed in 1864.[15] Upon complaint of the Italians, Greeks and Dalmatians who somewhat later comprised a majority of the fishermen about San Francisco, a law was passed regulating the size of the small-meshed shrimp nets chiefly used by the Chinese.[16] By 1870 the export value of the *abalone* was nearly one million dollars;[17] and in 1880 the Fish Commission complained that the Chinese shipped three million dollars worth of dried shrimps annually to China, and recommended a law against shrimp and drag nets.[18] As a result, the Legislature passed a law requiring fishermen to take out a license of two dollars and a half a month.[19] The tax proved both difficult and costly to collect and brought only a meager return, partly because the number of the Chinese in the business was rapidly declining.[20]

In 1888 the value of the shrimp meat exported to China was said to be $77,000 and of shrimp shells, $38,000; and there were in addition about two million and a half pounds of *abalone* shells exported. From this time on, other foreigners, chiefly Italians, rapidly encroached upon the fishing business. In 1893 there were about 2,500 fishermen in the vicinity of San Francisco, of whom less than one-fourth were native-born Americans, about one-fourth Chinese, and the remainder Italian, Portuguese and Scandinavian.[21]. During the last decade all nationalities including the Americans and the Chinese have been

---

[14] *Cal. Stats.* 1860, p. 307.
[15] *Cal. Stats.* 1864, p. 492.
[16] *Daily Alta California*, Jan. 2, 1876.
[17] Bancroft, *Works*, v. 38, p. 348.
[18] An. Rept. Com. of Fisheries, 1887-8, App. *Legis. Jos.* v. 1.
[19] *Cal. Stats.* 1887, Sec. 435, Penal Code.
[20] In 1887, $4,782.30 was collected from 1800 fishermen of all nationalities at a cost of $492.30.
[21] Walsh, *Cal. Illustrated Mag.*, 1893, v. 4, p. 833.

superseded by the Italians. The Chinese now supply only their own local markets and in recent years have been forbidden to export shrimps and shells to China.[22] It is an open secret that the Italians have obtained the monopoly of the business by intimidation—even an American cannot fish on the waters of San Francisco Bay without being in danger of his life.[23]

The exclusion of the Chinese from the fishing industry has been accomplished by laws nominally constitutional, but demanded by other foreigners and enforced so as to chiefly affect the Chinese. It does not appear that the export of dried fish and shells was more injurious to the State than the wanton destruction of fish in San Francisco waters by other foreigners or even by the unprotected sea-lions of which the Fish Commission constantly complained.[24] The result has been to raise the price of fish inordinately in the American markets. While the fish caught by Italians are sold in these markets at a monopoly price, the Italian housewives thriftily avail themselves of the lower prices in the markets of Chinatown.

A variety of other license taxes which discriminated against the Chinese have also been laid at times. In San Francisco, particularly, many ordinances have been passed affecting their occupations. The cubic air and queue ordinances of the Kearney period, described elsewhere, were only a part of them. The laundrymen have been subject to all sorts of interference for many years and the gambling houses, lotteries and brothels have been pursued vigorously, both as a source of city revenue and to divert attention from similar white establishments.[25]

---

[22] *Cal. Stats.* 1905, Sec. 628, p. 186.
[23] Interviews. *S. F. Chronicle*, Sept. 7, 1907.
[24] An. Rept. of Com. of Fisheries, *Legislative Jos.* 1880, vol. 1. 1885, vol. 1.
[25] See Chapter XV. A detailed list of these ordinances, compiled by a Seminary at the University of California under the guidance of Professor Kendric C. Babcock, and placed at the disposal of the writer, was unfortunately destroyed in the San Francisco fire of April, 1906. San Francisco *Municipal Repts.*, 1859–60; 1865–6.

From the foregoing outline of license and tax measures especially affecting the Chinese, it is evident that in later years the motive of exclusion gradually became stronger than the desire for revenue. As the Chinese question became a larger and larger factor in State politics, such legislation, though ineffective and unconstitutional, was the chief means by which the candidates of all parties strove to win the allegiance of the workingmen. But no small part of the persecution of the Chinaman was due to the fact that it was his misfortune to arrive in the United States at a period when the attention of the whole country was focussed upon the question of slavery.

The Chinaman, of whose civilization almost nothing was known in America at this time, was ignorantly compared with the negro and the Indian, merely because of the color of his skin. It was the habit of Congressmen and Editors to draw most alarming deductions from these comparisons, although the negro and the Indian belonged to primitive and comparatively undeveloped races as contrasted with the Chinese who had attained a high—if wholly different—civilization before the Caucasian race had emerged from the savage state. Such parallels, arising in part from ignorance, in part from instinctive color antipathy, were the pretext if not the sole cause of the denial to the Chinese of political privileges enjoyed by all other aliens. Yet even this scarcely serves to explain why the Californians were unwilling, even after persons of African descent were permitted to testify in the courts, to admit Chinese testimony.

As early as 1850 Indians and negroes had been excluded from testifying for or against white persons and an attempt was made at that time to exclude the Chinese also.[26] The question was finally settled for a generation by the decision of Chief Justice Murray of the California Supreme Court, that the word " Indian " included Mon-

---

[26] *Cal. Stats.* 1850, p. 455. Hittell, *Hist. of Cal.* v. 4, p. 112. *Ass. Jo.* 1853, p. 259.

golian. Judge Murray's opinion began with an attempt at ethnological discussion of the colored races and finally arrived at the theory that although the word "Indian" as commonly used, referred only to the North American Indians, yet as in the days of Columbus all shores washed by Chinese waters were called the Indies, therefore all Asiatics were Indians. In the second place the word "white" necessarily excluded all other races than the Caucasian; and in the third place, even if this were not so, he would decide against admitting the testimony of the Chinese on grounds of public policy.[27]

As a result of the Civil War and the predominance of the Republican party, the Legislature of 1863 removed the prohibition against the testimony of negroes but at the same time expressly prohibited the testimony of Mongolians, Chinese and Indians.[28] In 1865 there was an unsuccessful attempt at repeal and Governor Low in his last annual message protested against these barbarous and illiberal provisions.[29] Yet it was not until the revised Codes took effect on January first, 1873, that witnesses were admitted to the courts of California regardless of color and nationality.[30]

An even more important disability suffered by the Chinese and one not yet removed, was the denial of naturalization. The first constitution of California adopted in 1849, guaranteed the property rights of foreign residents, but limited the suffrage to "white male citizens of the United States and Mexico," with a provision that the Legislature might grant suffrage to the Indians. Partly because the Chinese were regarded as contract coolies and partly because their color caused them to be classed

---

[27] People v. Hall, 4 Cal. pp. 399–405. Sustained in Speer v. See Yup Co., 13 Cal. 73 and in People v. Elyea, 14 Cal. 144. *Ass. Jo. App.* 1855.

[28] *Cal. Stats.* 1863, pp. 60, 69.

[29] *Sen. Jo.* 1867–8, p. 34.

[30] *Cal. Code*, Civil Procedure, p. 493. People v. McGuire, 45 Cal. 56. U. S. *Stats.* 1870, Sec. 16. Sacramento *Union*, Jan. 8, 1866; July 2, 1867; July 28, Dec. 19, 1868.

Anti-Chinese Legislation in California 77

with negroes, it seems to have been taken for granted that they were inadmissible to citizenship. Now and then some intelligent editor or speaker would call attention to the fact that the Chinese were an old and highly civilized race, but with the majority of citizens ignorance and race prejudice prevented such arguments from taking effect.

The question of suffrage for the Chinese was never seriously discussed until the change in the status of the negro wrought by the Civil War precipitated the question of negro suffrage in Congress. The Burlingame Treaty of 1868 expressly excepted naturalization from the rights of the most favored nation guaranteed to the Chinese. The Western Congressmen of both parties were unanimously opposed to granting either naturalization or suffrage. Although, in the long debate in Congress which ended in the extension of suffrage to "aliens of African nativity and persons of African descent," Eastern Congressmen pointed out the inconsistency and injustice of denying naturalization to the Chinese, the united resistance of the representatives of the Pacific Coast prevented the extension of the privilege to them. In the light of later history it appears that the denial of political privileges deprived the Chinese of the only weapon which could have protected them against the lawlessness and jealousy of other foreigners and against local race discriminations.[81]

The association of the Chinese with the negro in the popular mind seems to have resulted in their being treated with even less justice than the negro in the matter of school privileges for their children. On account of the small number of Chinese families and children among the earlier immigrants, the question of school provision for

---

[81] See Ch. XV. The first application for naturalization made by a Chinaman appears to have been in 1854, see *Alta*, Dec. 3; an instance of actual naturalization in New York, 1873. See N.Y. *Sun*, Nov. 30, 1878; several were said to have taken out papers at St. Louis in 1876. Mr. Yung Wing was one of the very first to be naturalized in the East. Thirteen applied in 1876 to the California Courts—see Brook's *Brief*.

them did not arise until an agitation was started to provide for the schooling of negro children. The State Superintendent of Public Instruction in 1859 protested against the attempt to force "Africans, Chinese and Niggers," into the white schools, and the Statute of 1860 excluded Mongolians and Indians together with negroes from the public schools. Separate schools might be provided for them, and the statute of 1863 permitted school trustees to use public funds for this purpose.[32] The statute of 1864 was mandatory upon school trustees to provide a school whenever the parents of ten or more such children made application.[33]

In 1866, John Swett, a man of New England birth and ideals, became State Superintendent and he immediately recommended a specific provision for the education of the negro, Mongolian and Indian children in separate schools as one dictated by justice and common humanity.[34] The statutes of 1866, however, only reiterate previous provisions and add that if the parents of white children made no objection, colored children, whose education could not be provided for in any other way, might be admitted to white schools.[35] At this time there were only about 500 Chinese children altogether under fifteen years of age in the State, one-half of whom were in private schools supported by their parents. San Francisco established the first and only school for them, but not till 1885.[36]

In most towns in California after the Kearney period the Chinese children who desired to do so attended the school for white children. There were sporadic movements to exclude them, which generally arose simultaneously with labor agitations in the same localities. In San Francisco as late as 1905, the Board of Education

[32] *Cal. Stats.* 1863, p. 210.
[33] *Cal. Stats.* 1864, p. 213.
[34] *An. Rept. State. Supt. of Public Instruction*, 1866.
[35] *Cal. Stats.* 1866, 398.
[36] McClellan, *The Golden State.*

Anti-Chinese Legislation in California 79

voted to exclude Chinese boys of High-School age from the white High Schools but were shortly obliged to rescind the order by the threat of the Chinese parents that they would withdraw their children from the graded school.[37] The question as to whether Mongolian children may be excluded from white schools has now become a matter of international interest through the attempt to exclude Japanese children in the same manner.[38]

Some slight mention remains to be made of State Legislation designed to exclude the Chinese from California altogether, all of which was declared unconstitutional. The most extreme of these acts was that of 1858 forbidding Chinese to land upon the Pacific Coast except when driven by stress of weather. Any captain landing such a person was liable to a fine of $400 to $600 or to imprisonment not to exceed one year. The *Alta* pronounced the statute ill-advised and narrow-minded and, in view of the treaty, peculiarly obnoxious; and this appeared to be the general opinion of the Press and the Bar of San Francisco.[39]

While measure after measure of the types described was proposed, some of them passed by the State Legislature and all sooner or later declared unconstitutional, only two were enacted that had any guarantee of permanency. These were acts similar to the Federal Coolie act of 1862 prohibiting the importation of Chinese criminals and of women for immoral purposes; and to prevent the establishment of "coolie slavery." Every Chinaman must obtain from the Commissioner of Immigration at San Francisco a permit particularly describing that he came voluntarily and that he was a person of correct habits and good character. Penalties were provided for shipmasters and jurisdiction given to the counties.[40]

[37] See Ch. XXI, for details of discrimination in San Francisco.
[38] Newspapers of March-July, 1907.
[39] *Alta*, July 28, 1858; Jan. 1, and 12, 1859. Sacramento *Bee*, June 1, 1886.
[40] Declared unconstitutional, 7 Howard, 382; 7 Cal. 169.

The attempts of the State of California through a period of twenty-five years to drive out, limit or prohibit Chinese immigration are seen to have taken two general forms: *Taxation,* by license, commutation, capitation and police taxes—all of which were clearly unconstitutional and ultimately so declared by the courts, either as regulations of commerce or as discriminations against race and color; or *denial of privileges of citizenship* by exclusion from naturalization, suffrage, giving testimony for or against white persons in the courts, and exclusion from the public schools. This second class of disabilities would all have been done away by the Federal amendments of the Reconstruction period but for the fact that the Burlingame Treaty expressly excepted the right of naturalization.

It must not be overlooked that the Chinese were taxed, not merely because they were the most objectionable and the most submissive of all foreigners, but because they always had money and the state was always hard up. In a state whose population even now numbers only nine persons per square mile and in the first two decades numbered from one to two to the square mile, nothing but the most conscientious economy would have supplied funds enough for government, public schools and public improvements. The earlier immigrants from the eastern United States were mostly single men, adventurers and speculators. They had little thought of homes and families, of schools and churches in California. Such men as these had little interest in state government or concern with the duties of citizenship, except to protect their property rights and to keep foreigners from sharing the riches of the state. The State Controller, year after year, urged economy and complained of the difficulty of collecting the poll taxes because the male population was constantly moving. Of all the foreigners the Chinese were soon found to be the most thrifty and the most easily intimidated. The Tax Collector's salary was a percentage of the amount collected, and he therefore collected most diligently from those who paid with the least trouble and who were least able to escape. If the Chinaman lost his tax receipt or did not know enough to take one, he was held to pay a second and even a third time.[41] Although the Chinese did not invest in real estate to any extent and therefore escaped this form of tax, it is shown elsewhere that they paid an inordinate proportion of poll, road, and hospital, as well as license and capitation taxes.[42] In return for taxation they received neither protection nor privilege—not even so much as the negro. The Federal law alone prevented them from being deprived of everything except the right to labor in occupations which all the Americans and most of the aliens, scorned.

Race antipathy, on the other hand, lay at the bottom of the denial of citizenship. The yellow and the copper-colored man were classed with the negro by the Southern Democrats who dominated politics in California in the first decade. Even after the Civil War, no privileges were given to the darker races, except such as were made compulsory upon the adoption of the Reconstruction amendments. During the first generation, the exclusion of their testimony from the courts was an even more serious deprivation. Eaves says: " The results of the exclusion of their testimony from the Courts was most disastrous for the Chinese. It made it possible for unprincipled whites to commit crimes against them with impunity, so long as there were no white witnesses."

Much of the discrimination suffered by the Chinese was due to the fact that the administration of the law was in the hands of officials whose political future depended upon their pleasing the miners who constituted at that time the chief body of workingmen in the State. Although the judges of the local courts were not infrequently pro-Chinese in communities where public opinion

[41] Shinn, *Mining Camps*; Haskins, *The Argonauts*.
[42] See Ch. XXI.

was strongly anti-Chinese, the Chinaman had no protection against the unscrupulous constable and tax collector.

Doubtless the State legislators who passed these acts knew that they were unconstitutional—certainly the lawyers knew it—but the passage of them served to satisfy the anti-Chinese element and the courts could be left to make them ineffective.[43] In 1859 a special committee was appointed to frame a new law " free from constitutional objections " and their joint resolution, reported for transmission to Congress, laid the blame of previous failures upon the decisions of the Supreme Court of the State. But there was no pretense of framing a law that would be acceptable to the courts.[44]

By the time the Workingmen's party was organized, it was clear that any effectual limitation of Chinese immigration must come through Congress, by treaty or Federal statute; and that every candidate for office in California, whatever his private interests or opinions, would be compelled to range himself against the Chinese.

[43] The question had long before been decided in the Passenger cases —7 Howard 283—.
[44] *Ass. Jo.*, 1859, p. 469.

CHAPTER VI

THE CALIFORNIA SENATE ADDRESS AND MEMORIAL

"Impregnable to all the influences of Anglo-Saxon life, they remain the same stolid Asiatics that have floated on the rivers and slaved in the fields of China for thirty centuries of time .... We thus find one-sixth of our entire population composed of Chinese coolies, not involuntary, but, by the unalterable structure of their intellectual being, voluntary slaves .... Is it not possible that free labor, unable to compete with these foreign serfs ... may unite in all the horrors of riot and insurrection, and defying the civil power, extirpate with fire and sword those who rob them of their bread, yet yield no tribute to the State?"
—California Senate Memorial to Congress, 1876.

" As was expected and in fact perfectly understood beforehand, the report was violently anti-Chinese in character and suited the popular prejudice so well that 20,000 copies were ordered printed. Matters had so far advanced that nobody, particularly nobody that held or ever expected to hold office, dared say a word in favor of the Chinese, but on the contrary, everybody, the Republicans as well as the Democrats, seized every opportunity to make public profession on the anti-Chinese side."—THEODORE HITTELL.

AFTER 1877 the California Senate Address and Memorial was constantly referred to by Pacific Coast Congressmen as representing the opinion of the majority in the Far West and as replete with important facts about Chinese immigration. At the same time it was also referred to by the principal historians of California, by the independent newspapers and by many trustworthy citizens of the State, as a purely partisan document, concocted for campaign purposes; and as a misrepresentation of public opinion and of the Chinese. It must be remembered that this report and the Congressional Committee report made shortly afterwards, represented the greater part of the accessible information offered by the Coast states to the discussions in Congress which ended in the restriction act of 1882.[1]

The Democratic Legislature and the Democratic party of the State, with an eye to the national election of 1876, revived the Chinese question as one likely to be most welcome to a voting population more than one-half foreign born, of whom one-third were single men, owning little property and conscious of little civic responsibility. The Honorable Creed Haymond of Sacramento, offered a resolution in the State Senate in April, which was unanimously adopted, appointing a committee of investigation to ascertain the number of Chinese immigrants, their probable effect on the social and political condition of the State and the means of exclusion; and giving the committee power to publish the report. The tone of the resolution, the composition of the committee—one senator from Sacramento, four from San Francisco, and two only from the country—insured a strong anti-Chinese report consistent with the political interest of the only considerable cities in California, and the Democratic majority.[2]

In August, 1877, the Committee published and distributed to members of Congress, Governors of States and the newspapers, more than ten thousand copies of this document of three hundred pages. As might have been expected from the fact that it was published in the midst of the Kearney agitation, it was obviously intended to satisfy the workingmen of the State and to impress the reading public and Congress with the necessity of immediate federal legislation.

---

[1] Full title: *Chinese Immigration: Its Social, Moral and Political Effect. Report to the California State Senate of the Special Committee on Chinese Immigration.* The report consists of an address to the people of the U. S. on the evils of Chinese Immigration, a Memorial to Congress, the proceedings of the commission and the testimony taken.

[2] The committee was composed of five Democrats and two Republicans: McCoppin, Pierson, Donovan, Rogers (San Francisco), Lewis (Tehama county) Democrats; Haymond (Sacramento) and Evans (San Joaquin), Republicans.

A study of the careers of the witnesses and an analysis of the testimony shows that everything was prepared to accomplish these purposes rather than to ascertain the truth about Chinese immigration. Forty-two American witnesses were called whose occupations were as follows: four clergymen; one lawyer; one police judge; five officials and travelers who had resided in China; twenty-two public officials of San Francisco and Sacramento, including five regular police officers and five special police in Chinese quarters; one farmer, two journalists; two manufacturers; the captain and the mate of an English vessel carrying Chinese immigrants; an expressman and a man in the marble business. Of these forty-two, three understood the Chinese language, seven had lived in China for periods of from three to thirty years, and two had traveled there for a few months.

More than half of the white witnesses were officers whose positions directly depended on political favor, and one-fourth were policemen; four-fifths lived in either San Francisco or Sacramento, both strongly anti-Chinese communities, and the names of one-half of the witnesses were distinctly foreign. No representatives of the large employers of Chinese labor—the Pacific Mail Steamship Company, the Southern Pacific Railway, the Tide-Land Reclamation Company, the Merchants' Exchange—or of the large land-owners, or the mining interests, appear in the list.

Of the eighteen Chinese witnesses called, six were Presidents of the Six Companies in San Francisco, two interpreters, one a geologist, and eight workingmen. Of the twenty-three public officials, all but two (the surveyor of Customs and the State Senator from Tehama County) were anti-Chinese; but of the other nineteen witnesses not "in politics," seven were pro-Chinese, five moderate, one non-committal and six only, anti-Chinese.

The final report of the Committee constitutes the "Address to the People of the United States upon the Evils of Chinese Immigration," and consists of fifty-eight pages of statements and quotations of which ten are on Chinese slave women and prostitution, five on criminality, seven on the failure to Christianize, and four on the effect of the Chinese on free labor.

The *Address* states that there were in California in 1876, from 100,000 to 125,000 Chinese of whom at least 3,000 were women held in slavery for base purposes;[3] that they had no families or children and therefore could not assimilate by education; that they performed no duties as citizens—as jurymen, soldiers or *posse comitatus*—; that they were governed by secret tribunals in defiance of American law; that they could not be convicted in our Courts because their language was not understood; that their moral ideas were different from those of Americans, and they resorted to bribery, perjury and intimidation; that the criminal class outnumbered the others in the proportion of seven to one; that in their quarters they lived in the most unsanitary conditions,— opium smoking, gambling, leprosy and smallpox being common; and that they refused to become Christians in spite of the work of missionaries. On the point of competition with free labor the *Address* stated that the Chinese had monopolized twelve specified occupations and "many others," and that they lived so cheaply that they had already reduced wages beyond the point where an American could live; that their presence had created the "Hoodlum class peculiar to San Francisco" by keeping boys out of the industries and making work degrading; that the Chinese were in a condition of servitude "not involuntary, but, by the unalterable structure of their intellectual being, voluntary slaves."

The report states further:

"Not less than 180,000,000 of dollars in gold have been abstracted from the State of California alone by Chinese laborers,

[3] In 1876, there were 111,000 Chinese in the Coast states, of whom not more than 78,000 were in California. See Table in Appendix.

while they have contributed nothing to the state or national wealth. From a purely financial point of view, it is beyond question that the United States is loser nearly four hundred millions of dollars by Chinese immigration."

The report finally summed up the objections to the Chinese as follows:

"During their entire settlement in California they have never adapted themselves to our habits, mode of dress, or our educational system, have never learned the sanctity of an oath, never desired to become citizens, or to perform the duties of citizenship, never discovered the difference between right and wrong, never ceased the worship of their idol gods, or advanced a step beyond the traditions of their native hive. Impregnable to all the influences of our Anglo-Saxon life, they remain the same stolid Asiatics that have floated on the rivers and slaved in the fields of China for thirty centuries of time."

The emphasis both in the Address and in the Memorial was laid chiefly upon five matters: prostitution, criminality, non-conversion, competition and coolie slavery, and this order corresponds fairly to the amount of testimony upon the topics named. On the morals of Chinese women, the committee interrogated twenty-one witnesses at length, devoting about one-fifth of the testimony to a class which constituted at most, only one-fifteenth of the Chinese immigrants. The Presidents of the Chinese Six, Companies, men of intelligence and education, were asked whether they were married to their wives, and whether they were engaged in importing prostitutes. From the standpoint of Chinese manners, such questions were an extreme personal insult and they naturally refused to reply, or replied only in monosyllables. Further cross-questioning on Chinese gambling and criminality, coolie slavery, cruelty to the sick, and the genuineness of professed Christianity, did not tend to loosen their tongues. Only one of them was asked any questions on the subject of wages and occupations, and none was interrogated on the degree of political and social assimilation—

matters upon which they might have given valuable information if they had been courteously treated. In fact, these competent witnesses, having been insulted in the beginning, were dismissed by the committee as quickly as possible, their combined testimony amounting to less than ten pages.

On the subject of the criminality of the Chinese, twenty witnesses gave an opinion and, with three exceptions, substantially agreed that the Chinese were thieves and perjurers; but they differed widely in their estimates of the proportion of criminals to the whole Chinese population. On this particular charge, the report appears to have represented the testimony accurately. But the fact that fifteen of these witnesses were dependent for their positions on the political party then in power in San Francisco and Sacramento, and were probably subpoenaed with a view to their anti-Chinese opinions, discredits their testimony. Only one of the witnesses who had lived in China, or who had an intimate knowledge of the better classes, was questioned about the proportion of Chinese criminals, and the only statistics presented showed that the Chinese were 17 per cent of the prisoners of the State prison in 1876 and omits to mention that they were 20 per cent of the total population over twenty years of age; as compared to the Irish males, for instance, who constituted 9 per cent of the prison population while they were only 6 per cent of the total male population over twenty.

In connection with the subject of crime the *Address* states that the Chinese were not only not amenable to law but that they were governed by secret tribunals, formed by the Six Companies or Guilds, which levied taxes, intimidated witnesses and interpreters, enforced perjury, regulated trade, punished the refractory, controlled liberty of action, prevented the Chinese from returning home, and even executed the death penalty. Sixteen witnesses—fourteen Americans and two Chinese—

California Senate Address and Memorial

testified concerning this secret government. Twelve of them offered only hearsay evidence of a vague and contradictory character and did not even know the difference between the Six Companies and the Trade Guilds. Two missionaries, Mr. Gibson and Mr. Loomis, explained this distinction and said that they knew of no such tribunals, and Mr. Lewis of the committee, quoted the President of the Six Companies as denying any criminal jurisdiction whatever over their countrymen.

The Committee seemed to consider the question of conversion to Christianity only less important than prostitution and criminality. One-sixth of the report and one-ninth of the testimony is devoted to this topic with the conclusion:

"Of all the vast horde not four hundred have been brought to a realization of the truths of Christianity. . . . It is safe to say that where one Chinese soul has been saved . . . a hundred white have been lost by the contamination of their presence."

Twenty-four persons were questioned as to how many Chinese had been converted and whether these converts were sincere. Of these witnesses one-third were non-Christian Chinese whose testimony was wholly non-committal; another third were public officers confessedly anti-Chinese, whose experience with criminals scarcely fitted them to be dispassionate judges of the evidences of religion; and of the rest only six had been in such close contact with the Christian Chinese as warranted them in speaking authoritatively. One, the Reverend H. C. Bonte, Rector of Grace Church, Sacramento,—who believed in restriction of immigration—expressed the views of many thoughtful Christian workers:

"The Chinese in California are not in a favorable condition to hear the Gospel. They are here simply for the purpose of making money and as they find the great body of our own people engaged in the same enterprise, their love of money becomes intensified. . . . Again, the Chinese now in this country are continually on the move and it is almost impossible to keep up a continuous influence upon any one of them. . . . Again, the Chinese are very keen observers. . . . We teach them Christianity but they see hoodlumism and crime and wonder that our people reject a religion which we seek to give them. They easily discern that the Christian people are in a small minority. Under these circumstances we have no right to expect any special results in the conversion of the Chinese. . . . The Church has done its best but that is comparatively little. . . . The work in California, I fear, retards the final success in China. What they see of Christianity here from their standpoint must impress them very unfavorably."

It may be added that all this testimony on conversion was taken to prove that the one-hundred-and-twenty-fifth part of the Chinese immigrants who professed Christianity had not been true to a religion whose principles—from the Chinese standpoint—were exemplified chiefly by the mining tax collector, the police officers and the hoodlums of the cities, and shown with favor only by a handful of missionaries.

On the question of competition with white labor the committee admitted that in the earlier history of the State the Chinese had been very useful, especially in mining, gardening, general agriculture, and as domestic servants; but they went on to say that the Chinese had now monopolized the laundry business, cigar-making, the manufacture of slippers, the manipulation of sewing machines, domestic service, harvesting, fruit gathering, railroad building, placer mining, fishing, the manufacture of silk and wool, and many other occupations. They concluded that unrestricted Chinese immigration tended more strongly toward the degradation of labor than did slavery in the South.

Of the eight witnesses on this subject, three—only one of whom was a farmer—said that agriculture was held in high regard in China and that they would rather employ white labor if they could get it. This was the sole basis for the statement that the Chinese had monopolized harvesting and fruit gathering. The sole witness who testified on mining, said that the Chinese carried away the gold and were as injurious to the mines as to the cities. But the witness and the report both omit to mention the fact that every Chinaman had paid a license tax to mine at all, and that wherever placer mines had been profitable to them, they had generally been driven out by white men. Two policemen and two manufacturers testified on competition in manufacture. The woolen manufacturer said he could not run his factories without the Chinese, that he always employed white men when he could at a third more wages.

The police officers were strong on statistics: one had seen Chinese prostitutes working buttonholes for the business houses and concluded that there were 20,000 boys and girls growing up for state prison and prostitution because the Chinese had filled their places. Another had been detailed to secure statistics for the committee concerning the Chinese in San Francisco. He presented the accompanying figures as proof that the Chinese were fast monopolizing these occupations and had reduced wages to the starvation point.

On competition in the laundry business, cigar-making, the sewing trades and domestic service, there is no information whatever except that given in the policeman's table; and on the monopoly of railway building, fishing, manufacture of silk and the "many other occupations" mentioned in the report, there is none at all. The statement of the report that twelve specified occupations and many others had been monopolized by the Chinese, is seen to have been made—when there was any evidence at all —on the basis of the testimony of one farmer, one ex-miner, and two manufacturers, two of whom declared that Chinese labor was absolutely necessary in farming and in manufacture.

The fifth topic to which the report gave a relatively large amount of attention was the subject of "coolie slavery," which has already been discussed at length in

"STATISTICS REGARDING CHINESE IN SAN FRANCISCO,"

Digested from pp. 216-7 of Testimony taken before California Senate Committee, 1877.
(Collected in six days by Police Officer Rogers.)

Occupations.	Number of Chinese employed.	Number of Whites employed.	Wages.	Amount and value of product.	Number of establishments.	Remarks.
Cigarmaking	3,300	not given	40-90 c. sometimes $1 a day.	120,598,000 cigars 6,000,000 cigaritos.	260 about.	Small No. employ Chinese and whites jointly. Many made from butts of cigars picked up in street.
Laundries	1,500	1,500	?	?	300	
Peddling (fruits, vegetables, fish, etc)	300	?	?	?	?	Retailers cannot compete.
Clothing	?	?	?	?	30	Finishing by Chinese women.
Slippers	?	?	?	large quantities.	11	" " "
Shoes and Gaiters	Large number	?	?	Immense amount.	?	8 10 of all ladies' and children's used in S. F. made by Chinese.
Underwear	?	?	?	?	?	All violated "cubic-air" law.
Lodging houses	?	?	?	?	30	
Domestics	5,000	?	?	?	?	
Houses of ill-fame	?	?	?	?	150-200	Prostitutes worked on underwear in daytime.
Shirts	?	?	?	"largely."	"extensively."	Whites also frequent these.
Opium-Smoking	?	?	?	?	8	All now closed as far as practicable.
Gambling	?	?	?	?	"extensively."	No time to get details.

Nine others: (Brokers, butchers, carpenters, employment offices, jewelers, pawnshops, tinsmiths, barbers, and Josh-houses.)

California Senate Address and Memorial

Chapter III of this book. It is there shown that the Chinese were not " in a condition of servitude," nor " serfs," and as such, let out to service " at a miserable pittance," but merely free laborers, some of whom had borrowed money for their passage and were bound to pay it back with interest. In other words, some of them were assisted immigrants, exactly similar to those arriving at the Atlantic ports.

There may have been in 1876, a greater proportion of prostitutes to the male Chinese than of white prostitutes to white men, but the report affords no proof of it, nor that the Chinese woman's slavery was any worse than that of other prostitutes. There may have been a large number of Chinese criminals, but the testimony affords no proof that the proportion was greater than of other nationalities, and the figures given in the table on criminality in Ch. XXII show that the percentage was smaller than that of any immigrant nationality having a considerable representation in the male population. On the subject of competition, the testimony is very meager and contradictory, consisting for the most part of general assertions; while on the subject of " coolie slavery ' the report positively contradicts the bulk of the intelligent testimony.

It is significant that the testimony concerned the Chinese in two cities only. If the 30.000 Chinese in these two cities had all been criminals, prostitutes and competitors in manufacture there still remained the other four-fifths—at least eighty thousand—scattered throughout the Coast states, whose condition, character, occupations and contribution to the rural regions are scarcely mentioned.

After a critical examination of the California Senate report and the testimony of its sixty witnesses, it is difficult to suppose that it was meant to be taken seriously even at the time. Yet it was presented shortly afterward to the Congressional Committee by State Senator McCoppin as the opinion of the Senate of California, and as such, became a part of the foundation of the first exclusion law. Although it met the technical forms of an investigation the document might as well have been written without taking any testimony at all; for in order to produce an anti-Chinese report the committee ignored, emasculated or falsified most of the competent testimony, preferring in matters of religion the opinion of police officers to those of missionaries; on the subject of manufacture, the opinions of police officers to those of a large manufacturer; and again on the subject of coolie slavery, the opinions of city officials and policemen to those of persons who had lived many years in China.

In the Memorial to Congress the Committee proposed three remedies for the evils of Chinese immigration: co-operation with Great Britain in the prohibition of the coolie trade; abrogation of all treaties which permitted emigration of the Chinese to the United States; and Congressional legislation forbidding more than ten Chinese to be landed at any one time in this country. Without discussing the practicability of these proposals, it may be noted with regard to the first, that it displayed astonishing ignorance. The coolie trade had long before been forbidden by all the greater Powers, including the United States and China, and was being carried on in 1876—if at all, surreptitiously—from the Portuguese port of Macao to the South American countries.

Looking at this document after a lapse of thirty years and in the light of subsequent legislation which was in part based upon it, the question arises whether the anti-Chinese party in California dared not let the truth be told about the Chinese, or whether, knowing the power of race prejudice, they merely defied the intelligent minority who stood for moderate measures by the publication of a report based on distorted evidence, or no evidence at all. It must be inferred that the politicians who produced the Address and the Memorial, counted on the testimony never being read.

Theodore Hittell has said of this Committee that its special object was to furnish anti-Chinese thunder for the demagogues of the San Francisco sandlots. Certainly the desperate resort to misrepresentation, falsehood and vehemence, revealed the weakness of its contentions, and is probably to be explained by the fact that nobody who ever expected to hold office dared to say a word in favor of the Chinese.

CHAPTER VII

THE CONGRESSIONAL COMMITTEE ON CHINESE IMMIGRATION

" The Chinese are inferior to any race God ever made .... I think there are none so low. ... Their people have got the perfection of crimes of 4,000 years. ... The Divine Wisdom has said that He would divide this country and the world as a heritage of five great families; that to the Blacks he would give Africa; to the Red Man He would give America; and Asia He would give to the Yellow races. He inspired us with the determination, not only to have prepared our own inheritance, but to have stolen from the Red Man,' America; and it is now settled that the Saxon, American or European groups of families, the White Race, is to have the inheritance of Europe and America and that the Yellow races are to be confined to what the Almighty originally gave them; and as they are not a favored people, they are not to be permitted to steal from us what we have robbed the American savage of. ... I believe that the Chinese have no souls to save, and if they have, they are not worth the saving."—FRANK M. PIXLEY, representing the Municipality of San Francisco before the Congressional Committee of 1876.

"This Committee, containing no discordant elements, ... saw just what it wanted to see, saw nothing else, and reported in accordance. But the members might just as well have reported before leaving Washington."—Professor S. E. W. BECKER, 1877.

"But that they (the Chinese) have injuriously interfered with the white people of California .... may well be doubted. The great fact is, that there is to-day and always has been, a scarcity of labor on the Pacific Coast. There is work for all who are there, both white and Mongolian, and the State would undoubtedly develop much more rapidly were there more and cheaper labor. ... There is work and remunerative work for all who choose to perform it."—Senator OLIVER P. MORTON, 1877.

WHEN nearly all the legislation of the Coast States against the Chinese had been declared unconstitutional or a violation of treaty, it was evident that effective measures could only be obtained by the negotiation of a new treaty and by federal legislation. The exigencies of politics had already made the Chinese question the principal plank of both party platforms in the State, and an organized effort, therefore, was begun by the Pacific

Committee on Chinese Immigration 97

Coast Congressmen to obtain restriction of Chinese immigration from the National Government.

But they met with indifference, if not with active opposition, and the sole result of six years' effort on their part was the appointment in 1876 of a Joint Special Committee of Congress to investigate Chinese Immigration. The Committee as originally named, consisted of Senator Oliver P. Morton of Indiana, Chairman; Edwin R. Meade of New York, Wilson of Massachusetts, Cooper of Tennessee, and Senator A. A. Sargent and W. F. Piper of California. Senator Morton was already fatally ill, and although in attendance at nearly all the sessions of the committee, did not have any part in the preparation of the final report; Mr. Meade was present only a few days and then withdrew; and Mr. Wilson declined to serve. The working committee was thus reduced to three, Sargent, Piper and Cooper. Senator Sargent and Mr. Piper though of opposing parties, were one on the Chinese question. At the time they were serving on this committee, both were honorary Vice-Presidents of the Anti-Coolie Union of San Francisco and both had long been identified with the anti-Chinese movement. The majority report as finally published was written by Sargent.[1]

The committee sat for eighteen days in San Francisco and Sacramento, heard 129 witnesses, and published a report of only five pages, based on 1200 pages of testimony and statistics. Measured quantitatively, 52 per cent of the testimony is distinctly favorable to the Chinese, 40 per cent as distinctly unfavorable and the remaining 8 per cent may fairly be divided between the two.

An analysis of the witnesses by occupations shows to what extent Chinese immigration had become a question of class and politics.[2] The pro-Chinese witnesses in-

---
[1] *Sen. Misc. Docs.*, no. 36, s. n. 1786 (1877).
[2] Professor Becker says that the witnesses were chiefly officials of the city and State whose bias was well-known; and that, while the com-

cluded all the clergymen, diplomats, manufacturers and men connected with railroads, navigation and foreign trade. The anti-Chinese witnesses included nearly all the officials, journalists and workingmen; of those recently engaged in politics or dependent for their positions upon political favor, two only out of twenty-four were in the least favorable to the Chinese. Of the forty-four witnesses who had been in China or associated with the Chinese in business or as teachers or large employers, only six were anti-Chinese; and of the sixteen who had lived on traveled in China, only seven. Sixty-nine witnesses were asked directly whether they believed that Chinese immigration should be restricted; thirty-three thought it unnecessary at that time and six others thought it should be restricted somewhat, the same as all other foreign immigration; sixteen believed it should be limited to a greater or less degree and ten that the Chinese of all classes should be shut out; four thought public opinion divided on the question and one said frankly that property-owners were generally pro-Chinese and non-property owners, anti-Chinese.

It appears to be a fair inference from this alignment that the demand for restriction or prohibition came from the working class through the officials dependent upon their votes and the newspapers that voiced their wishes; and that the pro-Chinese party consisted of the large employing class, the humanitarians, and of those who had been intimately associated with the Chinese either in China or in this country. To this clear line of demarcation there is only one exception: the Chinatown Police, though in close contact with the Orientals, were anti-Chinese, but it must be noticed that they were also dependent upon political favor.

The Report of the committee states that laboring men

mittee sat, the anti-Coolie clubs were sending threatening letters to employers of Chinese and the daily press " brayed and argued, . . . lied and asserted." See *Humors*, etc.

Committee on Chinese Immigration 99

and artisans, perhaps without exception, were opposed to Chinese immigration but that the opposition was not confined to them; lawyers, doctors, merchants, divines, judges and others in large numbers thought the prosperity of California deceptive and unwholesome, ruinous to the laboring classes, promotive of caste and dangerous to free institutions.[3] Comparing these sweeping statements with the analysis of witnesses by occupations, we find however, that six of the fourteen lawyers, one of the two physicians, eight of the fifteen business men, all of the clergymen, half the judges and all of the diplomats were pro-Chinese. They either believed that no restriction of immigration was desirable at this time or at most only such as applied to other classes of immigrants. Very evidently the Report misrepresented the testimony on this point.

The Report professed to represent all classes of opinion and every variety of interest.[4] It granted that the conclusions from the testimony might be different to different minds; that the resources of California had developed more rapidly with the cheap and docile labor of the Chinese than could have been done without them, and that so far as material prosperity was concerned, it could not be doubted that California was a great gainer—" this was true at least of the capitalistic classes." The Report further acknowledged that the Chinese merchants were honorable in their dealings; that exclusion from suffrage had deprived the Chinese of their only adequate protection; and that the anti-Chinese views of the majority were " not unchallenged by a considerable and respectable class in California."

With these few extenuations the Report rehearsed concisely much the same objections to the Chinese as had been made in the Address of the California Senate. It stated that there were about 35,000 Chinese in San Fran-

[3] *Report*, p. iv.
[4] *Report*, p. iii.

cisco, who lived in filthy dwellings, on poor food, crowded together, disregarding fire and health ordinances and corrupting the young; that they did not assimilate and could not be convicted in the courts because of their want of veracity; that there was no European race which was not superior to them; and that there was not sufficient brain capacity in the Chinese race to furnish motive power for self-government; that they did not desire to become citizens and if they did, they would sell their ballots in such quantities as to determine elections; that Chinese immigration involved sordid wages, no public schools, the absence of families and a constant outflow of persons who had worked out specified years of servitude; that they bought their women, were cruel to the sick, and made their way in California as they had in the islands of the sea, not by superior force of industry or virtue, but by revolting characteristics.

Judged both quantitatively and qualitatively, the report and the testimony laid their chief emphasis on two subjects, vice and competition, and may therefore be fairly tested by an analysis of the testimony upon them.

On the subject of competition with white labor the report states that the evidence of twenty operatives, in nearly as many trades, showed that the Chinese had reduced wages to what would be starvation prices for white men and women; had crowded out the whites, monopolizing, or nearly so, many different industrial pursuits; that this had resulted in a bitterly hostile feeling exhibited in ordinances of doubtful propriety, the abuse of individual Chinese and sporadic cases of violence.

In the entire volume, thirty occupations are mentioned as examples of competition between white and Chinese labor. Seven of these employed less than fifty and twelve less than one hundred Chinese;[5] since no further

---

[5] Rice milling, wire springs and bellows-making, glass-blowing, glue-making, cordage, matches, brooms, fruit-canning, etc., candles and soap, furniture, gunpowder.

evidence was offered on these industries and since only about 600 Chinese were employed altogether, and these jointly with over 2000 whites, they may certainly be disregarded as examples of serious competition. Three other occupations, i.e., peddling vegetables, fruit and fish, gardening, and slipper manufacture, are mentioned as employing Chinese to some extent but no other information appears. The industries in which there were more than 100 Chinese and on which some testimony was offered, are thus narrowed down to fifteen; railway labor, laundry, domestic service, fruit picking, hop picking, grain binding and general farming, placer mining, tailoring, shirt-making, ladies' underwear, boots and shoes, cigars, jute and woolens. These may be examined in detail to see if they were monopolized and to what degree by the Chinese.

An analysis of the testimony concerning the fifteen industries upon which some information is given in the report, shows that in railway labor and farm labor of five different kinds, there was nearly unanimous testimony that white labor was scarce, unreliable and very high priced—wages in every case being far above the standard of the eastern states and white labor never obtainable in sufficient quantity. In laundry work and domestic service it appeared that wages were high and women very scarce. Judging from this testimony, competition in these occupations unquestionably did not exist, and there was plenty of room still for white labor at good wages.

In the sewing trades there was no evidence that wages were declining faster than elsewhere in the United States, or that women were crowded out; in fact the wages mentioned for both women and Chinese were still above eastern wages, for the same kind of work. As there is no statement either of the numbers of women employed or out of work, no conclusion should be drawn—and certainly no conclusion can be drawn that the Chinese had "monopolized" these trades and reduced wages to the "starvation" point.

Thus by a process of elimination, the number of industries in which competition may have existed in 1876 have been reduced to five; placer mining, boots and shoes, cigars, jute and woolens. It was not disputed that placer mining was almost exclusively in the hands of the Chinese; but there is nothing to show that Americans desired to mine the worked-out placers at this time, or would have been willing to do so for the two or three dollars per day which the Chinese were supposed to make. If this was monopoly, it was a monopoly which up to that time at least, white men had made no attempt to break.

In the four incipient manufacturing industries, there appears to have been some real competition between white and Chinese labor; yet large quantities of shoes, cigars, jute bags and bagging, and woolens were still being imported from the east and from foreign countries, and all of the manufacturers testified that the remuneration to capital in manufacture was much less than the current rate of interest on loans. There was no complaint of lack of employment except from the cigar makers and it appeared that this was partly due to the immigration of numbers of eastern cigar makers because of slack trade in the east. It was shown later that the jute and woolen manufactures would not have been started but for Chinese labor and could not at that time be wholly carried on with the labor of women and boys.

In these four trades as also in laundry work and domestic service, the Chinese competed, if at all, chiefly with women and girls. Much was made by the anti-Chinese witnesses of the poor women driven from their trades, but when it is remembered that there were two men to every woman in California at this time and even in San Francisco three men to every two women, it is difficult to imagine that any great number remained long

Committee on Chinese Immigration 103

unmarried or out of work.[6] Much collateral testimony was given showing that the cost of living had been steadily declining and that in 1876 it was cheaper than in the eastern states, because of low rents, a mild climate and the low cost of certain home-grown food products.

The statement that in nearly twenty trades the Chinese had reduced wages to what would be starvation prices for white men and women, and had monopolized, or nearly so, many different pursuits, is shown by the above analysis to be without foundation. When it is remembered that of the 30,000 Chinese in San Francisco, less than ten thousand were engaged in occupations in which any competition was shown, and that of the remaining 60,000 none were engaged in occupations in which there was not still plenty of room for all kinds of labor at high wages, the misrepresentation of the testimony and of the situation in California is apparent.

In contrast to the manner in which the true purport of the testimony was ignored by the majority report may be cited Senator's Morton's notes,[7] published after his death which represent his conclusions from the same testimony. Unlike the other members of the committee, he gave careful attention to the Chinese in the country where two-thirds of them were employed. The testimony showed—so he wrote—that they were industrious, temperate and honest; invaluable as servants and farm laborers where white labor could not be had in sufficient quantity; and on the overland railroads which would not have been built without them. It appeared that they worked often for lower wages but they performed drudgery which white men would not do in California, and, in his opinion, they did not interfere with white labor but

[6] Census 1870, Census 1880.
[7] *Cong. Docs.* Misc. Doc. no. 20, 1878, ser. no. 1785. Senator Morton died in November, 1877. He was a man of New England ancestry, Governor of Indiana, 1861-7, U. S. Senator, 1867-77, an advocate of negro and woman suffrage and of the protection of men of all races, classes and opinions.

rather opened new avenues for it. The testimony was conclusive, he said, that manufactures would not have been successful without their labor and in so far as they had been successful, white labor had been more and more employed. The inquiry failed to show that any considerable number of white people were out of work except the hoodlums and idlers who were wilfully so; and he finally concluded that but for Chinese labor California would not have half the property, production and population which it then had.

A tabular view of the conclusions of Senator Morton and of Professor S. E. W. Becker compared with the published Report, reveals the intentional perversion of the testimony in order to produce the desired anti-Chinese campaign document.[8]

The untrustworthiness of the report is still further indicated by the tone of the examination and the character of some of the witnesses whose testimony was most often referred to as convincing. Mr. Pixley, representing the Municipality of San Francisco, took the rôle of a prosecuting attorney and, in evident collusion with Senator Sargent, insulted reputable witnesses by questioning their motives and besmirching their character. He especially impugned the motives of all the missionaries to the Chinese as concerned only for their souls; while to all the other pro-Chinese witnesses he assumed that they were concerned only for the material interests of the State and not for its political and social welfare. Toward the anti-Chinese witnesses on the other hand, he assumed a most respectful, even flattering tone. He introduced Captain T. H. King as a merchant of San Francisco who

---

[8] S. E. W. Becker published a criticism of the Report in the *Catholic World* and afterward expanded it into a pamphlet entitled: "The Humors of a Congressional Committee." Mr. Becker had been a Professor in the University of Virginia and was at this time Secretary to the Bishop of Delaware.

See also analysis by J. C. G. Kennedy in *Cong. Docs.*, 1878, s. n. 1786, *Misc. Doc.* 36.

Committee on Chinese Immigration

COMPARATIVE VIEW OF CONCLUSIONS REACHED from the testimony given before the joint Special Committee of Congress on Chinese Immigration.

Of Majority Report.	Of Senator Morton.	Of Prof. S. E. W. Becker
Naturalization & Suffrage: Denial necessary to preserve republican institutions, but deprives Chinese of only adequate protection.	Denial caused by and retained by prejudices arising from negro slavery; Chinese should have ballot as self-protection, and would become as good citizens as other foreigners.	Cannot expect aliens who are denied naturalization to take interest in institutions or assimilate rapidly.
Prosperity of Capitalistic class of California due to Chinese; but laboring class crowded out of employment.	Much of prosperity due to Chinese; introd. manufacture due to them; as manufacture increased, employment of Chinese decreased, and of white labor steadily increased.	Difficulty due not to Chinese, but to refusal of Californians to change from mining and speculative era to farming, and attempt to hold wages above eastern states; reclamation, incipient manufacture, prosperity due to Chinese, who have made work for whites.
Prevents white immigration.	No; white immigration checked by disorders in California and persecution of Chinese.	White immigration increased by presence of Chinese, because they did low-grade labor whites would not do.
Intellectual capacity of Chinese below other races, even the negro; incapable of self-government.	Intellectual capacity fully equal to white people of same class.	Discrimination and persecution to which Chinese have been subjected would prevent any race from taking interest in American institutions; no proof of incapacity.
Slavery: Chinese "work out specified years of servitude" in California.	Chinese in California as free as any other persons.	Chinese no more "slaves" than any other men who have borrowed money. "Coolie contract" class does not exist in U. S.
Women: Buy their women; are cruel, sensual; make their way by "revolting characteristics."	Prostitution not greater than among whites; Chinese treated concubines and wives well and were kind to families.	Prostitution relatively less than among white men; could be suppressed by municipality. Chinese not encouraged to bring families. Number of respectable women larger than supposed.
Vice: Gambling, opium eating, corruption of society.	Gamble extensively, but not more than early white settlers under similar conditions. Number who practise opium taking, smaller than number of whites who drink hard.	Vices of gambling and opium not more than gambling and alcoholism among whites.

had been ten years in China assisting in the Consul's office, and as "the most intelligent person he could find" on this subject. Yet this was the same Captain King who helped Consul Bailey manipulate the immigration funds at Hong Kong and whose testimony, replete with misinformation and untruths, was couched in language so illiterate as to be almost unintelligible.[9]

Another of Mr. Pixley's favorite witnesses was Dr. Charles C. O'Donnell—a man who testified that there were 150 lepers loose in San Francisco—who had been several times arrested for abortion and whose subsequent political record was notoriously discreditable.[10] In questioning the witnesses Mr. Pixley assumed that there were 150,000 to 175,000 Chinese in California, 35,000 in San Francisco in summer and 75,000 in winter. Yet the figures of the Customs officers—who were certainly not pro-Chinese—and other testimony submitted to the committee, proved that there were less than 80,000 Chinese in the State and from 30,000 to 35,000 at most in San Francisco at different seasons.[11]

Representative Piper, too, was a very irascible interrogator. He became violently angry several times when references were made by witnesses to the well-known Irish prejudice against the Chinese. He insulted, badgered and contradicted the pro-Chinese witnesses; whenever the testimony was too favorable he cut it off abruptly as "irrelevant" and he tried to make the witnesses say what they did not mean by allowing them to make no qualifications whatever of any statement.

But Senator Sargent outdid all the rest of the com-

---

[9] For King's connection with Bailey see p. 51 *ante*; in refutation of his testimony see Gibson's, Loomis's and Olmsted's in the report of the Cong. Committee.

[10] Dr. O'Donnell was one of the most violent speakers at the sand-lot meetings in the fall of 1877; on his personal record see *Alta.*, Feb. 12, 21, 22, 1871; Nov. 1, 7, 1877; Mar. 20, Dec. 22, 1878. *Chronicle*, Dec. 20, 21, 1878.

[11] See Becker's characterization of Pixley in the pamphlet, *Humors*, etc.

mittee in his undisguised determination to suppress pro-Chinese and encourage anti-Chinese witnesses. He openly took the attitude of a prosecutor and was a continuous witness himself. He repeated the tactics of Mr. Pixley—entangling and confusing the witnesses, precipitating irrelevant economic arguments, and misquoting one witness to another. He too, had a special grudge against the missionary clergymen, aspersing their motives in order to discredit their testimony.

No investigation outside the Report itself is necessary to convince any reader that the Congressional committee came to its task committed to an anti-Chinese conclusion and that it had no judicial character whatever. In the face of a preponderance of evidence, judging both by quantity and trustworthiness, the committee arrived at the results which were required by the exigencies of politics. Costly and important as its labors afterward proved to be, it nevertheless did not clear up a single disputed point with regard to Chinese immigration.

Even in California the more conservative newspapers dared to comment adversely upon it. The *Alta* complained that not only did it not add anything to the knowledge of the question but that the eastern papers were commenting on it scornfully. It was indeed an unfortunate document from every standpoint and in this it shared the fatality which seemed to be pursuing the Chinese question. Two of the members of the committee from whom a dispassionate consideration might have been anticipated—Mr. Wilson and Mr. Meade—took little or no part in its deliberations; but the greatest misfortune of all lay in the illness and death of Senator Morton.

Secretary John W. Foster said of him in this connection:—

"From his strong personality, his great influence in Congress and his powers of debate, it was fair to presume that, his life being spared, if he had not been able to control the report of the committee he would at least have so restrained the legislation of Congress as to have prevented the radical action taken by that body." [12]

Yet unfortunate as were all the circumstances surrounding the collating of this document, and extreme as was the feeling on the Chinese question at the time in California, it was not foreseen that the report would be quoted from that time onward as if it were the dispassionate judgment of intelligent men worthy of the position they held as representatives, nor that in its train would follow persecution, injustice to the Chinaman and incalculable social and economic loss to the Pacific Coast whose end is not yet reached after thirty years.

[12] Foster, *American Diplomacy*, p. 293.

CHAPTER VIII

THE CHINESE MUST GO

"This party will exhaust all peaceable means of attaining its ends, but it will not be denied justice, when it has the power to enforce it. It will encourage no riot or outrage, but, it will not volunteer to repress, or arrest or prosecute the hungry and impatient, who manifest their hatred of the Chinaman by a crusade against John or those who employ him. Let those who raise the storm by their selfishness, suppress it themselves."—*Principles* of Workingmen's Party, Oct. 5th, 1876.

"To an American death is preferable to a life on a par with the Chinaman. What then is left to us? Our votes! . . . But this may fail. Congress, as you have seen, it has often been manipulated by thieves, peculators, land grabbers, bloated bond-holders, railroad magnates, and shoddy aristocrats—a golden lobby dictating its proceedings. Our own legislature is little better. . . . We declare to them that when the workingmen have shown their will that "John" should leave our shores, and that will shall be thwarted by fraud or cash, by bribery and corruption, it will be right for them to take their own affairs into their own hands and meet fraud with force. . . . Treason is better than to labor beside a Chinese slave. . . . The people are about to take their own affairs into their own hands and they will not be stayed either by 'Citizen Vigilantes,' state militia, nor United States Troops."—*Manifesto* of Workingmen's Party, Oct. 16th, 1876.

"Large gatherings of the idle and irrepressible element of the population of this city are nightly addressed in the open streets by speakers who use the most violent, inflammatory and incendiary language, threatening in plainest terms to burn and pillage the Chinese quarter and kill our people unless, at their bidding, we leave this 'free republic'. . . . We appeal to you, the Mayor and Chief Magistrate of this Municipality, to protect us to the full extent of your power in all our peaceful, constitutional and treaty rights. . . . We should also regret to have the good name of this Christian civilization tarnished by the riotous proceedings of its own citizens against the 'Chinese heathen'."—*Appeal* of the Chinese Six Companie Nov. 3d, 1876.

IN 1874 California was on the verge of political and industrial upheaval but the disaster was postponed by the temporary prosperity resulting from the opening of the Consolidated Virginia mines, and the abundant wheat harvest of 1875.[1] In 1876 the underlying causes of dis-

[1] See Ch. V.

content and disorder which had been preparing for
several years, began to come to the surface. During the
winter the rainfall was half the normal amount and less
than it had been for twenty-five years before. As a consequence the wheat crop failed, thousands of cattle died
on the ranges, and the output of gold from the mines
declined to fifteen millions—one-third what it had been in
1869.[2] In Southern California, where irrigation was not
then generally practised, the drought brought disaster to
the cattle and fruit industries. The decline of tourist
travel owing to its diversion by the Centennial Exposition at Philadelphia, cut off the income of a considerable
population in the towns. Land values had been highly
inflated and the combined catastrophe of the drought and
cessation of travel, produced a terrible slump in real
estate.[3]

The first premonitory sign of the coming upheaval was
the overthrow of the Republican party and the overwhelming victory of the Democrats in the State elections
of 1875. From the days of Governor Bigler this party
in California had been anti-negro, anti-Chinese, anti-
corporation and pro-workingman. In the campaign of
1867 the Chinese question had been made the foremost
issue, but while the more conservative Republicans were
in power it had fallen to a minor position, and its place
had been taken by questions of land monopoly and subsidies to railroads and steamships. With the return to
power of the Democrats, strengthened especially by a
large Irish immigration, and with the impending Presidential contest of 1876 as an incitement, the Chinese
question was again in a foremost position as a campaign
issue.

[2] Bowie, *Practical Treatise on Hydraulic Mining*, p. 288, (1885).
[3] On general causes of industrial discontent in California see: Hittell, T. *Hist. of Cal.*, v. 4, p. 594 ff.; Hittell, J. S. *Hist. of San Francisco*,
p. 422 ff.; Bryce, *American Commonwealth*, v. 2, p. 376 ff.; Bancroft,
Hist. of Cal. v. 7, pp. 348–55.

The Chinese Must Go

When the national campaign opened in March, 1876, the Republican State committee published a mild resolution in favor of a modification of the Burlingame treaty. The Democrats, on the òther hand, organized a gigantic mass meeting to consider the evils of Chinese immigration. The Mayor of San Francisco secured the appointment of a committee of twelve to work up a concerted movement throughout the State against them. The more conservative members of the Legislature and some leading citizens protested that these meetings would be likely to precipitate a disturbance on the part of thousands of discontented and idle men with which the city had filled up during the winter. The newspapers, however, while ranting violently about the danger of riot, reported at length the incendiary proceedings of the anti-coolie meetings, thus really urging on the lawless class.

The Chinese Six Companies sent a dignified and respectful petition to the Chief of Police, calling attention to the fact that Chinese were frequently assaulted while walking peaceably on the streets, and that their assailants went unpunished, while if a Chinaman resisted assault he was arrested and fined. They believed that the incendiary talk of demagogues to groups on the streets was the cause of the persecution and that it would result in riot. They were sorry to be so obnoxious and would willingly join in a movement to alter the treaty, but meanwhile they asked to be protected in their treaty rights.

How much danger there was of riot may be judged by the extraordinary precautions taken by the police at the time of the Mass Meeting on April sixth. Extra guards were stationed at the Pioneer and Mission Woolen Mills where Chinese were employed, one hundred extra officers were sworn in for the meeting and the militia was notified to be in readiness. The meeting, although said to have been attended by twenty-five thousand people, went off peaceably, and according to the *Alta*, " did not end in riot as was fondly hoped by the sensational press of the city." [4]

The meeting was addressed by fifteen prominent men, a majority of them Democrats and nearly all of them in active politics. The resolutions, proposed by Colonel Mark McDonald, Chairman of the Committee of Twelve, and read by Mr. Frank Pixley—and probably written by him—were of the most extreme description. They estimated the number of the Chinese west of the Sierras at over two hundred thousand, when, in fact, there were about 110,000; and the number in San Francisco at 75,000, when there were certainly less than 30,000. They declared further that the Chinese filled the prisons, asylums and hospitals, were a grievous burden to the taxpayers, and could not be used for civil or military service; that their diseases were infectious and horrible and their vices the result of four thousand years practice; that they imported prostitutes and *peons* and held them to slavery by means of a secret tribunal; that they monopolized whatever industry they entered and had driven thousands from employment. The document even went so far as to declare that Oriental trade was of no value whatever to California, that the Chinese were not industrious and that there were ten thousand Chinese in San Francisco belonging to the criminal classes— " Gamblers, opium-eaters, hangers-on upon dens of prostitution, and men of abandoned and violent characters,"—who lived by blackmail.

Finally the Committee declared unalterable hostility to Chinese immigration and advised the sending of a commission to Washington to demand an immediate abrogation of the treaty. Almost the only moderate word heard at this meeting was contained in a letter from Ex-Governor Haight who wrote, that, so far as the present number of the Chinese was concerned, they might, on the whole, not have injured but benefited white

Alta, Mar. 28, Apr. 6, 1876.

The Chinese Must Go

labor. He added that it was unfortunate that the question had been so largely influenced by prejudice rather than by reason and by passion rather than by argument.[5]

The Chinese question was at last launched as the vital political issue of California. During the whole summer of 1876 the excitements of the Presidential campaign increased and the closeness of the contest, and the Hayes-Tilden controversy, did not tend to quiet the turbulent masses, who were still further inflamed by industrial hardships. In January, 1877, the monthly dividends of one million dollars from the bonanza mines of the Comstock lode stopped and shortly afterward their value declined from eighty to ten millions. The stock market of San Francisco was nearly paralyzed and it was said that where there had been a hundred millionaires there were now only half as many. The estimated shrinkage in valuation of two mines alone, whose stock was nearly all owned in San Francisco, was one hundred and fifty millions. The passion for gambling, highly developed by the speculative type of all the earlier enterprises, had spread even to clerks, laborers and washerwomen. Everybody had dabbled in stocks—everybody hoped to strike it rich in larger or smaller measure. When, therefore, the yield of gold and silver ceased to meet expectation and the highly inflated stocks fell, all other values fell—down—down—into an apparently bottomless pit. The savings of the greater part of the common people were buried there and even yet the San Francisco Almshouse shelters the wrecks of humanity whose capacity and courage were broken by their losses.[6]

Nobody escaped—everybody was directly or indirectly affected. Miners and farm-hands, thrown out of work by the lack of water, drifted into the cities where the shrinkage of capital, failures of large houses and continued stagnation of business, threw other thousands out

[5] *Alta*, Apr. 6 and 7, 1876, full stenographic report.
[6] Smith, *Almshouse Women*, Amer. Statist. Assoc., v. 7, p. 332.

of employment. The transient male population of San Francisco, usually not less than ten or twelve thousand in winter, of whom more than half were foreigners and perhaps one-fourth of Irish birth or parentage, was thus largely increased by the invasion of those out of employment from the rural communities; and by those who had come from the panic-stricken East only to find no better conditions in the West.[7]

Governor Irwin, in his annual message in 1877, described these untoward circumstances and said that they had been the cause of demonstrations against the Chinese. While recognizing the duty of protecting them, he said it was not always possible to do what the Government was legally and morally bound to do and advised legislation in disregard of the treaty if it should be necessary. He acknowledged, however, that the demonstrations had later taken a wider range, menacing property of capitalists, but since they were due to the depression in business they would cease with better times. So long as the working classes had grievances they were justified in agitation until these were remedied.[8]

Such lukewarm support of the laws and treaty with China were certainly not calculated to check the rising spirit of mob-rule. Persecution and annoyance of the Chinese, which had heretofore been sporadic throughout the State, now became general. The more orderly members of society secretly disapproved, but no politician or office-holder dared protest, and many business men dared no longer employ them. The boycott, incendiarism, personal violence—every form of social and industrial intimidation was used against those who attempted to protect them. The more decent newspapers contrasted the temperate expression of the Chinese appeal to the Mayor of San Francisco with this alarming violence of speech and behavior on the part of the white population. But

---

[7] Bancroft, *Hist. of Cal.*, v. 7, p. 332.
[8] *Ass. Jo.*, 1875-6, p. 33; 1877-8, pp. 12 ff.

The Chinese Must Go

loose-tongued and violent speech had become the habit of all who wished to attract attention to their cause; and the example set by the prominent men and law-abiding citizens in the incendiary meetings of the previous year, was about to bear fruit in a harvest of hoodlumism, riot and arson, such as even San Francisco had never seen before.

For three days in July the rioters sacked and burned buildings occupied by the Chinese and raged almost unchecked; then a Vigilance Committee was formed and they were suppressed. In September, the Workingmen's party was formally organized and in October its leaders began a series of open-air meetings on the sand-lots at which they used the most violent language against the capitalists of the Pacific railroads and the Chinese. Dennis Kearney bade the men who put Chinese above American workingmen beware or they would import a tree from Oregon and set it up in the plaza where every morning it would be found bearing fruit. Day said that they intended to raise workingmen to their proper level even if they had to override law and civilization to do it.[9]

Upon being arrested for misdemeanor, Kearney and other speakers backed down and explained away much of this incendiary language; and were finally released upon technicalities. As a consequence of their arrest the demonstrations of the sand-lotters became less objectionable, the leaders confining themselves to the larger national questions of public lands, banks, currency and railroads. Kearney and Knight stumped the State on behalf of these issues, but were coldly received by the rural communities. On their return, the city had filled up as always in winter, with the vagrant and unemployed and they marched to the City Hall, demanding work from the Mayor. Again sand-lot meetings followed,

[9] Day, a Canadian, was called the brains of the movement; although he had been four years in the United States, it was said that he was not naturalized. Dennis Kearney was not naturalized till July, 1876. See *Alta*, Nov. 6, 1877.

at which the speakers expressed themselves more violently than ever against "thieving millionaires and scoundrelly officials." They threatened to lynch the railway magnates, burn the Pacific Mail Docks and drop dynamite balloons into Chinatown. This terrorism was cut short by the arrest of Kearney and other leaders for conspiracy and riot; but they were again acquitted on technicalities.[10]

Throughout this year and a half of financial depression, stagnation and social agitation, much had been threatened and done against the Chinese; yet it may be doubted whether Chinese immigration was, after all, the storm center of the disturbance. Rather, it appears that a mushroom prosperity and great extremes of fortune, arising from speculation and chance rather than legitimate industry, and the gathering of heterogeneous idlers under the leadership of demagogues, had brought to the surface all the elements of jealousy, envy and lawlessness which, inherent in human nature, now surged and frothed about the more stable elements of society. The indifference to public welfare characteristic of a society based on the pursuit of money alone, was bearing its legitimate fruits in a general disorder.

Of this unfortunate situation the Chinese were the victims rather than the fundamental cause; they were so many, so thrifty, so uncomplaining, so glad to work at any price, and above all so alien, so strange—so "heathenish." To the followers of the Workingmen's Party they seemed such a facile tool for the greedy capitalist that it was only natural to suppose that they were the chief cause both of his riches, and of their own hardships. Yet the Chinese had not caused drought, nor decline of mineral production, nor speculation and panic in stocks and real estate, nor land monopoly nor even the labor movement

---

[10] On Kearneyism and the Workingmen's Party the newspapers of the period and witnesses still living are the first authority. Good general accounts are given by: Hittell, T., *Hist. of California*, Vol. 4, p. 595 ff.; Bryce, *American Commonwealth*, vol. 2, p. 372 ff. (2d. Edition.) Davis, *Political Conventions*, 374 ff.

which was world-wide and which had taken on a special and violent phase in San Francisco.

If the Chinese had worn American clothes and been able to vote, even in California they might have suffered scarcely more persecution than the Spanish-Americans of the earlier time or than the Japanese of to-day—no more than the normal amount arising from color prejudice. But being constantly in the public eye by reason of their peculiar appearance and lacking political power for their own protection, they were the natural victims of ignorant men who were both malicious and cowardly, and of the politicians dependent upon the Labor vote.

For that the Workingmen's Party was now a serious factor to be reckoned with was recognized by both political parties. The members of the Legislature—overwhelmingly Democratic—hastened to make good their pre-election pledges and to stand right with the labor element on the Chinese question. Of seven anti-Chinese resolutions offered, four were passed. The Report, Address and Memorial prepared by the committee appointed to investigate Chinese Immigration was adopted, twenty thousand copies ordered printed, and the committee thanked and liberally paid.

One important measure, the so-called "Gag-law," passed at this session, affords opportunity for judging [11] how widely the sentiment of the time was divided as to the causes of the disturbance. The committee of five on the so-called gag-law made three separate reports. Tobin and Breen thought that the workingmen's movement was the result of the overstocking of the labor market by poor immigrants from the East and by Orientals, intensified by business stagnation and incited by Eastern labor riots. Long and Conroy said that as to the Chinese, beyond the fact that they had driven white

---

[11] Sec. 420 of *Penal Code*, Amends. to Codes, 1877–8, 117–8; *Sen. Jo.*, 1877–8, p. 122, Cal. Stats. 879; App. of *Jos. of Sen. & Ass.*, Vol. 4, 1877–8, pp. 240–1.

laborers from some of the industries which they had monopolized, there was no justification in the riots. They added significantly; " We look upon the Chinese evil as more of an excuse than a justification."

The fifth member—S. K. Welch—thought it must be patent to all thinking people that the widespread destitution was directly traceable to the presence of immense hordes of heathen Chinese. Since matters had come to such a pass that no politician dared to be pro-Chinese, it is doubly significant that only one member of the committee named the Chinese as the fundamental and inciting cause of the outbreak while two others regarded their competition as a secondary cause and two, conceding the fact of competition, regarded them as an excuse rather than the cause.

The old-line politicians were already dismayed by the sweeping victories of the Workingmen's Party; and in view of the election of delegates to the Constitutional Convention upon which the political interest of the whole State was now centered, they arranged a strong fusion ticket of Republicans, Democrats and non-partisans in the State at large. The Workingmen's Party, in which could now be discerned two factions, offered to the voters a lengthy programme of reform, in which opposition to the Chinese—not to employ them or to buy from them or sell to them—stood first, and opposition to land monopoly stood second.

When the Constitutional Convention assembled it was almost equally divided between the two old parties, but the predominance of workingmen from San Francisco, and of farmers representing the Granger element of the country districts who stood together on some of the most extreme propositions, gave the radicals the balance of power and produced the most extraordinary state constitution known in the history of the United States.[12]

[12] Sacramento *Union*, Sept. 30, 1878: The occupations of the delegates was as follows: 58 lawyers, 9 merchants, 5 physicians, 3 jour-

The Chinese Must Go 119

By this time even conservative citizens were so desperate at the lawlessness of the Workingmen's Party that they were ready to concede anything for the sake of industrial peace. The constitution, formed under this intimidation of the extreme laboring and agricultural classes, was permeated with two main ideas: hostility to capital, expressed in measures of taxation and limitation, and hostility to the Chinese, expressed in measures for cutting off their means of livelihood.[13]

For the purpose of this discussion the second Constitution of California is of no direct significance, except as it concerned the Chinese. In spite of an experience of twenty-five years during which all State anti-Chinese legislation had ultimately been nullified by Courts and Federal Constitution, the delegates to the Convention seemed to think that to check Chinese immigration only an organic act was necessary, regardless of treaties, courts or Constitution. The Workingmen's delegation brought in a series of anti-Chinese propositions of which the more important were as follows: aliens should not be allowed to hold property; Chinese should not be allowed to trade, peddle or carry on any mercantile business; no person not eligible to be a citizen should be allowed to settle in the State, and any person encouraging such should be fined; aliens, ineligible to citizenship, should be prohibited from bearing arms, giving testimony in the courts in cases involving white persons, from fishing in the inland waters of the State and from employment on public works; a per capita tax of $250.00 should be levied on each Chinese immigrant.

These propositions were remarkable not only for their display of rancor and ignorance, but for their total in-

---

nalists, 1 school teacher, 39 farmers, 17 mechanics, 5 miners, 1 telegraph operator, 1 music teacher, 1 restaurant keeper.

[13] Pomeroy, *Work of Stephen J. Field*, p. 405 ff.; Hittell, *Hist. of Cal.* Vol. 4, 610 ff.; Willis, *Debates of Constitutional Convention*, pp. 80–371.; Bryce, *American Commonwealth*, Vol. 1, pp. 683–724 (text), Vol. 2, pp. 383 ff.

applicability to the problem to be solved. Their tone is inhuman in its disregard of the common rights of men, as well as of the protection guaranteed to the Chinese under the Burlingame Treaty. At least two-thirds of them were on their face violations of the Federal Constitution, and several had been passed and declared invalid in previous years. And yet they were seriously proposed although it had become thoroughly understood in the ten years of previous agitation that no limitation or prohibition of Chinese immigration was possible except by Congressional legislation and treaty negotiation.

However ignorant or unused to questions of legality and method the workingmen's faction may have been, it cannot be supposed that the lawyers, physicians, journalists and other relatively well-educated men who constituted at least half of the Convention, were ignorant of the futility of such propositions. Yet they permitted the adoption of Article Nineteen of the Second Constitution, the provisions of which were not only unconstitutional but inhuman and silly.

Article Nineteen gave the Legislature power to regulate the immigration of paupers, criminals, diseased persons and aliens otherwise dangerous or detrimental to the State, and to impose the conditions of their residence or removal. It forbade corporations to employ any Mongolian, nor could they be engaged on any public works. Coolie contracts were declared void and companies importing them, whether formed in this or any foreign country, were to be penalized. The Legislature was even empowered to remove the Chinese beyond the limits of cities and towns and to prohibit their introduction into the State

It is no excuse for the adoption of this article that men of all parties were unanimous in desiring some check upon Chinese immigration, for the lawyers of the Convention certainly knew it was futile to that end. Two or three times a gleam of this knowledge appears in the de-

The Chinese Must Go

bates when it was suggested that a modification of the treaty was necessary; or, as when one member who, although a Democrat and opposed to Chinese immigration, plead warmly for legal and constitutional measures and declared that he had no taste for mobs and would never vote to withhold protection from any human being. One member and one only—Charles V. Stewart, a farmer of Sonoma County—made an extended and fearless speech in behalf of the Chinese. He reviewed the history of their favorable reception in the early days, their contributions in labor and money to the State, their superiority to most of the white tramp labor which was all that was available in California; and he pointed out frankly that it was white rioters and hoodlums that should be feared rather than the industrious and peaceable Chinese. In great detail and with great force and courage he went on and finally concluded with a demand that the Chinese should be accorded the privilege of educating their children in the common schools, in return for the school taxes which they paid; that the personal assaults to which the law was blind, should cease; that the disgraceful, heartless and inhuman special legislation against them should stop; and that the State, instead of allowing them to be outraged, should protect them in the rights of life, liberty and the pursuit of happiness guaranteed to all men under the American flag.[14]

Nevertheless, most of the sections finally incorporated in Article Nineteen, were adopted almost unanimously and many of the injustices to the Chinese were thus given a sort of constitutional approval. But when the Constitution was accepted by the Convention, most of the more intelligent members did not vote for it and when presented to the people for ratification, the majority was small. Even in San Francisco where the Workingmen's Party had been so strong the year before, there was a

[14] Willis, *Debates*, 1238-1240; see careful digest of thi speech in Hittell, *Hist. of Cal.* v. 4, pp. 622-625.

majority of 1600 votes against it which was only overcome by the Granger vote in the State at large.[15]

The result, so meagre in view of the original proposition of the Workingmen's Party—" The Chinese must go "—and yet so tremendous in the perspective of history in its consequences, was brought about not so much because the Convention favored Article Nineteen as because of timidity on one side, ignorance on another, and a shrewd forecast of its ineffectiveness on a third; not at all because the more intelligent believed there was such imminent necessity of extreme anti-Chinese measures or endorsed this method of securing them. The Constitution could not have been enforced as written; but fortunately by decisions of the courts and by legislation its most absurd and unpractical features have been nullified.

While the Constitutional Convention was still in session in January, 1879, San Francisco had been filling up as usual in winter with men out of employment and a new anti-Chinese agitation had broken out in the labor faction opposed to Dennis Kearney. Meetings were held at which the speakers advised driving out the Chinese with steel and torch because want and discontent prevailed and labor was paralyzed. They proposed cutting all queues, boycotting, compelling employers to pay a tax which should be used to return the Chinese to China, and lobbying at Washington to overcome the influence of Chinese money. The police were apathetic and the newspapers condemned the disturbances chiefly because they tended to keep the East from learning the truth.

But at last there were signs of a strong reaction against the radical measures of the Workingmen's Party. The Republicans were again conservatively advocating a moderate restriction of Chinese immigration, the Democrats still declared for a suppression of the " curse of coolies,"

---

[15] Hittell. *Hist. of Cal.* v. 4, 638.

while the workingmen continued to reiterate many of the propositions of the Convention, especially the limitation of the rights of foreigners and the enforcement of the law compelling corporations to discharge the Chinese. All three parties were now in varying degrees, anti-corporation, anti-monopoly, and anti-Chinese, but the reaction against Kearneyism had gone so far that the Republicans, conservative and capitalistic as they were, carried the State by a large majority.

At this election the popular vote on the Chinese question, called for by the resolution of the previous Legislature, was taken throughout the State. The whole number of votes cast was 161,405, of which 883 were for Chinese immigration and 154,638 against; 5,884 not voting.[16] This apparently indicated that California was almost unanimously against Chinese immigration, yet the manner in which the question was voted upon robs the result of any significance. There were four regular tickets in the field and the statute required that the words "For or against Chinese immigration" should be printed on each of them. Each ticket bore the names of forty-five officers from Governor to Constable printed in good-sized capitals; at the bottom of each was printed in much smaller type, quite inconspicuously, only the words "Against Chinese Immigration."[17] In order to vote *for* Chinese Immigration therefore, the voter was obliged to cross out the word *Against* and write in the word *For*. Scratching of tickets was much less common at that time than in modern elections, and it is easy to see that in an election where the adoption of the new constitution was the matter of prime importance, and where there was so long a list of offices, the question of Chinese immigration would be overlooked by many voters. If overlooked, it was necessarily a vote *against* Chinese

---

[16] App. *Legisl. Jos.*, v. 5, 1880; Hittell, *Hist. of Cal.*, v. 4, p. 647.

[17] See collection of ballots used in California State Library, Sacramento.

immigration, and under such circumstances it must inevitably have been overlooked by a large number.

A majority of the citizens of California were undoubtedly in favor of some measure of restriction by this time, if only because that was the only way to pacify the workingmen; but this vote, taken in a manner which violated the statute authorizing it, and which was calculated to mislead the voter, does not prove, as has been asserted ever since, that California was "practically unanimous against Chinese immigration."[18]

The Republican Legislature of 1879-1880 was occupied in suppressing a flood of bills offered by the radical minority and directed against vested rights and the Chinese. Bills to promote emigration from the State; to remove the Chinese outside the limits of cities and towns; to declare Chinese incompetent to hold real property; to prohibit the use of Chinese labor in any contract where the State or any subdivision of it was a party; to brand and banish Mongolian convicts; to make it a misdemeanor to secrete or store human bones in places other than those provided by law—these and many other propositions as wild, as vindictive or as unconstitutional, were lost.

But the combined minority elements—workingmen, Grangers and Democrats—succeeded in passing one important measure against both the Chinese and the corporations. It was made a misdemeanor with a penalty of one hundred to one thousand dollars fine (or imprisonment), for any corporation to employ Chinese and, on a second offense, the fine was to be raised to five hundred to five thousand dollars.[19] A few corporations dissolved but most of them resisted the law. The Sulphur Bank Quicksilver Mining Company, whose president was arrested for a second violation, took the question into the courts. The United States Circuit Court held that the

---

[18] Layres, A. *The Other Side, etc.* (Ed. 1886) p. 15.
[19] *Penal Code*, 1880, Art. 178, 179.

law was invalid because it conflicted with the Burlingame treaty and was, moreover, a violation of the Fourteenth Amendment—thus nullifying one of the most definite provisions of Article Nineteen of the Second State Constitution.

The reaction against Kearneyism still continued as shown by a multitude of protests to the Legislature against class legislation and injustice to the Chinese, and against the inferences from the referendum vote which, it was declared, did not represent the true feeling of California on the Chinese question. Governor Perkins attributed the cessation of white immigration in part to the turbulence on the Chinese question but thought that it might ultimately be beneficial in compelling the general government to give relief. On all sides it was now recognized that the restriction of Chinese immigration must be referred to Congress.

"The Chinese Must Go" had now become the dominant political issue with which the Coast States strove to make their rising importance felt in the National Legislature. Pacific Congressmen welcomed it as a definite and sensational cause upon which to make themselves known. Above all, safe, because the North and East, whose sympathies might naturally have been with an oppressed and alien people, were ignorant of the merits of the question. It appealed, they knew, to the race prejudices of even the most just-minded citizens and the Chinese had neither the weapon of suffrage nor the active protection of their own government with which to oppose injustice. Every other political issue in the West had powerful enemies to reckon with; the Chinese question engaged the sympathies of missionaries, humanitarians and scholars—the humane but politically ineffective minority.

The Chinaman, predestined by helplessness to be the convenient puppet of politics, had become, to the ignorant and antipathetic workingmen of California, the obvious cause of all his grievances. There were reasons enough—drought, lack of work, panic, monopoly, surplus of white immigration and decline of treasure yield—for the formation of an extreme workingmen's party; but when to these were added violent class prejudice against the rich monopolists, and instinctive antipathy toward a too-industrious, too-alien, and too-helpless people, the movement could not but take on outrageous forms.

It must be questioned whether California as a whole, or even the working classes, have profited enough by the exclusion of the Chinese to compensate for the lawless turmoil by which it was initiated and has been maintained. Certainly no dispassionate reader of the history of the State can fail to see that the incessant agitation of this question both at this period and later, has retarded the investment of capital and the diversification of industry, prevented, by giving the State a bad name, the immigration of a solid middle class composed of farmers, business men and skilled mechanics, while inviting at the same time the tramp and the turbulent adventurer; and, by giving encouragement to the ignorant and lawless to a degree rare even in pioneer regions, put even conscientious public men at the mercy of the least stable element.

CHAPTER IX

THE CHINESE QUESTION IN CONGRESS

" The Chinese question presents an eagerly seized hobby for the mountebanks to harp upon, humbug the people with, and ride into prominence and place on. . . . The fact is, the Chinese are mostly of excellent character as judged by American standards. They are intelligent, industrious, economical, ingenious and great money-getters and accumulators; are a persevering, vigorous, temperate and healthy race, enduring and energetic, all are free men and freedom-loving and compare favorably in morality with the Caucasians in California; hence all the more to be dreaded as competing rivals . . . and rooters out of other races. . . . England and America strove for generations to break down the Chinese wall of exclusiveness. . . At length they succeeded. . . . . We have at length ' Caught a Tartar.' The question is, what shall we do with the troublesome animal? "—PICKETT'S Pamphlet, 1876.

" We have received the Ambassador of the Chinese Empire with more distinction than we ever received the Ambassador of any foreign nation. Yet it is proposed to say by law that no subject of that Empire, no matter how long he has resided among us, and no matter what may be his character, intelligence or virtue, shall be an American citizen."— Senator CARPENTER—Debate on Naturalization law, 1870.

" While I am opposed to Asiatics being brought here and will join in any reasonable legislation to prevent anybody from bringing them, yet we have a Treaty that allows them to come. We have pledged the honor of the nation . . . that they shall be protected for twenty years, every obligation of humanity, of justice and of common decency towards these people has been violated by a certain class of men—bad men, I know; but they are violated in California and on the Pacific Coast.— Senator STEWART of Nevada, 1870.

By 1869 California had five representatives in Congress, Oregon three, and Nevada three—a total of six Senators and five representatives for the whole Pacific Coast. The economic conditions of these states and of the Territory of Washington—and a few years later of Wyoming and Montana—were similar, their populations recruited from similar classes and increased by similar immigration after the War. Their representatives, although dividing on party lines when voting on national measures, soon found it necessary, in order to make any impression in Congress, to stand together in all issues involving the states west of the Rocky Mountains.

The discharge of thousands of Chinese in Nevada and Washington upon the completion of the Pacific railroads, together with a panic in 1869, had brought the Chinese into sudden and conspicuous disfavor with the working classes. Although the Republicans of the West were still moderate on the question of Chinese immigration, the Democrats, augmented by the working classes and especially by Irish and other foreign Americans, were fully committed to an extreme pro-labor and anti-Chinese policy. Since the Chinese could not be naturalized nor vote nor testify in the courts for or against a white person, they were not likely to retaliate upon those who opposed them; and since, moreover, they aroused an instinctive race antipathy in the ignorant, they were a most effective issue with the local constituency. No more safe and picturesque party plank than Chinese restriction could have been invented nor one better adapted to attract the votes of workingmen.

At this period the Western representatives were by no means unanimous on the Chinese question. Senator Williams of Oregon, and Senator Casserley of California representing the extreme wing of the anti-Chinese element, made the most violent allegations against the Chinese in Congress, in defense of their bills against coolie immigration and immoral women. One said the Chinese Six Companies had an "*imperium in imperio*" without reference to the laws of this country; and that an allotment of 240 slave women had been sent to them; the other referred to the Burlingame treaty as the most one-sided, unnecessary and injurious treaty ever negotiated. Both were contradicted by Senator Cole of California, who thought the Chinese necessary to the prosperity of his State, and by Senator Stewart of Nevada, who advocated the exclusion of contract laborers but thought that California should be prevented from imposing unreasonable burdens on these people.

The Burlingame treaty had expressly excepted naturalization from the rights of the most favored nation guaranteed to the Chinese and the Western Congressmen of both parties were opposed to granting them either naturalization or suffrage. The inconsistency of the Republicans in refusing them naturalization was repeatedly attacked. In the long debate of the Forty-first Congress, which ended in the extension of the privilege of naturalization to "aliens of African nativity and persons of African descent,"[1] Senator Carpenter of Wisconsin said:

"The very men who settled the question of negro suffrage upon principle now hesitate to apply the principle . . . to the instance before us and now interpose the very objections to the enfranchisement of the Chinaman that the Democrats urged against the enfranchisement of the Freedmen."[2]

In this debate Senator Corbett of Oregon predicted the overthrow of civil and religious institutions and of the Republican Party unless Chinese immigration were checked; yet he was satisfied that if the numbers were limited the country might be able to absorb a few hundred thousand, perhaps a million. His colleague, Senator Williams, emphasized the danger of overwhelming numbers, in one paragraph declaring that the Chinese had no desire to be naturalized and later that there were eighty thousand on the Coast who would be naturalized in one day. Senator Carl Schurz, who appeared to be better informed about the Chinese than most of the Senators, called Williams' speech, "a heated fancy" since the immigration of Chinese had averaged only 6,000 per year for twenty years past, and even if it should rise to 20,000 per year it would take fifty years to bring a

[1] 41st. Cong. 2d Sess. *Cong. Globe*, p. 300.
[2] 41st. Cong. 2d Sess. *Cong. Globe*, p. 5160.

million. He advocated shutting out contract laborers, and admitting all other classes to naturalization for he believed that those who remained permanently would not long be cheap producers nor bad consumers but would acquire new wants and ultimately be absorbed among Americans.³

The House bill to enforce the right to vote was the occasion for all the Coast representatives to put themselves on record on the Chinese question. Mr. Johnson of California, said:

"You will never enfranchise the Chinaman. . . . I threaten nothing, but I know California and I know that the Army and the Navy are too small to protect the Chinese voters in that state." ⁴

Mr. Axtell said that citizenship would give these pagans power, in localities where they were in excess of Europeans, to substitute the brutalities of the Juggernaut for the religion of Christ, to convert the church into a Joss House, and the school-room into a brothel.⁵ But it was Mr. Sargent who, then and for many years afterward, surpassed all others in exaggeration and violence of statement. According to him the Chinese were pagan idolaters addicted to nameless vices, who could afford to work for twenty-five to fifty cents a day, who were already invading the manufactures of the Eastern and Southern states and who were depopulating certain districts of California. He predicted that the census of 1870 would show that the white population had diminished because their occupations had been absorbed by the Chinese.⁶ Although the Chinese were finally denied political privileges, they gained one substantial item of justice by the passage of the act to enforce the right of citizens to vote, in that it put an end to all dis-

---

³ *Cong. Globe*, 41st Cong. 2d Sess. 1870, p. 5158 ff.
⁴ *Cong. Globe*, 41st Cong. 2d Sess. 1869-70, Pt. I, p. 752.
⁵ *Cong. Globe*, 41st Cong. 2d Sess. 1869-70, App 5, p. 452 ff.
⁶ *Cong. Globe*, 41st Cong. 2d Sess., p. 4275 ff.

The Chinese Question in Congress 131

crimination in taxation under which the Chinese had paid nearly five million dollars for mining licenses alone.[7]

The bills of the Californians relating to Chinese immigration did not get further than the Committee Room in the Forty-second and Forty-third Congresses. At the end of five years, although the Chinese question had been continuously urged by the Coast members, almost nothing had been accomplished toward convincing Eastern legislators that the Chinese were a serious menace to a region where wages were so high and labor so scarce. The tone of extreme violence and exaggeration and the evident intention on the part of Western Congressmen to make the most of so sensational a subject for political ends, prevented their arguments from taking effect. Nor could any amount of ranting disguise the fact that while the rest of the country had been in the grip of severe panic, California was still relatively very prosperous.

But in 1876, owing to the effect of the national depression, to local drought, speculation, decline of treasure yield and real estate, and too rapid increase of population in proportion to capital invested in industrial enterprises, the general disaster was extended to California. In the winter of 1876-7 there were estimated to be 10,000 men out of employment congregated in San Francisco, whose grievances found expression in the sudden rise of the Workingmen's Party and in the riots of the sandlotters. In an earlier chapter the course of this agitation has been described, but it is pertinent to recall here that although the Chinese appeared to be the precipitating cause in the West, the violent labor disturbances were, in part at least, the reflection of a much wider industrial discontent throughout the country.[8]

During the sessions of the Forty-fourth Congress, therefore, these conditions were pressing upon its members. In the closely contested national election of 1876,

[7] Laws of the U. S. 114, sec. 16, 1870.
[8] See Coman, *Industrial Hist. of the U. S.* pp. 331-2; 341-2.

both parties had adopted anti-Chinese pledges, the one in order to divert the labor faction from its attacks on vested rights, the other as a necessary consequence of a habitual pro-labor attitude. As long as the Workingmen's Party held the stage in California it was inevitable that every Coast member of Congress should be unmistakably active on the Chinese question.

Senator Sargent was already known as an extremely skilful politician, but the advent of the able and it must be added, unscrupulous, Senator Mitchell of Oregon, greatly strengthened the Western forces. The effort to check Chinese immigration in the guise of shutting out coolies and prostitutes, was now abandoned for an attack on the Burlingame treaty. Senator Sargent offered a resolution in May, 1876, that the President should enter into negotiations with China to modify the treaty so as to check the influx of Chinese immigrants. He supported it in a speech full of extravagance and misrepresentation and was followed by Senator Mitchell who even exceeded him in venom. Senator Mitchell declared that all the Chinese except a mere fraction were composed of coolies and dissolute women—" vassals, criminals, lepers and debased "—who were brought in and controlled by the Six Companies. He even quoted approvingly the action of the mobs that had burned their buildings and driven them out.

In the interval between this debate and the renewal of the subject in Congress in July, Philip A. Roach, Democratic State Senator of California, was sent east to work up anti-Chinese sentiment. He found an unexpected degree of opposition and great difficulty in getting a hearing except before workingmen's assemblies. At Washington, although he interviewed the President and Cabinet and was given a two-days' hearing before the Committee on Foreign Relations, his efforts did not produce any substantial result for the anti-Chinese cause.

When, in July, Mr. Sargent modified his sweeping

resolution by substituting the words, "influx of Chinese coolies and criminals," for "Chinese immigrants," he obtained scarcely a more cordial hearing than before. The Eastern Senators were very critical of the motives behind the anti-Chinese movement; one said the Pacific Slope was trying to see which party would bid highest for its vote in the Presidential election; another said that it was one thing to shut out criminals but quite another to shut out labor. References were made to persecution and the misuse of the word "coolie" to mean a slave when in reality it merely meant a hired laborer, was pointed out. Finally, Senator Morton, after stating that neither the President nor the Senate would act without the fullest information, offered a substitute resolution to which Sargent agreed, that a Committee be sent to California to investigate the whole subject of Chinese immigration.

Between the Forty-fourth and Forty-fifth Congresses, the Committee of the California State Senate had published its report, already analyzed in Chapter VI., and the Congressional Committee went to California shortly afterward. Both reports were extremely anti-Chinese, as indeed, it was necessary that they should be, to meet the political requirements of the contending parties. The effort to obtain some kind of anti-Chinese measure was therefore renewed in the Forty-Fifth Congress with greater vigor than ever. The Westerners offered a variety of bills against contract labor, against the employment of Mongolians on public works, against naturalization of the Chinese, and many resolutions and petitions praying for the modification of the Burlingame treaty. The Committee on Education and Labor in the House reported back a resolution asking the President to open negotiations with China for such a modification of the treaty.[9]

Although the resolution itself was mild and judicious

[9] H. R. no. 123, Joint Res. re-committed.

the report made by Mr. Willis for the committee was as anti-Chinese as the Californians co d wish for. He said that the claim to protection of the Chinese residents here could not be denied and if money were the only consideration they should continue to be admitted; but they lacked self-respect and independence, were homeless single men, working for lower wages than white laborers and with a lower standard of living. They practiced the sale of wives, infanticide, concubinage, perjury and torture—he drew a fearful picture of "grovelling thoughts, low passions, parsimonious and degrading habits." They were impregnable to all influences and would always be. Since the Chinese emigrants sailed from the British port of Hong Kong the abrogation of the treaty would not solve the problem, and the committee therefore advised correspondence with Great Britain and China.[10]

In the Senate, Mr. Sargent presented several bills to restrict or regulate Chinese immigration and Senator Booth urged the necessity of early legislation to prevent a convulsion which would shake the foundations of social order in California, predicting that if the Government decided to continue free immigration, it must be prepared to maintain it by force. The California Senators presented several concurrent resolutions of the State Senate, one endorsing a bill introduced into the House by Mr. Shelley of Alabama, to restrict Chinese immigration by levying a per capita tax of two hundred and fifty dollars upon every subject of China entering the United States except officers of the Chinese government.[11] The Committee on Foreign Relations to which these measures were all referred, reported a resolution similar to the one passed in the House, inviting the attention of the Executive to the advisability of modifying the existing treaty with China.[12]

---

[10] *Cong. Docs.* s. n. 1822, H. R. Rept. 240, 1878.
[11] 45th Cong. 2d Sess. 1878, *Record*, pp. 2439–40; p. 301; p. 1155.
[12] 45th Cong. 2d Sess. 1878, *Record*, pp. 3226; 3772–3; 4782.

The Chinese Question in Congress 135

The struggles over the Second Constitution in California were reflected in the renewed vigor of the Coast representatives in Congress in the winter of 1879. Senator Booth presented the Memorial of the Constitutional Convention asking for the prohibition of Chinese immigration; Senator Mitchell, a similar one from the Legislature of Oregon; and the subject was finally brought to a head in the debate on a House bill which provided that no vessel should bring more than fifteen Chinese to this country at one time. Mr. Willis of Kentucky again repeated his charges of "sordid, selfish, immoral and non-amalgamating habits" on the part of the Chinese, reviewed the futile legislation of the Western States, criticised the inactivity of the treaty-making power, and concluded that the matter had now reached dangerous proportions.[13]

The Republican minority in the House fought the bill on various grounds: it was a revival of Know-nothingism; a measure reflecting the demands of the Kearneyites in California; a breach of faith with China in view of the Burlingame treaty such as the United States would not dare to perpetrate toward any European Power; it was even protested that the Chinese were not coolie slaves nor unassimilable. The Republicans particularly resented being told that California would go Democratic in the next Presidential campaign if the bill did not pass. The Democrats replied that the Chinese were filthy, vicious, incapable of self-government, unassimilable, contract coolies, and that China had not kept the Burlingame treaty. Some slight attempts were made to soften the bill by amendments but the Democrats would permit neither amendment nor delay and passed the bill by a large majority.[14]

[13] H. R. 2423, introduced by Representative Wren of Nevada but generally attributed to Willis of Kentucky, Chairman of the Committee on Education and Labor. See index *Record*, 45th Cong. 3d Sess. 1879. *Cong. Repts.* 1878–9. s. n. 1866.

[14] Vote 155 to 72, 61 not voting. Democrats 104 yeas, 16 nays; Republicans 51 yeas, 56 nays.

In the Senate the bill was reported back from the Committee on Foreign Relations without recommendation and the Chairman, Senator Hamlin of Maine, announced that he would personally move its indefinite postponement. Senator Sargent opened the debate with a reiteration of his former arguments to which he added the still more extravagant statement that there were now more Chinese in California than there were voters. When called to account for this later, he modified it and said there were about as many.[15] Senator Grover of Oregon, while assuring the Senate that he would much have preferred a modification of the treaty before legislating on the question, thought the demand of the people for immediate action should be met. The treaty was not reciprocal and the Chinese had got the best of us, anyway. Senator Booth, though more moderate in tone, supported his colleagues on the ground that American labor was in danger of being reduced to the Asiatic level and a conflict of races was imminent.

Senator Morgan while declaring his intention to vote for the bill thought the State Department should have dealt with the problem and did not hesitate to point out its political significance. He said:

"Politicians have seized upon it as a means of controlling votes in the Pacific states and each party is eagerly pressing its claim at present in forcing this bill on the attention of Congress. . . . This bill even is political and is expected to have much to do with the election of a President."

When, late at night, the question of adjournment was raised[16] and it appeared that with the exception of Senator Matthews of Ohio, only those in favor of the bill had been heard, Senator Hamlin said:

[15] In 1870 the white males in California over 21, numbered 186,823, the citizens 145,802; while the Chinese over 21 numbered 36,890.
[16] The vote on adjournment stood, yeas 29, nays 24, absent 21.

"I should be stupid not to know that from a concurrence of motives and circumstances, this bill is to pass this body, but may I not ask of the majority . . . that they treat the minority at least with courtesy."

Upon the resumption of the debate Senator Blaine of Maine took up the defense of the bill. He referred sarcastically to the fact that the vote on the naturalization of the Chinese had stood 31 to 9 in a Senate three-fourths Republican, and was of the opinion that the Chinese would be safer as a voter, dangerous as that would be, than as a political pariah. He protested against comparing Chinese to European immigration: the Chinese had no regard for the relation of the family, did not recognize the relation of husband and wife, did not observe the tie of parent and child, and were laborers under a mortgage.

When it had become perfectly evident that the bill would pass regardless of courtesy to the President, the State Department and China, and in violation of the treaty, the pro-Chinese minority attempted to kill it or to mitigate its harshness with amendments. Several were to the effect that if the Emperor of China did not consent to a modification of the treaty, Congress would consider the obnoxious stipulations as at an end after January first, 1880. This brought out a strong protest from Senator Hoar who said that Congress might have the legal power to abrogate the treaty but it was dishonorable and not justified by the emergency. Senator Sargent interrupted him to say that the Senator belittled the emergency, that the people of California had been trying to be heard for ten years, that the Chinese were coolies, servile labor, contract labor, which only the farmers wanted; and he referred scornfully to the "sentimentalities and generalities" of the pro-Chinese senators. Senator Hoar retorted that these were not sentimentalities but "eternal verities" and that the bill was a breach of faith and a violation of principle.

Senator Hamlin, who had registered his protest against the fixed purpose on the part of the majority to hurry the measure through, and against this legislation which catered to the Dennis Kearneys and the wild craze of Know-nothingism, was finally given the floor, in spite of strong opposition on the part of Senator Sargent, in order to make a full statement of his objections to the bill. He quoted Senator Morton's notes as authority for his facts concerning the Chinese and argued that although Congress had the power to abrogate a treaty it was absurd to say that one party to a treaty could change any part thereof. In this case it was a treaty which we had forced upon a friendly power. The subject should be left to the Executive and if Congress would be patient, there would be a solution satisfactory even to California. He asserted that the Chinese were not coolies under contract, that if they had the ballot the question of restriction would not be broached in Congress; that if treated with common humanity they would assimilate—if not rapidly yet within a reasonable time. He pointed out that California collected road, poll and school taxes from them, yet there were 3,000 Chinese in night schools because there was no other opportunity for them to learn English.

The amendment to notify the Emperor of China was voted down, but shipwrecked Chinese and students with a certificate from their Government were excepted from the operation of the act. Senator Sargent's amendment, that as soon as the bills passed the Emperor of China should be notified that certain sections of the treaty were abrogated, was passed. Again and again the minority returned to the attack with new amendments; at the last, Senator Edmunds once more expressed his abhorrence of the principle that without negotiation, without notice Congress undertook to abrogate by legislation a provision of a treaty with a friendly power.

The bill then passed by a small majority, the Republicans being equally divided, and the Democrats twenty-five to eight for the bill. Only two New Englanders—Blaine and Eaton—voted for it and ten Southerners voted against it. When it was known that the bill had been concurred in by the House the Californians made a tremendous effort to impress the President with their unanimity on the question. The Chamber of Commerce in San Francisco passed resolutions; an immense mass meeting was held to voice the public enthusiasm. One speaker only—General W. H. L. Barnes—had the courage to predict a veto by the President. When asked why Congress passed the bill if the President was sure to veto it, he replied:

"It was probably expected that the vote of California would have a great effect in the forthcoming presidential election."

On the first of March the bill was vetoed by President Hayes.

The President stated that the Burlingame treaty gave specific favors and privileges to Americans in China while the United States only guaranteed "permanent peace and good offices" in return. Already in 1868, a considerable immigration of Chinese had taken place, but the Coast States had asked for no modification of the Burlingame Treaty at that time. If the treaty fell short of what the Pacific Coast now desired, it nevertheless contained important advantages which, once relinquished, could not easily be recovered. The President regarded the grave discontent of the Western states as deserving the most serious attention, but he reminded Congress that while the power to abrogate treaties lay with that body, the power to make new treaties lay with the Executive and the Senate. The denunciation of any treaty was confessedly only justified by reasons both of the highest justice and the highest necessity. There was no emergency at present great enough to justify the withdrawal of protection from the Chinese in the United States or from Americans in China. Even if the delay necessary to obtain a modification of the treaty were fraught with inconvenience to the people of the Pacific Coast, the summary disturbance of our treaty relations with China would be far more inconvenient to other and more permanent interests of the country.[17]

The bill failed to pass over the President's veto. When this news arrived in California there was an outburst of disappointment expressed not only in wrath but in insulting personal attacks on the President and the Senators who had opposed the bill. But in spite of their anger, the Californians very soon acknowledged that the defeat of the bill had been chiefly due to Kearneyism and that it would seriously alter the political situation in the State. Senator Sargent said: "The chief obstacle in this fight has been the intemperate utterances of some of the anti-Chinese partisans."[18] The *Alta* said that the Kearneyites had only themselves to thank for the consequences which they had brought upon the State by their violence and ribaldry. Other papers, chiefly in the country districts, agreed with the Placerville *Herald:* "The question is not whether John Chinaman shall go but whether Kearney shall stay." The Republicans of the Coast, alarmed for the fate of the party at the next election, called meetings to repudiate the President's action and to point out that their Senator Sargent had been most energetic in getting the bill passed; while the Democrats, with ill-concealed glee, pointed out that it was a Republican administration which had betrayed California. Local politicians took advantage of the situation and indeed, temporarily, the grievances against the Chinese almost dropped out of sight in the readjustment of politicians to the new aspect of the coming campaign.

[17] Forty-fifth Congress, 3rd Ses. 1879, Cong. Rec. pp. 2275–6; Exec. Doc. 102, ser. no. 1838.
[18] Not many had been more intemperate in speech than Senator Sargent himself.

The Chinese Question in Congress

Thus at the end of ten years' almost continuous effort, the Californians had gained apparently no single step toward the restriction of Chinese immigration either by law or modification of the existing treaty. The measures proposed are of slight historical importance except as they foreshadow the lines of attack which ended in the first restriction law. Then and afterward, most of the Coast Congressmen showed themselves either grossly ignorant or—if the alternative be preferred—entirely willing to misrepresent the Chinese. The accusations that the Chinese were slaves, coolies under long-term contracts to capitalists or to the Six Companies, and that the Six Companies were a secret and tyrannical government importing contract coolies and prostitutes wholesale and punishing crimes outside the Courts, had been repeatedly denied not only by the reputable Chinese themselves but also by many American public men, scholars, Chinese interpreters and missionaries and even by the more reasonable and independent newspapers. The extreme anti-Chinese prejudice exhibited by most of the Coast Congressmen and their exaggerated statements made the Eastern members suspicious of their propositions and brought out many sarcastic references to their political intent. As in later years, the extremists prevented any legislation, even the most moderate, by their refusal to keep the question out of politics and to deal with it on a fair basis of facts. But for the veto of President Hayes the Fifteen Passenger bill would have become a law and Congress would have wantonly violated a treaty with a friendly power to satisfy the exigencies of party politics and the clamor of a few thousand workingmen in a region where wages were higher and the conditions of labor better than in any other part of the United States.

PART II
RESTRICTION AND EXCLUSION

CHAPTER X

TREATY RELATIONS BEFORE 1882

"Open wide ye gates of gold!
To the Dragon's Banner-fold!
Builders of the mighty wall
Bid your mountain barriers fall!
So may the girdle of the sun
Bind the East and West in one."
Poem of O. W. HOLMES, read at the dinner to
the Chinese Embassy, San Francisco, 1868.

"I believe that this occasion reflects more truly that enlarged spirit which is not alone devoted to trade but also to civilization and progress —the great and liberal spirit which would not be content with exchanging goods with China, but would also exchange thoughts with her; that would enquire carefully into the causes of that sobriety and industry; that would learn something of the long experience of that people; that would question those institutions that have withstood the storms of time, as to the secrets of their stability; that would ask what means that competition by which the son of the lowliest coolie may rise to the highest office in the Empire, and that makes scholarship the test of merit; that does not believe that genius is dead in the land of Confucius."—Speech of ANSON BURLINGAME at the dinner to the Chinese Embassy, San Francisco, April, 1868.

"We charge that Anson Burlingame sold his country's birthright for Chinese money . . . . For the purpose of obtaining prestige, with which he might work upon Great Britain in the interest of China and earn his fee, Mr. Burlingame induced his country to yield up a sovereign attribute, never before surrendered by any free people. Among them they bartered away . . . the right to determine who shall come and who shall not come to this new and growing country of ours, live on its soil, enjoy its privileges and mingle freely with its people. . . . It was conceived in fraud and chicane. It was negotiated at a time when no treaty was wanted by either country and not for the purpose named in the treaty. . . . The objection to terminating the Burlingame treaty has its stronghold in America with the cheap labor interests alone."—Anti-Chinese Memorial to Congress, 1886, drafted by JOHN F. SWIFT, A. A. SARGENT, MOREHOUSE, DAVIS and ANTHONY.

For the purpose of a history of Chinese immigration, only so much account of the treaties between China and the United States is necessary as relates to the subject of migration, other topics having been fully and carefully treated by writers on international law and diplomacy.[1] In the treaties of 1844 and 1858 nothing was said about the rights of the Chinese residing or trading in the United States. Nominally they possessed the same as the citizens of other nations; they were allowed to come and go freely, to engage in any occupation, and even, in a few states, to become naturalized citizens. But the words " free white persons " in the naturalization law of 1870 were construed to exclude them in most localities. As this operated against all colored persons of whatever nationality, and as the treaty of 1858 gave the United States the rights of the most favored nation in China but did not specify that the Chinese should have reciprocally the rights of the most favored nation in this country, this was not then regarded by them as an unjust deprivation.

The state of California had made various discriminations against Chinese immigrants, especially in the matter of taxation, which undoubtedly put them at a disadvantage as compared with other immigrants; but as the treaties had not stated their rights in detail and as most of this legislation was sooner or later declared unconstitutional, no diplomatic notice was taken of it.

At this time China was looked upon as walled in by tradition and incapable of entering into the reciprocity

[1] The best short account of the early treaties will be found in Smith's Emigration and Immigration; longer and fuller accounts from the diplomatic standpoint in Foster, *American Diplomacy*, Woolsey, *America's Foreign Policy*, Callahan, John Hopkins Studies, v. 19, *Our Relations with the Far East*. Minister Reed's own discussion of the articles of the treaty of 1858 in his dispatches to Secretary Cass are extremely interesting, see *Cong. Docs.*, ser. no. 1032 (1858), pp. 351–363 and pp. 429–435. On the Burlingame Treaty there is an immense mass of material, but the most illuminating is contained in the dispatches to the State Department, i.e. 1863, ser. no. 1181; 1867, ser. no. 1364; 1868, ser. no. 1316 and 1445. See also Williams, *Hist. of China*, p. 345 ff; *New Englander*, v. 38, p. 301 (1879); Godkin and Cunningham in the *Nation*, v. 10, p. 9; v. 7, p. 205, v. 9, p. 309; *Alta California*, Apr. 29 and 30, 1868; (Burlingame's speech, etc., at the San Francisco banquet); Knox in *Harper's Mag.*, v. 37, p. 593 ff. (1868); *Cong. Record*, 1882, Apr. 5, p. 2615; p. 1973; p. 1939 (being speeches on Burlingame's services.) For

Treaty Relations Before 1882   147

of nations; but the coincidence of a liberal movement there, led by Prince Kung, and the appointment of Anson Burlingame as Minister from the United States to that country in 1860, resulted in a remarkable extension of the relations of the two nations. Mr. Burlingame, as a New Englander, was thoroughly imbued with the earlier theory of free immigration. America had been for a long period the asylum of political and social refugees from Europe and had been obliged, for their protection and for the sake of democratic consistency, to grant them citizenship and to insist upon the right of expatriation. But the absorption of the whole country in the civil struggle and its consequences had diverted attention from the problems incident to the arrival of such large numbers of European foreigners on the Atlantic Seaboard and of the Chinese on the Pacific Coast.

Mr. Burlingame, after having served as Minister in China for six years, at the request of China and with the consent of his own Government resigned that post, and was appointed by the Chinese Government in 1868, Envoy to the United States and the principal European nations.[2] The Chinese embassy, with Mr. Burlingame at its head, was received in the United States with an almost continuous ovation, and even in California was heralded as the precursor of new and broader relations of trade and friendship between the two countries. Upon its arrival in Washington, a new treaty, to be known thereafter as the Burlingame treaty of 1868,[3] was drafted

further references, see Foster's Chapter on *China*.

[2] On the career and services of Mr. Burlingame, see estimate of Foster, pp. 257-9.

[3] At the banquet given to Mr. Burlingame in San Francisco, only two notes of dissent were heard: Gov. Haight said: "While opinions differ on the questions of immigration and other subjects, there can be no difference of opinion upon the desirableness of unrestricted commercial intercourse with China." The Hon. Eugene Casserley, in a letter of congratulation read on this occasion, repeated almost exactly the same sentiment. Both of these gentlemen had been conspicuously anti-Chinese in politics.

by Secretary Seward[4] and signed by the representatives of the two nations amidst the applause of the whole country.

The treaty secured, reciprocally, exemption from persecution or disability on account of religious belief, the privilege of schools and colleges, and the privilege of residence or travel on the basis of the most favored nation; it pledged the territorial integrity of China, disavowed any intention on the part of the United States to interfere with the internal administration or trade of China, and recognized the right of voluntary emigration, making the engaging in involuntary immigration by the subjects of either power a penal offense.

The purpose of the Chinese Government in sending the Burlingame Mission to the West was to establish the principle of reciprocity, that is, to secure the same 'privileges, immunities and exemptions' for Chinese in other countries as other aliens enjoyed there, and as the subjects or citizens of other nations were granted in China. Art. VII of the American treaty specifically stated this mutual guarantee in the following language:

"Citizens of the United States visiting or residing in China shall enjoy the same privileges, immunities and exemptions in respect to travel and residence as may be enjoyed by the citizens or subjects of the most favored nation. And, reciprocally, Chinese subjects visiting or residing in the United States, shall enjoy the same privileges, immunities and exemptions in respect to travel or residence as may be enjoyed by the citizens or subjects of the most favored nation. But nothing herein contained shall be held to confer naturalization upon citizens of the United States in China, nor upon the subjects of China in the United States."

At this period the questions of naturalization and of negro suffrage were being hotly contested in the United

[4] Secretary of State, Wm. H. Seward, was unqualifiedly in favor of Chinese immigration: "While in California in 1869 he did not hesitate to protest against the almost unanimous feeling pervading the community against Chinese immigration. He condemned the policy of exclusion and persistently maintained that immigration was an element of civilization, especially to the Pacific Coast, and that the attempt to suppress its 'invigorating forces' would ultimately prove a failure." Seward's *Works*, v. 5, p. 50.

States and the frequent parallels drawn between the negro and the Chinaman in the debates in Congress explain, in part at least, the reservation of the right of naturalization from the otherwise sweeping guarantee of mutual privileges. At the time, however, the naturalization clause was not taken to forbid the naturalization of the Chinese in the United States or of Americans in China, but was added to prevent the assumption that the article *per se* conferred naturalization. When public opinion shortly afterward began to change on the desirability of the free immigration of Chinese laborers the whole article became a source of great embarrassment to the government of the United States.

In the same year, Congress had declared the right of expatriation to be: "A natural and inherent right of all people, indispensable to the enjoyment of life, liberty and the pursuit of happiness." This declaration, from which the American government was so soon to recede by discriminating against a particular race and class, was reiterated in the treaty itself. The Preamble read:

"The United States of America and the Emperor of China cordially recognize the inherent and inalienable right of man to change his home and allegiance, and also the mutual advantage of the free migration and emigration of their citizens and subjects respectively, from one country to the other, for the purpose of curiosity, of trade or as permanent residents."

Professor Richmond Mayo-Smith states clearly the significance of these declarations and their effect upon subsequent legislation restricting the immigration of the Chinese. He says:

"This treaty of 1868 marks the dividing line between two distinct and contradictory policies on the part of the United States toward the Chinese. Up to that time our efforts had been directed toward compelling the Chinese to admit Americans to China for the pursuit of trade and commerce. In this contention we placed ourselves on the broad platform of the right of free migration and the duty of international intercourse. Shortly after this declaration we found that the influx of Chinese into this country was causing us inconvenience, and we immediately turned our backs on the principle of freedom of migration, and passed laws excluding the Chinese as effectually as they had ever excluded foreigners."[5]

At the time when the Burlingame treaty was negotiated California was on the eve of social and political changes which made her shortly afterward wholly dissatisfied with it. Under the pressure of local clamor and political interests, the Fifteen Passenger bill, restricting Chinese immigration, was passed by Congress in 1879; but it was vetoed by President Hayes as a violation of the obligations of the Burlingame treaty.

Meanwhile, not only in California but in the country at large, public opinion was undergoing a change as to the desirability of unlimited immigration. The extraordinary increase of European immigrants between 1840 and 1860, resulting in the congestion of Eastern cities, had given rise to a multitude of industrial, political and social problems which had not been foreseen by the advocates of the "asylum" theory. The state of New York, which had suffered most from the influx of European foreigners, attempted to send back pauper aliens and to make Steamship Companies responsible for them, and the Federal Government passed the act of 1875 shutting out paupers and criminals.[6]

Although the Californians based their demand for restrictive legislation on the ground that the Chinese were contract laborers, criminals, prostitutes and diseased, it appeared that such legislation as the Federal act was not what they really wanted. They desired, in fact, the exclusion of all except the merchant class, and for this purpose a modification or the abrogation of the Burlingame treaty was necessary. During the whole of the Kearney period the Workingmen's Party demanded the abrogation of the treaty and both the national political parties endeavored to pacify the voters of the West with promises of legislative relief which it was

[5] Mayo-Smith, *Emigration and Immigration*, p. 229.
[6] 18 Stat. L. 477.

doubtful if they would fulfil after the election was passed.

The State Department, meanwhile, recognizing that no remedial statutes could be enforced satisfactorily without the coöperation of China, was quietly bringing the evils of indiscriminate immigration to the notice of the Imperial Government. In April, 1879, Secretary Evarts wrote to Minister George F. Seward instructing him to bring to the attention of the Chinese Government the apprehensions of the Pacific Coast, to find out the facts in regard to the immigration of contract laborers, paupers, and criminals, and the measures which it might be willing to undertake in view of existing treaty stipulations.[7] Mr. Seward reported that his first task had been to allay the irritation caused by the hostile policy toward the Chinese in America and to assure the Chinese Government of the devotion of this country to the principles of liberal government and humanity. He continued:

"The sooner we rise to the idea of dealing with this Government as being actuated by very much the same motives of dignity, patriotism and public policy which actuate other governments, the sooner we shall be able to place our relations upon an enduring basis of good will and common interests."

Prince Kung, when approached by Mr. Seward on the subject of Chinese immigration to America, expressed willingness to negotiate for shutting out " criminals, lewd women, diseased persons and contract laborers" as a measure of friendship and good will. In regard to the Chinese who had already gone to the United States, he presumed that the government would make every exertion to protect them in their treaty rights. Mr. Seward assured him that his government was disposed to study the whole subject in a thorough and generous manner. These friendly overtures were suspended when

[7] *Cong. Docs.* s. n. 1991, Apr. to Aug. 1879; also s. n. 1842 (1878).

a commission was appointed to proceed to China and undertake anew the negotiation of a treaty which, with the least offence to China would nevertheless permit of legislation restrictive of the influx of Chinese laborers. This commission, composed of men well qualified by education and past experience to bring about an amicable agreement, assumed their new duties immediately, but the exigencies of party politics balked them at every turn.[8]

In preceding chapters it has been shown how and why the question of Chinese immigration had become a paramount one in Pacific Coast politics. The Burlingame embassy had scarcely left the country when the principle of free immigration was attacked in California as opening wide the Golden Gate to hordes of Chinese who would sooner or later, it was said, drive out white labor. During the three Presidential campaigns following the treaty of 1868 California went Republican, but only by an extremely narrow margin. As the campaign of 1880 opened both parties put themselves on record on the Chinese question in order to catch the unstable element of the Workingmen's Party.

James B. Angell, President of Michigan University and Chairman of the Commission to negotiate the treaty of 1880, thus explained the appointment of the Commission:

"The Fifteen Passenger bill was clearly in contravention of the Burlingame treaty, and the veto of President Hayes prevented it from becoming a law. The situation was growing critical. There was, perhaps, danger that some other law in violation of our treaties might be pushed through over a veto. In that case retaliation on our merchants and missionaries might have followed." [9]

The circumstances under which the Commission was appointed and proceeded to China to negotiate a modification of the Burlingame treaty, have been fully and

---

[8] George F. Seward was United States Consul and Consul General in China 1861-1876 and Minister to China from 1876 to 1880, when he was succeeded by James B. Angell.
[9] *Jo. of Soc. Sci.*, no. 17, (May, 1883), Pt. II, p. 27.

accurately described by Chester Holcombe, who as Secretary of Legation and Joint Interpreter of the American and Chinese Commissioners, was a member of the Commission and conversant with its proceedings. Concerning the purely political motive of the Commission Mr. Holcombe wrote as follows:

"Under these circumstances the Republican leaders planned a master stroke of policy. A bill was prepared and submitted to Congress directing the appointment of certain Special Commissioners who were to proceed to Peking and there to negotiate such a modification of our treaties with China as would permit of legislation restrictive of the influx of Chinese laborers. While the Democrats grumbled somewhat at the march thus stolen upon them, none ventured to oppose the bill and it was promptly passed."

"A most liberal appropriation was made for the salaries and contingent expenses. The Commissioners were at once appointed and summoned to Washington.[10] Upon arrival they were furnished with elaborate, and impracticable instructions concerning the 'likin tax' and 'transit pass' questions, which were widely outside of the object of their special mission, would require years of study and then still be beyond comprehension, and which they were not expected to touch. The subject of Chinese immigration was not discussed with them by either President or Secretary of State. It was not even mentioned, beyond the remark, made as they were taking leave and setting out upon their long journey, that instructions upon that most important subject were not quite ready, but would overtake them at San Francisco. They delayed a week in that city, and, when upon the point of sailing, received, in response to an inquiry by telegraph, directions to proceed and await their instructions in Japan. The same inquiry and response were repeated while they were in Yokohama. They reached China in July, but remained upon the coast until the end of September, awaiting instructions which never came. The only word of advice or direction of any sort which they received during their absence from the United States, bearing upon the object of this special mission or upon any other subject, consisted of a single line which covered and called their attention to the planks of the two great political parties upon the subject of Chinese immigration which had been adopted at the National Conventions held in June of this year. The Commissioners were left to draw their own conclusions from the strange and unexpected silence."[11]

[10] The Commissioners were Pres. James B. Angell of Michigan University, John T. Swift of California, W. H. Trescot, a former Asst. Secretary of State, and Chester Holcombe, Secretary and Interpreter.
[11] *Outlook*, 1904, Apr. 23, pp. 993-4.

In view of the fact that the first restriction law passed by Congress was ostensibly in execution of the treaty negotiated by this commission, and of the fact that a few years later there came to be a wide divergence of opinion with regard to the interpretation of the treaty, it is of the utmost importance to study the detailed account of the negotiations leading to it. After referring in a complimentary manner to the friendly relations and the benefits of international communication and trade between China and the United States, the American Commissioners stated the purpose of their mission in the following words:[12]

> "But we wish to ask the attention of the Chinese government to a species of intercourse which has increased to a large extent within the last few years, and which has subjected the Government of the United States to grave embarrassments. A class of Chinese subjects emigrating to the United States without the purpose of changing their allegiance and intending only a temporary residence claims all the privileges and exemptions provided by express treaty stipulations for 'permanent residents.' This same class, consisting entirely of laborers, coming in great numbers, with the avowed intention of early return, and concerted arrangements for a new supply, with the almost absolute exclusion of family and domestic relations in their association and jealously preserving their peculiar nationality in dress, language, creed and habits, claims that it is entitled to all the privileges of the subjects and citizens of the most favored nation; although the immigration from no other nation at all resembles this in its purpose, its methods, or its consequences. All other immigrants come to the United States with the express purpose of changing their allegiance, with their wives and children, to be in the course of a generation completely incorporated into the country of their adoption."

The Memorandum further said that of late years the the Chinese had congested in cities and that their competition with white laborers engendered popular discontent and raised questions which, if left unsettled, might ultimately disturb the friendly relations of the two countries; and besides the privileges of free immigration were

---

[12] The detailed account and memoranda of these negotiations are found in *Cong. Docs.* For. Rels. 1880-82, s. n. 2009, pp. 171-198.

Treaty Relations Before 1882 155

not met by equal privileges in China under the existing treaty. Understanding that China did not desire to encourage emigration and had already made a treaty of limitation with Spain, the Commission asked that the United States be allowed to regulate Chinese Immigration as might be most consonant with its own interests; acknowledging at the same time the duty of protecting resident Chinese against any opposition " whether it take the shape of popular violence or legislative enact ment."[13]

The Chinese Commissioners replied that the number of Chinese laborers in the United States was " certainly not small." They regarded America as a land of abundance and as furnishing great opportunities. The emigration had been entirely voluntary and they had rejoiced in the freedom of the country. During the years of Chinese Immigration many new lines of enterprise had arisen in California; the Chinese had given a large amount of their labor and the benefits of that labor had not been few. But that now, because the Chinese did good work for small remuneration, the rabble were making complaints. Since the amount paid to the laborers was small, the benefit still inured to the United States.

The Chinese Commissioners showed an accurate knowledge of the circumstances of the Hayes veto and of the discriminating legislation of the Western states. They quoted Senator Morton's report, the Constitution of the United States and the Burlingame treaty to show the justice and desirability of free migration. They went on:

"If now, because of temporary competition between the Irish and stranger guests, a decision is lightly taken to change the policy of the Government, contradiction with the Constitution of the United States and with existing treaties cannot be avoided. . . . In a word, there are Chinese who go to the United States as merchants and traders and there are also Chinese who go there as laborers. Formerly, when there was a demand for these laborers,

[13] Ibid. p. 192-3.

the only fear was that they would not go thither; and now, because of the influence of violent men, there exists a desire that they stay away. In consideration of the permanent friendship of the two countries, it is believed that the United States by no means entertains this idea. But as the number of Chinese laborers in California is daily increasing, there cannot but be abuses. . . . Hence last year the Foreign Office consented to enter upon negotiations with Mr. Seward to prohibit the four classes of contract laborers, criminals, prostitutes and diseased persons from going thither. . . . We are ready to discuss this proposition further . . . provided always that such negotiations shall not be contrary to the stipulations of the Burlingame treaty."

The Chinese Commissioners then called attention to the right of extra territorial jurisdiction as offsetting the right of free immigration and to the cordial jubilations which had taken place in America at the signing of the Burlingame treaty; but declined to consider the treaty with Spain as a basis for action with the United States in entirely different circumstances.

This bold and straightforward statement on the part of the Chinese Commissioners, showing an accurate knowledge of the real situation, and of the causes for the alteration of the treaty, was both unexpected and embarrassing to the Americans. In the conference which followed, they took exception to the phrases "rabble," "violent men," "competition between the Irish and stranger guests," though they could not deny that these were true to the situation. They reproved the Chinese Commissioners for going behind their written communication; for criticizing the motives of the United States and denying the good faith of its representatives; and declared that whatever they said represented not only the Government of the United States but the feeling of the American people and must be treated respectfully.

The Chinese Commissioners replied that their information came from the American Minister to China but that they had not intended to imply that the Government of the United States was influenced by unworthy motives.

Mr. Trescot, as Spokesman for the Americans, cited the current platforms of the two political parties in the United States as indicative of the unanimous sentiment against Chinese immigration. He then gave the foreigners to understand that Mr. Seward's propositions not only had not been authorized [1] but did not represent the motives of the United States Government. If the Chinese were not prepared to modify the Burlingame treaty, there was nothing to negotiate about. The Chinese replied that Mr. Seward's propositions were a modification of the Burlingame treaty, but if these were not satisfactory they would be pleased to discuss others.

Thereupon the United States Commissioners submitted a draft of their propositions: Art. 1—that, reciprocally, all citizens of either country visiting or residing for the purpose of trade, travel or temporary residence for the prosecution of teaching, study or curiosity, should enjoy all the immunities, privileges, *et cetera*, of the "most favored nation." Art. 2—that whenever the coming of Chinese laborers to the United States or their residence therein threatened to affect the interests of that country or to endanger the good order of any locality thereof, the Government of the United States might regulate, limit, suspend or prohibit such coming or residence after giving timely notice to China; and the words "Chinese laborers" as herein used should signify all immigration other than for teaching, trade, travel or curiosity; Art. 3—that all Chinese residents in the United States should receive the protection guaranteed by existing treaties.

In reply to these propositions the Chinese memorandum stated: that Article 1 was merely a repetition of rights then in force; Art. 2 separated the class of laborers in a way not in strict accord with the spirit of the treaties and which would, in practical operation, meet with many difficulties. They inferred that the word "regulate" was a general expression referring to the

[1] But see page 151 *ante*.

two other words "limit or suspend"; as for the word "prohibit", China "would assuredly find it difficult to adopt it." But they were ready to negotiate "to the end that a limitation, either in point of time or numbers, may be fixed."

In the conference following, the United States Commissioners asked the Chinese Commissioners just what they meant by "limitation in point of time or numbers." The Chinese said:

> "By limitation in numbers they meant, for example, that the United States having, as they supposed, a record of the number of immigrants in each year as well as the total Chinese now there, that no more should be allowed to go in any one year in future than the greatest number that had gone in any year past, or, that the total should never exceed the number now there. As to the limitation in time they meant, for example, that Chinese should be allowed to go in alternate years, or every third year or, for example, that they should not be allowed to go for two, three or five years."

The United States Commissioners replied that they feared that there was some misapprehension: the United States did not ask the Chinese Government to "regulate, limit, suspend or prohibit," but to leave the matter of regulation or prohibition to the United States itself. Whereupon the Chinese Commissioners asked if they could give them any idea what kind of laws would be passed to carry such a power into execution. The Americans replied that they could not but that it must be assumed between two great powers that both would act in good faith and with due consideration for the interests and friendship of each other. The United States might never deem it necessary to exercise this power. It would depend upon circumstances. If Chinese immigration concentrated in cities where it threatened public order, or if it confined itself to localities where it was an injury to the interests of the people, the Government of the United States would undoubtedly take steps to prevent such congestion. If, on the contrary, there was no large immigration, or if there were sections of the country where such immigration was clearly beneficial, then the legislation of the United States under this power would be adapted to such circumstances. For example, there might be a demand for Chinese labor in the South, and a surplus of such labor in California, and Congress might legislate in accordance with these facts. In general, the legislation would be in view of, and depend upon the circumstances of the situation at the moment such legislation became necessary. Mr. Trescot added that if the Commissioners failed to reach a satisfactory conclusion, the United States Government might be forced by the difficulties of the situation to take the question into its own hands and abrogate the Burlingame treaty. The Government did not desire to do this, but only sought a certain elasticity of action.

The Chinese Commissioners then prepared an outline of a treaty which would limit but not prohibit immigration; which would apply only to actual laborers and not impose disabilities on any other class; all other classes were to be allowed to come and go with perfect freedom; and all Chinese in the United States were to be protected as the citizens of the most favored nation. Whatever limitations were made were to be temporary in their nature—the number not excessively small nor the term of years excessively long; and all regulations were to be first submitted to the Chinese Minister at Washington or by the Chinese Government to the American Minister at Peking.

The project counter to this, drafted by the American Commissioners, repeated the words "regulate, limit or suspend," but omitted the word "prohibit"; defined laborers to include all Chinese who did not come for "trade, travel, mercantile pursuits, study or curiosity." These latter classes should be allowed to go and come with entire freedom. Chinese in the United States should be protected. The Government of the United States was to communicate such legislative measures as might be adopted by it in accordance with the foregoing articles and in case such measures worked unexpected hardship to Chinese subjects to give the fullest consideration to such representations as the Imperial Government might make in the premises.

This project was sent to the Chinese Foreign Office by the hand of Mr. Chester Holcombe, the Secretary, with a verbal message that it went as far in the way of concession as they could go and that the stipulations of Art. 1 were the least that would be accepted. The memorandum accompanying the project stated that the word "prohibit" was removed with the distinct understanding that the right of the United States to use its discretion should be recognized; and that the Chinese Government ought to assume that the United States would use this discretion in "a friendly and judicious manner"; that they must insist upon the interpretation of laborers as including artisans because it was this very class which gave the most trouble in the cities; and that the project must apply to the whole United States and not merely to California.

As a result of these exchanges the final form of the treaty of 1880 was as follows:

"Whereas the Government of the United States, because of the constantly increasing immigration of Chinese laborers to the territory of the United States, and the embarrassments consequent upon such immigration, now desires to negotiate a modification of the existing Treaties which shall not be in direct contravention of their spirit:—

Now therefore . . . the said Commissioners Plenipotentiary, having conjointly examined their full powers, and having discussed the points of possible modification in existing Treaties, have agreed upon the following articles in modification.

Art. I.—Whenever in the opinion of the Government of the United States, the coming of Chinese laborers to the United States, or their residence therein, affects or threatens to affect the interests of that country, or to endanger the good order of the said country or of any locality within the territory thereof, the Government of China agrees that the Government of the United States may regulate, limit, or suspend such coming or residence, but may not absolutely prohibit it. The limitation or suspension shall be reasonable and shall apply only to Chinese who may go to the United States as laborers, other classes not being included in the limitations. Legislation taken in regard to Chinese laborers will be of such a character only as is necessary to enforce the regulation, limitation or suspension of immigration, and immigrants shall not be subject to personal maltreatment or abuse.

Art. II.—Chinese subjects, whether proceeding to the United States as teachers, merchants or from curiosity, together with their body and household servants, and Chinese laborers who are now in the United States shall be allowed to go and come of their own free will and accord, and shall be accorded all the rights, privileges, immunities and exemptions which are accorded to the citizens of the most favored nation.

Art. III.—If Chinese laborers, or Chinese of any other class, now either permanently or temporarily residing in the territory of the United States, meet with ill treatment at the hands of any other persons, the Government of the United States will exert all its power to devise measures for their protection and to secure to them the same rights, privileges, immunities and exemptions as may be enjoyed by the citizens or subjects of the most favored nation; and to which they are entitled by treaty.

Art. IV.—The high contracting Powers having agreed upon the foregoing articles, whenever the Government of the United States shall adopt legislative measures in accordance therewith, such measures will be communicated to the Government of China. If the measures as enacted are found to work hardship upon the subjects of China, the Chinese Minister at Washington may bring the matter to the notice of the Secretary of State of the United States, who will consider the subject with him ; and the Chinese Foreign Office may also bring the matter to the notice of the United States Minister at Peking and consider the subject with him, to the end that mutual and unqualified benefit may result."

In announcing to the State Department the signature of the treaty the Commissioners carefully explained the reasons for its final form. They said they had struck out the word " prohibit " because the essential point was that the United States should have the right to limit, regulate or suspend immigration without abrogating the treaties by which it was recognized. They wrote further:

"We did not think that the public opinion of the United States would require so extreme a demand and we considered our instructions as warning us not to disregard the traditional policy of the United States. . . . We desired to define . . . with more precision exactly what all the negotiators on both sides understood by 'Chinese laborers,' but the Chinese Government . . . claimed that by Article 2 they did, by exclusion, provide that nobody should be entitled to claim the benefit of the general provisions of the Burlingame treaty, but those who went to the United States for the purposes of teaching, study, mercantile transactions, travel or curiosity. We have no doubt that an act of Congress excluding all but these classes, using the words of the treaty, would be fully warranted by its provisions."

In this confidential statement the Commissioners added:

"The representatives of the Chinese Government have met us in the fairest and most friendly spirit. . . . After a free and able exposition of their own views we are satisfied that in yielding to the request of the United States they have been actuated by a sincere friendship and an honorable confidence that the large powers recognized by them as belonging to the United States . . . will be exercised by our government with a wise discretion in a spirit of reciprocal and sincere friendship, and with entire justice." [14]

The internal evidence of the notes of negotiations sent to the State Department corroborates Mr. Holcombe's statement that the Commissioners received no specific instructions. The only reference to them is found in the final report of the Commission to Secretary Evarts, in which they wrote:

"We considered our instructions as warning us not to disregard the traditional policy of the United States and in your own words to give due weight ' to the widely diffused and, so to speak, natural sentiment of our people in favor of the most liberal admission of foreign immigrants who desire to incorporate themselves and their families with our society, and to mingle the stream of their posterity in the swelling tide of native population.'" [15]

Nevertheless, what the Americans desired and what the Chinese thought they were finally agreeing to, is

[14] *Cong. Docs.* 1880-2, s. n. 2009, *China*, p. 190-198.
[15] Ibidem, p. 196.

clearly indicated by the points raised, contested and conceded in the course of the negotiations. The Chinese first proposed to exclude the classes named by Minister Seward but were promptly told that Mr. Seward had no authority to negotiate any modification of the Burlingame treaty. After some rather frank discussion in which they showed too accurate knowledge of the causes of the anti-Chinese movement in the United States and the origin of the Commission, they agreed to discuss other modifications than those previously suggested. They yielded the point that the United States should regulate the immigration of laborers. but would not concede prohibition; they finally conceded that the word " laborers " should include artisans as well as unskilled laborers, and that the regulation should apply not merely to California but to the whole country.

The Americans in return, having gained the essential concession that regulation should be in the discretion of the United States, cut out the word " prohibit " and guaranteed that the regulation should be " reasonable " and should be communicated to the Chinese Government in order that a protest might be lodged against it if it were likely to work undue hardship upon Chinese immigrants. They guaranteed further that any suspension of immigration should apply only to " laborers " and if Chinese of any class should meet with abuse, the United States would exert all its power to devise means of protection. It thus appears that the Americans came with the intention of securing some discretionary control of Chinese immigration; and that the Chinese were entirely willing to grant this with respect to unskilled laborers and finally were persuaded to include skilled laborers; but that they would not agree to the suspension of immigration for more than a limited period and not at all with respect to any other classes.

The language of the most carefully drawn document is often open to misinterpretation when the circumstances and personages which originated it have passed away; and since in recent years, the interpretation of this treaty has been much disputed it is necessary to consider the disputed phrases from the point of view of the negotiators. The word "reasonable" for instance, as applied to the period of suspension, has been translated to mean from five to forty years. President Angell, chairman of the treaty commission, wrote a few years later: " a suspension of five years would have been quite long enough to make clear the effects of such legislation." [16] Mr. John F. Swift, the California member of the Commission, in a newspaper interview, is reported to have said that forty years would be entirely reasonable, while President Hayes and President Arthur both vetoed restriction bills on the ground that twenty years suspension was a violation of treaty. In the course of the treaty negotiations the Chinese commissioners, when asked what they meant by a "limitation in time" said they meant, for example, that Chinese should be allowed to go in alternate years, or should not be allowed to go for two, three or five years. They could not accept the word "prohibit" but they finally left the exact term of suspension to the "friendly and judicious" discretion promised by the American Commissioners, stipulating only that the limitations should be "temporary in their nature . . . the number not excessively small nor the term of years excessively long." Many thousand words were shortly afterward expended by Congressmen in debating whether ten, fifteen or twenty years' suspension constituted a prohibition under the treaty.

Another loophole for future disagreement was presented in the definition of "laborers" although in the light of the negotiations there would seem to be no question as to what the Chinese commissioners, at least, understood themselves to be conceding. The discussion shows clearly that the word as used in the treaty was in-

[16] *Jo. of Soc. Sci.*, no. 17, (May, 1883).

tended to include laborers only in the commonly accepted American use of that term; and that all other classes were to be admitted as before under the Burlingame treaty. This interpretation, corroborated by Mr. Holcombe[17], who as the Secretary of the Commission and Joint-Interpreter, would seem to be the final authority, was never authoritatively questioned until eighteen years after the treaty was signed. Then the Attorney-General of the United States decided that the words " for trade, travel, study or curiosity " were not used merely as illustrative, but as designating specifically the only classes entitled to enter the United States. Thus the word " laborers " was made to include a large number of persons of widely differing occupations and to carry a strained meaning which was not intended by the negotiators.

In proof of this, it may be noted that the Chinese negotiators only reluctantly agreed to the inclusion of artisans, *i. e.*, skilled workmen, in the term " laborers ", and in the last project sent to the American Commissioners they proposed, as the wording of Article II of the treaty, the following:

"Persons of all other classes, with the exception of actual Chinese laborers . . . will be allowed to come and go with entire freedom and will not be included in the limiting regulations."

When urged to make the definition of laborers more definite they replied that they had done so " by exclusion," that is, all except laborers skilled and unskilled, were still to enjoy the benefits of the Burlingame treaty.

The American Commissioners in reporting to the State Department commented on this as follows:

" As this was a clear and sufficient modification of the Burlingame treaty we did not feel authorized to risk such a concession by insisting upon language which would really mean no more, and

[17] Mr. Holcombe writes: "It was not the intention of the framers of the treaty, either American or Chinese, to have the words 'regulate, limit or suspend' apply to any Chinese immigrants but laborers, skilled and unskilled."

which was entirely unacceptable to the Chinese Commissioners. There is not in the treaty any language which modifies this concession and there was not, as we think, the slightest intention on the part of the Chinese Commissioners to diminish the full force of the discretion given to the United States."

There were only two concessions to which this explanation could possibly refer: the discretion conceded to the United States and the inclusion of skilled laborers in the term "laborers." In the light of the context it appears perfectly clear that the concession here referred to was the latter.

One other question with regard to the interpretation of the treaty has arisen in recent years. In a letter to Secretary Hay written in 1901, Minister Wu Ting Fang claimed that the words "officials, teachers, students, merchants or travelers from curiosity or pleasure," were followed in the Chinese text of the treaty by words equivalent to *et cetera*. He there contended that this proved unmistakably the intention of the Commissioners to concede only the exclusion of laborers.[18] Although as we have seen, the understanding of the Commissioners on both sides was clearly that laborers—skilled and unskilled—and laborers only, were to be affected by the restriction, yet Minister Wu is unquestionably mistaken in this statement. Mr. Chester Holcombe, the Joint Interpreter and the only person present at the making of the treaty who understood both languages, asserts positively that neither the Chinese text of the treaty of 1880 nor that of 1894 contains any word or phrase equivalent to *et cetera* or which could by any construction be rendered by that phrase.

Within two years after the signing of the treaty its meaning was disputed. Yet this examination of the negotiations preceding it shows that its terms were made by Commissioners who understood each other clearly; and

[18] This statement of the Chinese Minister was quoted and discussed in a debate in Congress especially by Senator Foraker and Senator Platt. See *Cong. Record* (1902), v. 35, pt. 4, p. 4098 ff.

Treaty Relations Before 1882   167

its language as interpreted by the context is unmistakable. Article I covers all that was secured from the Chinese Government; Articles II, III and IV, were added substantially at the request of the Chinese Commissioners and were intended to make more explicit the guards and limitations to the discretionary authority conceded to the United States in Article I. Article I in the first sentence conceded a discretionary limitation of skilled and unskilled laborers; in the second sentence it stipulates that this limitation shall be reasonable and that all other classes than laborers shall be free from such limitations. The statements, in English at least, are perfectly clear and it is evident that the enumeration of the other classes was intended to be merely illustrative. To assume that it was intended to further limit the classes of Chinese who were expressly declared to be at liberty to come to the United States—as was done shortly afterward by Congress—was to give the words a meaning directly opposite to that which they were designed to convey and was, therefore, a violation of the treaty itself.

CHAPTER XI

THE RESTRICTION LAW OF 1882

"It is an undisputed fact . . . that they are mostly coolies . . . who are brought here under contract for a term of years by one of the Six Companies; that their labor is controlled by the Companies . . . and many are detained here till their contract term expires. They monopolize many of the mercantile industries of the Pacific Coast . . . they take the place of the poor laboring classes . . . bring no families . . . have no children to support or educate . . . contribute nothing to the support of the Government, to the building of churches and schoolhouses . . . could not be called upon to bear arms . . . and have no desire to assimilate."—HORACE F. PAGE, California Representative in Congress, in Report of Committee on Education and Labor, 1882.

"The failure of this bill would be now to commission . . . all the speculators in human labor, all the importers of human muscle, all the traffickers in human flesh to ply their infamous trade without impediment . . . and empty the teeming, seething slave pens of China upon the soil of California."—Senator JOHN F. MILLER of California, 1882.

"California, Nevada and Oregon are supposed to hold the balance of political power in the next Presidential contest, and party leaders for party success, cater to the labor element of those three states which has possession of the ballot."—Senator MORSE of Massachusetts, 1882.

"Make the conditions what you please for immigration and for attaining citizenship, but make them such that a man may overcome them. Do not base them on the accidents of humanity."—Senator HENRY DAWES of Connecticut, 1882.

"It consigns to the grave all sublimated sentiment as to the equality of the races of men."—Senator BUCKNER of Missouri, 1882.

WHEN the struggles of the Second Constitution and the agitations of the Presidential campaign of 1880 had passed, California began to recover social sanity and industrial prosperity. The negotiation of the Chinese-American treaty and the pledge of a Republican President looking toward restriction still further allayed anti-Chinese feeling. But after the assassination of Garfield, and with the approach of a State election in California in 1882, the California representatives in Congress again became active on labor issues of which the foremost was Chinese exclusion.

Of the seven exclusion bills introduced during the first session of the Forty-seventh Congress, Senate Bill 71, offered by Senator Miller of California—much amended by the Committee on Foreign Relations—was reported back unanimously. It provided that sixty days after the passage of the act and for twenty years thereafter, the immigration of Chinese laborers was to be suspended; but this was not to apply to Chinese who were in the United States on November seventeenth, 1880, or who should come in before the act took effect. An elaborate system of registration, certification and identification was specified, with imprisonment and deportation as penalties for fraud.[1]

Senator Miller opened the debate by referring to the treaty lately negotiated in which the point of restriction had finally been granted by the Chinese Government. He argued that it would now appear inconsistent and vacillating if a measure of restriction should fail in Congress. Both political parties were now agreed that it was necessary and the vote on this bill would determine whether they were sincere or had been merely endeavoring to catch votes. The failure of the bill would, he said: "commission all the traffickers in human flesh to ply their infamous trade without impediment, and empty the teeming, seething, slave pens of China upon the soil of California." He attributed the great number of tramps and hoodlums in California during the late depression to Chinese competition, and ended with the assertion that thousands of white persons had quit the State because of it.

Senator Miller was supported not only by his colleagues but by the senators from Oregon, one of whom proudly alluded to the fact that the constitution of his state prohibited Chinamen from owning real estate or

[1] 47th Cong. 1st. Ses. 1882, *Record*, pp. 1480–81.

mining claims. Teller of Colorado and Jones of Nevada joined the anti-Chinese ranks; the one regarding it as a measure of self-preservation, the other because of future rather than present danger from the hordes of Chinese Coolies. The southern Democrats in general sympathized with the Californians, regarding the race issue as akin to their own.

The bill was as strongly opposed by the Republicans, led by the New Englanders in a solid phalanx. In a cutting analysis of its provisions Senator Hoar declared the cumbrous passport system an evasion of the treaty, and its distinctions by race and occupation rather than by character, degrading; for laborers would thus be classed with paupers, harlots and diseased persons.

Senator Dawes of Massachusetts said that one set of the supporters of this bill had granted that it was "invoked under the influence of overmastering passions," and that the mass-meeting in California confirmed that statement; while others acknowledged that their instincts revolted against it. Still others asserted that the Chinese endangered good order in certain localities, but did not explain whether the Chinese were disorderly or only the occasion of other people being so. Apparently it was not the Chinaman *per se,* only the laborer, that disturbed order; if he were only an idle, worthless, dissipated traveler, a gambler or an opium-taker, he might be allowed to come! To conform with the treaty, the bill could only limit as to time or numbers; and other limitation would be prohibition. This bill did not absolutely prohibit, it only declared that if the Chinaman came, he should go to the penitentiary!

Senator Platt of Connecticut said that he was utterly unable to support this bill because its object was not to regulate or restrict, but to prohibit and exclude. He reviewed the treaty negotiations, and showed that the Chinese had stipulated that the suspension should be "**reasonable**" and had finally left the term of suspension

The Restriction Law of 1882 171

to the discretion and justice of the United States. The bill violated the treaty by an elaborate system of registration; further, it violated an American principle in that it declared that no man should work in the United States unless he were a white man—no skilled labor should come, forsooth, unless the laborer were a white man. He denied that the Republican party was committed to this measure; it was, on the contrary, a violation of both the Republican platform and of President Garfield's pledge, for it struck not only at servile but free labor. The argument against cheap labor applied equally to any foreign laborer who would come here and work for less than those already here received. He closed by declaring the bill harsh in its provisions, "speaking the language of prejudice and fear;" but at the same time he protested his belief in the protection of American labor and his willingness to vote for any bill which was not in violation of the treaty.

Senator Hawley of Connecticut called it a "bill of iniquities" which based exclusion on color and birthplace, aiming only at the laborers of a particular race; it did not even say that the Chinese laborer was unlawful or dangerous or came with a bad purpose. It was furthermore, a violation of the treaty. The United States Commissioners had gone to China, disavowing any intention to prohibit immigration, because it was against our traditional policy; yet twenty years was prohibition, and so intended. The civilized world had bombarded China to obtain the right which we now proposed to deny to the Chinese. The bill besides violated the Fourteenth and Fifteenth Amendments. After an eloquent appeal to the Senate, he finally said: "Make the conditions what you please for immigration and for attaining citizenship, but make them such that a man may overcome them. Do not base them on the accidents of humanity."[2]

Two Southerners—Call of Florida and Brown of

[2] 47th Cong. 1st. Ses. 1882, *Record*, 1738–1740.

Georgia—joined the New Englanders. Senator Call declared many features of the bill unnecessary, harsh and objectionable; while Senator Brown protested against the unblushing violation of treaties by the enactment of a law which did not permit any Chinaman to come and go of his own accord, after having stipulated that all except laborers might come freely. Other members of the Senate—for the most part Republicans—though less emphatic, plead for "reasonable restriction" within the fair interpretation of the treaty and even divested of the proscriptive measures of imprisonment and deportation; Senator Ingalls said it went against all his instincts because it was so intolerant and so unfair.

The debate gradually centered about the amendments. The Californians succeeded in adding a clause forbidding naturalization and a definition of laborers to include both skilled and unskilled and those employed in mining. They were able to defeat the amendments to reduce the twenty-year suspension to ten or less; and a clause requiring that China should be formally notified before the act should be consummated. Although Senator Hoar and the New England group renewed the attack repeatedly they were able to secure only one amelioration: the extension of the period of 60 days to 90 before the act should go into effect. Senator Edmunds made an appeal for keeping the spirit of the treaty and referred to the bill as a political measure out of which the Democrats expected to make capital. In spite of this concerted opposition, the bill was finally passed by a vote of 29 to 15, 32 being absent.[3]

Senate Bill 71, so amended, was substituted for a similar bill then before the House, and discussed there a week later. The debate was far less concerned with treaty violation and injustice to the Chinese immigrant than it had been even in the Senate. Thousands of words were expended by the California representatives in re-

[3] 47th Cong. 1st. Ses. 1882, *Record*, pp. 1753.

The Restriction Law of 1882   173

peating the traditional anti-Chinese arguments, while the New Englanders contradicted their statements and demanded more conservative legislation in harmony with the treaty and the general immigration policy of the country. The Democrats taunted the Republicans with their inactivity on the Chinese question in past years; the Republicans replied with charges of low political motives. The principle of exclusion by race and occupation was neither discussed nor justified but was wholly obscured in the dust of party politics.

Eleven amendments, modifying the bill in the directions suggested by the debate, were then rejected in quick succession. Of these, two reduced the time of suspension by five or ten years, and four proposed substitutes for the word laborers such as " coolies," " contract laborers," " slaves," " paupers, diseased or lewd persons and criminals." But there was an evident determination on the part of the Democrats and the Californians to permit neither alteration nor delay and the bill was passed by a vote of 167 to 66, 59 not voting.

Shortly afterward, President Arthur transmitted to Congress a veto message on the bill together with the confidential papers concerning the treaty of 1880 upon which the veto was chiefly based. He stated that while he was convinced of the necessity of some legislation on this subject, and while he fully concurred with the objects of Congress in passing the bill before him, yet he regarded it as a breach of the national faith. His argument was clear and convincing: a nation was justified in repudiating treaty obligations only when they were in conflict with great paramount interests. The treaty of 1880 was understood to be " not reciprocal but unilateral " *i. e.*, granting equal but dissimilar privileges to either party, and the act proposed went much farther than Art. 1 contemplated. By analyzing the negotiations which preceded the treaty he showed that neither contracting party contemplated the passage of an act prohibiting immigration for twenty years or thought that such a period would be a reasonable suspension or intended to change the provisions of the Burlingame treaty to that extent.

Further, he criticized certain features of the act: he doubted if the passport system was a correct interpretation of the "favored nation" clause, while the registration requirement was an undemocratic imitation of a system fast disappearing in Europe, and liable to gross frauds. It was certainly our duty under the treaty to make the operation of the general laws upon the Chinese as like to that of our own citizens as possible, consistently with our right to shut out laborers. He noted the omission of any provision for transit across the United States of Chinese now in foreign countries; and pointed out that other regions than the Pacific Coast might desire Chinese laborers and that such an act might drive Chinese trade into more friendly hands.[4]

In the debate on the veto, Senator Sherman concurred with the President. He resented the incipient threat of Senator Farley of California that outrages might be perpetrated in California because of the veto. He urged that the bill be referred back to the Committee on Foreign Relations to remove the objectionable features, since both the President and the Chinese said the bill was unreasonable and since even in Australia, where there were severe police laws against Chinese laborers, other Chinese came and went the same as other foreigners. The bill was the result of passion, which doubtless, had some foundation, but which did not justify rash and unwise legislation.[5]

In support of the measure Senator Morgan of Alabama attacked the Republicans for wanting to bury the bill in Committee and objected strongly to the President's consulting with the Chinese minister about American

[4] 47th Cong. 1st. Ses. 1882, *Record*, pp. 2251-2; Exc. Doc. 148, ser. no. 1990.
[5] 47th Cong. 1st. Ses. 1882, *Record*, p. 2608 ff.

legislation. Senator Bayard of Maryland referred to the " coarse " language of the message and the lack of comity and respect toward Congress. He thought the Commissioners' interpretation of the treaty had nothing to do with this bill—the treaty was not ambiguous and should be read as it stood; twenty years suspension was entirely reasonable. As for the Burlingame treaty, he declared it a " humbug " and the Burlingame Embassy, a " circus."

The vote on reference to the Committee and the vote on passage of the bill over the veto, were both lost.[6]

There was a burst of newspaper wrath in California when the veto became known; President Arthur was severely criticised, and the Congressmen who had voted against the bill were vilified,[7] but louder than all rose the chorus of politicians. The Democrats either openly said that the veto would lose the state to the Republicans or covertly implied it by condoling with them on their misfortune. The Republicans of the eastern states very generally thought the President had done his duty and that the veto would not do the party much harm; but in the Western states they were apologetic or furiously angry in proportion as the veto affected their political fortunes. The Honorable John W. Swift, one of the Commissioners to negotiate the latest treaty, came out in an interview saying that the Commissioners and the Chinese Government had both understood that 33 to 50 years would not be too long a suspension, which drew a reply from President Angell of Michigan University, Chief Commissioner, to the effect that five years was the only time of suspension mentioned and that a longer suspension was not thought of by either of the parties to the negotiation.

[6] Vote on passage of bill over veto, 29 to 21–26 absent.
[7] The New England Congressmen were especially attacked, the general western feeling being that New England always got whatever legislation she wanted and was now pursuing an illiberal policy toward the West. See article by James O'Meara on the " Veto Power and the Chinese," in the *Californian*, June, 1882.

Within two weeks after the veto, four exclusion bills under differing titles were introduced into the House, and referred to the Committee on Commerce and Labor.[8] Mr. Page of California, speaking for the Committee, reported back a bill which differed from the one just vetoed in three essential and several minor particulars. The period of suspension was reduced to ten years, and the whole system of registration and the penalty clause against vessels bringing in Chinese illegally, were cut out. Mr. Page declared that the Committee had been careful to keep strictly within the stipulations of the treaty, but that he thought 25 years would be a reasonable suspension. Mr. Willis, in a minority report took an even more extreme view; he thought the bill should require a longer period to satisfy the Pacific Coast and should have such penalties attached as would secure obedience to its provisions.[9] Later, he characterized the committee measure as insufficient, weak and imperfect. He predicted dissatisfaction in California, an overwhelming immigration prompted by wealthy corporations, and the impossibility of distinguishing between lawful and unlawful Chinese residents. Mr. Prescott of New York pointed out as several members had done before, that California had one more representative in Congress because of the enumeration of the Chinese, yet refused them citizenship, and anticipated that the bill might be vetoed on this account.

The bill having passed the House by a large majority —chiefly Democrats and Pacific Coast Republicans— it went to the Senate Committee on Foreign Relations which reported it back within a few days amended in many particulars so as to be clearer, more exact and less sweeping.[10] Senator Morgan announced that the Committee was not unanimous, at least three members not

---

[8] By Willis, Van Voorhies, Berry and Page; no. 5804 was substituted for this latter bill.
[9] H. R., no. 1017, ser. no. 2068, 1882.
[10] 47th Cong. 1st. Ses. 1882. *Record*, p. 3262.

The Restriction Law of 1882 177

agreeing with the amendments. Most of these last, however, were accepted by the Senate without debate although all the Coast representatives objected to some of them and Senator Farley of California objected to all change. Section 12 was fundamentally altered by putting the control of deportation in the power of Federal officers, instead of the immigration officers of the district, after the case had been brought into Court. When Senator Call still urged that the clause laying severe penalties for aiding and abetting unlawful immigration was "perfectly unmeaning and perfectly outrageous," Senator Hawley said: "Why, that's what's the matter with the whole bill. * * * It reads like the old fugitive slave law. * * * If we have made up our minds to do it let us do it in silence and in mourning."

The committee recommended that the clause prohibiting naturalization be struck out but the Senate refused to concur. Senator Farley, the most extreme of all the Coast Congressmen, after disputing the statements of Ingalls, Dawes and even of his colleague, Senator Miller, imputed misrepresentation if not dishonesty, to Senator Hoar in the incident of the employment of the Chinese at North Adams, Massachusetts. Senator Dawes came out of a committee meeting to substantiate Hoar's statement that individual contracts were made by the employer with the North Adams' Chinese and to quote President Angell as saying that the "commission never dreamed of any exclusion which would exceed five years," while Senator Vest and Senator Grover came to the support of Farley.

The last skirmish centered about the definition of the word "laborer"; Morgan urged the necessity of a clear definition, though he thought the treaty negotiations showed that the Chinese Government understood the word to include artisans; Pendleton thought the word "skilled" should be used so as to indicate our interpretation of the treaty; Edmunds preferred to use the same terms as the treaty and leave the interpretation to the courts. The Senate finally refused to concur with the committee of the whole and left the words "skilled and unskilled" in the act.[11] The bill was finally passed on April twenty-ninth, 1882, and was signed shortly afterward by the President.[12]

Upon reading, after a lapse of twenty-five years, the treaty negotiations and exclusion debates it is at first difficult to explain the vehemence with which exclusion was pressed and the legal form which it assumed; but if considered in connection with the history of the development of California as a whole, many obscure things are explained. In 1880 a fundamental change had already taken place in the opinions of Americans generally on the desirability of unlimited immigration; and meanwhile, California, with her two local grievances, monopoly and the Chinese, had risen to an influential position in national politics. These two conditions produced a demand for the modification of the Burlingame Treaty shortly after it had been heralded with satisfaction as a compact of great importance to the commercial extension of the United States; and they resulted almost immediately in negotiations for a new treaty. When legislation in execution of this treaty was attempted, three types of opinion on the Chinese question were suddenly developed in Congress. The traditional policy—America the asylum of all nations—was represented by the New England Congressmen at one extreme; at the other, the doctrine of protection against non-assimilating and competitive races, was represented by the Pacific Coast delegation; while between them stood the moderate majority, composed of members of both parties, who were prepared to grant some degree of restriction of the undesirable immigrants of any race.

From the beginning of the struggle for Chinese restric-

[11] Vote—20 to 25, 31 absent.
[12] Vote—yeas, 32 Democrats, 9 Republicans, 1 Independent; nays, 1 Democrat, 24 Republicans, (of whom two were New Englanders).

The Restriction Law of 1882 179

tion, it was evident that neither the New Englanders nor the Pacific Coast minority could carry its view alone; and the logical issue would have been a compromise measure shutting out the vicious, diseased and contract laborers of the Chinese race, which would have met the approval of the moderate majority. But two conditions —the straits of party politics and the rise of the workingmen's movement in California—brought about the complete success of the anti-Chinese faction.

Before the War, California had been a Democratic State and had only narrowly escaped seceding from the Union.[13] It was inevitable, therefore, that, on the decline of the Union party, she should return to her natural allegiance, assisted as she was by a large infusion of Southerners and Irishmen. In the North the Democratic party, composed largely of naturalized foreigners and their immediate descendants, was committed to an anti-color policy which included with negroes, the Indians and the Chinese.

When, in the seventies, California had begun to attain some political importance on account of her rapidly increasing male population, the Republican constituency was strengthened by immigration until the State could no longer be safely counted upon by either party. As a result of reconstruction and other measures, the Republican party elsewhere had been losing ground; it was threatened with defeat in 1876 and 1880 before it was finally overwhelmed by the election of Mr. Cleveland in 1884. The struggle on the part of both parties during this period to carry California became fiercer and fiercer and gave her demands for legislation a prominence in the national legislature out of all proportion to their normal value.

For twelve years, preceding the Exclusion Law, Cali-

---

[13] "In 1859 the Southern Democrats in California had 62,000 out of 103,000 but in 1860 out of 71,000 Democratic votes, Douglass, the Northern Candidate, had 38,000." Hittell's *Hist. of San Francisco*, p. 325-6.

fornia had been in a state of incessant agitation against land and railway monopoly, and—incidental to these—against the Chinese, because of the rise of the Workingmen's party. Since it was much easier and safer for the politicians to fight the Chinese than to make war upon the great monopolies, it became their policy to divert and pacify these discontented workingmen with energetic anti-Chinese measures; and the national political parties as represented in Congress, in their turn pacified the Californians by yielding to their demand for Chinese exclusion.

This view is substantiated by the fact that the first restriction law was directed not merely against the Chinese, but against the *laboring* Chinese alone, although the rest of the country was prepared to exclude the vicious, the diseased, the criminal and the contract Chinese. Even the intelligent Californians themselves, if their current literature and the debates of their Congressmen prove anything, based their objections to the Chinese far more upon their alleged unsocial and vicious character than upon their injurious competition with American labor. Corroboration is lent by the fact that during the whole period preceding exclusion the most orderly and stable portion of California society both in city and country, employed these " vicious and diseased " Chinese by the thousands in their households, and about their homesteads and farms. Even the workingmen did not hesitate to avail themselves of Chinese laundries and the food provided by restaurants employing Chinese cooks. In short, the majority of Californians, though contemptuous towards Chinese peculiarities, liked their service and had no fear of them—and were only actively anti-Chinese when they were engaged in politics or about to vote.

If it be granted that the Exclusion Law was passed chiefly in view of the votes of workingmen in state and national elections, the form which the law finally assumed is easily understood. The negotiations for the

The Restriction Law of 1882

treaty of 1880 show that the Commissioners went to China determined if not instructed to obtain the right to *exclude laborers* of all classes—not to exclude the vicious, or diseased or even contract laborers. The Commissioners found the Chinese Government prepared to grant cordially the exclusion of all these undesirable classes, but not at all prepared for the exclusion of their skilled laborers. When the Commissioners attempted to obtain the prohibition of all Chinese labor, they found the Chinese ready only to limit in numbers or suspend for a time, the existing emigration. The Commissioners did not ask China to prohibit emigration but to allow the United States to use its discretion in the suspension or temporary prohibition, and that not merely for the State of California where the trouble lay, but for the whole United States. The resultant treaty, which granted the right to limit or suspend the immigration of all classes except those specifically named, for a reasonable time, was a compromise, the Americans yielding the point of prohibition and the Chinese all the other points of difference. It was clearly understood by the Commissioners that the suspension should be for a very limited period and should affect only laborers, all other classes being as free to come and go as before.

The first restriction law, enacted to carry out the treaty, suspended immigration for a period twice as long as the longest term mentioned in the negotiations, and established a system which greatly hampered the exempt classes of Chinese while visiting in this country. In the light of later and broader general immigration laws, it must be granted that the treaty of 1880 was defective in not shutting out effectively first—as suggested by the Chinese themselves—the vicious, diseased and contract laborers. The legislation immediately following it was still more defective in that it violated the treaty without reference to the solemn assurance of the American Commissioners that these large powers would be exercised "with a wise discretion, in a spirit of reciprocal friendship and with entire justice."

The Commissioners of the United States might indeed promise friendship and justice but both were impossible while workingmen newly come to power clamored in the ears of politicians; while California politicians feared to lose their foothold if they could not satisfy this demand; while the great parties contending for control of the government feared to lose the vote of California. The restriction law, whether wise and discreet or not—as time only could prove—was certainly not passed, nor was it intended to be executed, in a spirit of reciprocal friendship and with entire justice. Rather it appeared, that, urged on by political necessity, Congress went as far as a hardly-pressed Executive would permit, intending to take all and more than the treaty would allow and trusting that an unwarlike and inexperienced nation would submit to the humiliation. The clamor of an alien class in a single State—taken up by politicians for their own ends—was sufficient to change the policy of a nation and to commit the United States to a race discrimination at variance with our professed theories of government, and this so irrevocably that it has become an established tradition.

CHAPTER XII

THE SCOTT ACT AND THE ABORTIVE TREATY OF 1888

" Resolved: that we, as members of the Senate of the State of California, without regard to party, fully approve of the Scott Chinese Exclusion Act and pray to the authorities of the United States for its maintenance and enforcement."—Concurred in by the Assembly, 1889.

" I was not prepared to learn that there was a way recognized in the law and practice of this country whereby your country could release itself from treaty obligations without consultation or the consent of the other party, .. nor to learn that it is the practice of Governments to act on newspaper reports."—Minister Chang Yen Hoon to Secretary BAYARD, 1888.

" Believing that China did not intend to carry out or accept in full faith the (pending) treaty . . . the Scott Act was suddenly and without notice brought forward in Congress and passed with a unanimity in both houses which palpably rendered an interposition by a veto of the Executive, wholly futile."—Reply of Secretary BAYARD, 1889.

" In truth, so far as our former treaties were concerned, the Scott Act . . . was an outrage upon the proprieties, a gratuitous insult to a great yet defenseless nation. By it twenty thousand certificates were declared null and void—twenty thousand promises on the honor of the United States, that the holders should be allowed to return, were ruthlessly broken, to satisfy the clamor of irresponsible hoodlums led by sand-lot politicians in San Francisco. In a word, the political leaders of the Pacific Coast succeeded in committing the entire Government to an act that was a gross violation of the supplemental treaty of 1880."—CHARLES F. HOLDER.

" I believe that the Scott Act was one of the most vicious laws that has passed in my time in Congress . . . It was a mere political race between the two houses . . . in the face of a Presidential election."—Senator SHERMAN of Ohio, 1894.

THE Restriction Act of 1882 provided for the exclusion of laborers—" skilled and unskilled and those engaged in mining "—for ten years. All other Chinese except diplomatic officers, were required to bring a certificate from the Chinese government and any Chinese found unlawfully in this country were to be deported. The law was, however, full of ambiguities and omissions, precipitating all sorts of questions which had to be passed upon by the courts.[1]

To quote a single instance of the confusion arising in regard to Chinese in transit: several railway and steamship companies interested in returning contract coolies from Cuba via New York and San Francisco to Hong Kong applied to the Secretary of State for instructions. The Secretary referred the question whether such Chinese laborers in transit could be admitted to cross the United States, to Attorney-General Brewster, who decided that under the law they could not and a Treasury circular was issued to immigration officers to that effect; but six months later the Attorney-General reversed his decision.

The Chinese Chargé d'Affaires at Washington reported that the collector at San Francisco, who had been accepting the certificate of the Chinese Consul-General for merchants, students and others going to China or abroad, now compelled them to have a new kind of certificate provided by himself, and complained that the exempt classes were being treated like laborers.

The increasing difficulties of interpretation and the repeated assertions of the California newspapers and politicians that the number of the Chinese was increasing rather than decreasing resulted in a demand for the amendment of the Restriction Act. In 1884 Representative Henley of California introduced a lengthy bill which he said, was the joint production of the delegations from California, Oregon, Nevada, Washington and Arizona, and which, much modified, was reported favorably by a majority of the Committee on Foreign Affairs.[2] In the House debate the representatives from the Pacific Coast and the Democrats generally, supported the bill on the ground of the increasing numbers of the Chinese,

---

[1] *Cong. Docs.* ser. no. 2165, Exc. Doc. 62.
[2] H. R. 1798, 48th Cong. 1st Ses. 1884. The House had 201 Democrats and 119 Republicans at this time.

Scott Act and Abortive Treaty of 1888   185

the manifold evasions of the existing law and the danger to American labor. The Republicans, led by Hitt of Illinois and Rice of Massachusetts, showed that in the seventeen months previous, 12,000 more Chinese had departed than arrived and that of several hundred cases of so-called fraudulent certificates only thirty-three had been proven. Mr. Hitt declared the bill repugnant and unnecessary; Mr. Skinner of New York called it insulting, Mr. Browne of Indiana characterized it as "infernal persecution." The Californians replied that the bill was in response to the demand of five hundred thousand American workingmen; that unless it were passed the Chinese invasion would be complete, for there were twenty thousand in British Columbia trying to come over.

All the amendments to make the bill less severe were voted down and the bill passed the House by a large majority and, two months later, the Senate also.[8] Under the amended act the certificate was made sole evidence of the right of re-entry. The certificates of the exempt classes were required to be far more elaborate; the word "merchant" was defined to exclude hucksters, peddlers, and fishermen engaged in drying and shipping fish; the traveler's certificate must state where he proposed to travel and his financial standing; the certificates of identification from the Chinese Government must be verified as to facts and viséd by the United States diplomatic officer at the port of departure, to be *prima facie* evidence of right of re-entry and to be produced whenever lawfully demanded.

Although remedying some of the most conspicuous defects of the original act, the amendatory act, by its new provisions for the exempt classes and for the de-

[8] Vote in the House stood: yeas 184, nays 13, not voting 125; Vote in the Senate, yeas 43, nays 12, absent 21. The Senate was composed of 40 Republicans and 36 Democrats; the Pacific Coast Republicans almost invariably voted with the Democrats on the Chinese question.

portation of laborers, created still others.[4] Curious complications arose; as in the case of twenty-four merchants with proper certificates under the act of 1882, who arrived in San Francisco on July 28, 1882, and were refused admission although the amendatory act had been passed while they were at sea.[5] A party of Chinese laborers bound for British Columbia, arrived at San Francisco and were refused admission on the ground that laborers arriving at a port of the United States and departing from the same port were not "in transit." Thereupon the Chinese Chargé d'Affaires at Washington protested that there were no steamers running directly from China to British Columbia, Panama and other foreign ports.[6]

The Chinese minister reported several other cases of hardship. Several Chinese merchants who had been in business in the United States for many years and bearing certificates issued by the Chinese Consulate in 1882 were refused landing because their certificates did not comply with the amended act of 1884. While the Supreme Court was discussing the points involved the merchants were kept in the Detention Shed by the Steamship Company.[7] The Consul-General at San Francisco received applications for certificates from Chinese merchants wishing to go back to China temporarily but the Collector of the Port said he could not re-admit them on a certificate issued in the United States because the law provided only for merchants coming from China, and not for those leaving and intending to return.[8]

Twenty-four Chinese laborers without certificates were abandoned on a rock in the Straits of Fuca by the Master of a schooner who had failed to smuggle them ashore.

---

[4] For revised rules see *Cong. Docs.* ser. no. 2276, p. 118; ser. no. 2368, pp. 192-3.
[5] *Cong. Docs.* 1884, s. n. 2276, p. 99.
[6] *Cong. Docs.* 1884, s. n. 2276, p. 103.
[7] Chew Heong v. U. S., 112 U. S. 536, 5 Su. Ct. 255, 28 L. Ed. 770.
[8] *Cong. Docs.* 1884, s. n. 2276, p. 115.

The marshal was ordered by the Commissioner of the Court to take them back to British Columbia; the British authorities refused to receive them unless the Canadian head-tax of fifty dollars was paid. The Chinese were then confined in a jail on McNeil's Island; when brought into Court again Justice Greene of Seattle ordered the marshal to take them over to British Columbia regardless of the Dominion authorities; and the Chinese, supplied with provisions for few days, were so disposed of.[9]

The Chinese Minister represented to the Secretary of State that merchants having large commercial interests in British Columbia, Panama and other foreign countries could not obtain the required certificates since there was no Chinese consul there and they were not subjects of those states. A prominent mandarin from Hong Kong, who was a partner in a firm in San Francisco, having a United States' Consul's certificate and a first-class passage ticket, was refused landing, although he was well-known on the Pacific Coast and although there was no Chinese official in the British colony of Hong Kong to give him a certificate. To these representations Secretary Bayard replied that he must refer that matter to the courts as the statutes were ambiguous and " somewhat obscure and difficult of application." He concluded his courteous and apologetic reply with this assurance: " I do assure you that the Government of the United States has no other intention than to make their laws and their administration conform, in all respects, to every honorable obligation they have undertaken in their treaties." [10]

On the Pacific Coast the courts were being clogged

---

[9] *Cong. Docs.* 1885, s. n. 2340. Portland *Oregonian*, Dec. 5, 1885.
[10] The Treasury Department issued a circular in July, 1885, accepting the certificates of a United States Consul at any of these foreign ports, but was obliged to withdraw it because the statute required the certificate to be issued by the government of which the applicant was a subject.

with litigation growing out of the exclusion law, chiefly in the form of *habeas corpus* cases.[11] The Consul-General of the Chinese, Mr. F. A. Bee, declared that he had taken out over two hundred writs himself in order to enable well-known merchants to re-enter the United States; and that their difficulties far exceeded those of the restricted laborer. Judge Hoffman of the United States District Court said that the law worked manifest injustice and absurdity.

Meanwhile in other Coast territories a series of extreme attacks upon the Chinese were taking place, notably at Rock Springs, Wyoming, and at Tacoma and Seattle, Washington. At Rock Springs, 28 Chinese had been killed, 15 more or less seriously injured and property to the amount of $148,000 destroyed. In every case these outrages appear to have been precipitated by labor organizations chiefly composed of foreign-born persons, some of whom were not naturalized. The anti-Chinese contagion spread to San Francisco and was aggravated by the struggle already existing there between employers and Trade Unions and by the excitements incident to a municipal election in 1885, and a State campaign in 1886.[12] In San Francisco, a special Grand Jury was charged to investigate the workings of the Restriction Act. The majority report was violently anti-Chinese, even going so far as to misrepresent the figures of arrivals and departures by some thousands in order to show that the law was not stringent enough.

About the same time a committee of the Board of Supervisors of San Francisco, W. B. Farwell, Chairman (and candidate for mayor), made a report on Chinatown, describing in exaggerated terms the filth, crowding and disease of the quarter and asserting that the Chinese

---

[11] The California papers complained that the act was being nullified by the decisions; Morning *Call*, San Francisco, Oct. 31, 1882.

[12] In the presidential campaign of 1884, California went republican by a very close vote but the democratic candidate, Grover Cleveland, was elected.

Scott Act and Abortive Treaty of 1888 189

population was rapidly increasing.[13] Following this and constituting the principal feature of the gubernatorial campaign of 1886, was a series of anti-Chinese meetings ending in a State convention.[14] The report of the convention began with a reference to "the Mongolian hive with its 450 millions of hungry and adventurous inhabitants," and ended with an appeal for relief from "a situation which had become wellnigh intolerable."

The *Memorial* to Congress prepared by a committee of this Convention reiterated the usual objections to the Chinese and demanded that the United States absolutely prohibit this Chinese invasion; that no Chinese be employed on public works and that all persons employing Chinese or purchasing their products be boycotted.[15]

During these years there were repeated charges that the restriction law was evaded. It was said that thousands of Chinese were coming into British Columbia intending to cross the border; that forged certificates were for sale in Chinatown, San Francisco, and were used with the connivance of immigration officers; that certificates of the old Chinese who went home to die were used by new ones to return; that the Chinese in transit across the United States were allowed to escape; that many laborers came in in the guise of merchants and students with certificates from the Chinese government; and that the numbers of the Chinese were increasing rather than decreasing.

Special Agent Spaulding made an investigation and

---

[13] The San Francisco *News Letter* said this report was "more than usually sensational and misleading."

[14] In the campaign of 1886 there were six parties; a new Know-Nothing party polled 73,471 votes. The issue was very close.

[15] The Committee which made this report consisted of John F. Swift, (Rep. Candidate for Governor), A. A. Sargent (Rep.) U. S. Senator, 1873–9, H. V. Morehouse, E. A. Davis and Elihu Anthony. Horace Davis, Cong. Representative, 1877–1881, Pres. Elector, 1884, was Chairman of the Committee on the Memorial. General John Bidwell and Senator Sargent withdrew from the Convention on account of the boycott clause. *Cong. Docs.* 1886, ser. no. 2346. Davis, *Polit. Conventions*, p. 481 ff.

reported to the Treasury Department that the extent of the frauds had been greatly exaggerated. He estimated that the Chinese population had decreased by 20,000 in the three years since the Restriction Act and he was convinced that the Chinese Consulate had kept faith in the matter of Chinese in transit. There was opportunity for fraud undoubtedly, but no proof of it.[16] Other special agents, reporting on the opportunities for smuggling across the northern border, gave somewhat conflicting accounts but none of them found that any considerable number of Chinese had come over unlawfully. But the newspapers in California continued to reiterate the charges of fraud and evasion and to make political capital of them for the purpose of attacking immigration officials and Congressional representatives during the State campaign immediately following.

The renewal of agitation against the Chinese and the demand of the Chinese Minister for indemnity for the injuries done them, compelled President Cleveland to send two special messages to Congress rehearsing the facts and urging remedial legislation. The President attributed the outbreaks chiefly to race prejudice and thought, that, while the United States was under no legal obligation to give indemnity, yet in view of the failure of the Wyoming authorities to bring the guilty parties to justice, and in view of the absence of provocation, Congress should give indemnity for the outrages.[17] In the debate on the indemnity bill the Californians, with the exception of Mr. Morrow, urged that the remedy was severer restriction, that indemnity set a bad precedent, and that the massacre had been committed by foreigners in the United States and not by Americans. In opposition it was urged that indemnity was good policy, worthy of a "Christian" nation, under

[16] *Cong. Docs.* s. n. 2340, 1886, Senate Doc. 103.
[17] *Cong. Docs.* s. n. 2003, H. R. Exc. Doc. 102; also s. n. 2441, H. R. 2044 (1886).

Scott Act and Abortive Treaty of 1888   191

moral if not legal obligation, since the Chinese had not been protected according to the stipulations of the treaty.[18]

Although the immigration officials, the Treasury Department, and the special agents had all testified to the effectiveness of the restriction in lessening the numbers of the Chinese; and although the Courts, even in California, were obliged to discharge many for want of proof of fraud, the California newspapers, the politicians and the labor unions continued to demand severer measures. Governor Stoneman of California began his administration with a demand for the abrogation of the Burlingame Treaty; a committee of the State Legislature visited Chinatown in San Francisco and made a report containing such statements as the following:

"For thirty years China has dumped upon our shores all its refuse; ... all the incapable, the idiotic, the unfortunate, the criminal, the diseased, the vicious; the outcasts, have remained with us ... the men the most degraded slaves upon earth ... the women slave-prostitutes, ... the children the product of the most promiscuous miscegenation on earth." [19]

By 1887 the atrocities committed upon Chinese laborers throughout the Far West in the two preceding years, the hardships worked upon the exempt classes by the amended restriction law, and the complications arising from its administration, had produced several important results: an effort on the part of the President, the State department and the Chinese Minister, to protect and alleviate the condition of the Chinese by legislation; a demand on the other hand, from the labor unions and their political representatives for stricter exclusion; and a general crystallizing of opinion throughout the country that the whole situation should be adjusted by treaty modification.

On January twelfth, 1887, the Tsung-li-Yamen at

[18] 49th Cong. 1st Ses. 1886, *Record*, pp. 2886, 4055, 4425 ff.
[19] Cal. *Sen. Jo.*, 1887, p. 232–5.

Peking approached Minister Denby with a treaty project. They complained of the recent outrages upon Chinese in America, the lack of treaty protection and the denial of justice; and declared that China treated the Americans strictly in conformity with treaty stipulations but that the United States treated the Chinese as if the treaties were for no purpose.[20]

The Yamen proposed to prohibit all immigration of Chinese laborers even those already holding certificates, if without family or property in the United States; that the exempt classes should have a certificate issued either by the Consul-General in San Francisco to be viséd by both the American and the Chinese Consuls in Hong Kong or by the Chinese alone in Hong Kong; that Chinese in transit should have the same rights as before; that Chinese laborers resident in the United States and others holding certificates and having relatives or property there should have the same rights as before; and that the British Colonial government at Hong Kong be asked to coöperate in these arrangements.

On the same day that the Yamen made these proposals, Secretary Bayard proposed to the Chinese Minister at Washington the exclusion of Chinese laborers for thirty years. The Minister replied at once, that he could not proceed to negotiate a new treaty until the matter of justice and indemnity for outrages should be settled. Between January and March, 1887, he reported at intervals additional outrages upon the Chinese and the fact that so far no persons had been punished for them.

When, after three months, Mr. Bayard did not reply to these protestations the Chinese Minister finally outlined the propositions desired by his government under two heads: emigration and protection. Those specified under emigration were substantially the same as those named to Minister Denby by the Yamen. Under the

[20] These negotiations are found in *Cong. Docs.* 1887, ser. no. 2514, Ex. Doc. 272, 50th Cong. 1st Ses.

Scott Act and Abortive Treaty of 1888   193

head of protection he proposed a number of measures impracticable in a Democratic country.

Secretary Bayard promptly replied with a draft for a convention embodying under emigration three main points: a general prohibition of the immigration of Chinese laborers for twenty years; an exception to be made in the case of laborers who had been in the United States and who had a wife, child, parent, or property or debts to the amount of one thousand dollars; and a guarantee of the same provisions for the exempt and transit classes as in the existing treaty. As to the safety of the Chinese in the United States he argued that the United States was not under obligation to give protection in the form suggested, nor could the Federal Government so interfere with state and territorial administration under the American constitution.

Owing to the absence of Chang Yen Hoon in Spain for four months, the negotiations lapsed, but on his return he reiterated his demand for specific protection by treaty—" not in the same form but in equal measure " —and for indemnity, to be adjusted by a claims convention in accordance with the usual practice between foreign governments. To these suggestions Secretary Bayard made no reply whatever for several months until finally, Chang Yen Hoon wrote again reminding him that the original immigration project had been made by him in April, 1887, and that the Chinese government had replied, naming two additional articles which it deemed essential. He regarded Mr. Bayard's silence as inexplicable and insisted politely upon the discussion of protection and indemnity before he would proceed with the negotiations on the subject of immigration.

After a personal interview with the Minister, Mr. Bayard finally consented to three additional articles on the contested points. The first, that all Chinese, including laborers, should have the same protection as American law gave to citizens of the most favored nation; the second, that a lump sum covering all losses—without reference to liability, which the United States denied—should be paid; and the third, that the Chinese Government should arrange with the British Government to prevent Chinese laborers from coming into the United States from Hong Kong via British Columbia.

Chang Yen Hoon at once forwarded a statement of claims and, with some slight modifications, the treaty was completed and signed by the two plenipotentiaries on March twelfth. At this stage the treaty provided: Art. I—For a period of twenty years the coming of Chinese laborers shall be absolutely prohibited. Art. II—The preceding articles shall not apply to any Chinese laborer having wife, child, parent, or property or debts to the amount of one thousand dollars; and such right of return shall be exercised within one year of departure. Art. III—Chinese subjects, not laborers, to have admission and to produce a certificate viséd by the diplomatic representatives at the port of departure. Chinese in transit to have the same privileges as before. Art. IV—guaranteed to the Chinese residents all the rights of the most favored nation except naturalization, and the United States reaffirmed its intention "to exert all its power to secure protection to the persons and property of all Chinese subjects in the United States." Art. V—while expressly denying the legal obligation to grant indemnity, agreed to the payment of $276,619.75 as full indemnity for all losses and injuries suffered by the Chinese in the United States.

While these negotiations were proceeding, several resolutions were presented in the Senate inquiring what steps had been taken by the President toward a modification of the treaty of 1880.[21] Shortly afterward, when the President sent to the Senate the signed treaty, he included with it a confidential letter in which the Secre-

[21] *Cong. Docs.* 1888, 50th Cong. 1st Ses.; Sen. Doc. 115.

Scott Act and Abortive Treaty of 1888

tary of State explained the reasons for delay and for the insertion of Articles four and five. The letter said:

"It cannot be justly alleged that any discrimination has been made against the Chinese by the laws of the United States . . . but the fact remains that . . . there has been a failure of justice in the repression and punishment of crime and violence of which the Chinese were the victims, owing to the mingled causes of race prejudice, labor rivalries, their peculiar habits and segregation from other nationalities. The ill treatment to which Chinese laborers have been subjected by lawless and cruel men . . . has been a subject of just complaint by their government as well as mortification and sorrow to our own." [22]

The Senate, to which the treaty went for ratification, was Republican by a very small majority and the National Conventions for the nomination of Presidential candidates were impending. Just what took place in the secret session at which the treaty was amended is not known, but it was generally believed that it was done by the Republican Senate in order to embarrass President Cleveland and to prevent the Democratic party from claiming the credit of negotiating a satisfactory treaty and so influencing the labor vote in the impending campaign. The Senate added to article one the following clause: "and this prohibition shall extend to the return of Chinese laborers who are not now in the United States whether holding return certificates under existing laws or not." To article two was added, "and no such Chinese laborer shall be permitted to enter the United States by land or sea without producing to the proper officer of Customs the return certificate hereinafter required." [23]

Apparently the Chinese Minister did not fully understand the effect of these amendments in shutting out at least twenty thousand Chinese who held certificates of return; for in a note to Secretary Bayard he said: "I have carefully examined these amendments and *as they do not*

[22] 50th Cong. 1st Ses. 1888, Confidential Doc. O. reprinted in ser. no. 2626. Correspondence between the Chinese Minister and Secretary Bayard. p. 398 ff.
[23] *Cong. Docs.* ser. no. 2626, 1888, p. 398-9.

alter the terms of the original treaty, it will give me pleasure to accept them in due form." About the middle of May he forwarded them to the Chinese Government to be ratified and appended to the original treaty which had been signed two months before.

After the treaty of 1888 had been perfected, Mr. Cleveland was nominated a second time for the Presidency and it was at once apparent that the acceptance of the treaty by the Chinese Government would add considerably to his political strength in the Coast states, especially with the labor element. Although President Cleveland had exerted the Federal power to protect the Chinese from outrage and although he had urged the indemnity, it was known that he believed in strict exclusion. General Harrison, the Republican nominee for the Presidency, had on the contrary an almost pro-Chinese record. He had voted against the first restriction law with Senator Hoar, and for striking out the clause excluding the Chinese from naturalization. The fact that his attitude at that time was the attitude of the best men of his party and indeed, of the statesmen as opposed to the politicians of both parties, did not prevent his action from being called "pro-Chinese" by the Democrats in the campaign of 1888. Thus the Republicans, even more than the Democrats in Congress, were driven to put themselves on record on the Chinese question in order to secure the vote of the Pacific States.

In the late summer a bill embodying the main points of the pending treaty was discussed at intervals for a month in the Senate, each party attempting to prove that its record for anti-Chinese measures had been superior to the other.[24] When the bill passed the Senate and went to the House it was debated even more acrimoniously and wholly from a political standpoint.

The Republicans, led by Cannon of Illinois and Dingley of Maine, defended themselves by pointing to the

[24] The Senate was composed of 39 Republicans and 37 Democrats.

years between 1875 and 1881 when the Democrats had had a majority of the House and had yet done nothing for California. The Californians of both parties urged the passage of the bill on the ground that the treaty would probably be signed by China and legislation had already been too long delayed. Since, for political reasons, neither party dared to go on record as refusing such legislation, little time was spent in debating the bill itself, or the question of courtesy to a friendly power. Hooker of Mississippi did protest that the Chinese had acted in a most liberal manner and that it was most unfortunate that the Senate by its drastic amendments had jeopardized the treaty; and McCreary of Kentucky declared that there was no occasion for such extreme haste to anticipate its acceptance. But, the debate having degenerated into a wrangle as to which party should have the credit of furthering anti-Chinese measures, the bill passed, and was signed by President Cleveland to take effect as soon as the treaty should be ratified.[25]

Ten days afterward a press dispatch from London, to the effect that China had refused to sign the treaty, was published in the American papers. On September third, Mr. Scott of Pennsylvania, Chairman of the National Democratic Campaign Committee, and a friend of Mr. Cleveland, introduced a bill into the House shutting out any Chinese laborer who should not have returned before the passage of the act, prohibiting the issue of any more certificates under sections four and five of the act of 1882, and making all heretofore issued void.[26] The bill was passed by the House without debate and sent to the Senate where an attempt was made to pass it without debate or reference.

Although it was generally understood that this was a measure intended to strengthen the Democratic party in

[25] Debate, *Record*, 50th Cong. 1st Ses. 1888, pp. 7692 ff., 7748 ff.; Bill signed Aug. 20th, 1888.
[26] H. R. 11336. Senate Debate, *Record*, see index.

the West, the division in debate was by no means along party lines. Rather, the struggle was between the more dignified and conservative elements of the Senate on the one hand striving "to keep up appearances"—as Senator Morgan said—and the politicians on the other, openly attempting to further party interests. Senator Sherman of Ohio argued that to pass such legislation on newspaper information before official notice of the refusal of the treaty was received, was dishonorable and unnecessary; Senator Platt of Connecticut denominated it "a vote-catching performance," and Blair of New Hampshire said it was needlessly offensive.

A number of Southern Senators whose party affiliations and color prejudices were naturally anti-Chinese, protested quite as emphatically; George of Mississippi declared the bill a breach of national faith, urged in undue haste; Senator Butler of Tennessee said the United States would not dare to do it with a strong power. He continued: "It is a game of politics * * * and not a seemly one I must say. But for the fact that we are on the eve of a Presidential election and each party wants to get the vote of the Pacific Slope, this Senate would not be engaged in this debate." Senator Brown of Georgia offered an amendment excepting the Chinese holding certificates who were at that time on their way to the United States. He referred to the hardship, cruelty and outrage suffered by the Chinese and said apologetically, that the amendment was not so broad as it should be but he was aware of the motives that prompted both political parties to hasty action in the matter. Reagan of Texas declared that it compromised the honor and dignity of the Senate. Senator Morgan regarded the bill as a repeal of the treaty. Senator Call of Florida said that it was a case of seeing which party could "persecute the most."

On the other hand, the friends of the bill denied that the Senate amendments had jeopardized the treaty, arguing that it was five months since the original treaty and three months since the amendments had been sent to China. When, on September seventh, the President transmitted two telegrams from Minister Denby reporting that the Chinese had postponed the treaty for further deliberation, the bill was at once passed by a vote of 37 to 3 (Brown of Georgia, Hoar of Massachusetts and Wilson of Iowa), 36 being absent. Senator Gorman on a motion to reconsider, pleaded for delay, calling it indecent haste. When Senator Stewart pronounced the treaty a trick and a sham, which justified immediate legislation, Senator Gorman replied, "We all understand the pressure here in face of a contest between two great parties which has prevented fair consideration."

On September tenth Senator Blair urged, that the act be passed to take effect on November first if the treaty should not then be ratified. Senator Evarts of New York said it would be the first instance of legislative interference with a pending treaty; the bill was an absolute violation of the existing treaties; for it was not the fault of China if we could not pass laws strict enough, and enforce them; it was moreover a violation of the personal rights of the Chinese in the United States. He urged in the strongest terms that it should be referred to the Committee on Foreign Relations. George, Sherman, Hoar, Butler of South Carolina, Morgan and Saulsbury —even Teller—urged that the bill go to the Committee on Foreign Relations, "for decency's sake."

On September fourteenth a vote was taken on reconsideration—no quorum; and again on September seventeenth—yeas 20 (14 Democrats, 6 Republicans) nays, 21 (15 Republicans, 6 Democrats), absent 35. Thus the effort to obtain reconsideration failed. On September eighteenth the resolution of the Committee on Foreign Relations asking the President to withhold the transmission of the Scott bill to the House, was tabled and when brought up again the bill had already reached the House, to take the fate there or elsewhere that it deserved—as Edmunds said. It was passed by the House and sent to the President on the twenty-first.

On the same day the Chinese Minister cabled from Peru the counter amendments. The Chinese government asked for some reduction of the period of suspension; for some arrangement by which laborers having property in the United States might be allowed to return with a certificate from the Chinese Consul; and for the return of laborers with less property than one thousand dollars.

After a lapse of nine days President Cleveland returned the bill with his signature and a message justifying it. He referred to the urgency of the question and said that in now proposing further alterations the Chinese government had not coöperated with the United States as they had a right to expect. The President regarded this unexpected and disappointing refusal as an indefinite postponement and practical abandonment of the treaty; and he therefore joined Congress in substituting legislation for international agreement. He recommended, however, that an exception should be made of the Chinese already on the way and that the indemnity named in the bill should be paid.[27] In both houses the bill was referred to the committee on Foreign Affairs but no legislation was enacted to except the Chinese then on their way to this country. Shortly afterward the indemnity agreed upon was voted.

That the motives which produced the Scott Act were purely political was shown in the debates preceding it; but it is even more strikingly illustrated by the newspaper comment of the time.[28] The Republican papers early in the summer had united in declaring the Chinese question a dead issue and when the Scott bill came up the leading organs of the party were very sarcastic.

[27] *Cong. Docs.* 1888, s. n. 2514, Exc. Doc. 273.
[28] Full quotations in September and October issues of *Public Opinion*, 1888.

Scott Act and Abortive Treaty of 1888   201

Some called it demagogism and bullying; others thought the question should be left to diplomacy; and still others criticised the slowness of the State Department in negotiating the new treaty. The Democratic papers, which had attacked the Republican candidate's pro-Chinese record, now said that the treaty had failed because of the Republican amendments, and that President Cleveland had scored again against General Harrison.

But the Independent newspapers were unanimous in their comments that the measure was a race for the vote of the Pacific Coast, an unseemly scramble for the vote of hoodlums, and a violation of treaty without the courtesy of notice. The majority thought that Mr. Cleveland had done his best but had been balked by the Republican Senators, and that the existing law was quite sufficient.[29]

On his return from Peru the Chinese Minister began that stream of dignified and ineffectual protest which has continued to the present time. In January, 1889, he sent to the State Department an analysis of the act.[30] He said that it was a plain violation of the existing treaty which did not give the United States the power to restrict the free exit or return of Chinese laborers already in this country; and it was a prohibition without limit of time, not suspension or regulation. He reviewed the assurances of the treaty commissioners of 1880 already detailed in these pages, reminded the Secretary that the treaty of 1888 was still under consideration and that Mr. Bayard had assured him that the President would veto any legislation which might be passed in violation of the treaty.

Mr. Bayard replied enclosing the President's message of October first, and saying that the exclusion act had

---

[29] Independent papers: N. Y. Times, Evening Post, Herald, Commercial Advertiser, Harper's Weekly, Boston Herald and Post, Pittsburg Dispatch, Baltimore Herald. The last named was the only one in the least favorable to the Scott Act.

[30] *Cong. Docs.*, 1889, ser. no. 2714. For the following correspondence, see pp. 119-138.

been passed in consonance with the wishes of China and that he had only promised to influence the President to delay the bill as long as possible, since he was not in favor of it. Minister Chang Yen Hoon replied that the act was in direct opposition to the wishes of China, and that he had told Mr. Bayard that he had no authority to sign a treaty which did not provide for Chinese in transit and for Chinese laborers now in the United States. He enclosed also a memorandum of a conversation between Mr. Bayard and himself, approved by both the Chinese and the American Secretary, in which Mr. Bayard had said: "Unless you and I agree upon some satisfactory measures * * * Congress will certainly enact laws regardless of the treaty stipulations and the President would, of course, veto them."

The Secretary of State replied that he was not disposed to question the accuracy of the memorandum but that Chang Yen Hoon had admitted that the Senate amendments did not alter the terms of the original treaty. The delay in China, and the report in the newspapers that the treaty had been rejected, had caused the Scott act to be suddenly brought forward and passed with a unanimity "that palpably rendered an interposition by a veto of the executive, wholly futile."

Meanwhile the Chinese in the United States had raised a fund of one hundred thousand dollars to test the constitutionality of the act in the Courts,[31] but the Supreme Court decided that a treaty is subject at any time to be modified or changed by Congress, and that if the Chinese had any just ground of complaint, it must be made to the political department of the government.[32] Chang Yen Hoon wrote again to Mr. Blaine in July:

[31] Interview with attorney for the Chinese.
[32] *In re* Chae Chan Ping, (C. C. California, 1889; 36 *Fed.* 431, affirmed in *Chae Chan Ping* v. *U. S.* (1889), 130 *U. S.* 581, 9 *Sup. Ct.* 623, 32 L. 6d. 1068.

"I was not prepared to learn * * * that there was a way recognized in the law and practice of this country whereby your country could release itself from treaty obligations without consultation or the consent of the other party; it can hardly be contended that my government was exceeding diplomatic practice or courtesy in following out the example of the Senate and proposing amendments * * * I have yet to learn that it is the practice of governments to act on newspaper reports. * * * It was officially known that China had not rejected the treaty. * * *. So far as this legation knows the treaty is still pending and awaiting the reply of the State Department to the amendments proposed in the legation note of September twenty-fifth last."

The Chinese Minister further contended that the treaty had been brought about by the express solicitation of the United States; that the action of Congress was not justified by its conduct toward other nations nor by any action of the Chinese government; that it must be regarded as an affront to China.

In March of the following year Tsui Kwo Yin, successor to Chang Yen Hoon, reminded Mr. Blaine that the Chinese Government had waited eight months for a reply to its protests against the Scott Act, which the Supreme Court had declared was a violation of the treaty. He then recounted the hardships suffered under the act; at the time the act went into effect there were over 20,000 Chinese who had temporarily left the United States with certificates entitling them to return, and 600 of these were on the ocean on their way back and were refused admission;[33] some of these had families and property interests of many sorts. Those left here had to choose between perpetual banishment from their native country or abandonment of their interests. The right of transit was interfered with and in great measure cut off, although there had been no additional legislation affecting treaty rights on this subject; Chinese merchants

[33] The Chinese Minister notified Secretary Bayard, on Oct. 9, '88 that Chinese having certificates and Chinese in transit had been refused landing at San Francisco; on Oct. 18th, Acting-Secretary Rives replied that such certificates were now void, and enclosed a copy of the Scott Act.

had encountered much harsher treatment and increasing embarrassment from the Customs authorities; they were treated with much the same surveillance as is extended to vagrants and criminals; the certificate required was difficult to obtain, expensive and humiliating. It was serious enough when the Imperial Government beheld the manifest intention of Congress to obstruct and finally abrogate the treaties but it regarded with real alarm the apparent disposition of the Treasury Department to go even beyond the enactments of Congress.

He contrasted with this treatment the way in which the United States expected its treaties to be observed in China; in the case of the missionaries, " the most fruitful source of trouble ", not one had lost his life, none of their treaty guarantees had been violated with the consent or the connivance of the government, and an indemnity had been paid for every loss. The American Minister had even gone beyond the strict treaty rights in demanding protection and indemnity and an exact equality in the construction of the treaty clauses; and this doctrine was being insisted upon at the very time when Congress, the Executive and the Supreme Court were setting the treaty at defiance where its application was invoked in behalf of Chinese residents of the United States. The Imperial Government undoubtedly had the right of retaliation upon the American merchants and missionaries in China but the statesmen of China desired to observe a "more humane and elevated standard." A treaty between two independent nations was a contract; the nation which broke it was responsible for resulting injuries and the responsibility could not be escaped by any action or failure of the internal authorities of its government.[34]

In June, 1890, the Yamen sent a dignified protest to Minister Denby, recalling the fact that the Yamen had

[34] This correspondence is found in *Cong. Docs.* 1890, ser. no. 2830, p. 187 ff., and reprinted in ser. no. 3056 (1892).

sent three amendments to the treaty of 1888 and that to these neither the American Minister nor the Secretary of State had ever replied; that since the passage of the Scott Act the Chinese coming and going had all met with interference; that Minister Chang had written to Secretary of State Bayard in January and February, 1889, but had received no reply; that after Mr. Blaine became Secretary, Minister Chang wrote again and that the Department merely replied that they would give it careful consideration; that Minister Tsui had repeatedly written since, but without receiving any answer. The Yamen recounted the hardships of the new law which was entirely at variance with the treaties and a violation of the spirit of the negotiations; and they urgently demanded the repeal of the Scott act and an answer to their protests.

"We are humbly of the opinion that in the law of nations reciprocity is considered most important. Suppose that China should conduct herself towards American citizens in a similar manner, we ask whether Congress would not reproach China with a violation of the treaty? * * * Change your point of observation!"

In October the Yamen again protested to Minister Denby that they had received no reply to their previous communications; Minister Denby replied evasively that Congress can make and repeal laws, the President can only veto, and the Secretary of State can do neither—he did not know what Congress would do. But in a note to the State Department Mr. Denby wrote that he did not "deem it prudent to discuss the Scott Act" with the Yamen or "the mode of reconciling China to its results."

At the same time Tsui Kwo Yin wrote to Mr. Blaine that "it filled him with wonder" that no answer had been received to his note of six months before. He begged the Secretary to regard this as a friendly effort to restore their former cordial relations; China had learned to regard the United States as a model in the practice which should control governments in their reciprocal intercourse and because of this, had accepted its code of international law. "To this," he added, "we appeal." Mr. Blaine replied that the delay was not due to neglect or lack of appreciation of the importance of the subject but because he hoped soon to be able to convey the views of the President.

At the end of two months, not having received a reply, Minister Tsui conveyed the disappointment of his government that Congress had adjourned without repealing or modifying the Scott Act; he hoped this note would not be interpreted as a manifestation of impatience at the non-receipt of a reply but in view of the injustice and loss inflicted by the operation of the law his government wished to make known their urgent desire that something should be done to alleviate their injuries.

At the end of fifteen months Minister Tsui repeated his complaint, adding a protest against the new bill pending in the spring of 1892, but again he received no reply. At last, in December of 1892, more than four years after the passage of the Scott Act, the Acting Secretary of State undertook to answer the charges made by the Chinese government and advised China to adopt an "attitude of amicable concurrence instead of obstruction."

In the light of cooler judgment, in a later time, only two reasonable excuses can be offered for the passage of the Scott Act. If the first restriction law had been entirely ineffective, so that California was really suffering from surplus Chinese labor, it would have been justifiable for Congress to pass an amendatory act remedying its deficiencies in order to make it effective within the limits of the existing treaty; or, if China had delayed unreasonably long in offering her counter-amendments, or had finally refused to compromise them and to sign the Treaty.

There is apparently only one way of determining whether China delayed unreasonably and that is the test of our experience with other nations. The Senate amendments had been accepted by the Chinese Minister four months before the Scott Act was passed and had presumably been in the hands of the Chinese Government about three months. In 1885, the Senate had ratified the Claims Convention with Venezuela and had waited three years and two months before exchanging ratifications; in 1881 the United States Senate ratified the Consular Convention with Roumania and waited a year and two months; in 1888, it ratified an Extradition Treaty with Columbia and waited a year and eight months; in 1887 the United States concluded an Extradition Treaty with Russia, but it was six years and two months before the Senate ratified it.[35] Many of these treaties were also amended by the other party, after being ratified by the Senate. If the Senate amendments had been made in good faith and not as a mere political stratagem, the ordinary courtesies of diplomacy would have permitted the Chinese Government to discuss them. The blunder of the Chinese Minister in underestimating their importance to his government did not bind his government to accept them, though it might be cause for his removal from office. However regarded, the passage of the Scott Act under such circumstances was nothing less than an insult to the Chinese government. Indeed, it was generally so interpreted by foreign powers, some of whom professed to think that the United States were trying to provoke war as an excuse for taking a hand in the affairs of China.

As to whether California was in such imminent danger as to justify the cancellation of 20,000 certificates,—a discourtesy which fully warranted retaliation,—the official statements of the Customs Officers will show. During the six years preceding the Scott Act the departures

[35] See *Treaties in Force*, 1904.

of Chinese had exceeded arrivals by a net total of 11,300. But during the years of 1887 and 1888 arrivals exceeded departures by 4,700, a fact which lent color to the theory that California was in great danger. But it must be remembered that Congress had made no adequate appropriations for the enforcement of the Restriction Act up to this time, and therefore the Customs Officers were powerless to do more than enforce the obvious features of the law in plain cases. Nor should it be overlooked that the increase in Chinese immigration was always in the winter and spring and the decrease just before Christmas. It was known in China as well as in America in the winter and spring of 1888 that a new treaty was pending and that legislation, more restrictive, would be likely to follow. Unquestionably this caused a rush both of immigrant and returning Chinese and must be balanced against the excess of 5,500 departures above arrivals in the following year.

As to the "sad havoc and ruin" said to be occurring in San Francisco, a glance at the wage tables on page 354 of Chapter XX shows that wages in San Francisco in the year 1888 were far above those of any city east of the Rocky Mountains, and were steadily rising. The *minimum* average wage for twenty years (1870-1890) in 18 trades exceeded the average of eleven other cities by 39 cents per day per trade; and the wages of common labor ranged from one-quarter to one-third higher than anywhere else in the United States.

The passage of the Senate amendments and the Scott Act can therefore find justification neither in the delay of China nor in the failure of the Restriction law, nor in the danger to the working class on the Pacific Coast. It was, in truth, a mere vagary of American politics, due to the violence of the current Presidential campaign; and was so understood and so characterized shortly afterward by the men who were concerned in it.

CHAPTER XIII
THE GEARY LAW AND THE McCREARY AMENDMENT

" We have found that China has constantly violated the treaty and that is why we are here demanding this abrogation. There never was a treaty between this Government and China that was violated by any law passed in any American Congress since the time the treaty was made. . . . This registration law is not only not violative of the treaty but is expressly authorized by the terms of that instrument. . ."—THOMAS J. GEARY of California—Debate in Congress, 1892.

" Besides these reasons the Chinese consider that the law is unwarranted and an unnecessary insult to a friendly nation. . . . It is in violation of every principle of justice and equity and fair dealing between friendly powers. . . . If England or any foreign power was to pass a similar law in reference to the subjects of the United States, we think the United States would resent the indignity."—The Six Companies in reply to the Collector of the Port of San Francisco, 1892.

" The acts to which I have referred deny to the Chinese the right conceded to all other persons, of indictment and trial before conviction. The law also denies the universal rule of presumption of innocence. . . . There is no good reason for our Government to still further violate the treaty between the United States and China by requiring them (the Chinese) to be tagged, marked and photographed."—Representative J. B. MCCREARY of Kentucky, 1893.

" It contains within it the germs of the assertion of unlimited and arbitrary power . . . incompatible with the immutable principles of justice, inconsistent with the nature of our Government and in conflict with the nature of the Constitution by which that Government was created and those principles secured."—Opinion of Chief Justice FULLER, 1892.

THE ostensible reason for the passage of the Scott Act in so summary a fashion was the prevention of fraud and evasion, but before the new law had been in operation two years the charges of smuggling and spurious certificates were again revived. The statistics of the Treasury Department showed that although there had been a net gain of 4,700 between March, 1889 and December, 1890, the net loss during the seven and a half years after the Restriction Act was 15,369—an average of 2,000 per year for the whole period. Secretary Windom reported that the allegations of fraud and evasion were not supported by tangible proof nor reliable figures but he did not doubt that small parties did occasionally get across the borders and that the Chinese were attempting to use dishonest papers. As a matter of fact the whole number of Chinese seen, reported and arrested during the year 1890 was about 800, and if all had gained admission they might have added one per thousand to the Chinese in the country or one per 80,000 to the entire population.[1]

The officials of the Chinese service were no better pleased than the anti-Chinese party with the effect of the Scott Act for the confusion arising from its defects was often ridiculous. The special agent at Suspension Bridge, New York, reported that the Dominion Customs officers refused to admit the Chinese without the payment of the fifty dollar head-tax and that the American officers had to choose between smuggling them back or placing them on the bridge connecting the two countries—"where they were certain to suffer much discomfort, to say nothing of the annoyance to the Bridge companies." The special agent at Toronto complained that neither the Consuls nor the collectors knew what constituted a merchant under the act. Twenty Chinese having been tried and found illegally in the United States were sent over to Victoria—"whence they came." The Canadian authorities would not receive them, and the Captain of the vessel tried to bring them back to the United States; but the American Customs officers would not permit them to land and the Judge who had ordered them sent to Victoria fined the Captain for not landing them there. They were finally sent back to China

---

[1] See table of numbers, appendix, p. 500; Windom's report, 1890, *Exc. Doc.* 97, Pt. I, s. n. 2686. For evasion on northern border see Julian Ralph, *Harper's Mo.*, vol. 82.

on a showing that they had come to Victoria through Hong Kong.[2]

The immigration officials at the ports of entry were compelled to refer constantly to the Treasury Department for its interpretation. They agreed that the Chinese should be deported to China rather than to the country whence they came, and that they ought to be registered both for their own protection and the convenience of the service.[3] They were of the unanimous opinion that a large increase of appropriations and officers was necessary for the satisfactory enforcement of the law. Inspector Coon predicted that the law was likely to be an expensive toy, since the estimated expense of arrest, conviction and deportation in California from 1889 to 1891 was not less than five hundred dollars per head for each Chinaman. American officials abroad were equally puzzled. Minister Denby did not know how to procure an acceptable certificate for a Chinese physician in the employ of a Mission at Peking who wished to come to the United States to study medicine, and he wrote to the State Department: " the requirements of the statute are almost impossible of performance."

The Chinese Minister at Washington in the course of his repeated and ineffectual protests against the Scott act, described the insuperable difficulties of the privileged classes of his countrymen and the troubles of those in transit. The steamers sailing from Havana refused to take Chinese passengers in transit because they were denied landing at New York, unless they gave bonds to the amount of two hundred dollars each. Secretary Blaine replied that this new regulation was necessary because of the evasions of the law but that it had been amended so that common carriers might execute a general bond. The Minister protested that

[2] *Cong. Docs* H. R. 4048, s. n. 2890, 1891.
[3] *Cong. Docs*. s. n. 2920, May 29, 1891.
[4] *Cong. Docs*. s. n. 2714, Jan. 18, 1889.

this did not help the matter for the transportation companies would not take the risk unless each Chinaman gave an individual bond.[5]

It would have been reasonable to expect that the Coast states, having obtained exclusion of laborers and established a precedent of superseding treaties by legislation, would be intent upon perfecting the details of the law and securing adequate appropriations for its enforcement. But while the Treasury Department struggled to enforce the law without money or a sufficient corps of officers and endeavored to make up for the deficiencies of the statute by severity of regulation, the Californians introduced a measure for making exclusion practically permanent. Whether the original restriction act, as amended in 1884, expired in 1892 or 1894, was a disputed question; and upon the opening of the national political campaign in 1891 this afforded an opportunity for again bringing the Chinese football into the arena.[6]

The Congressional Sub-committee sent to California to investigate Immigration made a report far more reasonable in tone than those of earlier years and based on the testimony. The report stated that the number of the Chinese was decreasing though perhaps not as fast as desirable, and that the two chief abuses of the law were the accumulation of *habeas corpus* cases in the courts and the importation of contract laborers. The number of *habeas corpus* cases in 1888 had been over 7000, but between 1888 and 1890 only 1992. Of the 67 per cent remanded, only a very small proportion had been actually deported because of worthless bonds. As to the importation of contract labor a careful reading of the testimony does not substantiate the conclusions of the committee. The details, which were supposed to be conclusive proof, prove nothing more —to anyone familiar with Chinese methods of doing business—than that

[5] *Cong. Docs.* s. n. 2830, Jan. 9, 1899.
[6] *Cong. Docs.* s. n. 2815, Aug. 5, 1890.

there was a considerable amount of assisted immigration. The committee finally concluded that in spite of these abuses, all that was necessary was a re-enactment of the existing law and strict enforcement.[7]

Almost simultaneously with the presentation of this relatively mild report, Senator Dolph of Oregon reported from the Committee on Foreign Relations a bill extending all laws in force for ten years with some amendments making them still more severe. In spite of protests from the leading Senators of New England, the bill passed without debate and went to the House, where it was lost in the struggle over the still more extreme Geary bill. Congressman Thomas J. Geary, of California, had obtained a suspension of rules for the consideration of his bill and thirty minutes had been allowed for the debate.[8] The essential provisions of the bill were much the same as had been proposed by other Western Congressmen in previous years: it should be unlawful for any Chinese persons except diplomats and their servants to come or to return to the United States. The penalty for shipmasters bringing such persons was to be five hundred dollars for swearing falsely, one thousand dollars or a year's imprisonment and the vessel to be forfeited to the United States. Any Chinaman crossing the boundaries was to be liable to arrest by any party on behalf of the United States and to deportation—the penalty for violation five years imprisonment. All Chinese, whether subjects of a foreign power or not, were to be included under the law and no Chinaman was to be admitted to citizenship. Chinese residents must obtain a certificate stating minute particulars concerning themselves and must supply photo-

---

[7] *Cong. Docs.* s. n. 2890. H. R. 4048, 1891. The Sub-committee consisted of W. C. Squire, Ex-Governor of Washington, (Rep.), Lehlbach of New Jersey (Rep) and Stump of Maryland (Dem.).

[8] Thomas J. Geary was born in Massachusetts, practised law in California 1877 ff., was representative in Congress, 1883-4, 1890-3. Democrat and American.

graphs at a cost of three dollars each. The Secretary of the Treasury was empowered to make regulations for the temporary admission of Chinese, not laborers, desiring to visit the United States.[9]

Mr. Hooker of Mississippi (Democrat) and Mr. Hitt of Illinois (Republican) divided fifteen minutes between them in a vain attempt to bring the House to a reasonable consideration of the measure. Mr. Hooker protested against its many harsh features—the exclusion of all Chinese except diplomats, the registration fee of five dollars, the suspension of *habeas corpus* and the denial of bail—declaring them to be violations of the treaty. Mr. Hitt protested that he was unwilling to revoke a portion of the treaty while the Chinese soldiers were guarding Americans in China, and while the United States was demanding that China should keep covenant under the same treaty. The bill which had already passed the senate was so severe that it had driven from this country Oriental merchants who were known in every commercial center of the world. He ended with these words:

"We have had many anti-Chinese bills—each harsher than the preceding. They come every year with the elections.* * * This bill is wholly needless, it is mischievous. * * * It will result in non-intercourse and break up our trade with China." [10]

Mr. Geary, followed by Mr. Hermann of Oregon and Mr. Cutting of California, replied that the existing legislation was very defective, for in spite of it 60,000 Chinese had come in during the last ten years and they were still coming over the borders in large numbers. He quoted Judge Morrow as saying that a quarter of a million of appeal bonds had been forfeited in the *habeas corpus* cases. The Angell treaty had been obtained by misrepresentation on the part of the Chinese

---

[9] Cong. *Record*, 52d Cong. 1st Ses., p. 2913.
[10] 52d Cong. 1st Ses., *Record*, p. 2911.

and had since been constantly violated by them. The so-called merchants were really coolies and the American laborer must be protected from them.[11] At the end of a debate limited to thirty minutes, this Democratic bill passed an overwhelmingly Democratic House and went up to the Republican Senate.[12]

On April twenty-first the Committee on Foreign Relations reported back the Senate bill of February as a substitute for the Geary bill. The four days' debate was participated in by nineteen members of whom four only—Mitchell of Oregon, Felton of California, Teller of Colorado and Stewart of Nevada,—all Western Republicans, defended the bill. These advocates asserted that the Census of the Chinese was inaccurate, that in reality there had been an increase of 30,000 instead of a decrease as alleged; that the existing legislation was ineffective, that laborers came in as merchants and identification was impossible; that if the Scott bill violated the Treaty then the Senate bill did also, and in any case the Chinese had repeatedly violated it themselves; and had been unreasonable in refusing the treaty of 1888; that the Geary bill would not injure trade, and the trade with China was of no importance anyway. They acknowledged that the bill was harsh in some of its provisions but insisted that this was necessary because the influx of Chinese could not be prevented in any other way.

Eight Republicans and two Democrats—Butler of South Carolina and Morgan of Alabama—united in a vigorous attack on the Geary bill. Senator Sherman thought it "harsh and cruel, against the spirit of our civilization, far beyond anything before in severity," and not a necessity since the Chinese were decreasing in numbers; it would not only injure commerce but would

---

[11] 52d Cong. 1st Ses. *Record*, 2911 ff.; H. Rept. 407.
[12] Vote: yeas 178, nays 43, not voting 108. At this time the House had 236 Democratic and 88 Republican members.

endanger diplomatic relations. Senator Frye showed the financial loss to the United States by the exodus of Chinese merchants and by the check upon Chinese travel across the country.[13] Senator Dawes sarcastically referred to "keeping treaties as long as we had a mind to." and dwelt on the difference between what the treaty commission of 1880 had said and Congress had done. In this view Senator Davis concurred, denominating the Geary bill a rank, unblushing repudiation of every treaty obligation which remained and unwarranted by any existing danger—a violation such as the United States would not dare to commit toward any warlike nation of Europe. Other senators did not believe the civilization of California was threatened and thought the Senate bill quite severe enough. Senator Squire, who had been a resident of Seattle since 1879 and Governor of Washington Territory, regarded the Geary bill as unnecessary. While he understood the feeling of intense antagonism among the laboring people toward the Chinese, it seemed to him demagogy of the most arrant kind for Congress to pass act after act for the alleged purpose of their exclusion when it failed to provide money for the efficient enforcement of the law.[14]

When the Senate had by a strong vote substituted the Senate Bill for the Geary bill,[15] Senator Platt of Connecticut offered an amendment to re-enact all laws in force except the Scott Act. At once the crucial point of debate became the expediency of the Scott Act, and the most significant feature of this memorable discussion was its penitential tone. Senator Platt said he had voted for the Scott Act under protest but never would

[13] Based on a telegram from C. P. Huntington of the S. P. railway, which stated that the Chinese in transit had paid $350,000 to American railways and that hundreds of merchants had gone back to China.
[14] W C. Squire was a New Yorker and a Republican; a veteran of the Civil War, Governor of Washington Territory, 1884-7; United States senator 1889-1897; Chairman of the Senate Committee on Coast Defenses.
[15] By a vote of 43 to 14, 31 not voting.

again. Senator Dawes, referring to the haste with which it had been passed, said: "We see now that if we had not done it the way would have been clear for a law and a treaty sufficient to exclude all Chinese whose presence would be injurious here." Butler was ashamed of having voted for it, Davis regretted his participation in it; Gray did not approve its harshness but feared its repeal would cause embarrassment. Senator Sherman shared his hesitation but explained his position fully: "I believe the Scott law was one of the most vicious laws that have passed in my time in Congress. I believe now and I believed then that it was a mere political race between the two houses * * * in the face of a Presidential election. I believe the passage of that law prevented the negotiation of a treaty which would have accomplished its object." While conscious of inconsistency, however, he thought it better to continue the laws as they were until Congress could take up the whole subject calmly and deliberately.

Senator Dolph argued that the Senate Bill as it stood did "no great injustice" and even the repeal of the Scott Act would make no adequate restitution. Senator Vest of Missouri, while not choosing to be put in a penitential mood over the transaction, thought the law ample even if only partially enforced, and did not see any necessity for going further and ruthlessly offending China. Senator Chandler, the only eastern member who openly supported the Californians, thought that since the Scott Act already violated the treaty "it did not much matter now" whether it was violated again. Senator Mitchell alone, of all those who had been concerned in the Scott Act, was neither apologetic nor repentant.

Apparently because of the administrative complications which might arise upon the sudden repeal of the Scott Act, the Platt amendment was rejected, and the Senate substitute prevailed. The House having refused to concur, a committee of conference was appointed consisting of Senators Dolph, Sherman, and Morgan [16] and Representatives Geary, Chipman and Hitt. A week later, Senator Dolph presented the Conferees' report signed by only four members—Senator Sherman and Mr. Hitt having declined. The report consisted of the Senate bill plus certain sections of the Geary bill, *i. e.*, sec. 5—no bail to be permitted to Chinese in *habeas corpus* cases; Sec. 6—all Chinese laborers to obtain certificates within one year and if arrested, the burden of proof to be upon them; Sec. 7—the Secretary of the Treasury to provide certificate forms and opportunity for registration; Sec. 8—a penalty named for fraudulent certificates; Sec. 9—the Collectors to be paid by fees.

In presenting the report Senator Dolph said that he hoped that the Conference bill was within the treaty and added apologetically: " I had great misgivings about the Scott Bill. * * * It not only violated the treaty but was a great injustice to many persons." Senator Morgan would have preferred the Senate bill but pointed out that since a certificate was necessary for the protection of the resident Chinese, it was to be issued without charge and that they could only be arrested by certain officials and tried only before a Federal Judge. Senators Platt, Dawes, Call and Palmer again registered their protests against the Conference bill as unjust, unnecessary and a violation of treaty, Senator Frye because it discriminated between the Chinese and other foreigners,[17] and Senator Hiscock because it was bad policy to invite attempts at evasion.

Notwithstanding these objections, the Senate finally concurred in the report by a small vote.[18] and it was signed the day before the expiration of the existing law.

---

[16] April 26. The original Committee was Dolph, Dawes and Butler.

[17] Senator Frye said that when he visited Rock Springs, Wyo., he found U. S. troops defending the Chinese from a "horde of unnaturalized Poles and Hungarians."

[18] The vote was 30 to 1, 43 not voting. At this time the Senate consisted of 47 Republicans and 39 Democrats.

But the President's signature was scarcely dry when the defects of the new law arising through haste and inconsideration, began to be apparent. A number of distinguished lawyers pronounced it unconstitutional. On the strength of their opinions the Chinese raised a large sum of money and a test case was carried to the Supreme Court.[19] Secretary Foster reported that the standing appropriation of $60,000 would be quite inadequate to pay the salaries and expenses of additional officers to enforce the law and also the expenses of deportation, and asked for one hundred thousand dollars.[20] Awaiting the decision of the Supreme Court and lacking the necessary appropriation, Secretary Carlisle suspended the operation of the new law and the Chinese Six Companies of San Francisco issued a proclamation advising their countrymen not to register. The officers and courts charged with the enforcement of the law had already discovered that it did not create the machinery nor name the persons authorized to deport the Chinese; no mode of trial was prescribed, yet the Chinaman found unlawfully in the United States could be imprisoned and treated as a felon.[21]

The leading newspapers without regard to political affiliations, attacked Geary and condemned the bill. One independent newspaper said: "The whole barbarous business was a vote-getting one from the start." Others declared the measure "in the last degree insulting to China and unjust to the Chinese people"—"a sop thrown to these far western states." Even the *Call*, the independent daily in San Francisco at that time, said:

[19] At least one of the Attorneys of the Chinese in San Francisco believed the act (except sec. 4) constitutional; but Heber J. May of Washington, D. C., Judge James C. Carter, J. Hubley Ashton, and Rufus Choate rendered opinions that it was unconstitutional. The Attorney-General procured an advance on the Calendar of the Supreme Court for the test case.

[20] *Cong. Docs.* 1892, ser. no. 2957, Exc. Doc. 244.

[21] See *In re* Ny Look, C. C. New York, 1893, 56 *Fed.* 81, a laborer discharged by the court in New York because there was neither money nor machinery for executing the law.

"It is not supposed that every member of the House who voted for Geary's bill did so from conviction. Some of the Democrats saw a chance to make a little political capital out of a question upon which there has been no division of parties." [22]

Mr. Hitt and Mr. Hooker were especially approved for their vigorous fight in a hopeless campaign while Mr. Geary became the general butt of criticism and ridicule. Indeed the reaction of general public opinion went so far that the Californians began to apologize and to explain that only a little of Mr. Geary's original measure had been incorporated into the law. Even Mr. Geary undertook to justify himself in a magazine article in which, however, he contradicted many statements made in his speeches before the House, and denied that the bill had ever violated the treaty or contemplated the deportation of Chinese.[23]

The Collector of Internal Revenue at San Francisco wrote to the Chinese Six Companies, asking if they had directed the Chinese not to register and warning them that not only would their people be subject to fine and imprisonment but they themselves might be liable for damages and possibly responsible to the United States government for inciting people to disobey the laws. The Chinese Six Companies replied that they had issued a circular advising Chinese laborers that the law was unconstitutional and suggesting to them that they should not comply with it. They considered the law "an unwarranted and unnecessary insult * * * in violation of every principle of justice, equity and fair dealing between friendly powers." If enforced, it would subject every Chinese merchant to blackmail because he could be arrested anywhere as a Chinese laborer. Concerning their responsibility to the United States Government

---

[22] *Nation*, Boston *Herald*, Omaha *Bee*, Washington *Post*, and a large number of other papers united in condemnation. See *Public Opinion*, vol. 16, 1892–3.

[23] Compare Mr. Geary's speeches in April, 1892, with article in *N. A. Rev.*, July, 1893. See also editorial, *Nation*, v. 57, p. 23.

Geary Law and McCreary Amendment 221

they said: "We know of no law which makes it a crime for us to advise our fellow subjects that they have a right to disregard a law which is in violation of the constitution and treaties."[24]

Meanwhile the Chinese Minister at Washington, the Consul-General at San Francisco and the Yamen at Peking were also protesting against the act. The Chinese Minister had steadily protested ever since the Scott Act against the plain violation of treaty; just preceding the Geary Act he wrote six letters to Mr. Blaine only two of which were so much as acknowledged. He now declared that the Geary Act was worse than the Scott Act, for it not only violated every single article of the treaty of 1880 but also denied bail, required white witnesses, allowed arrest without warrant and put the burden of proof on the Chinese. He quoted our own statesmen on the harsh and hasty character of the act, not required by any existing emergency, whose political motive was well understood both in China and the United States.[25] In his final protest he said: "The statute of 1892 is a violation of every principle of justice, equity, reason and fair-dealing between two friendly powers."[26]

There was, indeed, nothing for the Executive Department to say, since the facts at least could not be denied, but at last, in December, 1892, Acting-Secretary Wharton attempted to justify the action of Congress and the regulative measures of the Treasury Department. He resorted to the ancient device of blaming the other party. The Scott Act, he said, was the result of China's refusal to sign the treaty of 1888, "which had exerted a prejudicial influence on American sentiment"; and had created a "belief that the attitude of China was obstructive and the claims of China unreasonable." It was idle to talk of repressive treatment and lawlessness toward the Chinese

---
[24] San Francisco daily papers, Sept. 15 and 19, 1892.
[25] *Cong. Docs.* s. n. 3076, 1892.
[26] *Cong. Docs.* s. n. 3056, 1892.

in the United States while Americans could point to mob violence and vexations in China. It was a mistake to suppose that the Chinese were on the same footing as other aliens in the United States—they were "immiscible * * * not willing to be engrafted on the national life and dwelling under the special license of an artificially created necessity." Finally, ignoring the questions of hardship, injustice and treaty violation—the chief points of the Minister's contentions for several years—he reproached Minister Tsui for not adopting ".an attitude of amicable concurrence toward a rational and practical end." [27]

At the same time the Tsung-li Yamen, in a dignified communication to the United States Minister at Peking, protested that they could not but regard the new law " in a strange and frightful light "; and asked for its repeal on the ground that it violated the Constitution of the United States and the favored nation clause of the treaty. They referred specifically to the hardships of the certificate system, the denial of bail and the penalty of imprisonment. Six months later the Yamen complained that they had received no reply to their protests and again asked for the repeal of the law as a violation of the treaty of 1880. Prime Minister Li Hung Chang also wrote to Minister Denby that the American treaty commission of 1880 had "pulled the wool over the eyes of the Yamen" and that China wanted not merely the repeal of the Geary law but a treaty of reciprocity.[28]

Minister Denby replied that the legislation, in so far as it applied to the laborers who came in after the act of May, 1882, was in accordance with the treaty;

[27] Mr. Wharton carefully avoided acknowledging that the Senate had amended the treaty of 1888 and then refused to allow the Chinese government to offer additional modifications; that the Chinese had paid large indemnities for every vexation; and that every obstruction had been put in the way of assimilation in the United States. For full text of correspondence, see *Cong. Docs.* 1892, ser. no. 3076, p. 157 ff.

[28] *Cong. Docs.* ser. no. 3076, under dates May, Aug. 5, Nov. 3, Nov. 29, 1892.

as to others, "it was not a practical question" since very few remained in the United States; the law was not a prohibition but a regulation and removal, "both a mild and necessary form of punishment"—the lowest penalty allowed for crimes in the United States. The requirement of a certificate was a benefit and the production of it would relieve the owner of all trouble. Finally, Mr. Denby, too, reproached them; all this would not have happened if they had signed the treaty of 1888.

Just one year after the passage of the Geary law the Supreme Court rendered a decision that it was constitutional, the Supreme Justice and two Associate Justices dissenting, and Justice Harlan being absent. The decision was received with surprise by many of the legal profession and with disappointment by the friends of the Chinese. By the leading newspapers, both partisan and independent, everywhere except in California, it was made the text for renewed condemnation of the law itself. The independent journals referred to it as an act of barbarism, humiliating America in the eyes of the world, impossible to enforce except at enormous cost, and justifying retaliation from China. Many of the Republican papers concurred in these strong expressions, one was very sarcastic—"there is no money to deport and we can't drown them"—another advocated making California pay for the enforcement, others thought the country could not expect a heathen nation to exercise a Christian forbearance which Christian nations themselves declined to exercise. The Democratic papers joined in the general demand for an extension of time for registration, while denominating the law as "inhuman", "brutal", "worse than the alien and sedition law" and suggesting that the Christianization of China would have to be left to some nation sufficiently Christian to practice the Golden Rule.[29]

[29] Washington *Post* and *Star*, Phila. *Ledger*, Baltimore *Herald*, N. Y. *Herald*, Harper's *Weekly*, N. Y. *Mail* and *Express*, *Recorder*, Baltimore

Only two of the leading papers in San Francisco remained as vehement as before: the *Examiner* (Dem.) said: "The Six Companies have played a desperate game and lost. * * * If China does not like the presence of Americans there she can order them out." The *Argonaut* said: "The decision is good law and good sense. The arguments against the law have been absurd." The San Francisco *Chronicle* (Rep.) was sure that the state would take no actively hostile measures if the Geary law was enforced, and urged a special session of Congress to extend the time of registration. It was willing to assume that the Six Companies seriously believed the act to be unconstitutional. The *Call* (Ind.) blamed the Washington officials rather than the Chinese for their failure to register.

As the end of the registration period approached the Chinese in some of the ruder districts of California were threatened with violence.[30] Minister Tsui, the Chinese Merchants' Exchange of San Francisco and the Consul-General, appealed to President Cleveland for protection. The President appealed to the Governors of the Pacific States. The Governor of California notified the President that he had carefully instructed the Sheriffs of certain counties to protect them. Secretary Gresham wrote to the Chinese Minister: "It is gratifying to be able to assure you that the sentiment of the people of the United States towards the Chinese grows perceptibly more tolerant." To Mr. Denby he wrote:

> "I have stated to the Minister that while the President cannot suspend a law of Congress . . . and while it was impossible to give assurance that the Geary law would not be enforced, its terms . . . will necessarily cause its enforcement to be attended with some delay; so that there is no reason to believe that the

American, Hartford *Post*, Phila. *North American* and *Press*, Denver *Republican*, Portland *Oregonian*, N. Y. *Sun* and *World*, Phila. *Record*, and *Times*, Denver *News*, Atlanta *Constitution*.

[30] Fresno, Tulare, San Bernardino—riots in Selma. See *Cong. Docs.* 1893, ser. no. 3197, p. 257, and newspapers.

Chinese who have refused compliance with the statute wi.. .c ue-ported in large numbers between now and the assembling of Congress at which time there is ground to anticipate further legislation on the subject." [31]

But the increase of the numbers of the unemployed in California due to the panic of 1893 and the closing of the silver mines, resulted in riots during which the Chinese were maltreated, driven out of many localities and their quarters pillaged. Governor Markham notified the Federal Government that assurances must be given that the Geary law would be enforced or the mobs would enforce it.[32] Meanwhile the financial distress of the whole country assumed such serious proportions that the President called Congress together in August. Minister Tsui requested the President to embody in his message a suggestion for the repeal of the Geary law, but Secretary Gresham replied that the President did not regard the moment as opportune but had reason to believe that the Geary law would be modified at the next regular session.[33]

The Chinese were agitated anew in September by the arrest of some of their countrymen for non-registration. The Consul-General reported to the Legation that 64 of the better class of laborers were in jail in San Francisco, Oakland and Los Angeles, not admitted to bail and likely to remain there for several months because of the delay of the courts. Judge Ross of the United States District Court of California drew further attention to the situation by certain decisions, more particularly that warrants could be issued for the arrest of unregistered Chinese on complaint of private persons and served by United States marshals, and that a highbinder and a gambler were laborers. He granted appeals to the Supreme Court but refused to grant a stay of proceedings.[34]

The Chinese Minister remonstrated strongly and the

[31] *Cong. Docs.* ser. no. 3197, (1893), pp. 234, 250.
[32] *Review of Reviews*, Oct., 1893, p. 376.
[33] *Cong. Docs.* ser. no. 3197, 1893, Aug. 19.
[34] U. S. vs. Ah Fawn (D. C. California) 57 *Fed. Rep.* 591.

Secretary of State took refuge, as the Department had often done before, in an explanation of the coördinate powers of the different departments of the Government, which made no one of them responsible for the actions of the others.

It became apparent, however, by the time the regular session of Congress opened that not only the Chinese and their defenders but the whole country demanded immediate modification of the Geary law. In the chorus of criticism and indignation California alone asked no amendment except in the direction of stricter enforcement. Mr. McCreary of Kentucky reported from the House Committee on Foreign Affairs several amendments to Section Six of the act in which the Committee, with the exception of Mr. Geary, were unanimous.[85] The amendments proposed were an addition of six months time for registration, a discontinuance of all legal proceedings begun under the act, the substitution of "one credible witness other than Chinese" for the "white" witness clause, and a definition of laborer as both skilled and unskilled, including certain specific occupations.

Mr. McCreary described the circumstances which had misled the Chinese and under which only 13,242 out of 106,668 had registered. Only twenty-five thousand dollars remained in the Treasury with which to deport 85,000 unregistered laborers. As the cost of steerage passage for the Chinese was $51.00 and other expenses at least $35.00 per head, it would cost $7,310,000 to deport them all and would occupy the time of three judges from twelve to fifteen years. It was therefore not only just but economical to extend the time, for, he said, "The act denies to the Chinese the right, conceded to all other persons, of indictment and trial before conviction. * * * It also denies the universal rule of presumption of innocence. * * * There is no good reason now for our government to still further violate the treaty * * * by

[85] 53d Cong. 1st Ses. 1893, *Record*, see index, H. B. 3687 (McCreary).

Geary Law and McCreary Amendment 227

requiring them to be tagged, marked and photographed." He spoke further of the extraordinary number of petitions, some for repeal and others for extension of time, received by the Committee.[36]

In support of these amendments Mr. Hitt of Illinois (Rep.) spoke of "the unexampled harshness of the Geary law which it was never expected would be enforced," and which he regarded as "a gross, palpable, and declared violation of treaty." He described the advantages of Americans over other nationalities in China —consular jurisdiction, trade interests and protection of missionaries—enjoyed under the treaty; he pleaded for the national honor—but, he said, the evil could not be cured by biennial bills in violation of national obligations, brought in just before elections. It was significant that this bill, the only bill for the relief of the Chinese, was not proposed on the eve of an election.[37] Many other representatives were equally pronounced in their condemnation of the un-American features of the bill and in favor of uniform legislation for all immigrants of whatever race.

In opposition to the McCreary amendments, Mr. Geary led the attack, supported by five of the six representatives from California. He said that the United States had never at any time violated the treaty with China while China had taken every opportunity to defraud us. California had a surplus of labor, wages had fallen to $1.50 and $1.00 per day and the Chinaman could live on ten cents per day; American labor could not survive such competition. As to numbers, the Census was all wrong, there were 200,000 Chinese in the United States, (Mr. Maguire of California interjected "300,000"), they had more than doubled in twenty years in spite of all restriction laws. He argued that it was impossible to identify Chinamen; "that deportation was not contem-

[36] *Record*, p. 2421 ff.
[37] *Record*, p. 2435 ff.

plated as a penalty for crime"; and that since the United States was responsible for the life of every Chinaman here, it would be cheaper to deport them than to pay indemnity. Finally, he complained of non-enforcement, asserting that $25,000 would have served as well as millions to demonstrate the intent of the law and he appealed to the Southerners in the House to oppose the McCreary amendments, as offering only another opportunity for evasion of the law.

Mr. Loud of California did not discuss the merits of the bills before the House but spoke bitterly of the fact that only on the eve of elections had the Pacific Coast been able to secure legislation; as soon as election was over their issues were no longer burning ones. He attacked indiscriminately, "the advocates of the Foreign Missionary system", "the petty Supreme Court of New York", the Democratic Administration, and the Chinese Six Companies, and assured the House that the Chinese had always been treated "with kindness and charity" in California.

Mr. Bowers and Mr. Hilborn of California also attacked the Administration and the Judiciary for inefficiency but, contrary to the other Californians, they emphasized the very virtues of the Chinese as making them more dangerous. Mr. Bowers described instances of the persecution of other foreigners besides Chinese and asked what the Chinaman had to gain by embracing a religion that produced such results. "In the late troubles in California," he said, "a large sprinkling of the whites who were attempting to drive the Chinese out were themselves aliens, and some of them dissolute characters. * * * The most pestiferous anti-Chinese howlers * * * in California, those who incite to riot, have themselves been employing Chinamen." He attacked the Democracy for "shifting, paltering methods", and finally culminated in threats: "If the Democrats pass this bill, * * * there will not be Democrats enough left in California to make a greasespot big enough to see with the naked eye."

Mr. Maguire of California loved humanity but believed in self-preservation. He quoted the San Francisco Building Trades as saying that Chinese competition threatened to reduce wages below the standard of family life. In his district there was a vastly greater number of adult Chinese males than Caucasian males, citizens and aliens combined, and this had been true of San Francisco till recently. Hundreds of white children were becoming opium fiends and there were thousands of professional Chinese criminals and highbinders, hundreds of whom had been pirates in China. He defended the Geary law as " mild and humane ", not a deportation but a registration law, merely a passport system and assured the House that the Chinese in California had always been protected from injury and insult.

All of the California representatives, in varying phrases, accused the Six Companies of importing contract laborers for profit and of opposing the Geary law for that reason. They asserted that the coolie laborers were " bond-slaves ", " substantially owned by the Six Companies ", " imported practically as slaves ".

Mr. Blair of New Hampshire (Rep.) occupied a unique position in this debate. He had been nominated by President Harrison as Minister to China in 1889 and had been refused as *persona non grata* by the Chinese Government on account of his part in the debate on the Scott bill.[38] Although a strict exclusionist, he spoke in favor of the McCreary Act on the ground that public sentiment having been so strongly aroused against the Geary law it would be impossible to obtain the necessary appropriation to enforce it. For the exclusionists to vote against the McCreary bill would be to defeat their own object.

After a five days' debate, Mr. McCreary said, briefly,

[38] Blair (Rep.) of N. H., member of Congress, 1875-9; 1893-5; U. S. Senator, 1879-91.

that he had voted for the Geary Act but that he did not therefore believe in making outlaws of the Chinese. The question before the House was not exclusion, but an extension of time for registration. He accepted Mr. Geary's amendments defining "merchant" more strictly, providing for deportation by a United States marshal and for photographs to accompany each certificate. These amendments, together with one offered by Mr. Caminetti of California providing for the deportation of every Chinese convicted of a felony were accepted and after a second trial for a quorum, the bill passed.[39]

At this time the Secretary of State, in reply to a resolution of the Senate, stated that the Chinese Minister had repeatedly said that an additional opportunity to register would afford his government great satisfaction.[40] The Committee on Foreign Relations therefore reported the House bill without amendment.[41] While many Eastern senators spoke apologetically of the Geary law and the necessity for its amendment, Senator George C. Perkins of California made it the occasion for an extended argument for stricter exclusion. This amendment, he said, was regarded by the Californians as another attempt of the Chinese Six Companies to delay the enforcement of the law. The requirement of photographs was not humiliating and without it the certificates would be sold to brokers in China and there would soon be a million. The merchants were not merchants but merely laborers who paid from twenty to fifty dollars to become one of a hundred members of a coöperative firm. He declared that there were 15,000 highbinders in San Francisco and closed with the traditional arguments: the Chinese had sent home 810 millions of dollars in thirty years, their labor was a curse, they were vicious and immoral and the people of California, as proved by the

---

[39] By a vote of 178 to 1.
[40] *Cong. Docs.* ser. no. 3144, (1893, Oct. 20), Exc. Doc. 31.
[41] For debate see *Record*, 53d Cong. 1st Ses., 1893, p. 3040 ff.

Geary Law and McCreary Amendment

Referendum vote of 1879, were unanimously in favor of exclusion.[42]

Senator White of California said, as most of the Californians had said for twenty years, that the Eastern senators knew nothing about the Chinese. The Chinese could not be believed, therefore the necessity of a "credible witness" clause; they could not be identified, therefore they must all be photographed as well as registered. He described the highbinders and the boiling of dead bodies by the Chinese in order that their bones might be sent to China; and declared that he had never seen a bona fide Chinese Christian. He, too, assured his colleagues that California had sought to deal with them in a humane manner and he considered the McCreary amendments exceedingly liberal.

The attempts of the Coast Congressmen to weaken the McCreary amendments aroused their advocates to strong protest. Senator Davis of Minnesota said that it was most unfortunate that these amendments had to be determined when adjournment was already fixed, every one was tired and attention turned to financial legislation. But he then proceeded to make the most logical and vigorous attack on the methods of Chinese exclusion that had yet been made. He reviewed the legislation of former years showing that the acts of 1882 and 1884 were plainly sufficient, that the Scott Act was attributable "to that conscienceless party spirit, concerning which neither the Democratic nor the Republican party had any particular right to reproach the other." As for the act of 1892, whatever might be said, of the devices, pretexts and glosses to which it had been subjected; "the actual object of it was to drive the Chinese out." The Supreme Court had declared it constitutional—"a decision which had taken a great majority of the legal profession by surprise"—but the Supreme Court did not dictate the policy. It only decided that there existed

[42] 53d Cong. 1st Ses. 1893, *Record*, pp. 3044-48.

in other departments of the government a power, vast, ill-defined, and liable to be perverted to the purposes of passion. In analyzing the Geary Act in detail he noted that it violated treaties with other countries than China, in that a Chinese who was a subject of one of those countries might be deported; it presumed the Chinaman guilty till he was proved innocent; it denied bail and consequently the right of *habeas corpus;* the Chinese must apply to the collector for a certificate but nowhere was it made the duty of the collector to grant the certificate. He pictured the plight of a Chinaman in New York or St. Paul if he should lose his certificate—he might have to send 2000 miles for a " credible " witness; and yet this Chinaman's testimony would be acceptable against a white man in a trial for felony.

He compared with the Chinese, the Italians who came intending to return and take their wages with them, who brought the *Mafia* with them to New Orleans and yet nobody proposed to deport them. Yet if the Chinese could be deported, any other aliens could be deported under the sanction of whatever treaty. If a hundred thousand Chinese with the right of personal liberty and domicile guaranteed by treaty could be turned over " to be taken bodily in a man-hunt ", who would say that this statute was not made for oppression? He concluded with an appeal to refer the whole subject to the committee on Foreign relations to frame suitable legislation.[43]

But in view of the imminent consequences of the Geary law, the clamor of California, and the demand of the whole country that something should be done at once, the appeal came too late and the Senate passed and the President signed, the McCreary compromise measure. Yet the Chinese still seemed to hope for some way of escape and did not begin to register in any numbers till March. The Secretary of the Treasury increased the facilities for registration and sent officers to Chinese

[43] 53d Cong. 1st Ses. 1893, *Record*, pp. 3080 ff.

camps to save them expense and trouble. A large number of deputies had been appointed and Chinese who could not appear before the Collectors were permitted to have their witnesses sworn before a clerk of the court or a notary public.

Thus, at last, was set in operation at great expense, a system of registration which the officials in charge of the execution of every act since 1882, had declared to be indispensable to effective administration. For the eighth time in fourteen years, anti-Chinese agitation had reached a successful issue in a statute approved by both houses of Congress. From suspension to restriction; from execution of treaty stipulations to flat prohibition of immigration and cancellation of certificates in violation of treaty compact, the movement went on until it culminated in the Geary law, which reiterated and legalized the severer features of them all and added the requirement of registration. It was, in the words of Senator Hoar, progression from vinegar to vitriol.

Let it be noted that all but one of these measures was passed on the eve of an election under political pressure for avowed political purposes; against a disapproving majority in the East and even against a respectable minority on the Pacific Coast. The McCreary Amendment alone, passed in a year of political relaxation, bore faint signs of compunction and marked the beginning of a reaction against both the principle and the methods of Chinese exclusion.

CHAPTER XIV

THE BEGINNING OF REACTION

"It is probable that the crusade against the Chinese will have to go on till it reaches a climax of mischief and unreason that must be followed by reaction, and then we shall wonder at our folly, just as we now do at the folly of a past age which declared 'America for Americans,' and denied the right of Europeans to become anything above menials. How absurd it must appear when he sees the Irish of Cork rebelling against the right of the Germans to work there because it is not their own country, while the Irish and the Germans of the United States are demanding laws against the right of Asiatics to come here for work."
—Sacramento *Union*, July First, 1870.

"To The Congress of the United States:
Your memorialists, land-owners farmers and producers of California and other Western States, ... are aware that heretofore the voices uttered and the objections urged from the large cities have been taken as the sentiment of the whole people. We find now that our silence has permitted the achievement of an exclusion policy, in no wise beneficial to those who have urged it, and at variance with correct economic principles. We get no benefit from the European immigration which crowds the Atlantic seaboard. If that immigration reach these far States, it is under the same limitations as the white labor that is already here and shuns the work in the primary processes of the industries we represent. Our only resource is Asiatic labor. We affirm that there is absolutely no evidence that these states have ever suffered industrial or economic injury from the presence of the Chinese here, prior to the Exclusion law."—Petition of Californians, 1907.

For several years after 1893, the excesses of the Geary Act and the disastrous results of that hasty piece of legislation both to Mr. Geary and his party in California, tended to throw the Chinese question into the background of American politics. At the same time the attention of the world was being centered upon China, whose wonderful resources and commercial opportunities roused the active interest of business men, cotton manufacturers and engineers. The Exposition at Chicago brought a number of distinguished Chinese to this country and the magnificent exhibit drew further attention both to their skill in the arts and to the value of their trade to American exporters. The trip to the

The Beginning of Reaction 235

Orient also, owing to its picturesque interest and to more comfortable methods of travel, became suddenly more popular.

Information concerning Chinese politics and national traits became accessible in a remarkable series of books, written by Englishmen and Americans who had lived in China, and who, almost without exception, put Chinese character and capacity in a far more favorable light than those of a previous generation. Californians themselves, who had formed their opinions of the Chinese by an occasional trip through the slums of Chinatown, a superficial acquaintance with the lives of a few washmen and cooks, and the ready-made tradition of the Sand-lot returned from China with some accurate knowledge and a wholly remodelled view of the possibilities of Chinese development. The Boxer outbreak, while revealing the treachery and weakness of the upper stratum of Chinese government revealed even more the inherent strength of the common people—the persistence of those fundamental virtues of patience, industry, filial devotion, integrity and stability, which the peasant farmer and the laborer had preserved in spite of misgovernment. While Boxers murdered and pillaged, the friends of the foreigners—Christian and heathen—risked their lives to protect them; and thus, at the end of that rebellion, the Chinese stood to the world as both more ferocious and more noble than had been supposed.

Not the least important factor in changing the opinion of the Chinese was the alteration in the character of the Caucasian immigration at the Atlantic ports. Where the Chinaman had formerly been compared with the Celt and the Teuton of northern Europe, he was now measured by the mixed and darker peoples of Southern and Southeastern Europe, whose standard of living was often as low and whose character was quite as questionable as his. The Austro-Hungarian and the Italian immigration, beginning twenty years after the Chinese, had both of them exceeded the whole Chinese immigration to the United States six times over. In the single decade, 1890-1900, the number of Russians arriving was twice the total Chinese in fifty years; and the social and economic problems precipitated by these later immigrants in congested cities, in the mines and in the shops of the eastern states, tended to reduce to their proper proportions the problems of Chinese immigration on the Pacific Coast. And, most potent of all, the contact of Californians themselves in their own domain, with a lower grade of "white" immigration drove them to do the Chinaman a belated justice.

California, having recovered rapidly from the panic of 1893, began a new era of development. Society became more stable, wages were steadily rising, agricultural industries were no longer overshadowed by premature manufactures and mining and, with more stable conditions and the decline of speculation, capital was satisfied with lower rates of interest in conservative undertakings. The elements of California progress, hitherto experimental and shifting, seemed to settle down and take strength; and with the decline in the numbers of the Chinese and their dispersion to other parts of the country, the source of irritation was to some extent withdrawn.

Immediately after the passage of the McCreary amendment the Chinese Minister at Washington intimated his wish to entertain new treaty negotiations and as a result a new draft was sent to the Senate in April, 1894. It was opposed by the trades unions throughout the country and the Pacific Coast Congressmen tried to prevent its ratification. As finally ratified it provided for the absolute exclusion for ten years of all Chinese laborers, except such registered laborers as had in the United States a lawful wife, child or parent, or property or debts to the amount of one thousand dollars; the right of transit was still to be enjoyed by laborers, subject to regulation; all resident laborers were to register

The Beginning of Reaction 237

and the Chinese Government might require the registration of American laborers in China. The privileged classes were to be admitted to residence and might—not "must"—produce a certificate from their government viséd by the American representative at that port.[1]

The treaty sanctioned, in fact, the acts of 1892 and 1893 for ten years and certain Treasury regulations then in operation. The substantial points gained by the Chinese were a slight degree of reciprocity in the registration of American laborers in China—an empty privilege as yet—the registration of all Americans except officials, residing in China; and the privilege of return guaranteed to a Chinese laborer having a family or considerable property in this country. In conjunction with a decision of the Attorney-General it repealed the still active sections of the Scott Act and thus removed a measure of injustice.

The treaty might have considerably ameliorated the situation of the exempt classes but for the undefined powers vested in the Treasury Department under the term "necessary regulation" to which the Chinese had pledged themselves not to object. Congress, in the following year, added to the act appropriating fifty thousand dollars for the enforcement of the exclusion acts, a provision making the decision of the immigration or customs officer, if adverse to the admission of an alien, conclusive—subject only to an appeal to the Secretary of the Treasury. This principle had been established by the general immigration law of 1891 which shut out idiots, paupers, convicts and diseased persons, and it had been upheld by the courts. As applied to the Chinese it had been attacked in several cases, notably the Ju Toy case in 1905, and at various times a majority of the Justices of the Supreme Court have held that the principle is both unjust and dangerous.[2]

[1] See *Treaties in Force*.
[2] Justices Field, Brewer, Peckham and Day, and Chief Justice Fuller.

The denial of appeal to the courts and the increasing severity of regulation by the Treasury Department, became subjects of incessant protest on the part of the Chinese Minister in the years following the making of the treaty. The definitions of the exempt classes were made so comprehensive by official regulation as to exclude many who had hitherto been admitted. In 1898, by a new decision of the Attorney-General, the previous interpretation of the phrase, "being officials, teachers, students, merchants or travellers," was reversed so as to exclude all who were not technically laborers whether belonging properly to these classes or not.[3]

If the protests of the Chinese Minister were justified the predictions of the opponents of the Geary law that it would invite perjury, bribery and evasion, were equally so. Chinese cunning and duplicity were more than matched by American greed and corruption; sheriffs, court commissioners, and United States marshals and deputies, were known to be in collusion with professional Chinese agents on the borders and money seemed to smooth the way even at the ports of San Francisco and New York. The law permitted any person to lodge complaint before a Commissioner; wholesale arrests of Chinese persons became notorious; prisoners were in jail at the expense of the Government, marshals receiving two dollars a day; and the salaries of attorneys, Chinese inspectors and interpreters went steadily on. Under such circumstances the cost of enforcement was rapidly increasing.[4]

The pressure at the borders and at illegal ports of entry was also increasing. The Chinese soon learned that if they attempted to enter at the appointed stations their papers might be taken away and there would be no appeal except to the Treasury Department. Certifi-

[3] Op. A. G., July 15, 1898; S. 19677.
[4] 56th Cong. 1st Ses. H. R. 13197, H. Rept. 2503, s. n. 4213 (1901); and H. R. 12665, H. Rept. 2516, s. n. 4212 (1901). *Record*, pp. 3441; *House Doc.* 471, s. n. 4163.

The Beginning of Reaction 239

cates were precious, negotiable property, and the Department rarely reversed the decisions of its inferior officers. But if the Chinaman were arrested at the border he must be brought before a court commissioner and had an appeal to the higher courts.[5]

The Treasury officials complained not only of the law's defects but of the difficulty of enforcement due to evasion and frauds practised by Chinese of all classes—unlawful entrance at the borders, transference of certificates, laborers posing as members of the exempt classes, and worst of all, younger Chinese claiming to be native-born citizens. It was even asserted that the wealthy Chinese were in collusion with governmental inspectors and interpreters to bring in laborers. Other factors besides increasing severity of regulation on one side and increasing dissatisfaction on the other were again tending to renew the anti-Chinese agitation. The Trades Unions were rapidly increasing in membership and in coherence and labor was better organized in San Francisco than anywhere else in the country. The struggles between the unions and employers for a decade, culminating in the Teamsters' strike in 1900, and characterized by methods of extreme brutality on one side and as extreme obstinacy and unwisdom on the other, have no part in this history except as they have resulted in flooding California with the most lawless and least desirable class of single workingmen. During this period the position of Commissioner-General of Immigration had been filled in the interest of labor,[6] but Chinese immigration re-

---

[5] To amend some of these defects an act was passed in March, 1901: Warrants of arrest must be made by an official or approved by the District Attorney who designated the Commissioner for trial. This act also provided for certification in Hawaii and for the exclusion of the Chinese there from the Continental United States.

[6] Commissioner-General, 1889-1897, Hermann Stump of Md.; Commissioner-General, 1897-1902, T. V. Powderley, Machinist, lawyer, Ex-Grand Master of the Knights of Labor, political speaker for the Republican party in the campaigns of 1896 and 1900. Mr. Powderley was removed from office by President Roosevelt.

mained in the control of collectors of the ports, subject to direct supervision by the Secretary of the Treasury, until 1900, when it was transferred to the Commissioner of Immigration.

The representatives of Union Labor were now in a position to dictate in California and to control the administration and interpretation of the Exclusion laws through the Commissioner-General. Nominally, the Secretary of the Treasury must approve all regulations; practically the Commissioner-General made all the regulations and decided all appeals according to his subordinate's opinions. During the period of Mr. Powderley's service it was perfectly understood that the Secretary of the Treasury disapproved of his methods. Mr. Powderley administered the Chinese laws and regulations with the purpose of shutting out all Chinese; the Secretary believed in shutting out laborers only and in admitting the exempt classes with as little inconvenience as possible.

For political purposes, the Chinese question was apparently dead. The national platforms of 1896 and 1900 made only slight references to general immigration. The President's messages defined the characteristics of good and bad immigration and recommended an intelligent educational test, a certain standard of economic fitness and close supervision, but made no reference to the Chinese in this connection.[7] But the acquisition of new territories which had among their populations a large number of Chinese, revived the subject in a new form. In 1898 Major-General Otis by military order, applied the Exclusion laws to the Philippines;[8] and Congress, against the protest of the white population, applied them to the Hawaiian Islands,[9] to pacify the labor constituency of the mainland who objected to the movement of the

[7] *Cong. Docs.* 1901, ser. no. 4268, pp. xx–xxi.
[8] *Cong. Docs.* 1899, ser. no. 3898.
[9] U. S. *Stat.* 1897–8, p. 751, Joint Res. of July 7, 1898.

The Beginning of Reaction 241

Chinese from Hawaii to California. There were, at th time, about 20,000 Chinese in Hawaii many of whom had lived there for years with their families and had risen from the status of laborers to positions of independence; while the number of white laboring men was less than 1000. That native American labor was neither obtainable nor practicable on the sugar and coffee plantations was perfectly known but it was deemed necessary to sacrifice the interests of both China and Hawaii to the demands of Union Labor in the United States.

While the policy of enforcing more and more strictly a peculiarly difficult statute was demanded by the organized labor element, a pro-Chinese reaction on the part of the general public was furthered by the remarkable personality of Minister Wu Ting-Fang. China had had other scholarly and worthy representatives at Washington but never one who could meet western diplomats on their own ground and fight them with their own weapons. To an extraordinary breadth of culture in English learning, he added experience in diplomacy, wit and charm of personality, and a keenly logical mind.[10] The conjunction in office of President Roosevelt, Secretary John Hay and Minister Wu Ting-Fang, gave promise of discussion for the first time, perhaps, on a plane of mutual and international interest, rather than a basis of merely local and class agitation.

Simultaneously with the anti-Chinese Convention of 1901 in California and the opening of Congress, Minister Wu availed himself of the stipulation of Article IV of the treaty of 1880, to present the hardships of the Chinese under the exclusion laws to Secretary Hay. After rehearsing the earlier history to show that the United

[10] Wu Ting-Fang was born in Kwangtung province, China, educated at Canton, studied law and admitted to the bar in England; Director of Kai Ping R. R. Co.; First Secretary of Embassy of Peace to Japan in 1895, and later, Plenipotentiary to ratify the treaty; in 1897, Envoy Extr. and Minister Plen. to U. S., Spain and Peru; author of many articles in English. Recalled to China in 1902; returned to the U. S. as Minister in 1908.

States was at first favorable to Chinese immigration, that the change of opinion had been caused by the growth of the labor unions, and that the treaty of 1880 did not permit prohibition but only a reasonable suspension, he traced the growing severity of legislation which, regardless of treaty obligations, had finally shut out even certificated laborers under the Scott Act. The supplementary treaty of 1894 had by no means satisfactorily relieved the hardships of the exclusion laws and regulations.

He argued that the treaty had been interpreted by the Bureau of Immigration in a way not intended by its phraseology nor by the intent of the negotiators; i. e. to exclude scholars, bankers, commercial agents, physicians, noblemen, etc., while admitting students, merchants and laborers with a certain amount of property; the definition of students and merchants had been narrowed without warrant and their admission beset with so many conditions as to very nearly amount to a prohibition. It was almost impossible to obtain an acceptable certificate; and even when technically correct it was not accepted. On arrival the exempt classes were imprisoned during examination, not allowed to see their friends nor to retain counsel or even an interpreter who spoke their own dialect; and every advantage was taken of technicalities to exclude them.

He asserted that the appeal from the decision of the local officers to the Secretary of the Treasury without a judicial hearing, was a mere travesty of justice for the Treasury Department had no evidence beyond that of its own subordinates and would rarely reverse the decision of its own officers. Furthermore, the Chinese resident in the United States were often harassed by over zealous marshals and inspectors. The argument contained many citations of instances and decisions illustrating his contentions.[11] During the discussion of the

[11] *Cong. Docs.* 1901, ser. no. 4268, pp. 75-971; also ser. no. 4231, *Sen. Doc.* 162.

The Beginning of Reaction. 243

various exclusion measures in Congress, Minister Wu again protested not only against the incorporation of the obnoxious Treasury regulations into law but also against their application to the Island possessions, on the ground that since these were no part of the territories of the United States at the time the treaty of 1894 was signed, it was a violation of international comity to extend the exclusion laws to them without the consent of China.[12]

These protestations coincided with a local political campaign in California in which the labor element was playing an unusually prominent part. The Teamsters' strike in San Francisco had consolidated the Union Labor vote into a party which planned to elect a number of workingmen's representatives to Congress at the approaching election. The party must have an issue and with the imminent expiration of the exclusion law Chinese immigration was a natural one. It was well understood that the conservatives in California wanted only the reenactment of the amended Geary law, if, indeed, they did not want it made less stringent; but the platform of the Union Labor party demanded exclusion of all Asiatics.

Once more political leaders seized upon a question which, though no longer vital, was sure to win the approval of workingmen and not likely to involve unpleasant consequences to themselves. Every aspirant whether in office or not, ranged himself on the question in order to attract the favorable attention of the labor party. Three years before the expiration of the treaty the governor of California urged a renewal of agitation against the Chinese because China was objecting to the application of the exclusion to the new territories.[13] In November of 1901 a Convention called by the Mayor of San

---

[12] Prince C'hing also protested to Minister Conger in China. *Cong. Docs.* 1902, ser. no. 4440, pp. 211-221, ser. no. 4361, *H. Doc.* 562.

[13] Message of Gov. Gage, 1901, App. to Cal. *Legis. Jos.* Gov. Gage was out for re-nomination.

Francisco,[14] met to frame a memorial to Congress for re-enactment of Chinese exclusion.

The Convention consisted, according to the committee on credentials, of 3000 accredited delegates from every part of the state; in fact there were on the list something less than 2000, and in attendance about 1000; these being, for the most part, the officials of towns—supervisors and other officers—and delegates from labor organizations. There were present at least nine candidates for Governor and United States Senator and most of the leaders and whippers-in of both parties. It was, in short, truly representative of only two elements—the Union workingmen and the politicians, for the names of leading men in trade, manufacture, commerce and agriculture, of physicians, lawyers and clergymen, educators and philanthropists—names that stood in California for public spirit, integrity and knowledge, were conspicuously lacking. The committee of five appointed to draw up the memorial consisted of three candidates for the State senatorship at the current election and one for the United States senatorship; the only consistent anti-Chinese member, and the only member not in politics, was Walter McArthur, a prominent labor leader. The memorial rehearsed the increase of white population, of trade and the general prosperity since the exclusion law of 1882 and the necessity of protecting American labor. It repeated the time-worn charges against the Chinese, some of which were gross exaggerations and others plain lies within the knowledge of all intelligent Californians. Having been duly accepted, it was sent to Congress by a special delegation.[15]

At the first session of the Fifty-seventh Congress twenty bills relating to Chinese immigration were introduced. Of these the most important was that offered by Mr. Kahn of California in the House, almost identical

[14] James D. Phelan, Mayor, 1897–1901, candidate for U. S. Senatorship.
[15] Text in *Sen. Doc.* 191 (1901), s. n. 4234; also in S. F. Daily papers, Nov. 21 and 22. For comments see amusing pamphlet by P. J. Healey.

The Beginning of Reaction 245

with Senator Mitchell's bill in the Senate. The Committee on Foreign Affairs in reporting a substitute for Mr. Kahn's bill said that all were agreed on the necessity of excluding coolies and of guarding against frauds but it was also important to avoid any unnecessary discourtesy to the genuine privileged classes. They had cut out some of the clauses in the Kahn bill because they were unconstitutional, and the clause excluding Chinese sailors from American vessels because it was injurious to American shipping; but they had excluded Chinese from the Philippines, leaving the regulation in the hands of the Philippine Commission.[16]

The debate on the Committee bill centered about three principal points: the definition of the exempt classes, the seaman's clause and the extension of the law to the Philippines. It was soon apparent that a good fighting minority, led by Cannon and Hitt of Illinois, Gillett of Massachusetts, Douglass of New York and Hooker of Mississippi, would endeavor to soften the majority bill. Kahn and Coombs of California succeeded in restoring the extremely narrow definitions of the privileged classes and in retaining the seaman's and Philippine clauses. As thus amended the bill was passed without a roll call and went to the Senate committee on Immigration.[17]

Meanwhile the friends and foes of exclusion were having a hearing before the Senate committee. Minister Wu had asked for a non-partisan commission to consider the whole question and report suitable legislation. But the five commissioners sent from California and representing, in reality, not California but the anti-Chinese Convention, had obtained an immediate hearing on the composite bill offered by Senator Mitchell of Oregon. The character, standing and motives of the now clearly defined opponents showed how far the Chinese question had pro-

---
[16] *Cong. Docs.* 1902, s. n. 4403, H. Rept. 1231.
[17] For debate see 57th Cong. 1st Ses. 1902, *Record*, pp. 3678 ff. Index H. R. 13031.

gressed in public opinion since the passage of the Scott Act. The advocates of the Mitchell bill, which purported to alleviate the hardships of the exempt classes while reenacting practically every severe feature of the Scott Act, the Geary law and of the Treasury regulations, comprised precisely the same classes as those of the Convention in California. Four politicians, all of them candidates for public favor, and six spokesmen for the labor organizations, with only one man to represent the general welfare, constituted the witnesses on behalf of the bill; while the advocates of mere reënactment of existing law were eight men of wealth interested in commerce and manufacture, a sea captain, a distinguished attorney for the Pacific Mail Steamship Company, and four men of high public station—partisans neither of trade nor labor —in behalf of the general interest.

The contrast in the animus and arguments of the witnesses was as great as between the groups of men themselves. The Californians and the Union Labor representatives urged the necessity of stricter measures on the ground of the danger of hordes of Chinese and the frauds practised by them. The spokesmen for trade and transportation urged the growing importance of Oriental trade, declaring that the United States could not hope to hold, much less to increase, its proportion if it gave needless offense to the exempt classes. They considered the danger to labor greatly exaggerated, and urged the reënactment of the amended Geary law without the Treasury regulations.

There was besides, a group of notable men presenting the claims not of California nor of trade labor alone, but of the whole country and of humanity. For the first time in the history of the Chinese question there was an organized attempt to present the broader humanitarian view, by men whose commercial and political motives could not be questioned. John W. Foster, Ex-Secretary of State, diplomatist and author, showed the

The Beginning of Reaction 247

manner in which earlier legislation and even the existing law and practice, violated the treaties, operating both as an insult and injustice to the Chinese people. Stephen W. Nickerson expressed the protest of New Englanders against such discrimination against a single race. But by far the broadest argument was made by Simon Wolf, Chairman of the Civil and Religious Rights Committee of the Hebrew Congregations. Mr. Wolf summed up his humane and convincing testimony briefly as follows: the exclusion laws were unjust because discriminative; objectionable because the general immigration laws might be applied to the Chinese precisely as to other nationalities; unnecessary for the protection of labor because most of the evils complained of were purely imaginary; unnecessary further because the economic conditions both in the United States and in China had wholly changed— the gold fever had passed, while the rapid development of China herself tended to keep her laboring population at home. The exclusion laws were a menace to peaceful relations between the two countries, they handicapped the American missionary and the American merchant and limited trade and commerce. They were, moreover, contrary to the spirit of American institutions and to the spirit of the age, for the period of exclusiveness was past.

In opposition to an argument like this, the exaggerations, personalities and animosity of the principal spokesmen for California showed up most unfortunately. For nearly a generation California had had her own way by virtue of her claim that no one knew the Chinaman as she did, and no one's interests were primarily affected by exclusion except those of the Coast, and the Coast was "unanimous." The political ear of Congress might have listened to the Governor of California or the Mayor of San Francisco, but nobody could be either deceived or influenced by such men as James R. Dunn of the Chinese Bureau and Edward J. Livernash of the *Exam-*

iner, whose testimony constituted two-thirds of that before the Committee. The venom and falsity apparent in their statements did as much to win adherents to the milder view as all the arguments of trade and humanitarianism. Certainly if California was unanimously anti-Chinese it had chosen strange representatives.

But that the Pacific Coast was by no means unanimous was shown by the protests of the Chambers of Commerce of Portland and San Francisco and the petitions and telegrams from many other civic, commercial and religious bodies. All of them demanded in one form or another, better treatment of the exempt classes and some even the unrestricted admission of all except laborers. The California Commissioners succeeded, nevertheless, with the help of Senator Penrose of Pennsylvania, in getting the Mitchell bill favorably reported. Senator Penrose said that there were several reasons for something more than reënactment of existing law. There were in operation eight acts and innumerable and inconsistent legal and executive decisions which needed codifying and the powers of officials required definition. There was necessity for stronger measures for the prevention and detection of fraud for which purpose he advised the incorporation into the law of those strict measures of practise which had been left hitherto to Executive regulation. He admitted that the bill did not have the unqualified approval of every member of the Committee, and the subsequent debate showed that four members out of ten altogether disapproved of the bill and others did not approve its severer features.

Senator Mitchell said, that the bill—which reënacted at great length the most stringent provisions of the existing laws and Treasury regulations—was the composite work of the Coast Commissioners, the Far-Western Congressmen, the American Federation of Labor and representatives of the Departments of the Treasury and of

The Beginning of Reaction 249

justice.[18] But Senator Hanna in the course of the debate denied that any of the Treasury officials had been consulted. It was, indeed, known by this time that none of the higher Government officials, except the Commissioner of Immigration, favored the incorporation of the Treasury regulations into the law and that they were all very critical of both regulations and practice. In the debate Senator Mitchell pursued his usual course of plausible argument and reckless misstatement, concluding with a threat that if the bill was not passed, the Republican party would be overthrown in the coming elections.[19]

The bill was strongly supported by all of the representatives from the states west of the Rocky Mountains but, with the exception of Senator Penrose, Senator Fairbanks was the only Eastern man of influence to speak on its behalf. The opposition desired either the reënactment of the existing law until a new treaty should be negotiated, or its modification; and objected to the seaman's clause and the extension of the law to the Philippines. Between these widely separated groups stood a third—that objected to the Mitchell bill but thought the reënactment of the existing law insufficient.

The debate disclosed that the Californians had overreached themselves—they were both too violent and too obvious; for the time had gone by when prejudice, ignorance and political exigency could be counted on to wring from a reluctant East this special concession to the West. Too many senators had been in California and were posted on the labor conditions there. California had gone Republican in two national and two state elections and the next campaign was two years away. But more than all the trade interests of the country were involved—representatives of transportation, lumber, flour and cotton rose up and hurled into the Senate hundreds of telegrams and petitions. The voice

[18] 57th Cong. 1st Ses. (1902), *Sen. Rept.* 776, Pt. 2.
[19] 57th Cong. 1st Ses. (1902), *Record*, pp. 3654 ff.

of labor was no longer the only voice heard. What the plea of justice and the protests of the religious bodies of the country had not been able to do, the interest of commerce accomplished. The Senate called a halt in anti-Chinese legislation and discussed the testimony of John W. Foster, Ex-Secretary of State and diplomatist, who since leaving office had steadily protested against treaty violation in the guise of Treasury regulation.[20] Minister Wu Ting-Fang was praised and hotly defended for his protests and arguments on his country's behalf. The unwarranted definitions of the exempt classes, the weakness of the consular system and the corruption of minor officials by the exclusion laws were exposed. Protests culminated in a general revolt against the Mitchell bill. Perhaps the most surprising spectacle of all was the defense of Chinese Christians by Senator Quay. As the reaction gathered head, Senator Platt offered a substitute amendment substantially reënacting the existing law until a new treaty should be negotiated, which the Senate passed by a vote of seventy-six to one, only eleven not voting. The seaman's clause and the Philippine question having been thus eliminated, the Mitchell bill was indefinitely postponed and the Platt amendment substituted for the House Bill.[21]

At the end of the debate the venerable Senator Hoar, who had maintained for a generation on this question, the course of a consistent idealist, said that the bill and the debate indicated a great progress in sentiment; but he protested once more against the principle of striking against labor as labor and of legislative descrimination against any race. His solitary vote against the mildest exclusion law that could be hoped for at that time, marks how far the United States had traveled from its earlier

[20] John W. Foster, Diplomatist, Secretary of State in 1892, author of *American Diplomacy*, etc.; see argument before the Senate Com. on Immigr. Test. S. Rept. 776, pt. 2, pp. 53 ff. See also articles on same subject in Chicago *Record-Herald*, Jan. 11, 1902; *Atlantic Mo.*, 1906.
[21] April 16, 1902.

The Beginning of Reaction 251

principles, when America was the asylum of the oppressed and manhood suffrage the seal of its democracy.

As had been anticipated, the House refused to concur in a bill so much less stringent than its own and a committee of conference was appointed which finally agreed to reënact all laws in force, extending them to insular territory in so far as not inconsistent with treaty obligations. The Secretary of the Treasury was empowered to make regulations not inconsistent with the law of the land; provision was made for admission of Exposition exhibitors and their assistants; for the certification of the Chinese in the Islands and for putting in the hands of the Philippine Commission, the regulation of the Chinese resident there. As thus amended the bill was signed by the President.

Thus the pro-Chinese reaction inaugurated by the commercial and manufacturing industries of the country found expression in the refusal of Congress to enact new legislation while a treaty was pending. The favorable impression made by this unusual self-restraint and by the reorganization of the immigration service at New York, enabled the President to negotiate a commercial treaty with China on a more satisfactory basis than before.[22]

In January, 1904, the Chinese Minister at Washington denounced the immigration treaty of 1894 and the question at once arose whether, upon the expiration of this treaty and in default of a new one, the status of the Chinese would be determined by the treaty of 1880.[23] Those in Congress opposed to the Chinese at once renewed the dying agitation, picturing the vileness and slavery of Chinese laborers and the danger of "unrestricted hordes." In the House, a bill to reënact existing legislation with certain new and extreme features was

[22] Message, 1903, *Cong. Docs.* s. n. 4627, pp. xii and pp. 91–119.
[23] 58th Cong. 2d Ses. (1904), H. R. 15054 (General Deficiency), *Record*, p. 5031; p. 5037 ff.

considered and passed without reference to the Committee on Foreign Affairs. When it arrived in the Senate it encountered another atmosphere; and the bill, stripped of all except the reënactment section and the phrase " in so far as not inconsistent with treaty obligations," went back to the House and having been accepted by the conferees, became a law.

Once more the changed temper of the times had been demonstrated. The California Congressmen, in deference to their labor constituency, had repeated the traditional arguments, but nobody had paid much attention to them; knowledge of the awakened and developing power of China, and self-interest, had combined to broaden the view of the relations of China and America. Phases of self-interest and self-preservation not represented by organized labor had united to modify legislation originally directed against a single race for the benefit of a single class.

As Californians have become more homogeneous and sympathetic with the North and East, the increasingly intimate relations of society, travel and trade have widely modified the opinions of the present generation. Where, even fifteen years ago, most Californians would defend the exclusion laws and excuse the violation of treaties in the guise of Treasury regulation, the more intelligent now apologize for them and regret as well as acknowledge the persecution of the privileged classes. Even the laboring Chinese have found defenders in the housewives and farmers whose straits for lack of domestic and agricultural labor have made the virtues and the scarcity of the Chinese doubly conspicuous; and the irony of the change is emphasized by the wholesale and exasperated condemnation of their vari-colored successors.

It may be surmised that the Californians are a little tired of the Chinese question. Anti-coolie meetings have died out. In 1904, for the first time in the history of the Democratic party in California, its platform contained

The Beginning of Reaction

no Chinese plank and the Republicans dismissed it with a line. More significant still, those candidates who were loudest in the reiteration of the traditional anti-Chinese view, were among the defeated. The anti-Chinese cry no longer deceives anybody in the West; whenever a faction, a journal or a candidate raises it now-a-days, there is a general smile of intelligence and the public understands perfectly that they want something of the labor element at the next election. No sooner are California politicians and Congressmen promoted to Federal and Diplomatic positions, where they are not dependent on local constituencies, than they drop the Chinese question into the abyss devoted to the worn-out tools of practical politics.

If the Japanese-Corean agitation seems to have taken the place of the Chinese Question, it is after all a superficial demonstration confined to a class of workingmen, and reflected by political aspirants of the lower grade but ignored by the majority. From these signs it may be hoped that California has arrived at a milestone in her devious golden trail, where she may be ready to let the yellow man take his chance with all the other colors under a general immigration law which already excludes prostitutes and contract laborers, paupers, insane and imbeciles, the diseased and disorderly,—the physically and morally unfit. Certainly the time is not far off when the wave of Mongolian Know-Nothing-ism will vanish as Celtic and Teutonic Know-Nothing-ism has already vanished, on the wider horizon of international comity.

CHAPTER XV

THE TREATMENT OF THE CHINESE IN THE UNITED STATES

" Had the first white immigrants to California found themselves met by a hostile population and hostile laws; had they been beaten in the streets, robbed and plundered by superior numbers; had discriminating taxes enforced against them under the guise of law; had they been refused citizenship and their children admission to the public schools and all of them police protection; the chances are they would not have fallen in love with the people, the country, the religion or the laws."—Professor S. E. W. BECKER, 1887.

STATEMENTS OF CALIFORNIANS IN CONGRESS:

" We have sought to deal with the Chinese in a humane manner."—Senator WHITE, 1894.

" The Chinese generally have been protected from injury and insult."—Representative McGUIRE, 1894.

" Only on the verge of political campaigns have we ever been able to secure legislation . . . . . the Chinese have always been treated with kindness and charity in California."—Representative LOUD, 1893.

" We have never at any time violated any treaty."—Representative GEARY, 1893.

" In the late troubles in California a large sprinkling of whites who were attempting to drive the Chinamen out, were themselves aliens, and some of them, dissolute characters. . . . The most pestiferous anti-Chinese howlers we ever had in California, those who incited to riot, have themselves been employing Chinamen. . . . What have the Chinamen to gain by giving up their religion for a religion that produces such results?"—Representative BOWERS, 1893.

" The people of California as a people have protected the Chinese from being violently treated, except by the rough portion of the people."—Representative FARLEY, 1882.

" The Chinese in California have been protected to the full extent of the law."—Senator SARGENT, 1876.

IN earlier pages it has been pointed out that at first the Chinese suffered incidentally, but perhaps no more than some other foreigners from the greed of the American miners.[1] After the expulsion from the mining camps

---
[1] See Chapter II.

Treatment of Chinese in United States 255

of the Mexicans, the South Americans and the French, the jealousy and race prejudice of the whites was concentrated on the Chinese, resulting in the Foreign Miners License, in capitation, police and fishing taxes; and in exclusion from the ballot, the witness-stand and the public schools.[2] In addition to these discriminations there is a tally of physical persecution and intimidation, which however incomplete,[3] discloses even more the lawless and inhuman spirit of the times. It would be impossible to estimate the number of victims unrecorded, who were driven from their claims, robbed, maltreated and murdered. In a period when white men carried their lives in their hands and when justice was attained if at all, by the rope and the gun, the despised and defenseless Chinese were inevitably the prey of every lawless adventurer and criminal.

The commonest form of attack was to drive the Chinese from any claim that seemed worth a white man's picking; sporadic and individual cases are many, but at times whole mining communities rose and drove them away, sometimes with warning, more often with violence.[4] In 1858 and 1859 when the placers were beginning to be worked out in many places, there was a wide-spread movement to drive them from their claims.[5] In Shasta county the Sheriff reported to the Governor that the mob was composed almost entirely of irresponsible men from districts where the Chinese did not work in the mines.[6]

During all the time of these assaults the Chinese were

---

[2] See Chapter V.

[3] The instances cited are collated from the newspapers and from contemporary accounts by witnesses. Before the fire of 1906 in San Francisco, the *Bulletin* had an excellent index which registered 262 outrages on Chinese; which are partly reprinted in *Statements for Non-Exclusion* and in *Brooks' Brief*.

[4] *Alta*, Nov. 6, 1858; Sacramento *Union*, Aug. 21, 1854; Shasta *Courier*, Jan. 1855.

[5] Sacramento *Union*, 1858, Dec. 29, 30; 1859, Mar. 5-10; July 16,25; driven from Vallecito, Douglas Flat, Sacramento Bar, Coyote Flat, Sand Flat, Rock Creek, Spring Creek, Buckeye.

[6] Sacramento *Union*, Mar. 3, 6, 7, 1859; *Ass. Jo.* 1859, p. 401-5.

paying the customary mining license tax, and sometimes paid it twice over. One collector said that he found that nearly every Chinese company had been robbed of sums of from four to eight hundred dollars and two had suffered to the extent of fifteen thousand dollars.[7] In fact, the Chinese were so often robbed in the guise of taxation that they worked for a white company when they could, as, for instance, on the Fremont estate where each paid a dollar a month to the manager for protection.[8]

The Chinese were often cheated or failed to obtain redress because their testimony was not admitted in the courts of California against a white man. Many instances are reported where Chinese who bought or leased claims and had papers to show for them could not be heard in the courts against the white men who drove them out.[9] Occasionally are mentioned destruction of Chinese miners' cabins by dynamite and by fire but by far the largest number of outrages were plain robbery often accompanied with assault or murder. From the time of Joaquin Murietta and his band [10] the criminal and cowardly of all races preyed upon the Chinaman because he was too timid by nature to protect himself in the manner of the brutal Anglo-Saxon, and had not even the modicum of protection afforded to other foreigners under the law.[11]

Yet this gloomy catalogue of outrage does not completely and justly represent the attitude of all classes toward the Chinese during the most lawless period of

[7] Shinn, *Mining*, p. 212; Downieville *Messenger*, July 29, 1864. *Alta* Oct. 12, 1855.
[8] Mariposa *Gazette*, Apr. 30, 1862.
[9] *Alta*, Sept. 22, 1857 (from the *Volcano Ledger*); 'Sacramento *Bee*, Feb. 23, 1857.
[10] Joaquin Murietta and his band of Spanish ruffians preyed especially upon the Chinese—see Ridgeley's history of Murietta; see also *Alta*, Feb. 16, 1853, for typical instance.
[11] John S. Hittell. *Resources of Cal.*, 1863, p. 375. The *Alta* said: "That the Chinese are hardly and even cruelly used is well known." Sept. 10, 1855.

California history. While it is true that the number of Chinese robbed, maltreated, despoiled and wantonly murdered undoubtedly mounts to thousands, it is also to be remembered that in this earlier period there was, in nearly every mining community, at least a minority of law-abiding and race-respecting easterners and northerners, who occasionally rose to restore order and to protect even the Chinamen. The citizens of Long Bar, Yuba County, are more than once mentioned as defenders of the Chinese from tax collectors.[12] In '53 the white citizens of Jackson lynched a Chileno for robbing a Chinese; and a white man in the Nevada district—the first on record—was hung for killing a Chinaman.[13] In '57 a white man was sentenced to be hung for the murder of a Chinaman in Shasta County and the *Republican* said:[14] "Hundreds of Chinamen have been slaughtered in cold blood during the last five years by desperados that infest our State. The murder of Chinamen was of almost daily occurrence, yet in all this time we have heard of but two or three instances where the guilty parties have been brought to justice." On one occasion the *Alta* said that so many instances of fiendish cruelty had been practised on the Chinese that it could scarcely express regret when a Chinese, who had been attacked by white men while getting them water to drink, shot and killed one of them; and the jury did indeed, acquit the Chinaman of murder. At Bangor, two white men were lynched for a series of outrages on peaceable Chinamen [15] and Shaw reports [16] that fifty Chinese bought a claim and, being driven from it by "Pikers" from Arkansas, were brought back by the organized white community.[17]

---

[12] *Alta*, 1853, June 10; *Bulletin*, 1857, Apr. 7.
[13] *Alta*, 1853, July 29, Oct. 14.
[14] Shasta *Republican* quoted by the *Bulletin*, Dec. 18, 1856.
[15] *Alta*, 1855, May 21.
[16] Shaw, *Ramblings in California*, p. 72–6.
[17] Wells and Chambers, *Hist. of Butte County* (1857), p. 157.

As to the number of Chinese who lost their lives by violence during the first eighteen years, there is only the most fragmentary information. Homicide of white men was so common as to create slight comment unless committed under circumstances of peculiar atrocity, and the murder of Indians, Mexicans and Chinamen went almost unnoticed in mining communities. John S. Hittell recorded for the year 1855, 538 deaths by violence, of which 32 were Chinese; six were killed by tax collectors, and it was his opinion that the numbers of the colored races recorded was far too small.[18] In 1862 The Six Companies reported to the California Senate a total of 88 Chinese murdered, eleven by tax collectors.[19]

The charge of persecution did not rest on the newspapers alone but was repeated in stronger terms by foreign travelers and by the pioneers themselves. There were all shades of opinion as to the character and desirability of Chinese immigrants but only one opinion as to the undeservedly harsh treatment which they received and the discredit which this abuse reflected upon the community.[20] The Senate committee of 1862 acknowledged that there had been a wholesale system of wrong and outrage practised upon the Chinese population.[21]

It seems clear, however, that up to 1867 the abuse of the Chinese was sporadic and generally confined to the adventurous and criminal elements of the community. They had still many outspoken defenders and in San Francisco, where their services were indispensable to decent living, they were even at times actively protected from the depredations of criminals, hoodlums and the police. But the tradition that a Chinaman had no rights which white men were bound to respect was being es-

[18] Hittell, J. S., *Resources of Cal.* 1861.
[19] Rept. Joint Select Com. California *Legis. Jos.* App. 1862.
[20] Mollhausen, *Mississippi to the Pacific*, 1858; see also Auger, *Voyage en Californie*, Frignet, Lambertie, *Echo du Pacifique*, etc.
[21] Commended by the Daily *Alta* of Mar. 12, 1862. See also Beadle, Bowles, Brace, Cleveland, Townsend, Shaw, Hittell, Tuthill, Lloyd, J. Ross Brown, R. W. Raymond.

tablished; and during the years between the Civil War and the Kearney riots certain influences united to produce systematic, concerted—and ultimately, official—persecution.

From 1867 onward the attacks on the Chinese were closely associated with political campaigns and movements incidental to the growing demands and organization of white workingmen. Simultaneously with the campaigns of 1867 and 1869, in which the Democrats were drawing workingmen from their allegiance to the Union party, riots against the Chinese broke out in a number of mining counties and the first of the serious labor riots, destined to become so frequent, occurred in San Francisco.[22] A mob of several hundred men attacked 30 Chinese employed in grading, because the contractor would not dismiss them. The white foreman as well as the Chinese was beaten and seriously injured. The rioters also threatened the rope-walk and the woolen mills and of the twelve arrested, five were convicted and sentenced but all were finally released on legal technicalities.[23]

With a variation in place and details, this outbreak might serve as a type of many, culminating in those of July, 1877. The juvenile criminal element, characteristic of San Francisco and known as "hoodlums," became conspicuous from this time on. Then, as now, they roamed the streets in small gangs, committing petty depredations and making the Oriental their chosen victim. The accounts of a few months, taken at random, mention many petty outrages in the streets—pelting Chinese with stones, beating, whipping, mud-throwing, stamping and kicking, stealing vegetables and laundry from basket men, cutting the queues from their heads, and snatching ornaments from the hair of Chinese women. It was

---

[22] Sacramento *Union*, Sept. 20, 1869.
[23] *Alta*, Feb. 11, 13, 24, Mar. 5, May 12, 1867. *Bulletin*, Feb. 12 ff. and Mar. 12, 1867.

common for the Chinese immigrant to be met at the wharf with a riotous welcome. Stones, clubs, potatoes and mud were thrown at them and many were knocked down.[24] On one occasion, one hundred and fifty Chinese landing from the Sacramento boat in San Francisco, were beaten, stoned and robbed, fifty of them injured, but no arrests were made. In 1869 the abuse had become so flagrant and the police so indifferent, that a Chinese Protective Society was organized among merchants and humanitarians in San Francisco, which employed a staff of special police to patrol the city day and night and to arrest those molesting the Chinese.[25] From 1871 onward throughout the period of the Kearney agitation, no Chinaman was safe either in person or property. It was generally conceded that the Chinese were rarely the originators of a quarrel or the provokers of attack, and they rarely fought back; but they often lost their lives because of the passive obstinacy with which they resisted the demands of the robbers.

About 1870 a new criminal element began to appear among the Chinese themselves which gave deserved alarm to the white population of cities. The conflict between the police and the so-called Highbinder tongs (secret societies of blackmailers and assassins) became a cause of riot in Chinatown and a temptation to corruption and outrage among the city police. One of the most disastrous of the earlier riots of this class occurred in Los Angeles in 1871. A war between Chinese factions having broken out in the Chinese quarter, a police officer, with the help of a citizen, undertook to arrest a Chinese rioter, and the citizen was shot. The Chinese quarter

[24] *Bulletin*, June 18, 1868. Descriptions of similar occurrences are found in the *Pioneer*, March, 1855; *Alta*, Dec. 13, 1877; Sacramento *Union*, July 14, 1873. Dickerman wrote in the *Congregationalist* of Dec. 21, 1881: "They have been stoned all the way from the wharf to Chinatown until their scalps hung down the sides of their heads, the blood on the streets showed the tracks which they had pursued and they were taken from carriages unconscious and helpless."

[25] Sacramento *Union*, Nov. 27, 1869.

was adjacent to the worst portion of the city and the toughs and criminals made the Tong war a pretext for attacking the whole Chinese population. Twenty-one Chinese were killed—fifteen hung on the spot—and their quarters looted by the mob before the riot was quelled. The grand jury brought thirty-seven indictments against the rioters and scored the city officials for their insufficient defense of the peaceable Chinese. Yet eight rioters only received sentences of from two to six years.[26]

Although by this time persecution of the Chinese was common among hoodlums, foreigners and the working class, it was still unofficial; or, at any rate, winked at rather than officially practiced. But in proportion as hard times brought the adventurer and the tramp to San Francisco, and in proportion as organized labor felt its power in politics, the petty and then the higher officials found it necessary to cater to the popular antipathy. An ordinance requiring lodging-houses to provide at least five hundred cubic feet of air-space for each adult person, on penalty of imprisonment or five hundred dollars fine, was passed by the Supervisors of San Francisco in 1870, but was not generally enforced. In 1873, it was enforced in the Chinese quarters only, and the jails were so crowded that prisoners had scarcely a hundred cubic feet of air-space apiece. No pretense was made of enforcement on other nationalities and when the Chinese combined to resist the ordinance by refusing to pay the fines, the Supervisors passed three other ordinances by way of retaliation. These were aimed at the Chinese customs of wearing a queue and of sending the bodies of their dead back to China, and at their monopoly of hand-washing.[27]

But they were vetoed by Mayor Alvord as violations

[26] For full accounts of this affair from different points of view see *Bulletin*, Oct. 24; *Alta*, Oct. 25, 26; Dec. 3, 1871; Sacramento *Union*, Feb. 19, Mar. 2, Apr. 1, 1872; Bancroft, *Works*, v. 35, p. 563; *Overland Mo.* n. s. v. 7, (1886), p. 230 ff. article by P. S. Dorney.
[27] Hittell, *Resources of California*, (1874), pp. 42–6.

of the treaties with China and of the Civil Rights Act. The California Press and people generally approved the veto and many references were made in the current newspapers to the fact that these measures were intended to influence the municipal election. From Mayor Alvord's time, however, we hear no more of any official defense of the Chinese in California. The historian John S. Hittell sums up the attitude toward them just before the Kearney outbreak:

> "Riots to beat and murder Chinamen, to destroy their houses, and to drive them away from the places where they are employed, have been frequent in the State. Many public meetings have been held to fan the feeling of hatred against them into flames. . . . Arson has often been used against them and their employers. . . . Half a dozen white men have been assassinated because they employed Celestials. . . . Hundreds of farmers, miners and manufacturers would like to hire Celestials but dare not offend the anti-Chinese ruffians." [28]

The causes which produced Kearneyism have been described in an earlier chapter and it is there shown that the Chinese were the victims or at most, the precipitating element, of the lawless unreason of the mobs that terrorized California in the name of the workingman. If we follow the yellow thread through those troublous years, it seems a miracle that any Chinaman remained alive in the country. The violence of anti-Chinese feeling can only be explained by that contagion of antipathy which sets one race upon another for the most trivial cause, or no cause at all.[29] During the spring of 1876 the Chinese were driven out of many small towns and camps, their quarters burned and in almost every case one or more were injured or killed.[30]

---

[28] *Bulletin*, May 20–29; June 2–3, 1873. *Alta*, May 27, June 8, 10, 24, 25, 1873. Ordinances discussed in *The Other Side* (3d ed.), in Pomeroy's *Work of Stephen J. Field* and in *Statements for Non-Exclusion*.
[29] *Alta*, Jan. 3, 1876.
[30] Sacramento *Union*, May 1st., mob at Antioch burned Chinese quarters; May 3d, 9 Chinese killed and 7 injured, near Tehachepi Pass; June 6, riots at Carson.

In June, a violent attack was made upon them at Truckee [81] and throughout the fall and winter they were terrorized in many counties by the attacks of men and boys who seemed to be acting under orders. In February, 1877, the employers of Chinese labor at Chico, in Butte County, received a series of threatening letters, and a number of outbuildings were burned. In March, six Chinese tenant farmers or wood choppers on the Lemm ranch, were attacked, five killed and their cabins and bodies burned. The murderers were arrested by a citizens' committee and confessed to being under the orders of an executive committee of a Workingmen's Protective Association.

It was generally believed that these organizations were responsible for the outrages at many other points. The eastern and the more conservative California papers declared them to be the legitimate results of the toleration of lawlessness.[32]

Meanwhile the fires of Kearneyism were smouldering in San Francisco. For some years there had been a spasmodic eruption of anti-coolie clubs just before elections; but in 1873 a " People's Protective Alliance " was organized out of the anti-coolie clubs, the Industrial reformers, and the Workingmen's Alliance, which sent a clergyman through the state to organize branches. The pledge of membership was not to vote for any candidate for office who was not opposed to Chinese immigration.[33] In the meetings thus organized constant prophecies of riot and bloodshed were made unless the Chinese were shut out.

[81] Truckee *Republican*, June 20, 1876; Sac. *Union*, June 20 ff., *Bulletin* Sept. 27.

[32] For full account see *Alta*, Mar. 16, 17, 19, Apr. 16, 1877; Sac. *Union*, Mar. 16-19, Apr. 11; May 28; *Hist. of Butte County ;* Sacramento *Bee*, Nov. 2, 1889, gives a trustworthy account by W. J. Davis. Bancroft's narrative, *Works*, v. 35, pp. 563-83, must be taken with much caution. Five of the murderers were sentenced to long terms but were all pardoned out before half the sentenced had been served.

[33] *Alta*, May 29, 1873. The Rev. M. B. Starr was sent through the state to lecture and organize.

Under the pressure of this concentrated discontent, the political machine in San Francisco became the organ of the most irresponsible portion of the working classes. The anti-Chinese ordinances were revived and passed, with additional ones. The Chinese were arrested, for carrying vegetable baskets on the sidewalks, for discharging firecrackers, for having theatrical performances in certain hours, and for beating gongs at such performances. The cubic air and the queue and the laundry ordinances were enforced. The hoodlums demanded cigars of the Chinese peddler and then had him arrested for having unstamped cigars in his possession. The poll tax collectors stationed themselves at the Ferry landing in San Francisco and compelled the Chinese who lived in Oakland to pay their poll tax a second time. The Board of Health refused to allow them to send the bodies of their dead back to China, and at times, enforced sanitary measures in Chinatown which were not in force anywhere else in the city.[34] The Legislature in the following winter incorporated the cubic air and the exhumation ordinances into state laws.[35]

Between 1870 and 1876 other discriminations, most of which were afterward declared unconstitutional, were legalized. The Legislature imposed a penalty of not less than $1000 upon any one bringing to the Pacific Coast, Chinese or Japanese without first presenting evidence of their good character. In 1878, a law was enacted forbidding aliens debarred from citizenship to acquire title to real estate; and another withholding business licenses from the same class. San Francisco and other cities passed ordinances forbidding Chinese labor to be employed on public works of any kind; and in the creation of irrigation districts it was also forbidden.

---

[34] Brooks' *Brief*, p. 87–9; *The Other Side*, etc., (3d. ed.); Becker, *Humors of a Congressional Committee*, Oakland *News*, San Francisco *Bulletin*, *Alta*, Sacramento *Union*, Pomeroy, *Work of Field*, p. 397 ff.
[35] Cal. Stats. 1876 and 1877.

The Supervisors of San Francisco even excluded Chinese granite from use in public works.[36]

In a few cases the Chinese sued for damages, on the ground that the ordinances were class legislation or outside the power of the Supervisors; but whenever a judge decided in their favor, the decision was greeted with a storm of vilification on the part of the radical papers and the workingmen's organizations.[37] During the spring of 1877 the lawlessness of tramps and hoodlums rapidly increased in San Francisco. The better papers deprecated the attacks on the Chinese, scolded the police for inefficiency, and prophesied greater troubles,[38] but the Sand-lot speakers continued to inflame the turbulent portion of the population without hindrance. The apathetic minority of decent, cultured and Christian people, sat still and let the Chinaman be scourged until at last the storm broke over the whole city in the great riots of July, 1877.[39] In the first riot alone twenty-five wash houses were burned at a loss of twenty thousand dollars and the laundrymen fled into hiding in Chinatown. Then followed an orgy of outrage; for months afterward no Chinaman was safe from personal outrage even on the main thoroughfares and the perpetrators of the abuses were almost never interfered with so long as they did not molest white men's property. The epidemic of arson, robbery and personal abuse spread to the surrounding country. In town after town Chinese laundries and quarters were set on fire by incendiaries; and when the inmates tried to escape they were often robbed and shot

[36] Bancroft, *Hist of Cal.* vol. 19, p. 340 ff. Ordinance of Los Angeles 1889.
[37] Judge McKee, Third Dist. Ct. S. F., decided in the case of Hong Hair, a Chinese laundryman, that the laundry ordinance was "unreasonable, oppressive and void." (May, 1876). Judge Field decided that the queue ordinance was "hostile and spiteful." (Ah Kow *v.* Noonan, June, 1876). Both were subjected to great public abuse.
[38] The *Alta* said: "These hoodlum outrages are becoming disgracefully frequent. The chronicle of the week's doings records no policeman to be found at all."
[39] *Examiner*, July 24, 1877 ff.

and sometimes left to die in burning buildings. Throughout the farming districts barns, outhouses and stacks owned by men who employed Chinese were burned by tramps who made the Chinese merely a pretext for crime.[40]

The Chinese could no longer safely attend the Mission night schools in the towns and fled to the mountains and the remote country districts for work.[41] Many, especially the rich merchants who then carried on a considerable part of the trade at the port of San Francisco, went back to China, never to return. The culmination of this insane resentment was reached in a riot at Truckee in November, 1878, when the town was in a state of anarchy and the Chinese population of about 1000 persons was driven out.[42]

After two years of almost incessant agitation and riot, the citizens of California began to protect themselves from the criminal classes. The better class had been awakened by the atrocities of the Kearney period to the necessity of enforcing order; and incidentally, as a degree of order was attained, the Chinese reaped the benefit, though in a lesser degree than the rest of the population. Thereafter, race resentment took more often the form of interference with their business by boycott, by strikes compelling employers to shut them out, and by legal discrimination.

Meanwhile, placer mining had declined and been replaced by mining on a larger scale, under the control of corporations. Riots and strikes were inaugurated in the mines, ostensibly for higher wages—although wages were still far above the eastern standard—for shorter hours, and for discharge of the Chinese, although white men were generally receiving twice the pay of Chinese. The

[40] *Bulletin*, Sept. 2, 17, 18, Oct. 23, 1877; *Napa Register*, Sept. 1, 29; *Alta*, Sept. 4, 10 ff; Healdsburg *Enterprise*, Sept. 29; Merced *Express*, Apr. 24, 1878; Carson *Appeal*, Dec. 28, 1878; *Bulletin*, Jan. 29, 1878.
[41] Second An. Rept. Cal. Chinese Mission, 1877, p. 12.
[42] Truckee *Republican*, Sacramento *Union*, Nov. 20 ff., 1878.

white men were seldom American citizens; it was, in fact, an uprising of European foreigners, generally led by Irishmen, against Oriental foreigners. At the Amador mines in 1871, just before election, three hundred Irish, Italians and Americans struck; the mines began to fill with water, the Governor and militia went to the scene, and the riots at last ended in a slight increase of wages and the displacement of the Chinese.[43]

At Martinez two salmon canneries had been started with Chinese labor because white labor could not be had at reasonable rates. The Greek and Italian fishermen attacked the Chinese, injuring nine seriously, and then sailed for the fishing grounds. It appeared that the mob was accompanied and encouraged by Americans, but the sheriff and other town officials, although at home, professed to know nothing about it. The Chinese Legation complained to the Secretary of State, the Secretary rehearsed the complaint to Governor Perkins, the Governor wrote to the District Attorney, and the four persons indicted—one a county official—escaped punishment by means of legal technicalities.[44]

These two instances, selected because they are typical of many others, illustrate the two principal causes of the persistence of anti-Chinese agitation in the country districts. In San Francisco the growing power of organized labor and the excessive race feeling of the foreign—especially of the Irish—population exhibited itself in other ways. For many years the Chinese had paid on arrival at the port a so-called hospital tax, but were denied admission to the City and County Hospital. In 1881 the Consul for the Chinese applied for the admission of a sick and friendless Chinaman and was refused on the ground that the hospital was too crowded.

[43] *Alta*, June 23-7; July 7, 25, 1871. The wages of white men had been $2.25-3.50 per day, and found, for ten years; while the Chinese received $1.00-1.25.
[44] *Morning Call*, Apr. 27, May 29, June 20, July, 1, 5, 1882. Similar instances reported in *Cong. Docs.* 1891, ser. no. 2920, p. 461 ff.

The Board of Health immediately passed a resolution that all chronic incurable diseases should go to the pest-house, and under this diagnosis the Chinese had to go there, no matter what their disease. Yet foreigners of every other nationality, even with tuberculosis or syphilis, were freely admitted, and are still. A few years later the Chinese colony raised $75,000 for a Chinese hospital and had let the contract for it, when the Board of Supervisors refused to allow them to have a hospital run by Chinese managers and physicians.[45]

One of the few things which all Californians admit in favor of the Chinese is their commercial honor. Many bankers and tradesmen, and even lawyers and customs officials, had been accustomed to accept the personal word or bond of Chinese merchants. For fifteen years prior to the Kearney period, bonds, stock in trade, and personal effects had been accepted by the Collector of the Port of San Francisco as security for the Chinese tobacco manufacturers. In 1879 Collector Higby, newly appointed, and instigated by the cigar-makers' union, insisted on real estate security. As the Chinese seldom invest in land in the United States, the result was that fifteen factories went out of business and the rest employed professional bondsmen who were notoriously much less trustworthy than Chinese merchants. The order of the Collector was ultimately rescinded by Commissioner Raum.[46]

Outside of their own quarters in the cities of California the Chinese have carried on only two lines of business to any considerable extent, *i. e.*, truck gardening and washing. The laundries were most frequently attacked and it has been necessary until within a few years for

---

[45] *Alta*, Nov. 20, 1881; test. of F. A. Bee, ser. no. 2890, *Cong. Docs.* p. 400. In Shasta County the county physician admitted one Chinaman to the County Hospital in 1869; when he was criticised for it he said that the Chinese had paid nearly 25% of all the money paid into the hospital fund in eight years. Shasta *Courier*, Feb. 6, 1869.

[46] *Cong. Docs.* 1879, ser no. 1902, p. 237-242.

every laundry to be barricaded against hoodlums with wire netting and bars until it looked like a prison. Official persecution generally took the form of declaring hand laundries a public nuisance and enforcing the prohibition on the Chinese wash houses regardless of the fact that the French laundries of the poorer class were quite as unsanitary and that the owner of the Chinese premises was a white man. In the months just before the passage of the first restriction law there was a general movement throughout the state to boycott the Chinese laundries and vegetable peddlers and dealers in handmade Chinese shoes.[47]

From this review of the treatment of the Chinese in California before the Restriction law was passed, it appears that as regards abuse it was divided into three fairly marked periods. The first when the Chinese, along with the French, the Mexicans, the South Americans and the Indians, were driven from the better placers by the Americans, who intended to keep the mines for the native-born or at any rate for Caucasians. The second, when the Chinese had become indispensable in towns and camps for their menial services and when they were squeezed by taxation and maltreated whenever they got in the way. The third, from 1867 to 1882, when the increase of the white foreign-born and of organized laborers put the Chinese at the mercy both of politicians and workingmen, while the general lawlessness of a period of economic upheaval let loose the worst elements of society to vent their race antipathies on the Chinese. During this period both political parties became more and more subservient to the labor element and the better class of citizens were indifferent or afraid to interfere.[48]

A minor cause of anti-Chinese movements was undoubtedly the large proportion of Irish among the for-

[47] *Alta*, July, 1882; Riverside *Press*, Apr. 15, May 6, 13, 20; July 8 Dennis Kearney was stumping the state for Governor Stoneman at this time.
[48] *Argonaut*, Dec. 26, 1885.

eign-born. Not only in California but elsewhere in the larger cities they have shown violent antipathy to the darker races, and have brought with them from Ireland the tradition of turbulency. The Irish immigrant has been a conspicuous factor in American politics; and in the second, if not in the first, generation has been a leading element as well in organizations of labor.[49] In California from 1870 to 1890 the Irish constituted from one-fourth to one-sixth of the foreign-born, and a far larger proportion in the active business of politics. The preponderance of Irish names in the leadership of mobs, anti-coolie clubs, persons arrested for attacks upon the Chinese, and also among legislators and municipal officers, bears witness to the rapidity of their assimilation—but it was a great misfortune to the Chinaman. The enforcement of anti-Chinese legislation before 1882 by state officers and the administration of the exclusion laws since that time, has also been largely in the hands of men of Irish birth or parentage.[50]

Before the passage of the Restriction law of 1882 the Federal Government was not unaware of the injuries and discriminations practised against the Chinese in the West;[51] and Minister Seward, in reply to a protest from the Yamen, assured them of the benevolence of his government and urged China to establish a Legation at Washington and a Consulate at San Francisco.[52] The Legation and the Consulate were established during the Kearney period and they became the conventional channels through which all complaints reached the President. When the treaty of 1880 was negotiated the Chinese Commissioners laid especial emphasis upon Article Three guaranteeing protection to Chinese immigrants. But the

[49] Ripley, *Atlan. Mo.*, v. 93, Race in the Labor Unions.
[50] During the earlier years of California history, it was generally accepted that the Irish led in Chinese persecution and though recently denied, there can be no question of the fact. See Hittell, John S., *Resources of California*, (1874.)
[51] *Cong. Docs.* (1868), s. n. 1364, Secretary Seward to J. Ross Brown.
[52] *Cong. Docs.* (1876), s. n. 1741, p. 57 ff.

Treatment of Chinese in United States

general government was powerless to prevent local discrimination and abuse perpetrated under state and municipal laws, although the Senate might and did promise protection. The anomaly has thus been presented, again and again, of a federal treaty habitually violated by states and territories for which neither redress nor adequate indemnity has ever been given.

The first Chinese diplomats sent to this country repeatedly invoked the treaty in an appeal for justice and were told in a variety of polite and evasive phrases, that the United States recognized its obligations but could not interfere with the internal government of states, and must therefore refer them to the courts.

After the Denver riots of 1880 in which without any provocation, one Chinese was killed, many injured and at least twenty thousand dollars worth of property destroyed, Minister Chen Lan Pin appealed to Secretary Evarts for compensation on the ground that the Chinese residents of Denver had been made a special object of persecution by the mob and that they came to this country under a treaty with the government of the United States, and not with the state of Colorado.[58] Secretary Blaine replied that the local authorities had done all that could be expected and the Chinese had the same protection as American citizens.

The year 1885 was marked by violent outbreaks against the Chinese in the territories. At Rock Springs, Wyoming, the Chinese were attacked, not because they were working for lower wages but because they would not join in a strike. Twenty-eight were killed, a number injured, and property to the amount of one hundred and forty-eight thousand dollars destroyed. The claim for indemnity, made by Minister Cheng Tsao Ju to Secretary Bayard, is one of the most dignified, discriminating and logical documents ever presented by a Chinese dip-

[58] *Cong. Docs.* (1880), ser. no. 2009, p. 318 ff.

lomat before the time of the brilliant Minister Wu.[54] He pointed out that this had occurred in a territory—not a state—under Federal control, and asked that the murderers and robbers be brought to punishment, the Chinese victims fully indemnified and measures for future protection of the Chinese be taken.

He argued not merely on the ground of treaty engagements, but of reciprocal kindness and moral principle. He recounted the fact that the Chinese had in a number of cases indemnified American citizens in China and that China in 1858 had paid for loss of life and property the sum of seven hundred and thirty-five thousand dollars without regard to treaty construction or examination of claims. It had been the constant practice of the representatives of the United States to insist on indemnification for almost all conceivable losses and upon the punishment of offenders. He could not believe that the United States had required of China what it would not do.[55]

In 1886 Secretary Bayard, while admitting privately to the American Minister in China the "shocking and inhuman character" of the treatment of the Chinese in the United States, assured the Yamen that maltreatment of Chinese subjects in the United States was the exception and not the rule.[56] When the City Government of San Francisco threatened to remove the Chinese from their quarter to a locality outside the city he referred the Chinese Minister to the courts. Minister Pung Kwang Ju replied that many of the Chinese were poor and friendless and unable to maintain their rights by means of expensive litigation in the courts. He said that the assurances of the American commissioners and the language of the treaty itself justified the Imperial

[54] *Cong. Docs.* (1886), ser. no. 2460, pp. 154 ff.
[55] For full correspondence concerning the Rock Springs affair see *Cong. Docs.* (1885), s. n. 2368, p. 187 ff; s. n. 2460, p. 101-140, s. n. 2379, p. 1223 ff.
[56] *Cong. Docs.* (1886), s. n. 2532, p. 159 ff; s. n. 2460, p. 75 ff.

Government in expecting some active measures of protection.[57]

The Rock Springs massacre seemed to inflame the working classes in the territory of Washington and in Oregon as well. The Chinese were driven from Tacoma and would have been excluded from Seattle but for the prompt protection afforded by the sheriff and leading citizens. The Federal Government was asked by the state authorities to interfere and the President demonstrated that the general government could maintain order and give a degree of protection if it cared to do so.

Aside from such exceptional instances, however, the Chinese were compelled to seek redress through the courts and by indemnity. The lower courts sympathized to a great degree with the strong anti-Chinese feeling of the common people, but unfavorable decisions appealed to the higher courts were often reversed. This was so expensive that only a few Chinese, comparatively, of all those entitled to a hearing ever made use of this recourse, to which successive Secretaries of State referred them. When, in the case of severe losses from boycott, the courts awarded damages, it was often found as at Butte, Montana, that the rioters had no property.[58]

On the question of indemnity there was a fundamental difference of opinion as to the proper interpretation of treaty obligations. The Chinese Minister and Foreign Office pointed to Article Three of the treaty of 1880 as having been understood and intended to afford special protection to the resident Chinese, in return for which China had agreed to the limitation of the immigration of laborers. When the Chinese Ministers quoted this

[57] *Cong Docs.* (1890), s. n. 2830, p. 219–26.
[58] At Butte, Montana, the Labor Unions organized a systematic boycott against the Chinese; but the boycotters were insolvent. When the Chinese Minister asked for indemnity the Secretary replied that the rights of Chinese subjects had been violated but that an adequate remedy would have been afforded by the courts if they had applied promptly, and therefore the United States Government was not responsible. *Cong. Docs.* ser. no. 4268, (1901), p. 100 ff.

guarantee, the Secretaries of State always pointed out that the Constitution of the United States did not permit the Federal Government to interfere to maintain order within the states, except at their request; and that the treaty gave the same protection and recourse to the Chinese as to American citizens. The Chinese must, therefore, appeal to local authorities and to the courts.

Without pursuing the legal technicalities of this interpretation, there are two considerations which seem to bear directly on the justice of the Chinese contention. For many years American traders and missionaries in China who had been subject to mob violence and to individual injury and loss of property and life had been under a similar guarantee of protection from the Chinese government. The missionaries had, however, often gone to localities in the interior where no guarantee of protection was given—but, having suffered there, the United States Government nevertheless claimed and received compensation for their losses. The situation was identical in all essential features, yet China neither quibbled over treaty obligations nor refused to pay fully for all such damage. The total sum paid by the Chinese government for the lives and property lost—far less in number and in value than that suffered by the Chinese in the United States—has amounted to more than a million dollars.[59] In the second place if such guarantees of protection had been negotiated between England, France or Germany and the United States, and if such atrocities and losses had occurred to their unnaturalized citizens resident here, any of these countries would unquestionably have demanded and received compensation; if, indeed, the Federal government would not have interfered with the states to protect them.

That the Federal government possessed a degree of power which it has not exercised in the case of China,

---

[59] See instances in *Cong. Docs.* ser. no. 2532 (1886), p. 159, p. 177; Marquis Tseng, in *China, The Sleep and The Awakening*, p. 199.

was demonstrated not only by President Cleveland in the case of the Seattle riots, but later by President Roosevelt in the Japanese school case in San Francisco. The fact that, in this latter case, the interference took the form of moral intimidation—exercised by the President upon a local school board and a state legislature—makes it no less significant as showing what might have been done to protect the Chinese. The difference of treatment was due not to any superiority of treaty rights of the Japanese over the Chinese but to the fact that Japan has proved her military prowess and the President of the United States deemed it prudent therefore to show a just regard for treaty rights.

After the exclusion law was passed, the persecution of the Chinese might have been expected to die out; and certainly the traditional forms of physical persecution should have become less and less frequent. Yet within five years Chinese of San Francisco have been stoned in the streets, have been arrested and held to pay all the fines of themselves and their white companions; fined for gambling and prostitution while white establishments close by flourished without molestation under police protection; fined for sanitary nuisances while the Italian quarter, no less bad, received no attention; and have been denied the right to buy or lease property outside the Chinese quarter. In the country districts of California they have had their ears and their queues cut off, their cabins burned, their property stolen and destroyed without being able to secure protection or redress. The tradition that a Chinaman has no rights is dying, but it is certainly by no means dead.[60]

Throughout these years, while the Chinese have suffered and protested in vain, it has been the habit of the Pacific Coast Congressmen, when they were urging some new legislation against the Chinese to please their labor

[60] All these and many other petty instances are within the personal knowledge of the writer and are by no means unusual.

constituents, to assure skeptical Easterners that the Chinese were treated and always had been treated "with kindness and charity," or at least as well as other foreigners. Yet since 1855 no other class of foreigners on the Pacific Coast has such a roll of outrage, robbery or murder to show, as the Chinese. If this be kindness and charity on the Coast, what would persecution be?

To the Occidental mind the most inexplicable thing about the Chinese people in the United States has been their failure to retaliate. Yet that after all, is most characteristic. Bred in a philosophy that looks upon war as a despicable occupation, they have been accustomed to settle difficulties by arbitration and to accept and give compensation for injury. The whole theory of American law and justice was foreign to them. Being slow to learn the English language, and not having the right to testify in the courts of California till after 1870, they settled petty cases of trouble among themselves by arbitration; and in larger matters they were either afraid or too ignorant of our courts to attempt to protect themselves or to obtain redress by law. Moreover, the minor officials of justice were all political appointees in sympathy with the laboring class and often of the nationality —the Irish—that persecuted them most. The Chinese were too intelligent to expect redress from courts whose officers were the representatives of their enemies, and the poorer class could not afford the expense even if they were not afraid.

Since the Exclusion laws, the Chinese have brought test cases to obtain their rights, the expense of which has been subscribed to by their countrymen. The Chinese government, the natural protector of its subjects, did not approve of emigration and was besides, immersed in political and military struggles which left no room for attention to the welfare of a few stray emigrants. Not until China began to seek a place in the rank of Western nations did the treatment of her wandering sons become a matter of importance. Since that time, the accumulated bitterness of returning immigrants who have told the story of their treatment abroad, has influenced the minds of Chinese statesmen and produced a reaction and a spirit of retaliation, the results of which are not yet fully comprehended.

CHAPTER XVI

THE CHINESE PROTEST

"I must find, however, that under the peculiar nature and language of these laws it is not possible to recognize the appeal to the consideration of elementary justice and humanity (even if well-founded) or to bring the case within the scope of an act of executive clemency. The Chinese exclusion laws are necessarily rigorous and of the highest degree of technicality, and do not permit the imposition of maxims of equity, which command judicial authorities to search with scrupulous care for a way to do justice when the technicalities of the law present obstructions."—Opinion of Attorney-General KNOX, 1902.

"The situation . . . is equally unsatisfactory to administrative officers and to Chinese aliens of the exempt classes; to the former because the certificate, though correct in form, is no guarantee that the holder can be admitted without violation of law; to the latter because it does not assure him that he will not be turned back after his journey of thousands of miles."—FRANK P. SARGENT, Commissioner-General of Immigration, 1906.

"No one need be surprised at these abuses. . . . So completely are these safeguards of human liberty withdrawn that if you, Sir, landed in San Francisco on a Pacific liner and had an enemy sufficiently virulent and of sufficient influence with some inspector, you could be deported as a Chinese and would find yourself utterly powerless to protect yourself or to make proof to the contrary. It is a most vicious system, and if it had been planned to foster a system of infamous blackmail, criminal ingenuity could have added nothing further to it."—JOHN P. IRISH, Naval Officer of Customs, San Francisco.

AT the time that the first exclusion law was passed only simple experiments had been made even at Atlantic ports in excluding undesirable aliens; and there was no body of trained officers and interpreters and no bureaucratic machinery with which to enforce the new law on the Pacific Coast. The work of putting in operation a statute new in principle and, as it proved, badly drawn, was thrust upon the heads of departments wholly without experience and already fully occupied with other duties. Even the money necessary to enforce the law was not forthcoming, for Congress appropriated only meagre sums for Chinese exclusion during the first six years.[1]

The enforcement of the exclusion laws was originally vested in the office of the Secretary of the Treasury. At first the division of Customs, later the division of Special Agents, was invested with general supervisory powers, but the various details of administration remained in the hands of the Collectors of Customs. In 1900 Congress transferred the administration of the Exclusion laws to the Commissioner-General of Immigration. In 1903 the whole immigration service and its officers was transferred to the newly-organized Bureau of Commerce and Labor, leaving the enforcement of the Chinese exclusion laws as before in the hands of the Commissioner-General of Immigration but subject to the Secretary of Commerce and Labor.[2] During a period of twelve years there were three Secretaries of the Treasury, two Commissioners of Immigration, a Secretary of Commerce and Labor, Collectors of the Port at San Francisco and a Supervisory Agent or two concerned in the administration of the laws. There were other officers, of course, at stations on the borders and in the interior, but since three-fourths of all the Chinese came and went through the port of San Francisco, and half of the remainder through other Pacific ports, the administration of the law is relatively unimportant except at these places.[3]

In the enforcement of an alien exclusion law a certain amount of hardship to the alien is necessarily involved and the officials charged with it are therefore always liable to the accusation of bias and cruelty. In the case of Chinese laborers the first and greatest in-

[1] Appropriations 1882-9 about $35,000; in 1889, $250,000; in 1889-1893, $340,000.
[2] H. R. 647, 1906, p. 5. U. S. *Stat.* 27, p. 251; 31 *Stat.*, pp. 588-611; 32 *Stat.* p. 825.
[3] In 1906 the Pacific Coast ports were: San Francisco, Portland, Port Townsend, Sumas, Wash., and San Diego, Cal. The other continental ports were: Malone, N. Y., Portal, N. D., Richford, Vt., Boston, New York, New Orleans, and Tampa, Fla.

justice suffered was due not to administrative methods but to the law itself. The Scott Act invalidated at least 20,000 return certificates held by laborers who had left the country with the promise to the United States that they might return. Very few had families in this country, but the majority probably had debts owing them or small shares in various business ventures, and all by accepting the certificate showed intention to return. It is the highest ambition of a Chinese laborer in the United States to become a member of a firm and it is the Chinese custom to build up small businesses by means of co-operation, each member of the firm having from two hundred to a thousand dollars invested and the management being delegated to several active members. Before the Restriction Act of 1882, many laborers had savings so invested and went on laboring from year to year and putting their capital in laundries, vegetable gardens and small dry-goods and produce stores. Some thousands of those shut out by the Scott Act had such investments and the inconvenience and loss resulting are impossible to estimate.

Aside from this hardship and injustice, there have been many others suffered by registered laborers, arising from the defects of the law and the severity of official regulation; but since even a perfect law impartially enforced would have involved some individual inconvenience, and since the principle of exclusion of laborers was acquiesced in by the Chinese Government, these might be regarded as incidental to the enforcement of the law. Only such instances have been selected, therefore, as seem to indicate serious defects in the system or a wilful neglect or bias on the part of immigration officers, producing unnecessary suffering.

With regard to classes of Chinese other than laborers, however, the United States government and its immigration officers were bound, both by treaties and express legislation, to treat them with the consideration shown

The Chinese Protest 281

to the citizens of the most favored nations. If the officials of the United States were so ignorant, so prejudiced or so incompetent as not to discriminate between laborers and the privileged classes, or if they treated the exempt classes with discourtesy; or even merely with a severity greater than was requisite to the enforcement of the exclusion of laborers, the Chinese government had just cause for complaint. In fulfilment of the international agreement the Chinese government was under a negative obligation not to encourage or abet the emigration of Chinese laborers to the United States; while the United States, in excluding them, put herself under a positive obligation to inflict no unnecessary hardship on laborers and, at the same time, to treat the exempt classes with the same courtesy shown to other nationalities. If the United States undertook to do an impossible thing, China could justly say that the restriction law had been made at the request of America for her own benefit and it was therefore for her to devise the necessary methods. China was not responsible if she were unequal to the task.

It would certainly not be just or conclusive to judge the expediency of the law or its results from the first ten years of experimentation. The irritating and almost insuperable difficulties under which the officials from the Secretary of the Treasury down labored have been sufficiently described in the chapters given to the history of federal legislation and treaties. But by the time the McCreary Amendment had been passed, fair appropriations secured, and a general system of registration organized, there should have been at least a small number of men competent to enforce the law reasonably.

Yet it will appear in the present chapter that in proportion as money was available and departmental regulations devised, the resentment of the Chinese Government and the indignation of the intelligent Chinese in this country steadily increased until it found trenchant expression in the diplomatic remonstrances of Minister Wu

Ting Fang in 1901. These complaints were politely evaded by the State Department and, although widely quoted and corroborated by the independent newspapers, were ignored by the immigration officials or met with denial and counter charges of fraud and misrepresentation. The boycott of American trade in 1905, occurring simultaneously with a pro-Chinese reaction in the United States, finally compelled the Commissioner of Immigration to defend the administration of the law. The contentions of Minister Wu and the defense of the Commissioner of Immigration refer almost without exception to the so-called period of Treasury regulation after 1894. The statistics and illustrations which follow will, therefore, be confined to this period.[4]

The adverse criticisms of the law made by Minister Wu Ting Fang concern chiefly the treatment of the admitted classes and are directed against the hardships arising through excessively strict interpretations of treaties and legislation, and against regulations devised by the Treasury department which made admission unduly difficult. The first related to questions of principle, determined by appeal to the Judicial department of the government; the second to methods from which there was no appeal except to the Secretary of the Treasury.[5]

In relation to the exempt classes the first and most important question of principle which arose was over their being limited to the occupations specifically named in the treaty of 1880. Up to 1898 the treaty and the restriction acts had been loosely interpreted to admit all classes except skilled and unskilled laborers. Although the practice had not been uniform and consistent, the principle that only laborers were excluded had been

[4] The papers of the Chinese Minister are in *Cong. Docs.* (1981-2), s. n. 4268 and s. n. 4440. The defense of the Immigration Commissioner is in *Cong. Docs.* (1906), s. n. 4990 and the annual reports of the Department.
[5] 21 Op. Attorney-General, 68

recognized and substantially followed for sixteen years.[6] In 1898, however, Attorney-General Griggs ruled that the true theory was "not that all Chinese persons may enter this country who are not forbidden, but that only those are entitled to enter who are expressly allowed," and even then, only upon compliance with the requirements of the laws, the treaty and the regulations. The Secretary of the Treasury at once made a regulation denying admission to salesmen, clerks, buyers, bookkeepers, accountants, managers, storekeepers, apprentices, agents, cashiers, physicians, proprietors of restaurants, etc.[7]

When the Chinese Minister protested against this ruling Secretary Hay replied that while treaty obligations were to be regarded as a sacred compact, and to be sustained if possible, they did not contain the ultimate decision of the question; and that the reversal of the previous view had been determined upon after careful consideration of all the facts and all the law in the case.[8] Although this is still the theory of the government, very strong arguments have been made against it by excellent authorities, not only on the ground that it is a violation of treaty but that it is not even borne out by the opinion of the Attorney-General on which it was originally founded.[9]

This narrowing of the exempt classes produced some curious inconsistencies. In 1899, the Secretary of the Treasury ruled out ministers, preachers, and missionaries, and under this ruling a Chinese who had entered the United States as a divinity student, was arrested as soon as he began to preach. The Court sustained the contention that he was a "laborer" under the law and he

---

[6] *Regs.* of 1893, series 7, no. 18, Int. Rev., Op. Secretary Carlisle; *Regs.* of 1896, Op. of Acting Secretary C. S. Hamlin.
22 Op. Attorney-General, p. 132; also Regulations, 1903, Rule 2.
[8] *Cong. Docs.* 1899, s. n. 3898, pp. 197-200.
[9] For full and very important legal discussion of this point see article by Max. J. Kohler in *Am. Jo. Asiatic Assoc.* Mar. 1906.

was deported.[10] A similar instance was that of a Chinese Professor who had passed his examinations and was a mandarin of the lower order, who came to the United States as a teacher; while here he taught only a few children but spent most of his time translating and editing copy for a paper. He went back to China to take higher examinations and when he returned to the United States was detained and ordered deported on the ground that he was an editor and that an editor was a laborer. The Secretary of the Treasury, by a special ruling, finally permitted him to land.

Not only did the strict limitation of exempts to five classes obviously exclude bankers, brokers, traders, agents of commercial houses, doctors, lawyers, farmers, engineers, priests, clerks and scholars—" and the countless avocations bordering on manual labor ", as Commissioner Sargeant seriously put it [11]—but the courts added many other occupations to the list. Gamblers, prostitutes, and criminals convicted of felony; bookkeepers, tailors and cooks (even if members of a restaurant firm); boarding-house keepers, laundrymen, peddlers; missionaries and preachers—if they were Chinese—all became " laborers " under the rule.

The principle of limitation of classes was carried still further by Treasury definition. In the regulations of 1900 a student was defined to be: (a) one who intends to pursue some of the higher branches of study or seeks to be fitted for some particular profession or occupation, (b) for which facilities are not afforded in his own country, (c) for whose support and maintenance in this country provision has been made, and (d) who upon completion of his studies, expects to return to China.[12]

At the time of the passage of the first restriction law there were 108 Chinese studying in the eastern schools

---

[10] Case of Wah Sang, 1905.
[11] An. Rept. 1905, p. 80.
[12] *Regs.* 1900, p. 351, based on Op. Solicitor of Treasury, June 15.

The Chinese Protest 285

and colleges of the United States to prepare themselves for the Chinese government service.[13] For some years after this the word "student" was construed to admit youths to study in the secondary schools who were evidently not of the laboring class; but the officials were not favorable to the admission of adult students.[14]

Up to 1900 every applicant, even wives and minor children of merchants, was required to have his own certificate. Not being able to comply with this regulation wives were generally excluded and minor children when admitted came in as students. When the Supreme Court in the Gue Lim case, declared the principle that Chinese minor children of merchants needed no independent certificate, the term student obviously called for a stricter definition. From that time onward the student class was restricted to post-graduate students in a few subjects who must return to China upon the completion of their work.[15]

This severe construction resulted in some peculiarly difficult situations. A Chinese boy of sixteen, son of a merchant at Shanghai with a certificate viséd by the United States Consul-General, and vouched for by the Consul-General at New York as a bona fide student, was obliged to return to China because his certificate stated that he came "to study the English language", this being neither a higher branch nor a profession.[16] A similar case in 1900 was that of a boy of fifteen with perfectly correct papers, who was refused landing at Honolulu whither he went to enter a high-class school for Chinese-Americans kept by American Missionaries. But on appeal to the Secretary of the Treasury, the decision was reversed and the boy landed, although as a

[13] Twing, *Scribner's Mag.* (o. s.) v. 20, p. 450.
[14] Case of Wong Hay, 1899, ruling of Mr. Spaulding; Case of Li Ip, Op. of Mr. O'Connell, Solicitor of the Treasury.
[15] Case of Yip Wah, 1900, *Cong. Docs.* ser. no. 4268, p. 59; also Test. of John W. Foster, *Cong. Docs.* 1901-2, ser. no. 4265, p. 46.
[16] U. S. *v.* Mrs. Gue Lim, 176 *U. S.* 459, 462-3, 467; Chew Hong *v.* U. S., 112 *U. S.* 563, 642-3; U. S. *v.* Jung Ah Lung, 124 *U. S.* 621.

student, he did not meet the requirements of the Treasury definition in two particulars.[17]

To what extent the Treasury definition acted as a check upon the immigration of the student class, cannot be known. Although the excuse offered by the Commissioner-General of Immigration for the stricter definition was "wholesale evasion", the exact number of students applying, and admitted or debarred before 1903 is not known. During the fiscal years 1903-5 out of 128 students, 116 were admitted and 12 denied—several of them under the provisions of the general law excluding contagious diseases, and the rest because their own testimony and personal appearance showed that their certificates were fraudulent.[18] This certainly does not justify the charge of wholesale evasion.

From this outline of the treatment of students, it appears that the interpretation of the law was vacillating; while as to definition the officials appear to have jumped suddenly from a very broad to a very narrow construction without reference either to the natural meaning of the word student, or the legitimate reading of the treaty. Concerning the definition of 1900 Minister Denby said that China had many colleges and many thousand students, but all her knowledge had never taught her the meaning of the word.[19] Wu Ting-Fang in his memorable protest against the reënactment of the exclusion laws wrote: "It would sound strange to read in a dictionary of the English language the only definition of a student to be 'one who pursues a super-graduate course and is provided in advance with a competency'."[20]

That the construction placed upon the word student from 1900 to 1905 went beyond the meaning of the

[17] *Cong. Docs.* 1901, ser. no. 4268, p. 73, case of Tong Tseng.
[18] Case of Liang Tu, May 1905, debarred for trachoma; *Cong. Docs.* 1906, ser. no. 4990, H. R. 847, pp. 57-8.
[19] *Forum*, v. 34, p. 132.
[20] *Cong. Docs.* 1901, ser. no. 4268, p. 81.

treaty of 1880 is evident,—the exclusion laws have repeatedly done that—but in this case the immigration officials acknowledged that it is comparatively easy to distinguish a student from a laborer; and they have further tacitly yielded to the protests by modifying and finally dropping the definition.[21] Under the administration of Mr. Oscar Straus, the new Secretary of Commerce and Labor, an entirely new and far more reasonable definition has been devised.

The right of transit had been enjoyed equally by all Chinese persons under the treaty of 1880. Few instances either of abuse or complaint arose until the period of Treasury regulation. In the years following 1888 an increasing number of the excluded classes applied for transit to ports in Mexico not far from the border of the United States and, as there was small demand in that region for cheap labor, it was inferred that they intended to come back surreptitiously into the United States. Upon this representation Secretary Windom refused to allow Chinese to pass through San Francisco to Mexican ports.[22] An elaborate system of identification was devised and soon afterward applied to all Chinese in transit. By the treaty of 1894 the right of transit was specifically guaranteed to all Chinese laborers in transit, but about 1900 the privilege was limited in various ways. At first Chinese laborers in transit had to have a through ticket across the whole territory and a bond of five hundred dollars each was required for their departure within twenty days; but by 1905 the rule had been elaborated to apply to Chinese *persons* (apparently including the exempt classes); the officer could demand any proof he chose to ask that the transit was in good faith—which included a photograph in triplicate—and if

---

[21] Secretary Metcalf said the rule was dropped because it "had been attacked as a narrow construction of the treaty and laws."
[22] Secretary Foster changed this order so as to allow Chinese in transit to go through to places south of Salina Cruz.

the traveler was not of the exempt class, an examination of the person by the Bertillon system.[23]

Up to 1901 about 37,000 Chinese in transit are known to have passed through the United States—an average of two thousand per year—and it was said that none had ever been denied.

The precise number in recent years is as follows:—

NUMBER OF CHINESE IN TRANSIT, 1901-1906.[24]

Year.	Passed through San Francisco.	Passed through Malone.	Total transits across U. S.	Rejected.
(25) Before 1901............			37,000	None
Year ended June 30, 1901.	3439	376		
" " " " 1902.	1958	694		
" " " " 1903.	1755	311	2493	95
" " " " 1904.	2090	252	3050	31
" " " " 1905.	1187	335	741	2
" " " " 1906.			611	5

In the latter half of 1901 out of 1000 transits 200 were suddenly denied landing.[26] This change of policy was suggested and inaugurated by James R. Dunn, Inspector in Charge at San Francisco, who suddenly began to examine minutely the baggage and persons of all transits. Of 107 arriving in July, 51 sought transit by rail under bond with tickets through to Mexico. Eleven of these were refused on the ground, either that they did not intend to make Mexico their ultimate destination or that they had been residents of the United States, were unable to enter the United States by lawful means, and had friends, acquaintances and business expectations only

[23] Regulations governing Chinese in transit, Dec. 8, 1900 are accessible in *Sen. Doc.* 776, pt. 2, pp. 189-192; *Regs.* 1902, Rule 69; *Regs.* 1903, Rules 14 & 44; *Regs.* 1905, Rule 39; *Regs.* 1906, Rule 42 a.
[24] Figures taken from H. R. 847, and from *An. Repts. of Com. of Immig.*
[25] Statement of Maxwell Evarts in *Sen. Doc.* 776, pt. 2, 1900.
[26] Annual Rept. of Com.-General of Immigration.

in this country and not in Mexico. A resumé of the evidence shows that four spoke English and had undoubtedly been in the United States before; six had American watches, knives and clothing on their persons and papers containing American addresses, and knew little or nothing about the places in Mexico to which they were booked; and one was a boy of twelve traveling with his uncle.[27]

In August, out of 98 transits, 20 were denied landing for similar reasons.[28] The Treasury department sustained the decision of the inspector and the Chinese appealed to the Supreme Court which ruled that the decision of the Secretary of the Treasury was final under the law.[29]

That the immigration officials were justified in their conclusion that the right of transit was being used by the excluded classes to gain admission and in devising means to prevent it, is unquestionable; but the methods employed were as unquestionably ill-judged besides violating the treaty. The transit regulations were published as applying to " all Chinese persons ", without discrimination between the two general classes entitled to transit privileges. That the Immigration officers soon became aware of this is suggested by the apologetic tone of the report of the Commissioner-General for 1906, and the change in the regulations.[30]

The change was precipitated by the unfortunate instance of four students, subjects of China, detained in transit from England at the port of Boston because they had no Section-Six certificates, no photographs and no one to give bonds for them. The Secretary of Commerce defended the action of the Boston inspector but the rule was afterward altered to read: " No Chinese person who shall satisfy the officer in charge that he is

[27] *Cong. Docs.* 1906, ser. no. 4990, H. R. 847, p. 80 ff.
[28] H. Rept. 847 (1906), pp. 86–9.
[29] Fok Young Yo case, 85 *U. S.* 296. *In re* Lee Gon Yung.
[30] *An. Rept.* 1906, p. 92.

other than a laborer (although not supplied with a Section-Six certificate) shall be required to comply with the rules which require transits to submit photographs or to be measured." [31]

But the severest criticism to which the Chinese Bureau has ever been subjected, arose from the treatment of the Chinese exhibitors at the Louisiana Purchase Exposition of 1904. No formal regulations had ever been issued before this time by the Treasury Department to insure the departure of those admitted to take part in such exhibitions. The Collectors of ports had been instructed to require proof that the persons claiming to be exhibitors held concessions and required the number of employes they brought in and would take them out òf the country within six months after the close of the fair. The collector made a slight description of exhibitors and employes to identify them and they were required to report to an officer of the department stationed at the fair ground. As to the total numbers admitted for the Omaha and Atlanta fairs, no statistics are available but in defending their action in 1904, the officials declared that 360 of those admitted for the Omaha fair " disappeared " and that of several hundred admitted to Atlanta the department had no assurance of their departure.

Chinese merchants and travelers could be admitted without special provision under a Section-Six certificate —a certificate from the Chinese Government in the English language, describing the holder so definitely as to secure his identification, and viséd by the United States consular officer. But in order to permit the exhibitors of all nationalities to bring in the necessary laborers for their concessions, both the contract labor law and the Chinese exclusion law were waived temporarily. The admission of these employes was, however, under such rules as the Secretary of the Treasury might prescribe.[32]

[31] *Cong. Docs.* 1906, ser. no. 4990, *H. Doc.* 847, pp. 134–6.
[32] Act of Apr. 29, 1902. 32 *Stat.*, pt. 1, p. 176.

The Chinese Protest 291

A special representative of the United States government having been sent to China, the Emperor issued a proclamation to the Viceroys of all the provinces requesting each to prepare an exhibit. Minister Barrett assured the officials and merchants that they would be admitted freely and received cordially. Apparently without reference to this invitation, the immigration officials proceeded to make such regulations as they thought necessary. As originally published in January, 1903, these rules required that each exhibitor upon arrival should be photographed for identification and should file a bond in the penal sum of five thousand dollars, the conditions of which were that he would proceed directly and by the shortest route to St. Louis, and would depart for China by the first steamer sailing after the close of the fair.[33]

The Chinese government protested against the rules and the American press attacked the immigration department violently for this breach of hospitality which would defeat the very object of their coming, the encouragement of trade. As a consequence the bureau modified the regulations in July, so as to except merchant exhibitors specifically from these conditions and to admit them on a simple certificate from their government, stating the purpose of their visit and viséd by an American consul. But some exhibitors and officials had already been catechised and detained in the Shed at San Francisco and had gone home much offended.

This tardy modification of the rules did not however wholly quiet the public clamor in the United States; and two years later the Secretary of Commerce and Labor, in a defense of the whole administrative system as applied to the Chinese, made an extended explanation.[34] He

---

[33] These rules were suppressed shortly afterward and are not accessible; the above statement is made on the authority of Chester Holcombe, formerly Secretary of Legation at Peking. See *Outlook*, Apr. 23, 1904, p. 976.

[34] *H. Doc.* 847 (1906), pp. 36-50. Commissioner Sargent also defended himself and the system in his annual report for 1906, p. 151 ff.

stated that Rule Forty-four did not apply and had not been intended to apply to the exempt classes who could come in on a Section-Six certificate; if they did not have this certificate it was their own fault or the fault of their government, and the immigration officials had no authority to relax the law by accepting any other kind of identification; furthermore, Rule Forty-four applied only to the excluded class, laborers, and was absolutely necessary as proved by the frauds perpetrated under the Chinese concessions at previous fairs and finally justified by the attempts at fraud in St. Louis.

Without analyzing the defense in detail, it may be said that since the immigration officials knew that a special invitation had been given, and since the act of 1902 setting aside certain laws had been passed at their instigation, they were assuredly under obligation to provide for the hospitable reception of all Chinese visitors and to make the regulations as little obnoxious as possible. The Viceroys of the Chinese provinces were not told that if they did not have a Section-Six certificate they would be refused landing; nor could they be expected to know that Rule Forty-four which began,—" every Chinese person " applied only to laborers, for even in this country the rule was not so understood. The Secretary of Commerce and Labor afterward stated that he had no authority to relax the law by admitting merchant exhibitors without a Section-Six certificate—yet when the public clamor became loud enough, he did relax it.

The only defense remaining—the frauds perpetrated at previous fairs and attempted at St. Louis—not only did not apply to the privileged classes but lacked the confirmation of authentic facts. The numbers admitted to Omaha and Atlanta are not given and since the officials state that they kept no record of departures of exhibition laborers, there is no proof either that they remained or that they departed. The 239 laborers admitted to St. Louis were in charge of James R. Dunn, formerly Chief

The Chinese Protest 293

inspector at San Francisco who, after keeping them all summer under the strictest surveillance, reported that one escaped but was recaptured; one died, twelve were arrested and deported, and the remainder returned to San Francisco by special train under the supervision of department officers and returned to China.[35] The Commissioner-General reported that it cost $18,214.84, plus the cost of arrest, trial and deportation of those who escaped and the services of officers in taking bonds and in identification to protect the laws from violation; but the United States does not yet know what will be the cost in loss of trade and good feeling, of humiliating the bona fide merchants and privileged exhibitors who had been assured that they would receive the same treatment as those of other nations. Nor does the trouble and cost of enforcing a law against laborers, made for the benefit of the United States, excuse the Department for not receiving the exempt classes in the most courteous manner.[36]

The law of 1893 defined a merchant as: "a person engaged in buying and selling merchandise, at a fixed place of business, which business is conducted in his name, and who during the time he claims to be engaged as a merchant, does not engage in the performance of any manual labor except such as is necessary in the conduct of his business as such merchant." To establish his status as a domiciled merchant for the purpose of being readmitted, the law declared: "he shall establish by the testimony of two credible witnesses other than Chinese the fact that he conducted such business * * * for at least one year before his departure from the United States and that during such year he was not engaged in the performance of any manual labor, except such as was necessary in the conduct of his business."[37]

---

[35] *An. Rept.* Com.-General, 1906, pp. 91–2.
[36] For effect on the Chinese see article by Wong Kai Kah (graduate of Yale), a Chinese official, in *N. A. Rev.*, v. 178, p. 422 ff (1904).
[37] McCreary Act, Nov. 3, 1893, 28 *Stat.*, p. 7.

The act of 1884 specified in detail the kind of certificate which an entering merchant must present; it must be issued by the Chinese government or the government of which the merchant was a subject; and the treaty of 1894 permitted the certificate to be issued by the government where the merchant last resided. It must be in the English language, showing signature, individual, family and tribal name in full, title, rank, age, height and all physical peculiarities, former and present occupation, and place of residence. It must state the nature, character and estimated value of the business carried on prior to and at the time of his application; and it must be viséd by the diplomatic representatives of the United States at the port of departure, whose duty it was, to examine into the truth of such statements. The certificate when thus viséd, was the sole evidence permissible for admission, but was nevertheless only *prima facie* not final, evidence of the right of entry; and the facts therein might be disproved by the United States authorities. After it had been approved and the holder admitted by the collector of the port, it must be shown whenever lawfully demanded.

Notwithstanding these minute requirements, the admission of merchants was guarded with greater and greater care. The Attorney-General ruled that only those were merchants whose names appeared as part of the firm name.[38] Although the Chinese minister explained that Chinese firms are usually made up of many partners none of whose names appear in the title of the firm and offered to furnish lists of partners, the Treasury Department excluded several hundred under this ruling. But the Circuit Court of Appeals finally determined that if the Chinaman could prove that he was an actual, *bona fide* partner of a legitimate firm he was a merchant even if

---

[38] 21 *Op. Attys.-Gen.* 5. Confirmed by U. S. Dist. Court of San Francisco; *In re* Quan Gin, 61 *Fed. Rep.* 395, 641.

his name did not appear in the firm name,[39] provided the firm books or articles designated such partner.

If any of the particulars enumerated in the law were omitted from the certificate or if the consular visé contained the required statements and the certificate did not, the certificate could not be accepted.[40] Under this ruling Yee Ah Lum and thirty other merchants of Canton who came to the United States in 1899 to buy goods were denied landing. It appeared that the particulars respecting the nature of their business, though plainly stated in the Chinese portion of their certificates, were not stated in the English portion. The Chinese Minister suggested that the merchants be released under bonds and that their certificates be sent back to China for correction. Although there was no suspicion of fraud, all these merchants were compelled to return to China.[41]

The movements of merchants were still further restricted by withdrawing from the consular officers in foreign countries and in the United States the right to issue certificates. The case of Lei Yok, a Chinese merchant partner returning to the United States from Havana, Cuba, is in point: he had a passport issued by the Chinese Consul-General at Havana, viséd by the British Consul-General on behalf of the United States and by the Spanish Governor of the province. Although he had a *bona fide* interest in a firm in San Francisco he was refused admission at the port of New Orleans because of the new ruling.[42]

Even the Chinese merchants who were naturalized citi-

[39] *Cong. Docs.* 1894, ser. no, 3292, p. 166 ff. Decision by Circuit Court of Appeals, Lee Kan *v.* U. S., 62 *Fed. Rep.* 914. Finally affirmed by the Supreme Court of the U. S. in Tom Hong *v.* U. S., 193 *U. S.* 517, though meanwhile at least one of the U. S. Circuit Courts of Appeals had held differently.
[40] Letter to Attorney-General, Sept. 6, 1892; letter to Grant and Skeans, Apr. 12, 1894, see *Regs.* 1902, rules 19 and 20.
[41] *Cong. Docs.* 1901, ser. no. 4268, *China*, pp. 73–4.
[42] *Regs.* 1902, Rules 11 and 21; Op. Atty.-Gen., Aug. 31, 1898; Op. Solicitor of Treas., Feb. 3, 1898; letter to Special Agent Hanlon, Sept. 1, 1893. Ser. no. 3898, p. 200.

zens of foreign countries could not be admitted on proof of naturalization and presentation of a passport, but only on a Section-Six certificate because—according to the Attorney-General—the exclusion laws "were based on moral and racial objections" and not on the fact that the applicants were subjects of the Emperor of China. Under this ruling the Chinese citizens of Mexico and Canada, although members of the exempt classes, were refused admission.[43]

The increasing stringency of the Attorney-General's rulings and of the Treasury Department between 1898 and 1902 led to an extended and formal protest on the part of the Chinese Minister. He objected to the fact that the merchant's certificate, obtained with difficulty, was not received as final evidence; that merchants were imprisoned, *incommunicado*, on arrival; that the method of examination was confusing and unjust; that misunderstandings arose from the incompetence and bias of interpreters; and that the Customs officers took advantage of every technicality even when there was no evidence of fraud. He protested further against the *ex parte* decisions of the Treasury Department, the denial of counsel and a judicial hearing, and declared the whole procedure to be a travesty of justice.[44]

The Chinese Minister complained further of *ex parte* decisions due to the unreasonable application of the statute of 1894 which made the decisions of the Secretary of the Treasury final in all cases of excluded aliens.[45] The rules allowed only two days for taking an appeal and no evidence could be submitted which had not been made the subject of investigation by the officer in charge. Of 720 appeals taken in two years, (1904-5). 80% were at the port of San Francisco. The evidence, witnesses,

---

[43] *Regs.* 1902, Rule 22; letter to collector at Burlingame, Feb. 5, 1895. Rule 23, letter to Secretary of State, Apr. 20, 1896.
[44] *Cong. Docs.* 1901, s. n. 4268, p. 81 ff.
[45] This statute, applicable to all aliens, was confirmed by the courts in 1905.

The Chinese Protest 297

inspectors and attorneys, were therefore three thousand miles from the Department to which appeal was made. The Secretary of the Treasury could know nothing except what had already filtered through officers who naturally wanted their decisions affirmed but who were often glad to throw the responsibility on a higher officer.

In reply to the Chinese protests, the Secretary of Commerce and Labor stated that the appeals received the personal attention of the head of the Department, every material detail being considered and discussed. Yet it must be questioned whether this could be strictly true, for there were in 1905, besides 438 Chinese appeals, 1921 appeals from the decisions of the Boards of Inquiry in the cases of aliens of other nationalities. If it were true, then he must have considered every material detail in at least seven cases per day on every working day in the year. The appeal system is acknowledged to be expensive and unsatisfactory but it must be doubted whether the remedy which the Commissioner proposed—the shutting out of new evidence on appeal—will be sufficient to satisfy the critics who insist on the fundamental distinction which exists in the law and should exist in practice, between the laboring and the exempt classes of the Chinese.[46]

The regulations have recently been ameliorated in some particulars: to permit five days instead of two for taking an appeal; to compel the inspector to hear all witnesses on behalf of the applicant; and, most important of all, to allow the attorney for the applicant to make copies of the evidence and the Chinese Consul-General to see the record.[47] This may not reduce the number of appeals but it will certainly allay some of the irritation arising from secret and apparently *ex parte* methods of taking evidence.

Some of the troubles incident to certification have been

[46] *An. Rept.* 1905, pp. 74-5.
[47] *Regs.* 1906, rules 5, 6, 12, 13, 14.

already suggested. The Chinese minister said further that at many places in China there is no American consul; that at Hong Kong where most of the Chinese go to ship for this country, it is impossible to obtain the required certificate, it being a British port and they not being residents of that place; and that the Chinese seeking to come from such foreign ports suffer great inconvenience.

As to the issuance of certificates, there has been incessant change and confusion, due to frequent changes of officers, to divided responsibility, to carelessness and corruption on the part of the administration; and to transference, alterations, pawning, and forgery on the part of the Chinese. As to the record and identification of certificates, there have been changes in methods of book-keeping with every change of administration, and until after 1902, the published reports did not even contain the numbers by classes of the exempts admitted and debarred.

The irritation caused by variations of practice in handling certificates is illustrated by the following instance. The law of 1884, as strictly interpreted by the Treasury department before 1902, prescribed that Section Six certificates should be cancelled by collectors writing across the face in red ink and should then be returned to such Chinese persons "*as evidence to protect them from arrest.*" Under this regulation there occurred occasionally such cases as the often-quoted episode of Hong Sling, a Chinese merchant who was detained and treated discourteously as a suspected laborer in an inland town, because he did not have his certificate on his person but in his baggage.[48]

But the regulation was afterward altered instructing officers to retain the certificates of the exempt classes.[49] The exempt classes regarded this as leaving them with-

---

[48] *Cong. Docs.* (1901), s. n. 4268, *China*, p. 84.
[49] *Regs.* 1903, Rule 23.

out any protection from officers who might be in search of laborers unlawfully in the country; for it has been a common custom throughout the West for the Chinese inspectors when not otherwise busy to round up all of the Chinese in their district at one time and demand their certificates. In Seattle such a raid resulted in several suits for damages by Chinese merchants against four inspectors.[50] Further, if the owner of an exempt certificate were required to identify himself in Cleveland, for example, and the original were in the hands of an officer in San Francisco, he must be detained till it could be sent for, a matter of ten days at least. Although the certificate was the sole evidence permissible of the right of re-entry, it was not final and its statements might be controverted. Under cover of this broad license the rules became more and more elaborate. The registered laborer in 1902 who wished to go home for a visit had to prove before he went, again three months before he returned and again on arrival, that he had the necessary family, relatives or property.

No one of the inconveniences incident to the enforcement of the law, has created more criticism and ill-feeling, than the place and manner of detention of all classes of applicants for admission. There is no immigration building at San Francisco. The detention station used by the department of immigration was provided by the Pacific Mail Steamship Company in order to avoid keeping the immigrants on board ship till they were admitted. The Shed—rightly so-called—is a cheap, two-story wooden building, at the end of a wharf, built out over the water where the odors of sewage and bilge are most offensive; unclean, at times overrun with vermin, and often inadequate to the numbers to be detained. The food provided was poor and the conditions even more unsanitary than the police cells of the city. Commis-

[50] H. R. 847, p. 140. Impounding of certificates declared illegal in Toy Tong v. U. S., 145 *Fed. Rep.* 343.

sioner Sargent, who compelled the Steamship Company to improve these quarters in 1903, said that they were lacking in every facility for cleanliness and decency.[51] It was in this place that the merchant exhibitors who came to the Louisiana Purchase Exposition were detained and it is not surprising that they reported: "The Americans are a race of pigs." No attempt to segregate the Chinese passengers, except by sex, has been made. Here were detained for days, sometimes for weeks, all classes of Chinese persons. Small-footed, high-born wives of merchants, and merchants' children, have been imprisoned with women held as professional prostitutes, and all under the guard of ordinary police whose duty it was to see that they were kept *incommunicado* for fear they might be coached by their friends.[52] If the friends of respectable women and children succeeded in getting an order for their removal, it was only to one of the Missions established by the Protestant churches for rescued slave-girls, where, though courteously treated, their pride of race and class was deeply offended by the association with women of an inferior class.[53] Commissioner Sargent said that the lack of government quarters and the necessity of depending on such a building as the Shed accounted for most of the odium which had so unjustly been charged against the enforcement of the exclusion acts.[54]

Finally the Chinese Minister, after objecting to denial of judicial appeal, *ex parte* proceedings, narrow regulations, confused and varying proceedings, complained of

---

[51] *An. Rept.* 1903, p. 63. The conditions of detention have been equally bad in other places, but not for long continued periods. At Plattsburg, N. Y., a hundred Chinese claiming to be native born were detained for several months, and 17 died on account of unsanitary conditions. See H. R. 847.
[52] Interviews and personal observation.
[53] "My Reception in America," by Fu Chi Hao, M. A., *Outlook*, Aug. 10th, 1907; *An. Rept.* 1905, p. 71.
[54] In 1905 a tract of land was set apart for an immigration building on Angell Island, and the buildings are being erected.

the unfriendly spirit of the laws and of the administration. All classes of Chinese were treated as suspects and criminals, and in every doubtful case the benefit of the doubt was given to the United States. This partiality was, indeed, only an elaboration of the theory of the law; but that the habitual attitude of immigration officials was one of suspicion toward all classes has never been denied. Certainly this brief and incomplete review of the grievances of the privileged classes shows that in the administration of the exclusion of laborers as well as in the legislation itself, the United States has completely ignored its treaty promises.

CHAPTER XVII

THE ADMINISTRATION OF THE CHINESE EXCLUSION LAWS

"The countless instances of imposture, the absence of an appreciation of the obligation of an oath, upon the part of some of the witnesses, the transfer of genuine papers and the fabrication of fraudulent ones, the abundant funds at the disposal of those who are interested in securing the admission of Chinese, the palpably false claims to birth in the United States, the absurd pretensions to a mercantile status of members of firms whose total business is out of all proportion to the number of alleged partners, the ingenious devices of counsel in some instances, and the numerous other obstacles to a just and effective enforcement of the law . . . are all a part of the story, a complete knowledge of which is necessary to an intelligent understanding of what may appear to the casual observer an unjust or unnecessarily rigorous action in the administration of the Chinese-exclusion laws."—GEORGE B. CORTELYOU, Secretary of Commerce and Labor.

"They call it exclusion; but it is not exclusion, it is extermination."—CHAN KIU SING, 1904.

FREQUENT references have already been made to a document—*Compilation of the Facts concerning the Enforcement of the Chinese Exclusion Laws*—prepared by the Commissioner-General of Immigration and transmitted in May, 1906, to the House of Representatives by the Secretary of Commerce and Labor.[1] That the officers of the Chinese service have been growing more and more sensitive to criticism since 1900, is evinced by the tone—sometimes complaining, often resentful—of the annual reports; but this paper is the first complete and reasonable attempt at defense from the Department itself.

Twenty-five pages of the defense was devoted to a statement of the general difficulties of administration; another twenty-five to the specific complaints brought to

[1] *Cong. Docs.* (1906), s. n. 4990, *H. R.* 847.

Administration of Exclusion Laws 303

the notice of the Department; and the remaining one hundred was given to a consideration of the regulations to which objection has most frequently been made, and which have been discussed in the preceding chapter.[2]

The document states that the exclusion laws are acknowledged to be among the most difficult on the statute books to enforce for three reasons: the system has been one of divided responsibility, resulting in lack of order and thoroughness; a certain element of the public, actuated either by interested motives or by the missionary spirit, has never believed in the exclusion policy and is often ready to oppose the enforcement of the law; and finally because the Chinese are deficient in a sense of the moral obligation of an oath, holding caste in higher esteem than law, and being clannish in the highest degree. To these difficulties is added the fact that the Chinese can always obtain money for litigation. Other aliens unlawfully in the country, are arrested and deported by administrative action almost entirely at the cost of the transportation companies; but Chinese aliens must be arrested on judicial warrants, have a judicial hearing, and be deported at the expense of the United States.

The administration measures fall into two general divisions; those arising from exclusion and those from expulsion. Other undesirable aliens are excluded by immigration officers and have no appeal except to the Secretary of Commerce; but Chinese aliens can be expelled, *i. e.*, deported, only by judicial process. The difficulties in the enforcement of exclusion lie chiefly in the disproving of fraudulent claims, the prevention of the " coaching " of impostors and the smuggling across the borders.

The Commissioner shows that the trouble begins in the visé of the Consulate in China. Of 1245 Section-Six

---

[2] Hereafter this document, which is found in *Cong. Docs.* (1906), ser no. 4990, will be referred to briefly as *H. Rept.* 847.

certificates issued in three years by the Chinese government and viséd by the American consul, 277 were found in the hands of persons obviously not members of the exempt classes.[3] In recent years there has been an increase in the numbers of native-born Chinese applying for admission, and extremely loose practice as well as much fraud has occurred in connection with them. There are no figures of the numbers admitted under this head before 1904; but since then, of 2218 applicants, 28% have been rejected.[4] The only trustworthy estimate of the numbers previously admitted as native-born has been made by the statistician of the twelfth Census. On the basis of 9,010 Chinese in the country claiming to be native-born, and assuming that the sexes are born and survive equally, he computed that there are 4,426 males and 122 females, that is, fifty per cent of the total, who are not native-born.[5]

Still another form of fraud is the domiciled merchant expedient. Small mercantile companies with a few thousand dollars capital often claim to have from ten to thirty members, under whose names laborers obtain admission. In 1904 and 1905 out of 1,302 applicants for admission as domiciled merchants, 12% were rejected. There are also "fake" firms whose chief business is selling opium, gambling, importing prostitutes and smuggling in coolies. The intelligent Chinese at the head of genuine mercantile companies are accused of aiding their countrymen in such frauds; and white persons assist by signing certificates without first-hand knowledge of the applicants. The Department has also found it necessary to guard the admission of wives and minor children very carefully to prevent the bringing in of prostitutes and young laborers. During the three fiscal years 1903-6 the statistics of this class are as follows:

[3] *H. R.* 847, pp. 52-3.
[4] *H. R.* 847, p. 91 ff.
[5] *An. Rept.* 1906, p. 90.

Administration of Exclusion Laws

NUMBER OF MERCHANTS' WIVES AND CHILDREN ADMITTED AND DEBARRED 1904-6.

	1904		1905		1906		TOTAL.	
	Admitted.	Debarred.	Adm.	Deb.	Adm.	Deb.	Adm.	Deb.
Wives	36	1	36	5	46	1	115	7
Minor children	180	52	123	22	345	33	648	107
Total in 3 years.	216	53	159	27	391	34	763	114
Per cent debarred		53		17%		8%		14%

The surprising thing about this table is that the number of wives and children debarred has fallen from 25% to 8% in three years while at the same time the total applying has been nearly doubled. If it was necessary to guard so carefully this class of admissions, precisely the opposite result would have been expected. It seems to be another of those contradictions of which the reports are full—fears and facts having no relation; and it may be set down to that change of heart which has overtaken the administration recently.

The Commissioner dwells at some length on "coaching" devices, and on attempts at smuggling across the border.[6] But since the border cases constitute only one-sixth of the total number this may be passed over, in order to dwell upon the more serious difficulties attending the expulsion of Chinese unlawfully in the United States.

The officers stationed at interior points have two classes of duties, the investigation of claims for re-admission when the evidence is within their district, and the apprehension of Chinese unlawfully in the country. In

---

[6] For full details of smuggling across the borders see *H. R.* 847, index, and also *Cong. Docs.* 1895–6, s. n. 3563, no. 167 (Byrne's Rept.); s. n. 3562 (1897).

the performance of the latter duty they complain of opposition from the white as well as the Chinese friends of the suspect and from the United States Commissioners before whom such cases are usually tried. The administration has not been adequately sustained, for the United States District courts have in some instances rendered decisions which, from the administrative point of view, are unduly favorable to the Chinese and, moreover, the courts and commissioners require affirmative proofs.[7] The Commissioner of Immigration in his annual report says that judicial officers sometimes justify the release of Chinese unlawfully here on the ground that they do not approve the law and one has even called it " a relic of mediæval barbarism."[8]

The true import of this official defense appears upon comparing the regulations of 1905 with those of 1906. Ten of the rules of 1905 have been dropped, four materially liberalized and three new ones which are apparently intended to alleviate the annoyances of the exempt classes added. The methods of hearing and appeal have been modified in the direction of openness and justice; the arrest of those who hold merchants' certificates but are now engaged in manual labor has been done away with; the Bertillon system of identification, the narrow definition of student, and a variety of petty restrictions upon domiciled merchants, have been omitted. It is evident that the incessant agitation against the administration since 1900 has at last taken effect among the officials.

The defense vacillates between the policy of loyally justifying the former rules, and excusing them by blaming the Chinese, the Courts, the missionaries and everybody else who has had anything to do with their enforcement. It says in substance: all Chinese are liars and in collusion to evade the law; the United States Com-

[7] *H. R.* 847, p. 17 ff.
[8] *An. Rept.*, 1905, p. 79.

Administration of Exclusion Laws 307

missioners and even the courts are ignorant of Chinese character, easily deceived and unduly lax; the critical public is ignorant and irrational; the American friends are either capitalists "strictly self-interested" or missionaries given to vagaries and interference. The blame for frauds is always turned upon the Chinese although the facts show that they were, almost without exception, initiated by white men and sometimes by white officers; and although it is evident that they could rarely succeed without the connivance of officers.

Exaggeration and even some degree of misrepresentation have been resorted to, to fortify the cause. Rumors of fraud are sometimes used in place of facts; it is stated that there was an attempt to bring in "large numbers" of women to the St. Louis fair and that the traffic in Chinese prostitutes was "extensively practised" along the Mexican border; yet the figures show that the number of women applying for admission was only slightly larger in that year than the year before and not nearly so large as the year after.[9]

But the recommendations for the improvement of the service in the recent reports of the immigration department witness even more than the defense to the degree of dissatisfaction created by the earlier administration and, as a result, to the difficult position in which the officers now find themselves. It is recommended that the phraseology of legislation should correspond to that of the treaties, that all investigations into class status should be made by an immigration officer stationed in China, and that all restrictions on the departure and return of registered laborers—except identification—be removed. Though the department does not directly yield the point that interpretation should coincide with the intent of treaties and legislation, it has at last urged that

[9] See especially pp. 43, 57, 77, 88, 116; many instances of the same sort are found in the reports since 1902.

the wording should be identical because of the trouble experienced by the officers.

As for the Consular visé, the exposures of fraud in the American service in China show that—so far as Chinese immigrants are concerned—no reform has taken place since the odious administration of Consul Bailey.[10] The Chinese Government has steadily protested ever since the treaty of 1880 that its certificate viséd by the American Consul ought to be conclusive evidence of the right to admission; but the immigration officers at the ports of entry soon discovered that the visé had been attached in a perfunctory if not in a dishonest manner, and therefore refused to accept it.[11] So long as the American consuls took no pains to make the visé authoritative or so long as they blackmailed the exempt classes, the coöperation of China in making the certificate truthful was scarcely to be expected. The boycott of American trade in 1905 drew attention to these abuses and President Roosevelt reminded the Consuls of their duty to ascertain the truth of the statements of the certificates before viséing them. As a consequence, only six per cent of such papers were rejected in 1906 as against 29% in 1905.[12]

Perhaps the most unexpected concession of all is the proposal to allow registered laborers to come and go at will on proof of identity. This proposal brings to light the retribution which has finally overtaken the United States for the passage of the Scott Act. The provisions relating to the going home and the return of domiciled laborers are so difficult of performance that many of them simply secrete their certificates on their persons, go home, and take their chances of being caught when they attempt to return across the Mexican border. If accosted by an inspector, they produce the certificate

[10] See also *Cong. Docs.* (1905–6) s. n. 5037; *H. Doc.* 665, p. 13 ff.
[11] See full discussion of the Visé by Commissioner Sargent in reports, 1903–6.
[12] *An. Rept.* Com. Gen. Immig. 1906, p. 83–5.

Administration of Exclusion Laws 309

and deny having been out of the country. During six months in 1905, 250 Chinamen returned in this manner. The unnecessarily exacting terms of the law discourages the leaving of laborers and hastens their return, thus defeating its avowed intention. Commissioner Sargent declared the law incapable of enforcement and added that these provisions tend to encourage perjury, deceit and smuggling.[13] He might have added that they have thoroughly corrupted the border officers.

At least 20,000—the exact number cannot be known—laborers had gone out of the country at the time of the Scott Act with certificates of re-entry. Since then it has been a noticeable fact that a very large proportion, sometimes half, of the attempts at fraudulent entry made by laborers have been made by men who had evidently been in the United States before and who even spoke English. The total number of Chinese deported is probably less than half the number shut out by the Scott Act who had intended to return. As each deportation costs the United States from ninety to one hundred dollars—not to calculate the cost of all other judicial and civil service—it has probably cost a million dollars to enforce the Scott Act.

The recommendations of the commissioner that the appropriations and the official staff of the Chinese service be consolidated hereafter with the general immigration service draws attention to their relative cost. The following table gives the essential particulars:

[13] *An. Rept.* 1906, pp. 86-7.

RELATIVE COST OF CHINESE AND GENERAL IMMIGRATION SERVICE, 1903–1906.

From Annual Reports of Commissioner-General.

Year.	Total aliens arrived, excluding Chinese. (14)	Expenditures for general immigration service.	Total Chinese disposed of. (15)	Cost of Chinese immigration service. (16)
1904	833,224	$1,296,808	7078	$356,684
1905	1,056,848	1,508,901	3827	465,492
1906	1,098,581	1,571,280	3547	372,640

Year.	Cost per Capita other aliens.	Cost per Capita Chinese.	No. of Chinese Deported.	Total cost of Chinese deportations.	Cost per Capita for deportation.	Total per Capita cost Chinese. (17)
1904	$1.55	$ 50	673	$75,536	$112	$ 55
1905	1.42	121	621	67,730	109	104
1906	1.43	105	310	27,882	90	96
Average for three fiscal years, 1904–1906.	$1.46	$92			$103	$85

From this table it appears that it costs as much to handle one Chinaman as it does to dispose of 58 other aliens. It might be argued that there should be added to the number of the Chinese seeking admission and transit, those voluntarily departing who must also receive the attention of the immigration officers; but even

[14] Including aliens in transit (not Chinese).
[15] Including Chinese in transit, of whom 131 were deported; not including voluntary departures of other Chinese.
[16] Excluding cost of deportations.
[17] Including cost of deportations.

Administration of Exclusion Laws 311

adding these, the cost of handling all arriving and departing Chinese amounts to fifty dollars per head.[18]

The four hundred thousand dollars expended yearly through the immigration service is by no means the whole cost of exclusion. During the three years 1904, 1905 and 1906, about 4500 Chinese have been arrested for being in the United States in violation of law. Of this number about 3200 have been taken before United States Commissioners, 800 before United States courts, and 100 before higher courts. It is impossible to estimate even approximately the enormous cost of these trials, of which one-fourth to one-half ended in discharge.[19] To reduce this inordinate expense the Commissioner-General urged in 1905 that Chinese aliens should be arrested and deported by administrative process as other aliens are; but it would certainly not be safe to authorize such purely administrative treatment until it shall no longer be regarded a crime to be a Chinese alien.[20]

Other recommendations, such as a complete re-registration of all Chinese regardless of legality of residence, and the issue of a durable certificate to exempts in lieu of the Section Six certificate, involve considerable expense and trouble. Still another—that the minor children of domiciled exempts should be admitted only on condition of not engaging in laboring pursuits appears to be a violation of treaty and possibly of constitutional rights. But the chief objection to them all is the irritation which they will probably cause among the Chinese. The very words "registration" and "certificate" have become so offensive to the Chinese because of the dis-

[18] The exact number of Chinese voluntarily departing is not given except for the port of San Francisco; in 1904 and 1905 the total departures from that port were 8970 which must constitute at least 90% of the total.
[19] Of all the cases before the commissioners about one-half were discharged; of those before the courts, one-fourth. See also Secretary Metcalf in *Cong. Docs.* s. n. 4966, *H. Docs.* Vol. 26, 1905.
[20] See article by Max J. Kohler, N. Y. *Times*, Nov. 24, 1901.

crimination between them and other immigrant races and because of the badgering which they have suffered, that it is doubtful if they could now' be induced to submit to it—certainly not unless concessions were made to them and the utmost tact employed.[21] Yet if the Geary law and its amendments are to be enforced, re-registration is absolutely necessary.

The complaints of the Chinese ministers and the defense of the immigration officials discussed in the foregoing pages relate for the most part to the character of the exclusion statutes, to the interpretations of them by the courts and to the administration of them in the form of arbitrary regulations. But a careful analysis of many Chinese cases and a consideration of the private testimony of lawyers, judges of the higher courts, consuls, legation officers, chiefs of police, missionaries, employers of Chinese and many private citizens has resulted in the conviction that after all the personnel of the immigration service and the traditions of the Chinese Bureau itself have been responsible for the larger part of the odium attached to the administration of the law.

The defenders of the Chinese Bureau assert that, aside from the Chinese, their critics are confined to "missionaries and strictly self-interested persons";[22] but everywhere in California, Oregon, Washington and Arizona, the most casual mention of the immigration service brings out stories of the treatment of the Chinese illustrating the ignorance, prejudice, untrustworthiness or incompetence of some immigration officer. There can be no question that the service has long been in disrepute; it is important therefore, to trace the causes in order to judge whether the recent changes in administration are likely to allay Chinese opposition and to secure general public acquiescence.

[21] During the spring of 1905 the Chinese inspectors of the various districts attempted to take a census of the Chinese, "not with a view to making arrests at all but in order to compile data." Such a storm of protest arose that it had to be discontinued. *H. R.* 847, p. 77.

[22] See *H. R.* 847, p. 5, Commissioner Sargent's statement.

Administration of Exclusion Laws

In earlier years the small appropriations made it impossible to investigate thoroughly each case or to secure the services of suitable men. Since 1894 the bulk of the work has been done by inspectors and interpreters at salaries ranging from twelve to eighteen hundred a year and the higher officials have based their decisions on the investigations and testimony of men of this grade. Such men as these have been detailed to receive not only Chinese laborers but officials, scholars and cultivated travelers. It could scarcely be expected that their manners would be equal to the social requirements of one of the politest nations in the world, but it appears that they have often omitted the ordinary American courtesies and hospitality. On one occasion when a party of Chinese gentlemen escorted on board the steamer a Chinese official who was on his way home, the immigration officials made difficulty about their return on the ground that they had technically left the United States. The Chinese wives of Americans and of Englishmen have been compelled to register in order to pass through the port of San Francisco. In various ways the officials have shown a lack of tact and judgment in the rather delicate task of cross-questioning their social superiors. In dealing with the Chinese they were attempting to ascertain the truth about a race whose language is particularly difficult and whose customs and character are far less understood than those of the immigrants from Ireland, Germany or Italy. The employes of the immigration bureau have generally been appointed by political influence solely, and from a class imbued with the tradition that the object of the exclusion law is not only to exclude laborers but all Chinese as well. To this class tradition has often been added the race prejudices of the European-born against the Oriental, for the service has been largely recruited from Irishmen and others of foreign extraction.

With the exception of a very few individuals of American parentage, the position of Chinese interpreter in the immigration service has been filled by half-breed Chinese-Anglo-Saxons. Their knowledge of both languages is imperfect and in the interpretation of Chinese documents and testimony this leads to technical mistakes which make it appear that the Chinese immigrant has been coached or that there are discrepancies in the testimony of himself and his witnesses.

The variety of dialects spoken by the Chinese from different districts makes it impossible for any but a thoroughly trained interpreter to translate accurately, and in so apparently simple a matter as the transliteration of names, mistakes have been made resulting in a failure to identify the man or his certificate, and consequently in his exclusion. Davis S Jones, an authority on Chinese names, says that lack of uniformity in English spelling of the names of Chinese persons has been a prolific source of confusion to immigration officers and of injury to Chinese immigrants. If a Chinaman should have a certificate issued to him in the name of *Tsam Gow* and should apply for a duplicate in the name of *Jaam Gow*, the chances are his certificate would be overlooked by the Department and a duplicate refused. Again, the names of Chinese merchants are often misspelled in the partnership lists and they have difficulty in returning to this country because they are not the same as those on their steamer tickets.[23] There is sometimes misunderstanding arising from the several sets of names common to Chinese persons, any one of which might be regarded as an *alias* by Americans unfamiliar with Chinese customs. As unobservant people are apt to think they all look alike, the variety of names and the apparent similarity of appearance adds to the likehood that an ignorant, over-zealous, or suspicious officer would make frequent

---

[23] Jones, *Surnames of the Chinese in America*. Mr. Jones has lived five years in China and for the past eight years has been interpreter of the United States courts in San Francisco.

mistakes in identifying them as the persons described in their certificates.[24] Even if the interpreter knows the Chinese dialect well, his knowledge of English has often been so imperfect as to distort any testimony offered on behalf of the immigrant.[25]

Interpreters of nondescript social class and superficial linguistic attainments have been despised and distrusted equally by Chinese and Americans. There is abundant evidence that in collusion with inspectors they have held up the exempt classes for bribes and that they have for the same reason been the chief instruments of all the Chinese schemes for securing the admission of laborers.[26] Among many instances of bribery the following may be quoted: A native-born Chinaman went to China and was married there six months before his return. When he started back he was married over again, American fashion, at the consulate in Hong Kong. His citizenship papers were all right and he was sure he had done everything necessary to comply with the law. But he was detained twelve days in the Shed at San Francisco on the charge that his marriage certificate was a forgery. He knew that the officials wanted a bribe and he knew his papers were correct, and he would not pay. If he had not had influential white persons to testify for him he could not have landed. At the same time his own cousin, native-born, who had never been in the country, who had bogus papers and an eruption on his face that should have detained him, paid a certain sum to an immigration official and came in without detention.

[24] See Smith, *Chinese Characteristics*, Douglas, *China*, pp. 226-8, on the mistakes arising even in China.

[25] See explanations of Kee whom Commissioner Powderly brought before the Committee on Immigration in 1902: *Cong. Docs.* s. n. 4265, p. 69 ff.

[26] Obtained from trustworthy persons and fully corroborated. See also criminal prosecutions of Chinese inspectors and interpreters for corruption: Williams *v.* U. S., 168 *U. S.*, 382, 93 *H. R.* 396; Dillard *v.* U. S. 141 Fed. Rep. 303 (C. C. A.); U. S. *v.* Wilson, 60 *Fed. Rep.* 890. *In re* Yee See, 83 *Fed. Rep.* 145.

The native-born more often refuse to pay a bribe than others, but sometimes they cannot get in in any other way. One such man cut off his queue and went back to China, dressed in American clothes. He got a passport from the American consul in Hong Kong and traveled in China as an American citizen; finally going to Manila and acting as interpreter to an American officer there; yet with his passport as an American citizen and with his certificate as an American born, he nevertheless had to bribe the officials to get in again.

If it be thought that these are exceptional cases it may be said that plenty of similar ones can be had not only from lawyers but from white persons who have acted as witnesses for returning Chinese. It has long been currently understood in Chinatown that money properly placed would secure the admission of almost anyone if those interested had not already incurred the ill-will of an official. It is always difficult to obtain proof of bribery and ill-treatment; but in the case of the Chinese it is almost impossible because their friends will suffer if they testify against any American official. The immigration officers can make and have made all kinds of trouble for certain merchants importing goods and for their friends and relatives returning from China.[27]

In the defense of the Bureau much is made of the cleverness of Chinese rings organized to secure the admission of the excluded class and of the practice of " coaching " which is a necessary adjunct to it. There has long been a traffic in expired certificates; that is, Chinamen who go back to China to stay sell their papers to be used by new Chinamen coming in, and the coaching process has grown up chiefly in connection with this. Coaching devices all depend on a routine schedule of questions and answers from which a competent and skilful interpreter can deviate enough to prove the

[27] Corroborated by many persons in interviews and by instances in *H. R.* 847, pp, 153-4.

Administration of Exclusion Laws 317

fraud;[28] and such schemes have almost invariably depended upon the coöperation of white officers secured by bribery. Whenever official interpreters and inspectors of known probity have handled the cases not only have all excluded classes been successfully kept out but others of doubtful right to admission have been detained and debarred. As illustrating that it has often been easier for a Chinaman to come in by bribery than by means of his legal papers, the following instance is quoted. It illustrates as well, the network of technicalities and trivialities in which the service had become involved.[29]

Chang, a Chinese laborer, who had been in the United States fifteen years and had worked for a well-known business man, saved money, bought a share in a mercantile firm, practiced his vocation of merchant for a year, then went away to cook at high wages for a few months and then returned to his store. Wishing to go to China for a visit, he got his former employer and the President of a Bank where he was well known, to sign his identification certificate. On his return he was detained at the port of entry as a suspect. His certificate was identified by the two gentlemen who signed it, and one of them went to the detention jail and identified Chang himself among several Chinese. But the Collector nevertheless refused to land him. A few days later a subordinate in the Collector's office came to the former employer's house and offered to "fix it up"; but the gentleman refused to bribe him, and appealed through the Senator from his State to the Commissioner of Immigration, who declined to interfere on the ground that the "case had been disposed of." After a month's imprisonment, Chang was deported, but three months later he appeared at his former employer's office, having spent all his money in getting himself smuggled in. The gentleman warned him that he was well-known and liable to re-arrest and advised him to go into the country. But Chang stayed in town, was re-arrested and thrown into jail. His former employer then engaged a good Irish lawyer, got the case taken before a U. S. Commissioner, six business men testified that Chang was known to them as a merchant, and the Commissioner allowed him to remain.

It is commonly said that lawyers have made a great

[28] See translations of coaching papers and intercepted letters reprinted in *Cong. Docs.* 1902, ser. no. 4265, p. 469 ff.
[29] See instances on the Southern border offered as testimony by Mr. Gompers (1902), *Cong. Docs.* s. n. 4265, p. 271 ff; 470; p. 477; also Byrne's report, s. n. 3563 (1895–6) p. 154 ff.

deal of money out of landing cases but this is true only in an occasional case. Ordinarily a lawyer makes only his contingency fee which is not more than fifty or seventy-five dollars. The money spent does not go to lawyers, for the Chinese have learned that a lawyer can do very little for them; the only man who can do anything for them is the examining inspector. If he approves the certificate it is accepted. But the Chinaman is examined before one or more inspectors; and as the inspectors cannot understand Chinese the interpreter can say whatever he pleases. If the interpreter and the inspectors agree the Chinaman is landed, and if money is spent it is probable that it goes to one or the other.[80]

The opportunity for biased and unscrupulous subordinates to misuse the immigrant is well illustrated by the examinations for *trachoma,* a contagious eye disease. Since 1903 all Chinese have been examined under the general immigration law as well as under the exclusion laws. Such cases have occurred as that of a merchant's wife returning to San Francisco having been held at Canton for several months under treatment for *trachoma;* again detained at San Francisco for *trachoma* and ordered deported. When her lawyers insisted in calling in outside experts they decided that she *had never had trachoma* and she was finally landed.[81]

A case of peculiar outrage was reported by an English missionary and her friends who took passage in the European steerage and were thrown with the incoming Chinese. The ship's doctor examined all of them for eye diseases five times during the voyage, and

[80] Statement of several reputable business men familiar with the service for a number of years. Chinese cooks are in great demand in California and usually remain in wealthy families for years; when they return from a visit to China and have trouble in landing it is customary to place a few hundred dollars in the hands of a lawyer who puts it "wherever it will do the most good."

[81] Eminent eye specialists do not hesitate to say that the doctors connected with the service are either incompetent or have no regard for the rights of immigrants.

Administration of Exclusion Laws

without washing his hands at all as he passed from one to another. A Chinese boy of twelve, the son of a San Francisco merchant, who had been examined before sailing for *trachoma* and pronounced free, and whose eyes appeared to be clean was detained at San Francisco for *trachoma*. His father was not allowed to call in another physician nor to see him a second time and the boy was deported by return ship.[82]

Certain individual officers retained for their zeal or by their political connections, have also been the cause of much irritation and injustice. It is noticeable that every attack on the administration has centered about certain inspectors and several of the most violent ones have been caused by James R. Dunn, whose extreme anti-Chinese prejudices were especially displayed before the Senate Immigration committee of 1901. Many instances of his arbitrary, discourteous and exasperating conduct and rulings have become matters of public knowledge. His irascible personality and his physical infirmity unfitted him for any public office;[83] and his disregard of the ordinary rights not only of Chinese persons but of their witnesses, attorneys and friends finally resulted in his removal from the port of San Francisco to a less conspicuous post.[84] But wherever he has been stationed he has made the service detested and the unfortunate treatment of the Chinese merchants who were invited to the Louisiana Purchase Exposition was chiefly due to regulations suggested if not drawn up by him, and to the offensive methods of his administration there.[85]

It will be remembered that as Chief Inspector, Dunn

[82] Letter published in *Statements for Non-Exclusion* by P. J. Healey and Ng Poon Chew, verified by interview.
[83] Mr. Dunn is afflicted with extreme deafness.
[84] First to Canada and then to St. Louis.
[85] For details see *H. R.* 847, pp. 36 ff. The record of other inspectors at New York, was quite as objectionable, but they are not now in the service; see for instance, N. Y. *Times,* Jan. 18; Brooklyn *Eagle,* Feb. 4; N. Y. *Tribune,* Feb. 4, 1903. The record of J. Thomas Scharf, at New York, was almost as bad.

was stationed at the port of San Francisco, through which three-fourths of the Chinese come and go, during the period of Minister Wu Ting Fang's Ministry in Washington, and under him Treasury regulations culminated in a sort of reign of terror. He not only enforced the law and the regulations to the very limits of technicality but he constantly devised new and more irritating rules and secured their adoption by Commissioner Powderly, whose prejudices against the Chinese apparently urged him on. He did not hesitate to overestimate the testimony in order that' his rulings might be sustained in cases appealed to the Department, nor to give undue weight to trivial details of the testimony in order to debar the applicant. His trivial maneuvering to distort the testimony represents fairly a large amount of the investigations and reports on which many Chinese have been debarred, and which are the chief occupation of a large staff of inspectors and interpreters.

That portion of the act of 1892 which made the penalty of unlawful entry a year's imprisonment at hard labor, was declared unconstitutional;[86] but nevertheless the penalty of imprisonment has been enforced to a considerable extent at the will of immigration officers, not only upon those ordered deported, but also upon merchants who were afterward released. In September, 1905, there were in detention at Port Townsend 18 Chinamen, some of whom had been there since February. Two merchants of Mazatlan, who were ordered deported in 1899 not because their certificates were defective but because the inspector at Los Angeles thought their calloused hands proved them to be laborers, were imprisoned awaiting the order of deportation from February to August.[87]

Inspector Dunn frequently seized papers from the persons of Chinese, used them and did not return them;

[86] Wong Wing *v.* U. S. 163 *U. S.*, 228.
[87] *Cong. Docs.* 1901, ser. no. 4268.

he detained members of the exempt classes for months in the Shed at San Francisco on technicalities and in several cases he ordered deportation when the case had been appealed within the legal period allowed. The extent, and the consequences, of his arbitrary power is illustrated by the case of Ho Mun, a Chinese merchant who came to San Francisco from Macao in September, 1899. He had a certificate issued by the proper Portuguese authorities of that city and viséd by the American Consul at Hong Kong, but it was rejected on the ground that it did not state the exact time during which he had been engaged as a merchant. He was kept in the Detention Shed pending orders for his deportation and soon became seriously ill. Inspector Dunn refused to allow him to have medical care and it was not until he had been in detention for two months that he was rescued by means of a writ of *habeas corpus*. He was then removed to the County jail and died there a few days afterward. There was in this case no presumption of fraud to excuse the isolation in which he was kept and the refusal of ordinary medical attention.[89]

But the most terrible of all the stories which are told of the reign of James R. Dunn is the story of little Lew Lin Gin, the baby whom he ordered deported and who has been lost ever since.

The father of Lew was a merchant in an interior town, a native Californian, and therefore a citizen of the United States. While on a visit to China he had a son born by his legally wedded wife and the child was therefore a citizen of the United States also. The mother died in China and subsequently the father married again and came back to this country leaving his son in China with the step-mother. When the boy was five years old the merchant sent for them both and when they arrived in San Francisco in 1899 the step-mother was landed but the boy refused on the ground that he was born in China. The father of the boy immediately sent to China for documents to fix the status of the boy and of himself, and meanwhile the Collector of the Port permitted the child to be placed in a Protestant mission. The step-mother was

[89] *Cong. Docs.* 1901, 4268, p. 74, *China.*

at first not allowed to see the child, but at last after obtaining a permit from the Chief Inspector she went to the Mission to see the child and take him some clothes. But when she arrived she was told that the boy had just been taken to the steamer for deportation by order of the Chief Inspector. This was only about two hours before the steamer was to sail. At the request of the stepmother and a reputable Chinese merchant, a writ of *habeas corpus* was issued directing the steamship company to produce the boy in the United States court on the evidence that he was the son of an American citizen. The writ was served upon the Steamship Company by the United States Marshal about three-quarters of an hour before the sailing time of the steamer. The Chinese quarters were thoroughly searched by the Marshal and the passenger agent of the Steamship Company, but the child could not be found. Missionaries who sailed on the same ship reported later that such a child, dressed in American clothes, had been concealed in a stateroom in the part of the ship reserved for white people, and that he was afterward placed in the steerage, whence he was taken ashore by other Chinese at Shanghai. The child has now been lost seven years, although his father has done everything possible to trace him.

For a short period Inspector Dunn appears to have usurped the functions of all his superior officers. Nominally the rules and practice of the Chinese service were under the Collector of the Port and the Secretary of the Treasury,—and later under Commissioner Powderly of the Immigration department; but in reality, the Chief Inspector at San Francisco did just as he pleased. He suggested rules and secured their adoption, and then under their sanction refused landing. If the case were appealed, he presented the testimony in any shape he chose, colored with his own interpretations. The department at Washington, in default of other information, naturally supported his decisions. Thus the exclusion law was superseded by regulations which were both made and applied by the Chief Inspector.[40]

The methods thus inaugurated by Inspector Dunn at San Francisco were imitated by his subordinates. Inspectors who were sent to verify the witnesses and claims of domiciled merchants, invaded premises as if they were

---

[40] Since the above was written three cases of arbitrary and outrageous procedure by Mr. Dunn and his subordinates in St. Louis, have been reported to the State Department.

Administration of Exclusion Laws 323

lairs of criminals, extracted information by intimidation, and if the information were refused, made an adverse report. If the Chinese merchants complained of bribery and intimidation, they soon discovered that their friends and relatives could not be landed, no matter how correct their credentials. Even their white witnesses were put to so much inconvenience and so discourteously treated by the Chinese Bureau that the merchants began to find it difficult to procure them. At other stations the Chinese were almost equally harassed even after the removal of Commissioner Powderly. At Boston in 1903 the whole Chinese colony of several thousand persons was surrounded in the evening by police and immigration officers and 234 of them who could not at once produce certificates were taken to the Federal building, of whom 45 only were afterward deported. They were put in two small rooms where they could not lie down; although a few were released during the night the greater part were kept till the next day when friends or legal proceedings brought relief. The citizens of Boston held an indignation meeting and the Press attacked the Immigration department, which defended itself with the excuse that the arrest was necessary to rid the Chinese quarter of Highbinders and pointed to the deportation of 45 of those arrested and the escape of a few more released on bonds. But the Department apparently did not consider the outrage inflicted upon the whole colony of peaceful Chinese holding certificates of lawful residence and entitled by treaty to the protection of the laws.[41]

Nor was it an isolated instance as the Department asserted. Several years before the Chinese Minister had complained formally of just such raids and his description would serve as an accurate account not only of the Boston raid but of others.[42] In 1905, in Seattle, two

[41] *H. R.* 847, p. 128–9. See also Foster in *Atlan. Mo.*, Jan. 1906; newspapers, Oct., 1904.
[42] *Cong. Docs.* (1901), s. n. 4268, p. 84.

Chinese inspectors not only blockaded the doors of a Chinese night school for boys, demanding to see their certificates, but also the entrance of several Chinese stores. They searched the premises, arrested those who could not at once produce certificates and took them to jail. All of them had certificates and as a result three suits for damages were brought by Chinese merchants. The jury awarded three hundred dollars damages each against Inspectors Wells and Hamer, but they were not removed from the service.[43]

All Chinese are treated as suspects, if not as criminals. The Inspector at El Paso was in the habit of invading mercantile establishments unexpectedly and justified himself on the ground that "all of them were engaged in smuggling." A single small firm in Montana received nine such unexpected visits in two years. The subordinate officers in their zeal to enforce the law, have taken advantage of the ignorance of the poorer Chinese. An old Chinaman on his way home to China with a through ticket to Hong Kong, had lost or destroyed his certificate. The conscientious inspector took away his ticket and had him deported at the expense of the United States.[44] Commissioner Powderly himself requested the passage of a law to permit Chinese inspectors to make arrests, quoting the case of seven Chinese who *had been arrested* by the inspectors and deported; for, he said, if the Chinese had known that the inspectors had no authority to make the arrest they could have successfully resisted it.[45]

Commissioner Sargent excused three inspectors at Buffalo who had brought four Chinamen across the Canadian boundary and then had arrested them for being unlawfully in the United States.[46] As far back as 1891, the same sort of thing was being done, for a

[43] *H. R.* 847, p. 140.
[44] *H. R.* 847, p. 61.
[45] *Cong. Docs.* 1901, ser. no. 4163, *H. Doc.* 472.
[46] *H. R.* 847, p. 137-8.

Administration of Exclusion Laws   325

Master in Chancery said: "The Custom House was in the habit of stopping Chinamen without any regard to their rights."[47] In the case of eighteen Chinamen arrested on Whidby Island, Washington, a number of white citizens complained to Secretary Blaine that it was the custom of immigration officers of the United States to arrest Chinese without warrants on mere suspicion and to deport them if they could not clear themselves by white evidence. When the cases were brought into Court a United States Commissioner released eight of these Chinamen and the Court on appeal, the other ten.[48]

To show what can happen to a decent, inoffensive Chinaman who holds a certificate of his right to be in the United States, the following story is related:[49]

A Chinese cannery-man, whose name for the purpose of this story shall be Li Toy, shipped from a Pacific port, carrying his proper laborer's certificate, to the Alaskan fishing grounds for the summer season. In the fall when with fifty or sixty others he was returning, he was detained at an Alaskan port by a new and zealous inspector who thought that his paper was a forgery. The inspector gave Li Toy no receipt for the certificate but wrote his own name upon an envelope and gave it to him telling him his certificate would be examined, and if not a forgery would be sent to the immigration office at the port to which he was returning. When Li Toy arrived at this port he went to the office and inquired for his certificate, but nothing was known of it. He went so often for it that he became a nuisance and the officers finally arrested him for being without it. He was taken before a Commission and sentenced to deportation because his certificate could not be found. Li Toy went to jail and quietly notified his friends; and at the end of three weeks a friend came from several hundred miles away and engaged a lawyer for him.

Meanwhile the period during which appeal may be taken from a decision of deportation had long expired. The lawyer went to the Commissioner of the Court, showed the envelope which was Li Toy's only receipt for the certificate which he had given up, and got a suspension of the sentence of deportation pending an investi-

[47] Test. of S. C. Houghton, *Cong. Docs.* 1891, ser. no. 2890, p. 344.
[48] Case reported by Minister Tsui, *Cong. Docs.* 1891, ser. no. 3076, p. 138 ff.
[49] The story and all its details are fully vouched for. For a similar, but less complicated case, see *H. R.* 847, p. 131, case of Pong Bow, which occurred in 1904.

gation. The Commissioner said, however, that this was only as a special favor to the lawyer. In order to prevent any further mistakes, the attorney informed the United States Marshal that the sentence of deportation was suspended and the marshal crossed from the book of deportations the name and sentence of Li Toy. The lawyer then obtained from the Alaskan Inspector a statement that the certificate had proved not to be a forgery and that he had sent it to the office as he had promised. As it had not been received there the attorney appealed to the department in Washington for a duplicate which was granted. Pending its arrival Li Toy remained in jail and the lawyer supposed that as soon as the duplicate arrived the officers would release him.

Two or three weeks later when the attorney was in jail on other business he inquired casually about Li Toy and was told by a Chinaman that he had been deported. When the attorney went to the United States Marshal he acknowledged that Li Toy's name had been on two different lists in the office and having been crossed off from only one, a deputy had deported him. The lawyer then went to the immigration officers, who had meanwhile received the duplicate certificate, and insisted that they should direct the United States Marshal to aid him in having Li Toy brought back. But before the immigration officials would instruct the Marshal to send for Li Toy they required the lawyer and Li Toy's friends to guarantee his round trip passage which amounted to over one hundred dollars. The steamer on which he had been deported being then about due at Shanghai, the Marshal signed a cablegram to the Captain of the vessel to release Li Toy—but the cable did not reach the port in time and another was sent to the port of Hong Kong. There Li Toy was finally found and returned to the United States by the same ship.

When he again arrived in the United States, he was examined by the Surgeon-in-Charge at the port of entry and detained for incipient consumption under the general immigration law. The attorney finally succeeded in getting him landed, however, under the legal fiction that he had never really landed in Hong Kong and was not therefore a returning Chinaman.

When the attorney suggested to the Immigration officials that since Li Toy had been deported through no fault of his own but through the negligence and mistakes of the immigration service, his steamer passage should be refunded to him, they derided the idea and pointed out that he was lucky to be landed at all and but for the personal favor of the United States Commissioner he would have long before been *legally* deported!

It has already been shown that under the present conditions of administration no Chinese person in the United States is safe from arrest. There are, nevertheless, in this country thousands of Chinese persons who have a legal right to be here without a certificate under the amended Geary law. In 1894 the Commissioner of Internal Revenue reported to the government that substantially all laborers had registered.[50] The classes of persons who could not or did not need to register at that time, were: 1—native-born Chinese of whom there are at present not less than 4500; 2—those who were too young to have been manual laborers in 1892;[51] 3—those who were merchants in 1892 but have since become laborers; 4—those who lawfully entered the United States after the registration period but have since become laborers.

The lack of a certificate is no proof that a laborer is here unlawfully, but since 1899 it has become increasingly difficult for such a person to prove that he has a right to be here. Before that time very few prosecutions for non-registration were brought, but about that time the officers suddenly became very vigilant and in 1905 no less than 1100 Chinese were arrested of whom *one-half* were discharged by the courts. The Department regulations take no account of the fact that these classes have a right to be here and the consequence is that a large number of Chinese persons—as for instance wives and minor children—who either could not or at least understood that they could not, register between 1892 and 1894 are now without certificates and subject to arrest and deportation.[52]

If the Chinese statutes had been carefully drawn to meet conditions of pauper labor and non-assimilation such as have arisen in the East as a result of indiscriminate European immigration, they might ultimately have had a chance of enforcement as measures of public welfare. But in consequence of their partisan and local origin, they have never received the support of general

[50] *Cong. Docs.* For. Rels. 1894, p. 166.
[51] There were 1400 Chinese children under 15 in California in 1890.
[52] Kohler, *Am. Jo. Asiatic Assoc.* July, 1905, 176 ff.

approval, much less the sympathy of the higher public officials whose duty it was to enforce them. In the earlier years Secretaries of the Treasury, Judges and Commissioners of the Courts and even Immigration officers showed leniency; sheltering themselves behind the looseness of the statutes and the lack of adequate appropriations, with the result that the policy of enforcement was vacillating, inconsistent and indifferent. But as soon as organized labor became a conspicuous political factor it demanded the chief positions of the immigration service as its perquisite and stricter enforcement of the laws.

Meanwhile the Chinese immigration service, about which nobody cared very much not even the politicians who had brought it into being, had been filled up with ignorant, narrow-minded men whose idea of effective enforcement was simply to shut out more Chinamen, no matter of what class, by constantly greater severity, suspicion and intimidation. Under Mr. Powderly those officers who pursued the Chinese most unremittingly were apparently most favored. In California an invariable symptom of official ambition for political preferment has been zeal in administering the exclusion law; and the sword hanging over the head of every officeholder for twenty-five years past, has been leniency to the Chinaman.

Under such circumstances it is not to be supposed that anybody was taking very much pains to make the law really enforceable. Before every Presidential campaign successive politicians tinkered with it hastily and successive officers of varying degrees of anti-Chinese prejudice and inexperience enforced the patched-up legislation by means of regulations that suited their own notions of technical efficiency. Nobody except the Judges of the Courts who occasionally called a halt in this improvised law, took the Chinaman into account at all. If the Chinese government complained it was told

Administration of Exclusion Laws 329

that the treaty was to be kept, if convenient, but that it was not the final authority. If China objected to regulations which did not even correspond to the legislation, she was told that even legislation was not the final authority. In short, it amounted to this: the Secretary of the Treasury in name, the inspectors in fact, were the final authority. Any rule, provided it had the appearance of greater severity, would not be disapproved by the Secretary of the Treasury or the Commissioner of Immigration or the Collectors of the Port at San Francisco, because the Chinaman was the pet antipathy of the workingmen on the Coast and the workingmen must not be offended.

If it be assumed that the law was or is unenforceable; if it be granted further that many of the difficulties of the administration were due to obstruction and fraud on the part of Chinese immigrants; if every reasonable defense that has been made were accepted—there is still the conspicuous fact that neither conscience nor intelligence seem to have applied to the solution of the problem. Thirty years ago the Californians complained that the Chinese were contract laborers, diseased and vicious; but the general immigration laws made to shut out European immigrants of these classes were not applied to Chinese immigrants till 1903. The squalor and inconvenience of the Detention Shed at San Francisco have been familiar to officials for many years and a subject of chronic grievance against the Pacific Mail Steamship Company; yet neither officials nor zealous California politicians compelled the company to alter it. California has gone to Congress for a generation with projects requiring millions of dollars but not one little bill for a grant of land and a suitable immigration station at San Francisco to make the exclusion law decent and enforceable.

From 1880, when the lax methods of the American Consul in China were exposed, until now, it has been no secret that the consular visé was of no value. Even when the Consul was honest it was impossible that he should investigate thoroughly the facts stated in the certificates so as to vouch for their truth. Yet no vigorous effort has been made to make the consular visé authoritative or, in default of that, to send, as Commissioner-General Sargent proposed, a trained officer of the immigration service to China whose business it shall be to ascertain the truth of the statements made by Chinese officials.

The first obstacle to the effective exclusion of the Chinese laborer encountered by the immigration officials was the thousands of miles of unprotected border on the north and south; yet the agreement with the Canadian authorities, securing a most satisfactory coöperation in the exclusion of Chinese was not made until 1903. We have not yet secured such an agreement with Mexico although it takes fourteen officers to guard less than two hundred miles of border from San Diego to Yuma and two other stations to guard ineffectively the remainder. And while the Immigration service makes desperate efforts to catch a few Chinamen crossing over without certificates, the pauper Mexican Cholos, by the hundreds, freely come and go under contracts to labor.

It would have seemed a perfectly natural thing for the United States, after having extorted from reluctant China the exclusion of her laboring class, to conciliate her by inviting her to coöperate in making exclusion as little of a hardship as possible. It is obvious enough after twenty-five years that without her active coöperation it has been and probably always will be impossible to enforce such a law except at enormous cost of money and good-will. Yet we have refused the proffered help of her accredited officers stationed in this country in making the law effective; and have only recently arrived at the idea that the only way to make the certificates

Administration of Exclusion Laws 331

truthful would be to enlist the services of her Provincial officers.

It has been assumed that the Chinese would obstruct and defeat the law before they had even attempted to do so. When the statutes and regulations, which were made with little reference to the treaty, have proven inefficient or unenforceable, the blame has been laid upon the cunning of the Chinese. It is small wonder that the exclusion laws have become a synonym for perjury and cunning on one side and bribery and graft on the other. The degree of irresponsible and discretionary power vested in the inspectors and the absolute secrecy in which all the examinations and records gradually became enshrouded invited abuse. Periodically the newspapers, voicing the ambitions of politicians and the general race prejudice baited and hounded every officer who showed the slightest inclination to give the Chinese a fair chance. Thus it came about that no man could stay in the immigration service who was not violently anti-Chinese.

To corruption was added oppression, prejudice and intolerance. When the Chinese minister complained of violation of international agreements and of the common principles of justice, the Chinese Bureau, ignoring the question of principle, justified the administration with complaints of Chinese evasion and deceit which, it said, made oppression and intolerance necessary. Yet the very officers of the service as well as of the courts and the law, were notoriously, in many cases, in collusion with the Chinese who were trying to come in. No one who has carefully read the testimony on both sides can doubt that with trustworthy and competent subordinates in the Chinese service every laborer who should be excluded by the intent of the treaties and a fair construction of the law, could be kept out.

Whether the exempt classes could, at the same time, be admitted as courteously as the citizens of the most favored nations, under the present form of the exclusion law, is quite another question. As now administered it has operated to keep laborers in the country who would have gone home and on the other hand it has put a premium on the admission of laborers who were shut out by the Scott Act. It has made it so difficult for the wives of the exempt classes to come in as to operate almost as a prohibition, while at the same time, any prostitute could be brought in if there was money enough spent. It has driven out of the country all the great merchants who contributed to the prosperity of California in the pioneer days, and encouraged the common laborer to become a " fake " merchant in order to get in; it has left in the country the insane and criminal Chinese, who might have been deported, and driven away scholars, missionaries and commercial men who would be the natural advertisers of American products and manufactures in China.

As the number of the Chinese in the country has steadily declined and the exempt classes have been discouraged from coming, the service has nevertheless cost more and more. From sixty thousand dollars in 1894 to two hundred and thirty thousand in 1903, and five hundred thousand in 1905, the appropriations have risen. In 1905 in the San Francisco Bureau there were forty men to handle 2200 Chinese persons coming and going, at a cost of sixty-five thousand dollars for salaries alone. The majority of Chinese should be landed without question since their papers were looked up before they went and again before they returned. There were less than forty landing cases per month with which these forty employes occupied themselves. They seem to spend their time trying to find out whether a man is a merchant or a laborer when in reality, if the certificate is correct and he is the person to whom it belongs, it makes no difference which he is. And to assist in this busy search there are stationed at other districts in the United States twenty-two inspectors-in-charge with their subordinates,

Administration of Exclusion Laws 333

besides the officers of the Chinese service attached to the general immigration service at New York, Philadelphia and Boston.

At the time when most of the Chinese in the United States refused to register under the original Geary law, the Secretary of the Treasury—to show the impossibility of carrying out the act—estimated that it would cost not less than ten millions of dollars to deport the 83,000 then unregistered. It has probably cost more than that already to enforce the exclusion law and there are still almost as many Chinamen left in the country. Since the treaty was after all not to be kept except when convenient, and since the exclusion law has never satisfied anybody, it would have been a saving of trouble and expense and perhaps of " face " if they had all been deported. The exclusion law has been " an expensive toy " as Inspector Datus E. Coon predicted, and we could scarcely have offended the Chinese more by wholesale deportation than we have contrived to do by the ingenious discourtesies of regulation.

The treaties and the laws distinguish between laborers and the privileged classes and guarantee specifically to the latter all the rights of the most favored nations except the right of naturalization; but the regulations of the Immigration Bureau have almost obliterated any distinction between them and the officers have in fact often ignored it. In the various compilations of the regulations, every third or fourth rule begins " Every Chinese person " and it is very nearly impossible for the uninitiated reader to discover what registered laborers must do and what the exempt classes need not do, to come and go from the United States.

The regulations have conspired more and more to make the exempt classes conform to the same technicalities as registered laborers. The practice of the ordinary courtesies shown to other most favored nations, and the simple expedient of publishing separate rules for the exempt classes, separate officers to catechise them and a separate place of detention, would have allayed much irritation, prevented much bribery and evasion and would have saved the United States millions of dollars in Oriental trade. The Chinese are justly outraged, not because their laborers have been excluded nor even primarily because they have been ill-treated, but because their honorable men and women have been harassed and insulted within our own borders. Granting that exclusion was inevitable if not necessary, the facts show that the legislation enacted to execute the treaties and the methods of administration have made it degrading to both parties. Whether a law which discriminates against nationality and occupation is justifiable can only be demonstrated by a fair interpretation of treaty and laws carried out by unbiased and conscientious officers.

PART III

COMPETITION AND ASSIMILATION

CHAPTER XVIII

LABOR IN CALIFORNIA BEFORE THE KEARNEY PERIOD

" The Chinese will maintain their hold in this country, if they maintain it at all, not by the cheapness but by the excellence of their labor. Their wages are constantly rising. Before long they will receive everywhere as they do now in many localities, as much as any man should receive in view of the cost of provisions and clothing; and finally, the question of wages is likely to settle itself by a rise in the demands of Chinamen and a fall in the price of Christians."—R. W. RAYMOND, Commissioner of Mining Statistics, 1871.

" The industrial situation in California is not to bring occupation to labor, but labor to occupations."—JOHN C. ENOS, State Commissioner of Labor, 1883.

" In the early settlement of the State . . . when mining was the chief industry and labor by reason of its scarcity, well paid, the presence of a few thousand Chinamen who were willing to work in occupations then seriously in want of labor, and at lower wages than the standard, caused no serious alarm or discomfort. . . . Thus civilization was possible in the very early days in the California mines. Many writers refer to the services rendered by the Chinese in those early times, and there is a general agreement that his labor was a blessing.—SAMUEL GOMPERS in *Meat v. Rice*, 1901.

IN order to understand the views of the post-bellum generation in regard to Chinese competition in labor, it is necessary to revert to conditions which have long since passed away and to opinions which, among the intelligent at least, are obsolete. These were the days when European immigration consisted almost wholly of Northern Teutonic and Irish stock; when pauper and contract labor laws had scarcely been broached; when labor organizations had no part in the control either of industry or politics.

We must also remember that before 1869 California immigration came by sea or overland at tremendous cost of money and hardship. It necessarily consisted of the strong and adventurous, who possessed money enough to carry them far beyond the limit possible to the newly arrived immigrant. They might be borrowers or assisted or even contract immigrants, but they were none the less a selected class. Whether skilled workmen or farmers or mere handy adventurers, they came to California to escape by gold mining or some other speculation, the drudgery of hum-drum occupations. Such men as these, however hardy and adventurous, had no intention of working by the day for wages even a good deal above the Eastern standard—they meant to make their fortune, "to strike it rich." From the beginning, then, California presented the anomaly of almost continuous scarcity of day labor while at times overstocked with capable men out of employment.

During the first twenty years, its unskilled labor class was composed of the prospector and the speculator, "down on his luck" and the workingman trying to accumulate a "stake"—in short of those, unstable or unfortunate, who had no intention of being permanent day laborers but who meant to quit the job at the first chance. In times of mining excitement or stock speculation, even the skilled workmen dropped their trades and joined the stampede for fortune. If successful, they left a vacuum of labor behind them; if unsuccessful, they returned, usually to San Francisco sooner or later, there to swell the ranks of the discontented employed, or quite as often the mass of the unemployable.

In any community such as early California, whose lure lay in its gold mines, the first immigrants were inevitably those who came to make fortunes, as inevitably followed by those who provisioned camps and supplied the daily wants of life and who, in their own line, were gamblers also. In such an aggregation of men there was, properly speaking, no laboring class and those who were driven, at times, to day labor, were, therefore, discontented, incompetent and unreliable. The man who had set out to be an independent prospector, investor, or miner and failed; or who had lost his capital, invested in groceries, blankets or tools, did not make an ideal workingman. He was likely to add to the high wages characteristic of a pioneer community the extravagant demands of a man who had set out for better fortune.

At first the adventurers did their own crude housekeeping, but in proportion as the better class among them succeeded, the demand increased for cooks, launderers, and laborers,—for women, Chinese, negroes, Indians—any kind of domestic or unskilled labor to do the necessary drudgery of even semi-civilized living. Because of the great cost of travel westward before 1869, neither laborers nor servants would come in sufficient numbers from the congested cities of the East; even skilled workmen could seldom afford to exhaust their savings in the hazard of emigration to California unless they hoped there to abandon their trades for that of the successful miner. For the same reasons the small farmer, enticed by the rumor of a gentle climate and enormous crops, seldom remained a farmer after he reached California.

The isolation of California and the extraordinary rewards of mining prolonged the era of generally high wages to 1870, and stimulated the immigration of laborers from the Orient as much as from the Eastern states. When, by the completion of the Pacific Railway, the industries of the States were suddenly brought into close rivalry with the East, and when almost simultaneously, placer mining gave place to other methods requiring the investment of larger capital and the coöperation of common labor, a sudden readjustment of occupations and wages became inevitable. Owing to the high cost of transportation of bulky manufactures and of passengers, labor in certain lines received a kind of artificial protection. A classification of occupations and wages brings out the fact that, while wages fell rapidly in some lines, they fell slowly in others and not at all in others. For the purpose of demonstrating this inequality the classification used by Professor Carl C. Plehn has been adopted.[1] According to his grouping the first class consists of labor occupied in producing goods for a wider market than California, whose wages would necessarily exceed wages elsewhere by so much as the natural advantages of location exceeded the cost of transportation—as for instance, gold, fruit, wine and for a time, wheat. The wages of this protected class have always been high in the West.

The second class consists of labor employed in producing goods which competed in the local market with goods that could be imported from outside the state, the only considerable advantage of which lay in the cost of transportation. To this class belong nearly all the manufacturing industries, such as woolens, boots and shoes, cigars, woodenware, *et cetera*. These industries were started comparatively late, the wages were never very high, and their wage scale had to fall to very nearly the Eastern level if the industry survived. The only exception was where California could produce an article distinctly superior to the Eastern importation—as for instance, woolen blankets. It is probable that superior raw material and a knowledge of the local market were more than offset by the higher interest on capital.

The third class of labor consists of skilled labor performing services which were rendered on the spot, such as the building trades. These were required very early, their wages were always high as compared with the Eastern standard, and still remain so in direct proportion to skill. The residue constitute a fourth class—the unskilled—which in any pioneer community gains relatively most from local advantages, but which is the first to feel competition and therefore the first to accept a lowered wage. The wages of this class have at times been only a little above the Eastern level but at

[1] Plehn, *Yale Review*, 1896, pp. 408 ff.

other times have fluctuated far above, generally returning to a scale distinctly above that of the East.

The miners and the farmers were the only classes producing for an outside market without local competition; and the natural advantages were such that wages remained extraordinarily high long after the wages of other classes had begun to fall. During the first twenty-five years miners seldom received less than four dollars per day and the wages of farm laborers steadily rose until they were double those of the Eastern states. The earliest manufacturing industries (class II) owed their origin either to the high cost of transportation of their products, as for instance, the iron industries, or to some local advantage, such as the sugar refineries, flour mills, saw and woolen mills. The high cost of production due to the scarcity of labor and high wages, to the lack of fuel and the exorbitant interest reaped by capital invested in other fields, made it unprofitable to initiate manufacture of many articles for which the raw material lay close at hand. Of the 2,700 men employed in manufactures in San Francisco in 1866, 1,700 were in foundries and woolen mills and 550 more in sugar refineries, saw mills and breweries. The only one of these in which the Chinese were employed to any extent was the woolen industry where they took the places filled by women employes of the Eastern mills.[2]

The two most reliable newspapers of this period refer frequently to the fact that, money being plentiful, good workmen of certain classes were always in demand, while there was no demand at all for others because the products of their labor could still be imported by sea and sold cheaper than they could be manufactured on the ground.[3]

[2] Assessor's reports, 1866–7. *Twelfth Census*, Vol. 8, discussion of California manufactures by Professor Carl C. Plehn.
[3] mor detailed tables of wages and comments thereon see: *Alta*, 1853, May 2; 1855, Jan. 3; 1857, Aug. 11; Aug. 21; 1866, June 8; 1861, June

Before 1867 there is very general acknowledgment that the Chinese had been of great value to California. In mining they had been allowed to take up only poor or abandoned claims, and as day laborers in the mines they received about half the pay of white men. In the country districts, where they were chiefly employed as farm laborers and domestic servants, white labor was not to be had in any amount even at exorbitant wages, and the Chinese soon demanded wages approaching those of white men and women. Although highly skilled as handicraftsmen in their own country, they did not quickly learn mechanical trades and never competed at all with the most highly paid labor in the State. The supply of unskilled day labor was so fluctuating and always so meagre in proportion to demand at this period that the Chinese were in reality as great a benefit to the white laboring classes as to the capitalistic employers.

Up to 1862 about fifty per cent of the Chinese were engaged in mining, and forty per cent more in trade (chiefly among themselves), truck-gardening, farm labor, washing and household service, fishing and common labor; less than one per cent were engaged in manufacture. Between 1862 and 1867 from twelve to fifteen per cent of them left the mines and most of them went to work on the Railway.[4] About six per cent, *i. e.* three thousand, were drafted into the manufacture of shoes, slippers, cigars, woolens, jewelry and blacking. In the towns they had already become what they remained for a long time afterward—gap-fillers. Whatever the white man would not do, that the Chinaman undertook; washing—in a country where washerwomen were and always have been unattainable; household service—where women were as one to three of the adult male population and would not go into service while there was an

7; 1854, Aug. 9. Chicago *Tribune*, (San Francisco Correspondent), 1865, June 3.

[4] In 1862 there were about 55,000 Chinese in the Coast States; in 1867 there were only about 51,000. See Table, p. 500.

Labor Before the Kearney Period 343

abundance of well-paid work of a less menial character; day laborers at $1.25 per day where white laborers demanded from $2.50 to $4.00—when they would accept anything less than a chance for a fortune; truck-gardeners, to supply the cheap vegetables of which California boasted when it invited white immigration; fishing, small fruit raising, and fruit picking, peanut and chicken raising, wood cutting, stubble clearing, rag picking—all the hundred petty, drudging tasks to which the native-born American is so averse—these the Chinaman assumed.[5]

The early historians of the state are unanimous in their statements that the Chinese were not only not injurious competitors of white labor, but were a great benefit to the state. Tuthill says: "The cleanliness, politeness and good behavior of the Chinese was in everybody's mouth and what they contributed saved several counties from bankruptcy." Cronise estimated that in 1868, 40,000 were engaged in mining abandoned claims and about 8000 in the construction of the Central Pacific Railway; of the rest some were scattered over the country, others remained in towns as cooks and domestics, a few hundred were at work in the woolen mills and small factories, a considerable number in laundries, or engaged in trade, gardening and other pursuits, their customers in these latter branches being found mostly among their own countrymen. He adds: "Certain of our manufacturing industries could not without their aid have gained a foothold thus early; nor could the Central Pacific Railway, an enterprise vital to every interest in the state, have been pushed forward with the speed it has been; not so much in the latter case, from their cheapening labor as in their filling a demand that must otherwise have remained unfilled."[6] Lloyd said: "We cannot believe otherwise than that the Chinese in California have contributed largely to her prosperity.

[5] Sacramento *Union*, January 17, Feb. 5, 1859.
[6] Tuthill, *Hist. of Cal.*, 1867; Cronise, *Wealth of Cal.*, 1868.

344 Competition and Assimilation

They have in no instance retarded her progress, but have aided in the development of her vast resources."[7]

Equally unanimous upon the industrial value of the Chinese, were the distinguished travelers, journalists, and experts who visited California during this period. Charles Loring Brace said they were an absolute necessity to the material development of California. Mr. Beadle of the Cincinnati *Commercial* wrote: "It is evident at a glance that less than one-fifth of them come into competition with white labor. The rest are doing work which white men would not do at all. * * * It is cheap labor in California but would not be in the East. * * * California needs and can employ a quarter of a million Chinese without displacing a single white." Mr. Bowles of the Springfield *Republican* wrote: "Labor, cheap labor, being the one great palpable need of the Pacific States, we should all say that their immigration would be encouraged. * * * Certainly here in this great field * * * their diversified labor is a blessing and a necessity." Even Mr. Gompers has said of this period that the Chinese caused no serious alarm or discomfort to white labor.[8] It seems clear then, that before 1867 the absorption of white labor in other and more remunerative fields than those in which the Chinese were engaged, and the small amount of white labor in proportion to the work to be done, left an immense vacuum which the Chinese only partly filled. But the year 1867 marks the beginning of certain political and industrial changes in California which in the following decade brought the Chinese question into prominence. For the first time in the history of California the trades

---

[7] Lloyd, *Lights and Shades of S. F.* 1876. See also Frignet, *La Californie*; Bancroft, *Hist. of Cal.* v., 38; Hittell, *Hist. of Cal.* v., 3, 4; John S. Hittell, *Overland Mo.* (N. S.) v. 7, (1886); McClellan, *The Golden State*, p. 471.

[8] Brace, in *The New West*, 1868; Beadle, correspondent of the *Commercial*, 1869–1873; Bowles, in 1865; Townsend, July 10, 1871; Gompers (presumably) in a pamphlet called "Meat *v.* Rice," published by the Amer. Fed. of Labor, 1902.

unions were in a position to dictate to the leaders of the established political parties. Although many unions had been organized from 1851 onward [9] they had not been very stable until united by the eight-hour movement which had spread over the whole country. The Republicans in California, disrupted by factions and the Democrats, weakened by the defection of many workingmen, felt alike the necessity of winning the labor vote in the current State election.

In the winter of 1866–7 there were labor riots in San Francisco stimulated by similar agitations in the East. Although they were the accompaniment of the efforts of organized labor throughout the country to obtain a shorter working day, the anti-coolie agitators attributed them entirely to the presence and competition of the Chinese. Nevertheless, as has already been shown, the Chinese were almost wholly engaged in occupations in which there was the greatest scarcity of laborers.[10] The Sacramento *Union*—an independent paper—said:

"California has about a half a million inhabitants . . . a queer place this, to raise a clamor about the ruinous competition of labor. Farmers complain of lack of hands . . . skilled mechanics get more dollars a day in gold than their fellow craftsmen in the East receive in depreciated paper money. Honest miners are in demand . . . while the prospecting field is immense. Land is cheap and the productive capacity unrivalled yet vast tracts remain untilled. . . . Factories would be closed without them [Chinese]; rail-

[9] Prof. Ira Cross of Stanford University has furnished from his material on the history of Union labor in California the following information as to the dates of organization: 1851, draymen, and teamsters, riggers and stevedores, lightermen; 1852, typographical, bricklayers, bakers, tailors; 1853, nearly all the trades; 1856, musicians; 1863, unions composed of seven trades representing 2000 to 2500 men, which lasted till 1866; 1866, Industrial League; 1867, Mechanics' State Council. From other sources, 1867, ironmoulders; 1868, shipwrights; 1869, Brotherhood of Locomotive Engineers; 1872, (reorganized) Typographical Union; 1873, tailors; 1877, glass-blowers; 1878, barbers, boilermakers, iron shipbuilders, caulkers; many others from 1880 onward. See Bonner, *Cal. Illust. Mag.*, v. 1.; Plehn, *Yale Rev.* 1896.

[10] *Alta*, 1867, June 2, 4; July 20, 22; Aug. 8; Oct. 5; *Call*, July 23, 27. *Examiner*, Feb. 14.

roads remain unbuilt; washing, cooking, ironing could not be hired by moderate means. . . . Whatever the case may be in San Francisco . . . the fact is that in the country more labor is wanted than can be obtained. . . . In mining regions as a rule, poor John confers more benefit than he receives. . . . In the towns the Chinese do not compete with the whites in mechanical pursuits. Cigar-making occupies many in San Francisco but that hardly rises to the dignity of a trade and is largely given up to women in Eastern cities. . . . How then can the presence of the Chinaman raise a square issue between capital and labor?" [11]

At this time the California Press, politicians and the public did not attempt to disguise the fact that the anti-Chinese movement was chiefly political and incidental to the agitation of reconstruction measures and workingmen's reforms. While politicians and workingmen fulminated against the Chinese "invasion," Democrats, Republicans and Labor Party alike availed themselves of their services in house and factory, on ranches and in mines. The single workingman himself had no other resource when he wanted a clean shirt or a decent meal.[12]

There were, undoubtedly, a considerable number of unemployed men in San Francisco every winter between November and April. The intermittent character of the early mining industries and of agricultural operations, the roving disposition of the California laboring men, the short inclement season and the allurements of one large central city, drew all the unemployed and the traveling adventurers to San Francisco. Then as now, certain streets were full of idle men warming themselves against sunny walls in the daytime, spending the earnings of the previous season in gambling and sport at night, and reluctantly yielding to the necessity of taking another job as spring approached. As regularly as March came on, contracting engineers of construction works throughout the country, in the mines and moun-

[11] Sacramento *Union*, 1867, Feb. 14.
[12] Richardson, *Atlantic Mo.*, Dec. 1867, p. 741; Sac. *Union*, Feb. 20, 26, 1867; Daily *Alta*, Oct. 15, 1868. S. Wells Williams, *Soc. Sc.* paper, 1879. John Bidwell, Address before the State Agricultural Society, 1881.

Labor Before the Kearney Period 347

tains, complained of scarcity of labor; on their heels came the ranchers, apprehensive that their crops of grain and fruit could not be harvested for want of hands; to be followed almost invariably in midsummer by complaints from the builders in San Francisco of a like scarcity of workmen.

This mal-adjustment and unequal distribution of labor was probably even worse before the Pacific railways were finished than it is at present; and it was early recognized by employers and labor organizations as a condition requiring special effort to remedy. In the spring of 1868 the merchants and influential citizens of San Francisco organized a private labor exchange—" to be a means of communication between the employer and employe and to supply information to immigrants." [18] The detailed report of this exchange for eighteen months, during which 15,022 men and women were placed, has been condensed into the table following, on page 348.

The most striking feature of the table is the peculiar list of occupations in which applicants were "very numerous"; and on the other hand, the large orders for classes of labor apparently not supplied. The significance of this grouping is that the over-demand was chiefly for heavy, common, and domestic labor at wages from $1.50 to $4.00 per day and board; while the oversupply consisted of two general classes—white-handed or indoor men, and men of low-grade city occupations.

In the middle groups, II and III, the demand and supply met in five occupations (waiters, painters, dishwashers, grooms and teamsters) which require little skill and are oftenest resorted to by incompetent or dissipated men who cannot do ordinary manual labor. It is to be remarked also, that the skilled trades are only slightly represented in Groups I and III. When orders

[18] The *Alta* of April 15, 1868, said: "The demand for laborers and several classes of mechanics ... is extraordinarily urgent ... especially for labor on docks, waterworks, railways and for carpenters, machinists *etc.*, in mining and manufacturing."

CALIFORNIA LABOR EXCHANGE (1868–9).
DATA RE-CLASSIFIED BY OCCUPATIONS TO SHOW DEMAND AND SUPPLY.

I Demand Excessive Occupations numbers ordered.	II Occupations numbers ordered	III. Supply Excessive Occupations (Applicants "very numerous.")	IV Occupations in which Chinese could have competed.
Laborers ... 5859 " (Farm) 2720 Carpenters .. 1788 Cooks (women).. 838 Lumbermen 763 Boys....... 752 Miners..... 724 Blacksmiths (Machine) ... 493 Total..... 13,937			Laborers " (Farm) Cooks (to replace women.) (To replace boys.) Miners.
	Waiters .... 485 Painters...... 297 Dishwashers.. 242 Boot and shoe makers.... 202 Grooms. ... 189 Potato Diggers.,...... 187 Bricklayers... 186 Teamsters.... 181 Total...... 1,968	Waiters Painters Dishwashers Grooms Teamsters	Waiters Dishwashers Boot and shoe makers.
		Porters (applications by the thousand) Bookkeepers Clerks Salesmen Storemen Warehousemen Barkeepers Coachmen Engineers Machinists Hostlers Laundrymen (Steam) Stewards Shepherds Watchmen	Laundrymen (Hand) Stewards

for carpenters and blacksmiths are numerous and applicants are still more so, it probably means that the competent were first employed leaving the demand still unsupplied, while there was at the same time a surplus of the poorer grades of men in the same line. The contemporary newspapers frequently mention the fact that highly skilled workers could always get employment at high wages in California while numbers of half-trained workmen were out of work.

It must not be forgotten that this exchange came into existence in the Spring of 1868—an extremely prosperous year on the Coast—when the Central Pacific had been compelled to employ nearly 10,000 Chinese because of the scarcity of common white labor. Practically all the unskilled and recently arrived Chinese had been drawn off to railroad construction.[14] Whatever competition with white labor there was, was necessarily narrowed down to a few occupations, such as did not have an adequate supply of white labor—laborers, family cooks, boys, miners, waiters, dishwashers, boot and shoe makers.

In short, this table, covering the bulk of the unemployed and unemployable in the State from 1868 to 1870 suggests that the objections to the Chinese were due to causes none of which were understood or ever mentioned. The first was a lack of distribution and adaption on the part of the casual white labor, resulting in the concentration in San Francisco of a large number of semi-skilled and probably more or less disappointed men who had come to California to make the traditional fortune; or, who were incapable of doing the ordinary manual labor for which there was such an extraordinary demand; or who would not go to the country at all, or at least not for moderate wages. The table proves conclusively that skilled labor felt no occasion to avail itself of the Labor Exchange.

[14] Chinese on the S. P. Railway received $30–$35 per month.

The reports of the Exchange give other information of an instructive sort on the labor situation. Women's wages remained at $20–$30 per month and found and the supply was never sufficient; the wages of ordinary labor which had for some years been rising, began to fall in 1869 and 1870, yet "sober, industrious" men could always find work at fair wages; the distant counties which needed labor most could not obtain it at any price partly because of the high cost of transportation, but chiefly because labor would not go far into the country at any price.

Fifty per cent of the applicants were Irish, 19 per cent American, 10 per cent English and Scotch, 10 per cent German,—the rest scattering. If it be assumed that a considerable number of the Americans were of Irish parentage, as they must have been, it will be seen how large a part of the problem of distribution and employment was due to the Irish race alone. The report says that the immigrants who could not speak English generally went to the country and had money to pay their transportation; thus leaving the Irish and Americans in the city.

Between 1869 and 1874 serious changes took place in the conditions of labor both in city and country, due to a coincidence of depression and over-immigration. The Central Pacific Railway was completed in 1869 and at once discharged its thousands of white and Chinese laborers, many of whom drifted back to San Francisco in search of work. The stimulus of railway building, the phenomenal prosperity resulting from extraordinary stock sales in 1868, and two successive years of abundant rainfall, had brought to California a net gain of 35,000 white immigrants in 1868 and 24,000 more in 1869—the largest influx of population since 1852 and 1854 and more than double the number for ten years previous. Chinese immigration, which had been almost at a standstill since 1863, suddenly showed a net gain in the three years, 1868-1871, of 22,000 chiefly due to the demand for labor on construction works.

At the moment when California thus had for the first time a fair supply of common labor, there came a severe panic in silver stocks, the treasure yield of the state in 1871 fell to one-half what it had been in '69, one-third what it had been in '64—and two severe droughts in succession materially lessened the demand for agricultural labor. Real estate in the city fell rapidly; exports of merchandise, which had risen to an amount equal to the gold product in 1867, fell off nearly one-half. By the winter of 1870-1 there were three men—two white and one yellow—for every job in San Francisco, and immigration of both classes received a sudden check within the year.

The depression in every line of business was suddenly, but by no means completely or permanently relieved in 1872 by the discovery of the Belcher Bonanza mines and by a heavy rainfall. Owing to this degree of local relief, and the fact that California was on a gold basis, the Eastern panic of 1873 affected business very little directly. Indirectly, however, it added to the unstable conditions of markets and labor. Great numbers of men were out of employment in the East and the rumors of continued prosperity in the West, combined with an ease of transportation hitherto unknown, again precipitated upon California, in the three years before 1874, as many white immigrants as had come to the state in the whole ten years from 1857 to 1867. This immigration was not, like the earlier influx, of the class of hardy adventurers and agriculturists, but largely factory operatives, men of indoor trades, and recently arrived European immigrants, whom hard times in the East had driven to pursue their fortune in the West, but who lacked very generally the initiative and hardihood of the pioneer population, and who were, for the most part, both unwilling and unfit to settle in the country districts, or to do heavy manual labor.

The later Chinese immigration was undoubtedly of a lower grade than that of the first eighteen years, consisting of mere manual laborers enticed by the demand for unlimited common labor on construction works and having their passages guaranteed by the contractors who employed them. They, too, had less initiative and adaptability, for they were not so generally of that class of sturdy peasant farmers that had come in early times enticed by the golden adventure, and able to pay their own passages. In short, the conditions already described, brought to the cities of California a relatively less adaptable and less sturdy class of workingmen of all races, for whom capitalists were not yet prepared to provide employment in their chosen occupations at the high wages that had prevailed for so many years.

Not only were the conditions of labor rapidly changing but the conditions of production also were altered. After 1869, cheaper and quicker transportation by railway brought California products suddenly into a much closer competition with Eastern products and manufactures than ever before. Capital still brought such high rates in other ventures in the West that manufacture could only be carried on by reason of some extraordinary advantages of raw material, location, climate or cheap labor over competing industries elsewhere.

Throughout the Eastern and Middle states wages had been rising rapidly after the War till the time of the panic; even in California they had risen in some lines and, up to 1870, had not fallen perceptibly in any. But Young's Tables for 1874 show that the inevitable fall of wages—so long postponed by isolation, mining discoveries and absence of real competition—was just beginning.[15]

[15] Young, *Labor in Europe and America*, (1875–6), *Cong. Docs.* s. n. 1686, pp. 745-7.

Labor Before the Kearney Period 353

In the twelve trades covered by these tables all groups of states except the Pacific, show an increase of from 20-40 per cent in wages between 1869-1874; for the same period California shows a fall of from 2 per cent to seven per cent in six trades, and stationary or slightly rising wages in the other six. Measured by the Eastern standard, wages in these lines in California were still high; but measured by the local standard, they had fallen terribly. It must be remarked that these trades belong to those "services on the spot" which are slow to feel the effects of outside competition.

But even in industries open to the competition of Eastern production, wages still held up. In ready-made and custom-made clothing; in sole leather, upper leather and calfskin, morocco and patent leather work, wages were higher than the average of New York, Kentucky and Wisconsin; in carriage making 33 per cent higher; in the iron industry $13\frac{1}{2}$ per cent higher than in Pennsylvania and Delaware. For women domestics, wages had been rising all over the country—in the Middle states they had doubled—between 1860 and 1874; in California they had remained practically stationary throughout the period and were still three times the average Eastern wage. The wages of farm and common labor also rose steadily from 1860 to 1870, and fell only slightly between 1870 and '74 east of the Rocky Mountains; in California, they were at least one-third above the average Eastern rate.

In 1875 Mr. W. H. Martin of the California Immigrant Union, in a comment intended for the eye of the white immigrant, pointed out the impending difficulty:

"Young men not afraid to work can almost always get employment in the country at from $25-$30 per month (and found). It is much easier to get employment in rough or mechanical work than in clerking, keeping books or in school-teaching; and persons who have no money and no friends in California able to assist them and no special knowledge that will certainly command employment, should not come here in expectation of an easy life. Men who expect to make their living by the shovel, plow and ax are wanted. . . . Chinamen are a necessary evil at present, for the reason that most of the young men of our state and newcomers generally, will not work for small wages. As soon as this is remedied by an importation of Eastern and European labor willing to work for $1.00 to $1.50 per day the employment of Chinese will gradually be diminished."

From a bulletin of the United States Bureau of Labor, a much wider view through a much longer period may be had of wages. The wage-scale was obtained from the actual pay-rolls of twelve cities of the United States, including San Francisco. It has been condensed and rearranged to show a comparison of San Francisco with the eleven other cities in the Table VIII below. For the nineteen trades named during 1870-1890 the schedule shows when the maximum and minimum wage occurred.

COMPARISON OF MAXIMUM AND MINIMUM DAILY WAGES OF 19 TRADES IN SAN FRANCISCO AND IN 11 OTHER CITIES, 1870-1890.

Trade	Max. 11 cities.	Min. 11 cities.	Range.	Max. S. F.	Min. S. F.	Range in cents.	Amount by which Minimum of S. F. exceeds Maximum of 11 cities.
Blacksmiths	2.70	2.43	.27	3.80	3.33	.47	† .63
" Helpers	1.59	1.41	.18	2.34	2.09	.25	† .50
Boiler makers	2.69	2.41	.28	3.46	3.15	.31	† .46
Bricklayers	4.13	3.00	1.13	5.00	4.00	1.00	† .13
Carpenters	2.60	2.28	.32	3.85	3.09	.76	† .49
Compositors	2.82	2.64	.18	3.54	3.27	.27	† .45
Engineers (R. R.)	4.02	3.49	.53	4.79	4.53	.26	† .51
Firemen (R. R.)	2.03	1.75	.28	3.06	2.54	.52	† .51
Hod carriers	2.20	1.58	.62	3.00	2.35	.65	† .15
Iron moulders	2.79	2.36	.43	3.71	3.40	.31	† .61
Laborers (street)	1.63	1.45	.18	2.50	2.00	.50	† .37
" General	1.57	1.40	.17	2.00	1.97	.03	† .40
Machinists	2.52	2.22	.30	3.36	2.95	.41	† .43
Masons (stone)	3.62	2.81	.81	5.00	4.83	.17	† .21
Painters	2.66	2.16	.50	3.72	3.00	.72	† .34
Pattern makers	2.98	2.68	.30	3.89	3.15	.74	† .17
Plumbers	3.15	2.79	.36	3.69	3.55	.14	† .40
Stone cutters	3.64	2.66	.98	4.11	3.66	.45	† .02
Teamsters	1.95	1.71	.24	2.67	2.62	.05	† .67
Averages	2.69	2.27	.42	3.55	3.13	.89	.93

Labor Before the Kearney Period 355

The table shows that the fluctuations of wages in San Francisco had a wider range than in other cities, but it also shows that notwithstanding these fluctuations, wages in San Francisco remained extraordinarily high. During twenty years, 1870-1890, the *minimum* average wage in San Francisco in every one of the nineteen trades except the bricklayers exceeded the *maximum* average wage in the other cities, the total average excess amounting to 39 cents per day per trade. When it is remembered that this extraordinary superiority of wages in San Francisco continued through the period of the greatest Eastern panic as well as through the period of severest depression in California, and after a continuous line of railway had made California relatively easy of access, it may be conjectured but scarcely measured, how great the local scarcity and local advantage of labor must have been.[16]

The foregoing examination of authorities—the most reliable California papers, the reports of the Labor Exchange, of the Immigrant Union, Young's special report, and Wright's Bulletin—establishes the fact that in the skilled and semi-skilled trades, in general labor both in city and country, in domestic and farm labor, wages in California both before and during the Kearney period, ranged habitually far above the maximum of Eastern wages. No further proof is necessary to show that, in these lines, the Chinese not only had not lowered wages to any appreciable degree, but that there was room for many thousands more. There was an unfillable vacuum in the lower grades of labor which must have tended to prevent the expansion of industry and of construction work. Thus by a process of elimination

[16] The San Francisco Bulletin made an investigation of wages in Feb. 1878, to ascertain whether "the Chinese had dragged down wages below living rates." The *Alta* of Nov. 20, 1879, published a table showing the comparative wages of San.Francisco, New York and three foreign countries. Both papers concluded that wages in California were uniformly higher than elsewhere and the *Alta* said that living was cheaper in S. F. than in New York.

it has been shown that if there was serious competition with American labor, and rapidly falling wages, in California anywhere, it must have been in manufacture, for it was certainly not in the mechanical trades, in agriculture, general construction or domestic labor.

CHAPTER XIX

THE CHINESE IN MANUFACTURE

" Beginning with the most menial avocations they gradually invaded one industry after another until they not merely took the places of our girls as domestics and cooks, the laundry from the poorer of our white women, but also the places of the men and boys as boot and shoe makers, cigar-makers, bag-makers, miners and farm laborers, brick makers, tailors, slipper makers, *et cetera*. In the ladies' furnishing line they have absolute control, displacing hundreds of girls who would otherwise find profitable employment. . . . . As common laborers they have throughout California displaced tens of thousands of men . . . they have crowded out the native population and driven the country boy from the farm to the city where he meets their skilled competition in many branches of industry."—SAMUEL GOMPERS, *Meat versus Rice*, 1902.

" In mining, farming, in factories and in the labor generally of California the employment of the Chinese has been found most desirable; and much of the labor done by these people if performed by white men at higher wages could not be continued nor made profitable. . . . Indeed it is conceded that while in physical powers they are inferior to the white men, they are superior in diligence and sobriety. . . . . There are many large importing houses and wealthy firms. . . . Thousands of Chinese are employed in the city's factories."—MCCLELLAN, *The Golden State*, 1876.

" We cannot believe otherwise than that the Chinese in California have contributed largely to her prosperity. There are few if any, in this whole country that have suffered because of forced idleness or little compensation for work performed. Thus, taking things as they are, and as they have been, we cannot see that the presence of the Chinese among us in the past has resulted in evil but the benefits they have wrought are seen on every hand."—LLOYD, *Lights and Shades of San Francisco*, 1876.

It has been shown in the preceding chapter that the Chinese were an important element in early California progress and also that they were not competing in the mechanical trades and could not fill the labor vacuum still existing in agriculture, general construction and domestic services. But as early as 1862 there was complaint of Chinese competition in cigar-making and in the decade 1870–1880 there was constant agitation against them, led by the cigar-makers, the boot and shoe and woolen operatives, and the workers in the sewing trades.

The origin and growth of certain manufactures in California before 1880, and their decline after that time, is of peculiar interest but only so much of it can be touched upon here as relates to Chinese competition. The Federal Census of 1870 shows that of 430,444 persons over ten years of age, 238,648 were engaged in gainful occupations, of whom 92 per cent were men and 5.3 per cent women, between sixteen and fifty-nine years of age. At least 95 per cent of the Chinese in California at this time were within the same age limits. Of the total workers only 46 per cent were native-born; 14 per cent were born in China, 13 per cent in Ireland, 8 per cent in Germany, 4.7 per cent in England and Wales, 2 per cent in France and 1.3 per cent in Italy.

If we set aside all the Chinese engaged in agriculture, personal and professional service, trade, mining, lumbering and general labor, there are left in four principal manufactures 2,316 Chinese. Since practically all manufacturing was in San Francisco at this time a study of the conditions should show whether the Chinese were seriously competing in these lines: whether they were causing wages to fall more rapidly than elsewhere or were displacing white labor. The accompanying table gives the distribution of the different sexes and nationalities in California manufactures.[1]

---

[1] Besides the Census there is available the Assessor's reports from San Francisco and Young's report in 1874; the natural presumption would be that the Census and Young would underestimate and the Assessor over-estimate the numbers of operatives. The Assessor's figures (which he acknowledges are in many cases "estimates") are far above those of the Census in the cigar and woolen industries, but far below in the other two. The Census is undoubtedly defective but it is not a mere estimate; and there is no reason to suppose that more Chinese were omitted than other foreigners as they were exceptionally isolated and conspicuous.

The Chinese in Manufacture

EMPLOYEES IN SPECIFIED MANUFACTURES.

By Age, Sex and Nativity. San Francisco, 1870, U. S. Census.

Manufacture.	Total Number.	SEX. 16-59 years.		NATIVITY.				
		Males.	Females.	United States.	Germany.	Ireland.	England and Wales.	China.
Boots and Shoes—								
Number	1551	1462	50	312	294	403	57	296
Per cent		94	3	20	18	26	3	19
Cigars and Tobacco.								
Number	1811	1799	2	38	45	5	2	1657
Per cent		98		2	2			91
Woolens—								
Number	393	377	4	69	7	34	17	253
Per cent		95	1	17	1	8	4	64
Sewing Trades—								
Number	1223	621	574	243	300	280	50	110
Per cent		50	46	19	24	23	4	9
Totals—Numbers.	4978	4239	630	660	646	722	126	2316
Per cent		85	12	13	13	14	2	46

One of the most striking things in this table is the almost entire absence of women and children in all except the sewing trades. As the Chinese constituted only 9 per cent of the 1,223 employees in these trades and women nearly 50 per cent, it may be set aside temporarily for the consideration of shoe-making in which they were 19 per cent, cigar-making in which they were 91 per cent, and the woolen industry in which they were 64 per cent, of the total operatives.

In the shoe industry the Irish constituted 26 per cent of the total employes, the native-born Americans 21 per cent and the Germans and Chinese each, 19 per cent. Assuming that the overseers were generally native-born, it appears that the competition was not so much between the Americans and the Chinese as between the 19 per cent Chinese and the 50 per cent of other foreigners, one-half of whom were Irish.

The boot and shoe industry was begun in California immediately after the Civil War as a result of the large quantity and superior quality of hides and leather produced there. From 1867 to 1869 many coöperative factories were started in San Francisco and those that had no dissensions flourished and made excellent wages. In 1870 the industry in California engaged about 1,500 workers and the total production was valued at a million and a half dollars. Men were making four to five dollars per day and women (at home) from two to four dollars. As soon as the Pacific railway was completed transportation charges were lowered and local manufacturers began to complain that in spite of cheap raw material it was impossible to compete with the Eastern product. Some employed Chinese and others sent East for white workmen who would presumably work at the lower rates prevailing there.

The organization of the Knights of St. Crispin—a union which had suddenly attained great strength in the East—in San Francisco precipitated a struggle between employers and employes in this industry. The Knights of St. Crispin not only demanded an increase of wages but attempted to drive out the Chinese and to intimidate those who employed them. The struggle was intensified by the rapid introduction of machinery in the boot and shoe factories throughout the country which superseded much hand labor and enabled employers to replace adult operatives with women and children and in California, with Chinese.[2]

[2] In 1875 in Massachusetts there were 4,731 less shoemakers than in 1865 although there were manufactured $33,000,000 worth more shoes than ten years before.

The Chinese in Manufacture

By 1875 the number of employes had risen to 2,600 and the value of the California product to three millions. It was generally believed that the proportion of Chinese operatives was rapidly increasing although there are no reliable statistics on this point. Wages in California as elsewhere, were falling, though still above the average of the Eastern states and double those of Massachusetts.

The Tenth Census compares the pay-roll of one establishment in California with eight others in the Eastern states.

AVERAGE WAGES IN BOOT AND SHOE INDUSTRY,
1875-1880.
In one establishment in each of the States named.
(CENSUS, 1880)

Classes of Employes	Cal.	Ills.	Ind.	Me.	Md.	Mass	N.Y.	Ohio	Pa.	Average.
Cutter......	$3.00	2.50	2.97	1.91	2.75	2.13	2.17	1.86	1.76	2.34
Fitter.....	2.73	1.50	1.77	.94	1.75	1.70	1.55	1.00	1.06	1.557
Laster	2.66	2.00	1.75	1.85	2.25	1.94	.....	1.50	1.43	1.922
Treer	2.83	.....	2.00	1.84	1.75	3.00	.....	2.02	1.76	2.17
Bottomer .	2.75	.....	1.75	1.97	2.50	.....	1.77	1.50	1.77	2.001
Finisher...	3.00	2.50	2.50	1.95	3.00	2.24	2.44	2.00	2.47	2.455
Averages...	2.845	2.125	2.123	1.71	2.333	2.20	1.98	1.646	1.708	

This table indicates that wages in the establishment in California were uniformly higher than in other states, there being only one case—treers in Massachusetts—in which employes were paid as high. This conclusion is corroborated by information from the San Francisco *Bulletin* of 1878 which said that San Francisco shoe operatives were then receiving $12-$20 per week—"twice as much as in the East and three times as much as in Toronto."

The editorial continued:

"Leather will average less in price here than in the East, yet much of the material used by the Eastern boot and shoe manufacturers is shipped from this coast, manufactured and sent back to us to be sold at as great if not greater profit than can be made on the same articles manufactured here." [3]

The Joint Special Committee of Congress to investigate Chinese Immigration, which sat in California in 1877, took the testimony of four shoe operatives, an editor and a miner, on the manufacture of boots and shoes. The operatives estimated the number of Chinese employed in the business at 2,000 to 3,000; of whites at 1,000, of whom one-half were women and boys. They agreed that since the war wages had fallen in their trade all over the country from 20 per cent to 25 per cent, and although the fall in California had been proportionately as great or greater than elsewhere, wages were still as high or higher than those prevailing in the Eastern states. There was no complaint that any considerable number of shoe operatives were out of employment. From two-thirds to three-fourths of all the boots and shoes manufactured by Chinese were made in Chinese shops and sold by Chinese, many of them to Chinese.[4] It was testified that formerly all boots and shoes consumed in California were made in the East and that in proportion as both white and Chinese labor had increased, the consumption of home-made goods had increased.

Although the exclusion law took effect in 1882 it did not reduce the numbers of the Chinese, materially for some time after. The second Biennial Report of the California Bureau of Labor contains the results of an investigation of the boot and shoe industry in 1883. Although the conclusions of the Commissioner of Labor are contradictory the testimony itself leads clearly to the following inferences: (1) The Chinese in San

[3] San Francisco *Bulletin*, Feb. 9, 1879.
[4] Sold to Chinese in the country who quite early gave up the impracticable Chinese shoe.

The Chinese in Manufacture

Francisco were receiving higher wages than whites in Massachusetts; (2) white men could turn out one-third more product in a given time than Chinese; (3) at least 50 per cent of all the boots and shoes used in San Francisco were imported from the East and sold cheaper than the same class of Chinese goods; (4) the Chinese could not make an expensive shoe, a first class ladies' shoe or dress boot, or even a first class miner's boot, their product being chiefly confined to cheap, coarse shoes and boots such as laborers and farm-hands wore, and to cheap slippers; (5) the number of Chinese shoemakers was greatly exaggerated, less than 300 being employed by white manufacturers and about 2,000 being employed by Chinese manufacturers; (6) the cost of living among the Chinese was not so low as had been stated—their diet, consisting of pork, fowl, fish, rice and vegetables, averaging from $8-$12 per month.[5]

The First Annual Report of the United States Bureau of Labor compared the numbers and wages of two establishments in California with those of seven other states. The most striking thing in this comparison is the large number of women (48 per cent of total employes) employed in the business in the seven states and the absence of women (except a few sewing machine operators) in California. Wherever women were largely employed in the East, as fitters, lasters, and sewing machine operators, the wages fall below those of Chinese in California. The wages of foremen in California—Establishment No. 2—were nearly twice those in other states; but the average wage of all classes of employes in California—Establishment No. 1—were considerably below the Eastern standard, and in Establishment No. 2 just about the same.

---

[5] See Testimony before the Commissioner, Second Biennial Report, Cal. Bureau of Labor, pp. 419–438. See also article by P. J. Healey, an Irish shoemaker, *Overland Mo.* (N. S.) v. 7; and article by John Bonner, Cal. *Illust. Mag.* v. 1.

364   Competition and Assimilation

It does not require statistics to justify the inference that an industry, 48 per cent of whose operatives in the Eastern states were women, must have some extraordinary advantage in California in order to enable local manufacturers to employ male adult labor at the prices then prevailing and to compete with the Eastern product. The only considerable advantage was the local production of hides and leather. But several shoe manufacturers and shoemakers testified before the California Commissioner of Labor that the raw product was shipped to New England, manufactured and sold in the local market at a lower price than it could be manufactured in the state. Again in 1886 similar testimony was given before the Commissioner of Labor. It was said that besides cheaper labor the East had other advantages in cheaper capital and fuel to which California opposed only a cheap raw product and Chinese labor, which was, after all, not so cheap as the labor of women and children. By this time the Chinese shoe manufacturers had a monopoly of the coarsest grades of boots, shoes and slippers which the white dealers either imported from the East or bought from the Chinese secretly.

Already the industry had begun to decline. In 1893 there were only 14 shoe factories in San Francisco, employing about 1,400 operatives of whom one-third were women and girls; while there were still about 700 Chinese in separate factories engaged in the rougher grades of work. The Commissioner of Labor reported that the total manufacture was only about 60 per cent what it had been six years before and he attributed the decline to Eastern competition. He added:

"This is not due to Chinese competition, so often alleged, as statistics show a corresponding decrease in Chinese production. They, too, have had to compete with Eastern-made shoes. . . . In the struggle to get rid of Chinese labor the white labor stamp was devised, but with its use there were imposed conditions which led to strikes and lockouts."

The Chinese in Manufacture 365

Before the Kearney period the State was fast becoming the chief supply depot for the Western and Southwestern states, for British Columbia and the Hawaiian Islands. The incessant strikes and labor agitations from 1876 onward, demoralized the trade and caused a partial transfer to the Eastern manufacturers. Some authorities say that this was the chief cause of the decline of the trade from which it has never recovered.[6] Certainly the fact is indisputable that whereas boots and shoes ranked fourth among the manufactures of the State in 1870, to-day the industry has not even a place among the sixteen leading industries. Meanwhile the Chinese have disappeared altogether from the trade as competitors of white labor. It is evident from this brief review that the evils of which organized labor complained in the Kearney period—falling wages and lack of employment—were due to a number of causes with which Chinese competition had nothing to do and which would have operated quite as severely had there been no Chinamen in the industry.

The cigar industry was established in San Francisco by Germans about 1860[7] but most of the cigars used for some years after that time were imported from Manila, Havana or New York. By 1870 there were, according to the Assessor, 2,500 employes—according to the Census only 1900—in the industry in San Francisco and the product amounted to a million and a half dollars. All authorities, though differing on most other points, agree that the trade had fallen largely into the hands of the Chinese. There was no extensive introduction of machinery, though the use of molds and pressers for fillers which came in about 1871 permitted the employment of less skilled labor. In that year a California

---

[6] Receipts in San Francisco by rail from the East: 1876, 49,321 cases: 1886, 73,076 cases plus 29,891 cases by sea. Population increased 40% between 1889 and 1890.
[7] Bancroft, *Works, Hist. of Cal.*, v. 38, p. 347; Tuthill, *Hist. of Cal.*, p. 638.

establishment employing Chinese exclusively paid cigar-makers $7.00 per 1,000 while Ohio and Virginia were paying $8.00 and $7.00 per 1,000 respectively; strippers, $1.00 per day the same as in New York, while the wages in D. C., Wis., Ohio, and West Virginia ranged from 25 cents to 84 cents per day; packers received $1.25 per 1,000 where Ohio paid $1.50. Young's report in 1874 shows that the wages of the three classes—makers, strippers and packers—averaged 10% lower in California than in twenty other states.

The Joint Special Committee of Congress to investigate Chinese Immigration which came to San Francisco in 1877 took the testimony of one cigarmaker, one editor and one lawyer, on cigar manufacture. The number of the Chinese in the trade was variously estimated at from 3,200 to 6,300 and one witness estimated the number of whites employed at 150, of whom one-third were said to be out of employment. Two witnesses estimated Chinese wages at six dollars per week and the cigarmaker testified that the wages of whites was eleven dollars per week. The only statistics submitted gave the names of seventeen firms—all but one of them German—employing a total of 263 Chinese at an average of $2.75 per day, several other firms employing 133 Chinese at $3.00 per day and 2,800 more Chinese employed by Chinese firms at $0.50 to $1.25 per day.[8] The three witnesses agreed that wages in this trade had been falling all over the United States for some time past and that there were numbers of cigarmakers out of work in all the Eastern cities; they also agreed that formerly all cigars consumed in California were imported while now two-thirds of them were made at home, and still cost more than in the East.

The San Francisco *Bulletin* stated in 1878 that Chinese

[8] It is an almost universal custom with Chinese employers to furnish board and lodging in the manufacturing industries. This would add from $0.33½ to $0.50 per day to the wages of the 2800.

cigarmakers were receiving $6.00–$6.50 per 1000 as against $4.00 per 1000 paid in the East. In 1885 the wages of Eastern male cigarmakers ranged between $1.50 in West Virginia and $2.25 in Connecticut; of female cigarmakers between $1.00 and $1.50.[9] In California the wages of white men averaged $2.00 per day and of Chinese in factories from $1.–$1.50.[10] During this year the White Labor League of California asked the cigar manufacturers to replace Chinese makers with white men in order to give work to the unemployed. Twenty-one firms agreed to do so provided the whites were competent men, and agreed to pay the Union prices of New York City. It was at once discovered that there were very few unemployed cigarmakers in California and the Unions sent East for men. Four hundred came out on this agreement to work for one year, and one hundred and nine came on their own account. Two hundred and forty returned East shortly; the manufacturers said, because they were incompetent, the Unions said, because the manufacturers violated the agreement. Shortly afterward the remainder of the imported men demanded an increase of wages; the manufacturers thereupon reduced the number of white employes and re-employed Chinese.[11] Other cigarmakers, finding that they could make better wages in the fruit districts and in other industries, left the occupation and the members of the White Labor League were finally compelled to work again alongside the Chinese.[12]

From this time onward cigar manufacture steadily declined in California as the Assessor's reports show. The causes of this decline are given by the Report of the

[9] First An. Rep. *U. S. Bureau of Labor.*
[10] A difference in the unit of payment makes the Census of 1880 of very little use for comparison.
[11] *Second Biennial Rept. of Cal. Bureau of Labor,* 1885–6, pp. 438–442.
[12] The accounts given by the Unions, the Manufacturers, the Commissioner of Labor and the current newspapers do not agree in many details, but the essential facts appear to be as above. See also Bonner, *Cal. Illust. Mag.* v. 1. and *Oregonian,* Dec. 28, 1885.

California Bureau of Labor for 1891. The Commissioner, after saying that the industry had increased 500% in California between 1866 and 1882, continues:

> "The factories up to a few years ago employed mostly Chinese, while the Atlantic States employed mostly girls. . . . The year 1882 brought with it labor troubles and the anti-Chinese movement and opened wide the door for Eastern competition. The Eastern manufacturers took advantage of our unskilled and dissatisfied state of affairs and flooded our importing houses with their goods."

Four manufacturers testified before the Commissioner as to the causes of the decline: Mr. Wolf said: "It is the natural outgrowth of persistent antagonism of the Trades Unions to Chinese cigars * * * the importation (of Eastern cigars) is encouraged * * * and yet the consumers do not stop to think that the filth of the tenement house cigarmakers of New York and those of Key West, are far worse than exists here, even in our Chinese dens." Mr. Liebes and Mr. Plageman said that the present condition of the trade was directly due to the agitation against Chinese cigars. Mr. Hoffman testified that in 1881 California was shipping cigars East by the car-load, factories were multiplying, and Chinese were in great demand; but as a result of the anti-Chinese movement, white men were imported from the East to replace them, many firms that would not employ Chinese lost money, and some sold Chinese cigars under white labels; as a final result the California manufacturers lost their Eastern trade, the white cigarmakers were thrown out of work and the Chinese were driven from the trade. In 1891 an agent sent by the California Bureau of Labor to investigate the trade, reported that the Hong Tuck Tong—Chinese Cigarmakers' Union—which had once been a strong and formidable body now had only one-fourth as many members as formerly and that Chinese manufacture had decreased at least 52% since 1882.

From the above review of the cigar industry, it ap-

The Chinese in Manufacture 369

pears that the wages of cigarmakers in California after 1874 were about on a level with those in Ohio and West Virginia and with those of women in other states, and considerably lower than men's wages in New York and New England. But other factors besides Chinese competition must be taken into account of which the foremost is the general depression in the trade all over the country from 1873 onward. After 1861 the introduction of some machinery, of improved methods, and particularly the imposition of a heavy revenue tax, along with the competition of the Havana product, drove the business into large factories and tenements and compelled the cigarmaker to become either an employe working for wages or a mere retailer without the privilege of manufacture.[13] After 1873 the conditions of tenement house manufacture became increasingly bad. The wages of cigarmakers in Massachusetts in 1872 were $4.00 per week higher than in 1860 but by 1878 had fallen almost to their previous level. In that year, out of 4,260 cigarmakers in Philadelphia, Detroit, Utica, New Haven and Brooklyn, one-third to one-half were unemployed between February and July, while cigarmakers in Ohio were only making from 83 cents to $1.35 per day.[14]

Mr. Strausser, President of a Cigarmakers' Union, testified before a Senate Committee in 1878 that although production was rapidly increasing (tripling between 1868 and 1878) the condition of cigarmakers was becoming worse. He attributed this to tenement house making in the East and to Coolie labor in the West;[15] the decline of wages in the East he chiefly attributed to the heavy revenue tax and to severe competition with the cheap labor and superior products of Manila and Havana.

The most recent report on the Cigar trade in California made in 1900 by Thomas F. Turner, Special Agent of

---
[13] See useful report on the cigar industry, Ohio *Bureau of Labor*, 1877.
[14] *Tenth An. Rept. of Mass. Bureau of Labor*, 1878.
[15] Testimony of A. Strausser, Report on *Causes of Depression* in 1878, *Cong Docs.* ser. no. 1863.

the Industrial Commission, devotes one-third of one page to the subject, and quotes the President of the Cigar-makers' Union to the effect that the Chinese have monopolized the industry. It does not state what wages were paid to either white or Chinese cigarmakers, and the statement that there were 1,200 cigarmakers in San Francisco is manifestly untrustworthy, being nearly double that given by the Census and the Assessor.[16]

The implication of this report that if it had not been for Chinese competition the cigar trade would now be in a flourishing condition, is wholly unwarranted by the facts as can be easily shown from the Assessor's Reports and the reports of the Census. In 1870 San Francisco had 1,800 cigarmakers of whom 90% were Chinese; by 1880 the number had increased to 3,500 but owing to labor agitations only 33% were Chinese. In 1890 the total number had fallen to 2,500, in 1895 to 750; but in 1905 the total had risen to 1,253 while during the last fifteen years the Chinese had been gradually decreasing. In 1900 the California Bureau of Labor reported that wages in cigarmaking had been decreasing while the number of Chinese had not been increasing; and at the same time the importation of cigars was rapidly increasing because white cigarmakers in the East were paid even less than Chinese in San Francisco.[17]

The question of competition is narrowed still further by a consideration of the nationality and sex of cigarmakers. In San Francisco in 1870 only one-fourth were native-born and even yet the native-born do not constitute one-half of the whites engaged in tobacco manufacture. The local competition has been between Germans and the Chinese, the Germans making the high-grade product and the Chinese the cheaper grades. As has been pointed out before, in this trade as in all the

[16] *Rept. Industrial Commission*, vol. 15, s. n. 4345. pp. 747–802.
[17] Assessor's repts. in Municipal Repts. of San Francisco; Census 1900, vol. *Occupations*; Census Bulletin, 49, 1906.

lighter manufactures, the ease and cheapness with which cigars could be imported has made the standard of both white and Chinese wages dependent on the conditions of Eastern production, which have been for many years more advantageous than those in the West.[18]

The chief of these advantages was the cheap labor of women and boys so largely employed in Eastern manufacture; but the white cigarmaker has been competing not only against female and child-labor but against the still cheaper labor of Havana and Manila. From this and other considerations, it seems clear that cigarmaking was one of the premature manufactures arising in California before the completion of the transcontinental railway because of a temporary artificial protection. As soon as cigars could be cheaply imported, the manufacture suffered in the West as well as in the East from the general demoralization which occurred in the eighties. The local manufacture of the cheaper grades probably would not have survived at all but for the Chinese; and the manufacture would not now be increasing but for the cheap labor of women and children who constitute one-fourth of the employes.

The woolen industry was founded in California in 1860 by a Scotch weaver and produced chiefly blankets, shawls, flannels, and cloakings. There were five mills, four in San Francisco and one near Marysville, and as early as 1867 it was found that the high price of labor made it impossible to compete with Eastern mills in many lines of production. But the superior quality of California wool for certain purposes and the employment of Chinese in place of the cheap labor of women and boys enabled the industry to survive. It declined in numbers of employes and amount of product between 1874 and 1880 and was said not to have paid any dividends until after Chinese were employed.[19]

[18] Of 194 cigar-makers, registered voters in San Francisco, in 1889, 58 % were foreign-born; in 1891 28 % were Germans; 95 % were single men.
[19] *Alta*, Aug. 16, 1868; *Atlantic Mo.*, 1869.

Young's special report gives the wages of the woolen industry in California compared with Connecticut, Massachusetts, Virginia, West Virginia, Wisconsin, Iowa and Kansas in the year 1874. Of the twenty-five classes of employes listed, eighteen were receiving lower wages in California than in the general average of states, and eight higher wages. The total average weekly wage of 25 classes of employes in California was $9.44 as against $10.30 in the other seven states. Wherever the reelers and burlers were women in the eastern states, their wages were from 25% to 40% lower than those of the Chinese who were their substitutes in California; and wherever the carders, weavers and drawers were women or youth their wages approached those of the Chinese. California employed one woman and one youth to nineteen men (white and Chinese) while the other states employed one woman and one youth or child to every two to five men.[20]

One of the proprietors of the two most important mills in California testified before the California Senate Committee in 1876 that the Chinese were paid from 90 cents to $1.12 per day after they had learned the processes.[21] This testimony is corroborated by a much fuller and more careful comparison of wages in the woolen industry furnished by the census of 1880. The figures of the Census table are taken from the pay rolls of eight establishments in the northern, eastern and middle-west states for a period of sixteen years (1867-1880) and from the pay-roll of the principal mill in California. Of the twenty-one classes of employes listed in California, eight were Chinese and two were a boy and girl respectively, leaving eleven classes of white adult men. Of the twenty-one classes listed in eight other states, four were in most cases boys and girls. The wages in California

[20] Young lists all Chinese at $5.25 per week which is the minimum wage of other authorities and undoubtedly too low.
[21] Testimony of Max Morgenthau, Cal. State Senate report, 1876.

The Chinese in Manufacture

and in the eight other states are shown in the condensed schedule below.

WOOLEN INDUSTRY.

Comparison of Wages in California With 8 Other Northern States, 1867-1880.

Classes of Employees	Average of eight states	Average of California	Amount of California above or below.
Superintendents	Per mo. $91.00	Per mo. $160.00	Per mo. $69.00
Woolsorter	Per day $1.60	†Per day $1.08	Per day — .52
Picker	.83	*1.08	+ .25
Carder (boss)	1.70	4.00	+2.30
† Carder No. 2	.69	*1.08	+ .39
Spooler	.73	†1.00	+ .17
Warper	1.48	2.75	+1.27
Spinner	1.72	1.89	+ .17
† Spinner No. 2	.83	*1.00	+ .17
Weaver	1.27	1.25	— .02
† Weaver No. 2	.97	*1.08	+ .11
Loomfixer	1.70	4.00	+2.30
Fuller	1.60	$1.25	— .35
Shearer	1.54	4.00	+2.46
Scourer	1.51	*1.25	— .26
Dyer	2.90	3.26	+ .36
" helper	1.34	1.17	— .17
† Gigger	1.16	*1.17	+ .01
Engineer	2.18	3.07	+1.11
Machinist	2.12	3.00	+ .88
Laborer	1.35	*1.00	— .35

† Boy or girl. * Chinese.

If the total average wage of the eight classes in which Chinese were employed in California be compared with the total average of the same classes for the eight states, it will be seen that the result is exactly the same, *i. e.* $1.11 per day; if the remaining 12 classes in which white adult men were employed in all the nine states be compared, it appears that although in three cases (woolsorter, weaver and dyer's helper) California paid slightly lower wages than the Eastern establishments, yet in the other nine, California paid very much higher wages, the total average being one dollar per day per class higher for all white labor. If one further crude test be applied, *i. e.* the proportion of wages paid to the value of product California still appears to have been leading the States, for she paid one dollar in wages to every $4.80 of product, while New England paid one to $5.60, the Middle West one to $5.80 and the South one to $9.00 of product.

Two conclusions may be drawn from these facts, (1) the employment of Chinese in the woolen industry had not, up to 1881, lowered wages to the level of Eastern establishments; and (2) that they were employed for the most part instead of the women and youth employed in the Eastern States. The introduction of a variety of new machinery during this period tended to substitute the cheaper labor of women and children for that of adults. The most conspicuous instance of this substitution was the introduction of the self-acting spinner between 1873 and 1875 which replaced an adult receiving $1.75 in the Eastern factories with a boy at $0.83 and in California an adult at $3.00 with a Chinese or boy at $1.08 per day.

In 1880 the Pacific Woolen Mills shut down until the Courts decided that the clause of the Second Constitution forbidding corporations to employ Chinese was unconstitutional.[22] In 1883 and 1884 the woolen trade was much depressed, it was said, because of over-production and low prices; whatever the cause the industry began to decline about that time. From a total of 819 employes in 3 mills and nearly $1,700,000 product the industry in San Francisco fell to 125 employes, and the product to $350,000 in 1890, where it has remained ever since.

In 1890, Commissioner Tobin of the California Bureau

[22] The Pioneer and Mission Woolen Mills discharged between 500 and 600 Chinese at the demand of the unemployed. The Pacific Mills were paying $6,000 per week to whites and $16,000 per week to Chinese when they shut down.

of Labor investigated the reasons why manufacture was not succeeding in the State. In regard to the woolen industry he states that where California had until recently twelve mills altogether with an invested capital of from three to four millions, now only half of them were running. The reasons given by the manufacturers for this state of things were many: over-production for the local market and the necessity of meeting Eastern competition on its own ground where it had the advantages of lower interest on capital, lower cost of fuel and water, lower taxes on plant and buildings, lower insurance rates and lower wages.

It has been demonstrated by the preceding study of three principal lines of manufacture in which the Chinese were most generally employed, that Eastern competition rather than Chinese competition set the standard of wages and of success; and that at the time when the Chinese were most numerous, wages in manufacture itself with the exception of cigar-making—were still much higher than in Eastern factories.

In an anti-Chinese memorial entitled "*Meat v. Rice*" addressed to Congress in 1901, published by the American Federation of Labor, Mr. Gompers mentions particularly eight industries as having been seriously affected by Chinese competition.[23] But between 1890 and 1900 not only did the value of the output in these eight industries decrease from eighteen million and a half to eleven million and a half dollars, but the number of the employes diminished from 10,175 to 6,705; the Chinese employed in them diminished from 3,900 to 1,820, while at the same time the population of the state increased 22.9%.

These figures certainly do not bear out Mr. Gompers' statement that 4,000 white men had been displaced by

[23] Gompers, *Meat v. Rice*. (pamphlet, 1901). These eight industries were cigar, shoe, broom, chemical, clothing, woolen manufacture, fruit-canning, match-making.

Chinese in these industries. They suggest rather that such manufactures could not thrive under the existing conditions, and that the relatively low wages in them was due to the narrow margin of profit rather than to Chinese competition. The manufactures which have thriven in California for any considerable period are those which have had such unusual advantages either in abundance and superior quality of raw material or in the high transportation charges upon the competing Eastern product, that they could afford to pay the extraordinarily high wages prevailing generally in the state.

Professor Plehn, in discussing the manufactures of California, said in 1900:[24]

> "Four important conditions have limited the growth of manufacture in California and have determined in large measure the particular lines established. These are the geographical position of the State, the high rate of wages, the high price of fuel and the exceptional attractions offered by mining and agriculture."

Of the fourteen industries which at present engage 45 per cent of the capital and 41 per cent of the labor engaged in manufacture in the State, five are dependent on agriculture or horticulture, viz: cheese, butter and condensed milk; flour and grist milling; canning and preserving of fruits and vegetables; malt and vinous liquors; and slaughtering. The other nine in order of importance are: sugar and molasses—due to the proximity of the Hawaiian Islands; lumber and timber products; foundry and machine shop products—due to the demand for mining machinery, and the high cost of transportation; car construction; tanning, etc. of leather; printing and publishing; manufacture of explosives—chiefly for the mines; clothing—men's factory product; lumber and planing mill products.

An analysis of the reasons why these industries have succeeded emphasizes still more strongly the fact that tobacco, shoe and woolen manufactures—the only indus-

[24] *Census*, 1900, Vol. VIII, Manufactures.

tries of importance in which the Chinese were largely employed—could not hope to compete with imported products which were neither perishable, bulky nor dangerous, and which had been produced in part by the labor of women and boys. It is obvious, that, except in times of general unemployment, the Chinese did not shut out white men but in fact kept those industries alive. If it be contended that it compelled white men to accept "Chinese wages" there still remains the inexorable fact of the competition of a product made in the East by white labor at wages as low and even sometimes lower.

Ten years ago Professor Plehn pointed out that the argument against the Chinese on the ground of competition proved too much. The fact is, that in 1870 the three industries in which the Chinese were chiefly engaged ranked among the leading industries of California; while in 1906 their combined product did not reach the amount of the least important of the seventeen leading industries. If it were true that the Chinese originally shut out a considerable number of white men from these industries, then it may now be argued with equal reason that the exclusion of the Chinese and the return of white labor has seriously limited their development.

CHAPTER XX

LABOR AND CHINESE COMPETITION

"Their presence keeps away half a million people directly and another half million indirectly."—JOHN C. ENOS, 1883.

"I have no disposition to belittle the claims which American labor has upon Congress, but it is reasonable to insist that these claims shall be made to harmonize with the principles of international justice and with other great interests of the country. It cannot be consistent with the genuine spirit of labor to violate treaties."—JOHN W. FOSTER, 1901.

RACE antipathy undoubtedly accounts for the greater part of the bitter feeling of workingmen toward all Orientals and the explanation of lack of employment for large bodies of men at times in a prosperous and rapidly developing region must be sought for in the character and social and climatic circumstances of the laboring class. In California the conditions of labor have never been conducive to continuous industry or sobriety of living. In the earlier years all industry was speculative; men came to get rich quickly, not to earn a decent living by steady, hard labor. Everybody—servants, laborers, clerks, bookkeepers, small tradesmen—speculated in stocks and real estate, if not in mining claims. Even in agriculture " bonanza " farming and the " boom " prices of all accessible farm lands, offered little opportunity to the small farmer and only intermittent employment to hired labor. Until recently, the kinds of products raised required considerable numbers of hands in the plowing season from November to February; and in the harvest from April to September more than has ever been supplied. Thus there were three months in late summer and early fall and three months in midwinter when most ranches discharged three-fourths of their men. The harvesters, fruit and hop-pickers, workers in canneries and general laborers, for many years moved from Southern to Northern California each season working as they went. They became a peculiar class of tramps, without homes, saving no money from season to season, hard drinking and irresponsible. The majority drifted to San Francisco, congregating on Grant Avenue during winter evenings to listen to the wild speeches of street fakirs and agitators; gambling, drinking, committing petty crimes, swelling the ranks of the unstable class and drifting away again as their money gave out and the spring demand for labor came on.

The habit of intermittent employment and the fact that three-fourths of these wanderers were single men to whom sleeping out of doors in the California climate was no hardship for nine months in the year, resulted in the practice of providing no proper accommodations for working men on farms and construction works. They slept in barracks, or in barns on the hay, and ate at the table provided by a Chinese steward and cook. Since mining and any kind of trade-labor paid better than farm and common labor, only the least competent, the most dissipated and unreliable were available for these kinds of work; and this class was therefore necessarily unemployed for from one-fourth to one-half the year. The employment agencies in the state show year after year, thousands of men on their lists, two-thirds of whom apply between July 15th and November 1st, one-third of whom have been less than a year in the State, and less than half of whom are American-born.[1] When a dry season occurred the demand for harvesters and cannery hands has been greatly reduced and in consequence, there has been a larger concentration of this floating labor in the towns and cities. Formerly, too, the placer mines discharged their quota of men into the towns every winter and in dry seasons. Coincident with this congestion—and partly as a result of it—there have

[1] *Cal. Bureau of Labor Rept.*, 1895-6; *Alta*, Mar. 9, 1880; Apr. 28, 1881; James Budd, *Legisl. Jos.*, App. 6, 1887.

been regularly recurring labor agitations, formerly anti-Chinese and latterly anti-Japanese.

The Kearney agitation produced a general lack of confidence, preventing the investment of capital in new enterprises and bringing to a standstill those already begun. The vagaries of the Second Constitution still further paralyzed certain industries and created an impression of instability which has only subsided in recent years.[2] Meanwhile about 1878 wages in California began at last to approach that minimum level which they had already reached in 1876 in the Eastern states.[3] At the time when many industries in the State were seriously checked and when wages were falling, the immigration of white employes received a strong impetus from the panic of 1873 and the consequent wide-spread lack of employment in the East.

Before the Kearney period there was great scarcity of labor in almost every line, but between 1876 and 1880 the unemployed became conspicuous in the towns and cities of California. Yet even at this time, while workingmen were crying out against monopoly and the Chinese, the Municipalities were paying two dollars a day of eight hours for common labor, the farmers were paying a dollar a day and board even in winter, and the manufacturers were paying more than their Eastern competitors and earning no dividends. In 1878 hundreds of single men loafed in San Francisco refusing to work at less than the high rates which they considered "white men's wages"—refusing even to accept relief work in the city because the wages were only a dollar a day—and the newspapers catered to them by talking of grinding men to starvation wages.[4] But as soon as the State

[2] Seattle *Chronicle*, Oct. 15, 1885; *Alta*, Feb. 23, 1880.
[3] See Wage Chart on p. 354.
[4] The Central Pacific railway in 1878 offered work at filling in land to 1000 men at $1.00 per day, cash daily, with tools furnished; and a private fund was raised to give the unemployed work in the Park of San Francisco, but only a very few men would take it. See *Bulletin* and *Alta* of 1878.

Labor and Chinese Competition 381

began to recover from the paralysis resulting from Kearneyism the demand for certain classes of labor again became pressing. Year after year farmers, contractors and mine-owners demanded laborers, depicting the charms of climate, high wages and cheap living. Successive labor exchanges, agricultural and horticultural societies and promotion committees urged the great opportunities open to the immigrant workingman and the need of his services. But no sooner did the workingman arrive from the East than he found an opening in more remunerative, more independent or more congenial lines in the urban districts.

The first report of the California Bureau of Labor, published in 1884, stated that the State had no pauper labor except that which was voluntary; that there were not enough boys and girls at certain seasons to supply the labor market; that, although a few industries were over-supplied with help, in others there was a positive scarcity all the year round. It describes the fruit unpicked, the hay and grain uncut; the impossibility of establishing and carrying on manufactures at the current rate of wages; and the activity of the building trades under which wages were constantly rising while the hours of labor decreased. It dilates on the advantages of the workingman in California—" even taking into account the slightly higher cost of living "—and points out with pride that they do not have to put their children at work. Yet in this same report the San Francisco Labor Council reported that half the men in the following trades were idle: painters, harness and collar makers, teamsters, printers, blacksmiths; house, ship and carriage smiths, draymen, coopers, woodcarvers, bricklayers; that there were ." multitudes of car-drivers " and one-half of the city employes, out of work. Here again the fact is noticeable that, granting this was true, these were lines in which the Chinese had not been and could not be employed.

In 1886, the Bureau of Labor reported an investigation made at the request of the State Horticultural Society as to whether enough white laborers of equal efficiency with the Chinese could be supplied for the fruit harvest of that year. Commissioner Enos roughly estimated the number of Chinese employed in fruit harvest at 30,000, or seven-eighths of all labor on farms. The employment agents for white labor testified that the average number of unemployed in San Francisco was 6,800; that they could supply from 2000 to 10,000 on demand and would agree to import from Europe and the east at $20 to $30 per month and found, enough more to replace all Chinese in sixty days to one year, but that white labor must have good food and accommodations and kind treatment. An employment agent handling Chinese labor exclusively, testified that the Chinese constituted seven-eighths of all farm labor at an average of $20 per month without board; that they had an advantage over white labor in their previous agricultural experience in China; that white men would not work for $30 per month and board; that the Chinese were industrious, reliable, honest, docile, cleanly in habit and able to board themselves and live decently in accommodations which white men would not accept; and that employers were always willing to advance the transportation of Chinese because they knew it would be repaid according to contract but that they would not do so for white hands.

The farmers' testimony was very nearly unanimous on the following points: that there was not nearly enough labor—the estimates were from one-tenth to one-fourth of the amount necessary—to replace the Chinese; that it would take more whites to do the work because of their inexperience; that when whites could or would do as much as Chinese they were less reliable, less steady and less punctual; that the Chinese were better handlers of small and dried fruits which required great care; and that ranchmen did and would habitually give from 15 to 25% higher wages to white labor.

The Restriction Act of 1882 and the Scott Act of 1888 reduced the number of immigrant Chinese laborers, while at the same time on account of unfriendly treatment some went back to China and many to other parts of the country. From this time to the present all sorts of societies and committees have been engaged in replacing them with the assistance of low fares on the railways and the lure of high wages and exceptional opportunities. The scarcity of labor in many lines has increased out of proportion even to the decrease of the Chinese. In harvest young girls earn from .75 cents to $1.50 per day and boys from $1.50 to $2.50 per day in picking, packing, drying, and canning in the fruit districts. In some localities the opening of the schools has been postponed because the growers could not harvest the crops on which the community chiefly depended without the aid of children. For the last twenty-five years there has been a temporary—and in some places and industries a permanent—labor " famine " every season.

The newspapers have at times grown irascible and outspoken on the effect of the removal of the Chinamen. One said in 1902:

"The feeling here against the Chinese is almost insane, in view of present conditions. . . . Will the white people do the work? Anyone with experience knows that they will not. The demagogues know it too. . . . The hoboes and tramps that float around the country will not accept steady employment at any wages."

Another thus describes the situation familiar to every Californian:

"Will they [the demagogues] tell us where we are to procure labor for our orchards and ranches ? . . . They are perfectly aware that every year thousands of dollars' worth of fruit and grain spoil because help cannot be procured to harvest it. Yet while this condition exists the town is full of men, . . . big, husky men, more than able to work. The country is full of them camping in creek beds, beating the railroad trains, working only when absolute necessity demands. The Chinese are the only people who will do ranch work faithfully. They are the only ones who can be depended upon to do housework. . . . Native Americans do not seek the work the Chinese are after."[5]

Still another comments on the scarcity of labor:

"It is not to be supposed that we have no working people on the Coast for we have, although not in due proportion; but that solid class of men and women who take daily toil cheerfully and as a matter of course are conspicuously absent . . . partly because the working classes as well as those of wealth are shifting and unsettled—but chiefly because the workers as a class are utterly unreliable."[6]

The history of general labor in California since about 1886 is the story of efforts to find substitutes for the vanishing Chinese. As a result of the labor agitations of 1877-9 many Chinese cigarmakers and boot and shoe operatives were discharged and hundreds of whites were imported by the trade unions to fill their places; girls were brought in at great expense to work in small factories and in domestic service; negroes, Apache and Yaqui Indians, Mexicans and Cholos, Italians, Greeks, Austrians and Portuguese, Hawaiians and Hindoos, Porto Ricans, Filipinos and Japanese, to work on ranches, railways, and construction works.[7] During the last twenty years—except during the panic of 1893—there has been no pretense on the part of anyone outside the Labor Unions that there was enough common labor to supply the demand.[8]

If the vacancy already existing and that created by the decrease in the number of the Chinese had been

[5] Los Angeles *Times*, Mar. 2d, 1902, San Francisco *News Letter*, Feb. 16, 1902.
[6] California Correspondent of the New York *Independent*, Apr. 1903.
[7] In 1900, of 5,846 railway employes employed on the Southern Pacific R. R., 346 were Chinese, 377 Mexicans, 137 Japanese, and 45 % of the remainder alien whites. *Rept. Ind. Com.* 1900, ser. no. 4345, p. 750.
[8] Layres. *The Other Side of the Chinese Question* (1886); Prof. W. J. Wickson, (Univ. of Cal.) *California Illustrated* (1888); Cal. Bureau of Labor Reports, 1886-1904; interviews with police officers, town officials, farmers, ranchmen, miners, in all parts of California; many newspaper references.

filled by native Americans of the thrifty sort or even by the better grade of European peasantry, the going of the Chinese might be regarded as no great loss. But it may well be doubted whether the state is better off for the importation of such labor as the instances mentioned, nationalities which have no more assimilative power than the Chinese, and far less ambition, integrity and industrial efficiency. The Cholos, for instance—a mixture of Indian, Spanish and Mexican blood—were brought into Southern California because neither white nor Chinese labor could be obtained for railway and construction work. The officials of the southern towns report that they make more trouble than all the rest of the population; that they settle in a quarter by themselves; that they are a hard-drinking, fighting, treacherous and revengeful class, incapable of assimilation. In 1900 of 13,956 railway employes on California lines, 9,475 were white, of whom not more than half were native-born. The remaining 4,500 were Mexicans, Japanese, and a few Chinese. The wages of white laborers were $1.50 to $2.25 per day; of colored men $1.00. On construction works where Japanese and Chinese were employed they received $1.75 per day.[9]

During 1906, the Southern Pacific and Santa Fe Railways were shipping in two or three carloads of Cholos and Mexicans per week with the avowed intention of filling up the Southwest with cheaper labor. The railroads pay $1.25 per day and provide box cars to live in; but on account of employment fees and being compelled to buy of the agency stores, the *peons* seldom receive in actual wages more than fifty cents per day. The ranches and mines adjacent to the railway, pay $2.00 or more and the *peons* leave the railways shortly for the better paid work, leaving their places to be filled by other *peons* at the lower wage.[10]

[9] Information from railway men in the Southwest.
[10] See also testimony of H. S. Hudson, Ass't. Chief Engineer of No. Pac. R. R., *Cong. Docs.* s. n. 2890, H. R. 4048, p. 161.

The Yaqui Indians, as another example, have been going back and forth across the border between Mexico and the United States for twenty years. An official says of them:

> "They come over here to work on the railroad, buy guns and ammunition, go over the border, fight the Mexicans till their stuff gives out and then come back. While the United States Immigration officials are patrolling the border to catch the stray Chinaman, the Yaquis and Cholos come freely and are a thousand times worse. If the railways could get Chinese they would not bring such as these." [11]

Of the Greeks, for instance, who in Central California are among the least desirable laborers, an employer says:

> "They run in bunches of from ten to sixty, speak no English and are under the control of a boss who keeps a per cent of their wages, charges them for writing and sending money home, and for every time they move to a new job. They are lazy and quarrelsome." [12]

Nothing perhaps bears stronger testimony to the comparative superiority of the Chinese laborer over the substitutes than the way in which common labor in California is now generally measured by them. A Chinese cook is a luxury which only the well-to-do afford, commanding from $35 to $60 per month in private houses and from $60 upwards in hotels and restaurants. One constantly hears among housekeepers praises of "the China boy I used to have" and unflattering comparisons of the Japanese and immigrant women cooks who have to some extent taken their places. Wherever other nationalities have taken the place of the Chinese the employer almost invariably makes Chinese efficiency the criterion of his successor's incapacity or unreliability, or stupidity.

---

[11] Interviews, (1904) immigration inspectors and police officers.
[12] Since the fire of April 18, 1906, large numbers of Greeks—at one time 3000 in a body—have been employed in San Francisco in default of native labor, at $2.25-$2.50. They have proved themselves, as a rule, lazy, unstable and extremely quarrelsome.

Labor and Chinese Competition 387

Mr. H. V. Ready, of the firm of Murray and Ready, the largest employment firm in San Francisco who have been in business eighteen years and handled last year 60,000 men, said in an interview [13]; that since 1894 the demand for labor, skilled and unskilled, had been increasing all over the state, but especially for railroad, general construction, street improvements, sewer work and general improvements. Wages in February, 1905, were $2.25-$2.50 for common labor—twice what they were in 1894 with a shorter day. Ranch hands now receive $30-$40 per month and board. Railway and construction work is now done almost altogether by foreigners who have largely replaced the blanket man.

Mr. Ready added:

"The trouble with all Americans in common labor is their roving disposition and unsteady habits. They will quit any job, good or bad, in about ten days and wander to the next place, knowing well that they can get work anywhere. The worst rovers are the railroad men—the passing of the trains seems to make them restless." [14]

Mr. Ready predicted a labor famine of perhaps 80,000 men just before the earthquake and fire of 1906 and in January, 1907, this prediction had been more than justified.

Although there are less than half as many Chinese in California as in 1882, nearly all are receiving twice as much wages. In laundry work, one of the lowest paid of their occupations, the Chinese proprietors complain that the high wages demanded by their countrymen will drive them from the business. Although they have raised their prices to customers fully fifty per cent, they pay double the wages they did twenty years ago. The Chinese have nearly deserted the factory trades because

---

[13] Quoted by permission.
[14] The report of the California Bureau of Labor in 1895 stated that the average time that the fourteen thousand men who passed through the Agency, remained in the place to which they were sent, was two months. See also *Legisl. Jos.*, 1889, App. 1.

they can earn so much more in small independent businesses—in salmon fishing in the north for half the year, in gardening, in fruit-raising on shares—and in domestic service. The Chinese who have acquired skill in any line invariably receives as much and sometimes more—as in cooking—than the naturalized foreigner.

Labor pamphlets, the anti-Chinese papers, and political speakers, since the exclusion law was passed, have continued to assert that the Chinese had a monopoly of a large number of trades and businesses, that they excluded men, women and boys from them, and that they lowered the wages in these lines below a living standard. As to wages, the matter has been carefully canvassed in these pages with the conclusion that wages in California even in times of greatest depression never fell to the level of eastern cities except in one manufacture and occasionally, for short periods, in common labor. As to monopoly, monopoly assumes that there are persons waiting to take the places of the monopolizers who are prevented from doing so by the lower wages accepted by those already in the industry. The Chinese were chiefly engaged in mining, horticulture, truck gardening, domestic service, washing and common labor; a few were in manufactures; and a considerable number in independent business, chiefly among their own countrymen. It can scarcely be called a monopoly when the wages of an industry continue above the level of other states, as in all lines of farm labor and domestic service, nor when there was a vacuum wholly unfilled, as in the case of laundry work; nor when there was an almost complete lack of the cheaper and lighter kinds of labor employed in manufactures in the East, without which manufactures in the West could not develop.

It has already been demonstrated that, at the period when there were the most Chinese employed in manufactures, there were few or no competent operatives out of employment; and that the wages and opportunities in other lines were so much more inviting that there was no inducement for white men to become operatives. California could have continued to grow without many of these manufactures but, having them, she could not expect to maintain a wage scale above her Eastern and foreign competitors in addition to paying from two to five per cent more for capital, and twice as much for fuel, taxes and insurance.

· Without pursuing the theoretical statement farther, there are two facts which disprove the monopoly theory as far as the Chinese are concerned. In the first place the occupations having the largest number of whites unemployed in all the tables for many years, are not the ones in which the Chinese were chiefly engaged. From the report of the State Employment Bureau (1895-6) it appears that out of 14,251 men who applied for work over 4000 were bookkeepers, clerks, blacksmiths, carpenters, painters, engineers, machinists, teamsters and porters; another 4000 were farmers and laborers and a last thousand were cooks and waiters. In the first group the Chinese never competed at all; in the second there was a chronic scarcity throughout the country at wages higher than those paid east of the Rocky Mountains; as to the third, the Chinese were seldom employed as waiters in cities because of the prejudice against them and as cooks they were in private families supplying the demand never filled by women at wages *above* the current rate of white labor.[15]

The second fact to be named in disproof of monopoly is that Chinese labor has never remained cheap labor for any length of time. The Chinese were thoroughly organized into *tongs, i. e.* trade unions, long before white laborers in California and being, as a race, disciplined in coöperative action they were able to divert their own immigrant competitors into the occupations where opportunity was best. For many years the two largest

---
[15] Compare this with similar results shown on Chart, p. 348.

tongs were the cigarmakers and the washmen.[16] Into these many of the young, ignorant and newly-arrived went, accepting low wages as apprentices and graduating from them into better paid occupations. Many immigrants who came directly from farms in China and were not skilled in handicrafts, went directly to the country to engage in vegetable raising, orchard work and general farm work, or to the mountains for placer mining. For many years California has been districted, as it were, by the older Chinese immigrants, in order to avoid excessive competition among themselves in any locality, as well as to avoid the prejudice which made their work alongside white men too dangerous or disagreeable.[17]

Like many ambitious and thrifty immigrants from Europe the Chinese came to make and to save money; one-third at least were married men, and all were imbued with that extreme sense of filial obligation characteristic of their race. They have, therefore, exacted as much for their labor as possible, but being non-aggressive and often skilled in two or more lines they have followed the lines of least resistance. As white men crowded into one line, the Chinese "moved on" to the less inviting task, so long as it was comparatively well paid; when it was not, he took up another. He might work cheaply to learn, to get a foothold, but he soon demanded all that the business would bear.

This *fluidity* of Chinese labor as compared with the instability of American labor available for the same lines of industry is, perhaps, its greatest advantage, combined as it is, with the thorough discipline of the *tong* organization and an almost universal tradition of honesty in

---

[16] Fong, *Chatauquan*, 1896, two valuable articles on Chinese Trades unionism.

[17] Layres, *The Other Side of the Chinese Question;* American *Free Press,* Apr. 21, 1876; Chronicle, Apr. 14, 1876; Becker, *Humors of a Congressional Committee,* 1877; Joseph McShafter, *Address* before State Agricultural Society, 1878; John Bonner, *The Labor Question, etc., Californian Illustrated,* 1892; interviews with many employers. *Report of the California Bureau of Labor,* 1898-1900.

Labor and Chinese Competition 391

keeping contracts. The Chinese drives a hard and haggling bargain with the employer through the agent or boss of his group; but, having made it, he lives up to it strictly as long as the employer does and quits at once if he does not. Thus his characteristic reliability constitutes another advantage, for he will stay with his job and never get drunk; postponing his pleasures and his vices till China New Year or the convenient slack season; work his full time without a boss, at a moderate gait and with scrupulous skill.

It adds an especial value to his service in the homeless life he leads that he can take care of himself anywhere; he cooks, washes, mends his clothes and keeps himself clean as few white men can or will do. In a lumber camp the last thing seen at night, when white men are asleep in their bunks, is the Chinese bathing themselves from the huge kettles of hot water which their boss has stipulated for in the contract.[18]

Chinese farm laborers are, as a class, neither inventive nor quick, nor handy with horses and cattle; but they have great patience and capacity for continuous labor, combined with the unusual deftness of hand characteristic of women and mechanics. They are, therefore, especially adapted to fruit handling, vegetable gardening, and to factory operations.[19] On this account they have appeared to take the places of women and boys in some lines of industry. Having greater physical endurance than either, they might have supplanted them—if there had been any number to supplant—or if they were not too intelligent and ambitious to remain long in labor paying from 0.75 cents to $1.25 per day when there was plenty of other labor open to them at much higher wages.

In all discussions of Chinese competition the factor

---

[18] Interviews with lumbermen in Washington.
[19] Witnesses before the J. S. Com. of Congress, 1877; interviews with ranchmen in various parts of California.

most frequently overlooked is the intelligent ambition of the Chinese immigrant. He is, in the first place, a Cantonese, that is to say, a Chinese "Yankee" from the most progressive province in China; he is, again, often a picked member of his family sent abroad to elevate the family fortune in much the same way as a son is often dedicated to education in China, in order that he may become a *literati* and an official. He is not at all stolid and servile but keenly alive to the better chance, and is, consequently, only cheap when he is newly arrived and unusually stupid.

As soon as he has served his apprenticeship and saved some money, he looks out for a small partnership into which a dozen of his own kind put their little hoards, hiring a manager, while each individual partner goes on with day labor to add to his capital. Or, with a few others, he leases a strawberry farm and works it on shares with the white owner; or he becomes a petty truck gardener peddling vegetables from a basket or, in more prosperous case, from a wagon. If he is a laundry worker his *tong* sets the price of his labor and makes the contract with the Chinese employer. The Chinese agent through whom the bargain is made with American employers receives a percentage on wages for his intervention, and it is to his interest to keep up wages as much as possible.

Because of his thrifty habit of never spending more than he earns, the Chinaman generally has money in his pocket and can better endure the intermittent employment which is the undoing of the American workman. The Chinese fishing gangs and cannery hands are often idle for several months of the year; but they receive for their short intense working season as much as the common laborer can save in a year. When paid off they send money home to their wives and parents and, if they get nothing else to do in the interval, they live frugally in Chinatown, at the headquarters of their *tong*,

Labor and Chinese Competition 393

gambling a little, smoking a little, going to the theatre occasionally but self-restrained in their pleasures as in their virtues.

It is a mistake to suppose that the ordinary Chinese laborer lives penuriously—the truth rather is, that he always lives within his income, whatever that may be, and will very nearly starve before he will beg. He can and does live cheaper than the American workingman because he knows how to feed himself better. In place of bread and potatoes, he uses rice which costs from two to three times as much but is far more nutritious. If very poor, he eats fish, and an immense variety of vegetables rich in starch and nitrogen, but he will have chicken and pork whenever he can afford it. The Chinese spend a good deal of money in feasts and banquets and are fond of good eating. Chinese manufacturers board their operatives in San Francisco at two dollars per week. The budgets of a large number of American families published in the San Francisco *Bulletin* in 1904, showed that many families of clerks, small tradesmen and workingmen fed themselves quite as cheaply. In the country throughout California the allowance of wages for a workingman's board is ten dollars per month, and many a student working his way through the Universities of the State lives on $8 to $10 per month.[20]

If the facts and contentions of the foregoing pages are in the main accurate, it may naturally be asked why for two generations in California the laboring class have been unanimously opposed to Chinese labor and why other classes have appeared to believe their assertion that they were crowded out of industries by the Chinese. It is not a sufficient answer to say—because

---

[20] Lloyd, *Lights and Shades of San Francisco*, p. 345; Kerr, *The Chinese Question*, p. 12; Gibson, *The Chinese in America*; Professor Jaffa, Testimony before the J. S. Committee of Congress, 1877; see index.

of race prejudice; though race prejudice was unquestionably the foundation of the opposition. Nor is it enough to say that for selfish reasons—local, political, racial—politicians and workingmen united in habitual exaggeration of the numbers of the Chinese and of their competition in certain lines.

Undoubtedly, it may be explained in part by the influence of "mob mind" but its origin lies in the natural human tendency to create a monopoly of a good thing. In California this tendency has reached an extreme development in the field of labor as well as in other fields. From the earlier days in California there was a tendency to concentrate land and resources in the hands of a few. The Miners of 1849 first attempted to shut out all foreigners, then to shut out all who were not naturalized; failing in both of these attempts, they finally succeeded in shutting out one class of foreigners —the Chinese—from all but the least desirable claims. The holding of immense tracts of land by a few owners, either for cattle ranges or for bonanza farming or for speculation simply, delayed the development of diversified agriculture by preventing the settlement of the small farmer; while the concentration of railway and steamship facilities in the hands of a very few kept transportation at prohibitive rates.

Workingmen, too, very early began to take advantage of the scarcity of labor, to hold up wages by artificial means. The miners of each locality organized themselves to maintain exclusive control by minute regulations and judicial functions exercised without reference to either state or Federal law. Between 1865 and 1878 a large number of unions, not strictly for trade purposes, were organized to press the claims of laboring men for an eight-hour day, for a mechanics' lien law and for the exclusion of the Chinese. Between 1878 and 1890 all the more important trades were organized thoroughly. By 1891 the labor leaders boasted that labor was better

Labor and Chinese Competition 395

organized on the Pacific Coast than anywhere else in the United States.[21]

The Eastern labor movement had to contend with a long established system of low wages and long hours; on the Coast the trade unions had only to maintain the high wages produced by pioneer conditions. The Eastern workingman had to raise wages and shorten hours in spite of constantly increasing European immigration; in the West, they had only to prevent overland and Asiatic immigration. The task was not difficult until after the railway was completed; but in the next decade overland immigration increased rapidly while the state was experiencing a period of depression during which all wages fell somewhat, while the wages of unskilled labor fell temporarily to the level of the Eastern states. From 1878 onward the organization of labor developed very rapidly, until in 1892 there were sixty unions in San Francisco alone, with an average of eighty members each.[22]

As early as 1866 the labor clubs of San Francisco scattered circulars through the Eastern states to discourage white laborers from coming to California. While immigration societies and committees painted the advantages to the workingman on the Pacific Coast, the labor journals painted its disadvantages, dwelling on the low wages in manufacture, the high cost of land and living, the monopoly of transportation facilities and resources which, they said, shut out the poor man from his rightful chance—at the same time omitting to mention anything that would attract immigration. Pursuing this policy, when small parties of workingmen arrived in

[21] Mr. Gompers of the American Federation, visiting California in 1891 made this statement.

[22] Bonner, *Cal. Illustr.* 1892, gives the numbers and membership of Unions from 1886 to 1892. The article on *The Labor Question on the Pacific Coast* is of very great value. Mr. Bonner was a Canadian who lived 16 years in California. He was editorial writer for the New York Herald and Harper's Monthly, Editor of Harper's Weekly and author of a large amount of historical and biographical material.

California they were compelled to join a union in order to get work; or if too many, they were refused admission to the unions and advised to return home; and if without money, they were sent out of the state, sometimes at the expense of the unions. If they persisted in remaining they were treated as "scabs" and not infrequently attacked, injured and even killed. The assaults of non-union laborers in San Francisco have been by no means confined to strike periods but have been a quiet, persistent, concerted practice among certain of the lower grades of men for the purpose of maintaining a monopoly.[23]

Before labor was organized sufficiently to form an appreciable block of voting power the attacks on Chinese laborers were occasional and sporadic, though at times severe; but from 1876 onward they became increasingly systematic and irrational. The Chinese had no votes, wore queer clothes, did not speak English and were noncombative. The citizens outside the trade unions were not enlisted for them, though they availed themselves of their service and praised their industry and sobriety. But the organized body of labor was determined to shut out all competition and, because of their race prejudice and because of Chinese peculiarities—bent upon shutting them out most of all.

In the earlier years there were so few boys growing up in California that all who would work could easily get into a trade by serving a hasty apprenticeship. But even then there were concerted attempts on the part of adult laborers to prevent them from being employed in place of the lighter and cheaper common labor, for which there was constant demand. The Miners' Union had a by-law that the rate of pay for all underground men must be $4.00 per shift, regardless of age, experience or ability. This prevented the superintendents from

---

[23] See valuable article by John S. Hittell, Statistician of California, in *Overland Mo.*, 1886, entitled *Chinese Immigration*.

Labor and Chinese Competition 397

hiring boys—miners' sons—and there being almost nothing else for boys to do in a mining camp, these boys grew up without trade skill, drifted into towns and formed the "hoodlum" element. This by-law prevented the working of low-grade mines for many years—mines that would have warranted wages of two to three dollars a day—and thus left them to the thrifty and astute Chinese who admit boys to the trade *tongs* as soon as they begin to learn the trade.

Nearly all the trade unions organized after 1870 limited the number of apprentices to the number of adults or to the shop.[24] In the cigar trade, for instance, where boys could most profitably be employed the allowance was only one apprentice for each ten journeymen and one for the shop, not more than three in all to any shop. The unions which denied having any such regulation did, in fact, threaten employers who took on too many boys and so shut them out. This policy grew to be the habit of organized labor and led to incessant conflicts with employers. But its worst effect is seen in the class known in California as the "hoodlum"—a class of roystering, idle, semi-criminal boys and young men recruited from the prosperous working population. Their guardians neither keep them in school, put them to a trade nor make them earn a living. It was this class that formed a considerable portion of the earliest Kearney mobs and that has recruited the vagrant, disorderly classes in all the larger towns in California. The Juvenile Court and the Reform Schools find them incorrigible; the settlements and night clubs and classes invite

[24] Bonner gives a list of apprentice apportionments, as follows: Iron moulders, one for each eight moulders and one for the shop; bag and satchel union, one to six, bricklayers, two for each employer; caulkers, one for each employer; coopers, one son to each member of the union; glassblowers, one to each fifteen men; hatters, two to each shop; patternmakers, one to every four journeymen; stone cutters, two to each yard; wood-carvers, one to each six men, and one to each shop; printers of morning papers, one to fifteen, of evening papers, one to ten, of weekly papers, one to five.

them in vain, for they have neither the desire nor the capacity for industry. If they ever work at all it is in those intermittent and high pressure occupations which pay well for a short season and turn their employes adrift at its close.

At the meeting held in San Francisco in July, 1877, to organize a committee of safety, two speakers attributed the large number of boys and young men among the rioters, to the fact that they were shut out from learning trades.[25] From that time onward the Unions have pursued either openly or secretly a steady policy of limiting the number of apprentices which has made it impossible for a considerable proportion of their own sons to learn a trade. Moreover, the wages of the fathers have been such in many trades that the children had no need to work and if disinclined to go to school they have roamed the streets and become the material out of which the hoodlum class was ultimately made.[26]

Thus the misfortune of intermittent labor demand in the country, combined with a policy of shutting out Chinese labor—the only labor to be had at a reasonable rate for occupations requiring patient drudgery; and the shortsighted practice of extreme limitation of trade opportunities, has resulted as Hittell says, in "handicapping the state by a larger number of tramps, vagrants, and disorderly classes in general in proportion to the population than is found in any other." [27]

It has been shown in the preceding pages that before 1867 in California there was an immense labor vacuum which not even the Chinese could fill and that in consequence wages in all lines were extravagantly high. In 1867 Chinese immigration was temporarily stimulated by,

---

[25] *Alta*, July 25, 1877.

[26] In 1904 the estimated membership of the unions in California was 110,000—more than half of the unions had regulations restricting apprenticeship. If one-half of the workingmen belonging to them had even one son, there would not be room for nearly all in these trades. See Rept. Bureau of Labor, 1902–4, pp. 18 ff.

[27] Hittell, *Hist. of Cal.*, v. IV, p. 721.

Labor and Chinese Competition

the demand for laborers on the railway; and from 1869 onward the closer economic and social connection of the Pacific Coast with Eastern states, the growth of labor organizations and agitations and the depression following the panic of 1873, resulting in a check of California industry, at the same time producing an unprecedented immigration of white workers who would not do heavy manual labor. As a result of all these conditions there were some thousands of men at times—especially in winter—out of work; yet wages though slowly falling, still held up in all lines except common, casual labor above the standard of the Eastern states.

It has been shown also that the only place where the Chinese really came into serious competition on the same plane as white laborers was in certain specific manufactures; that these industries were probably initiated because of a local advantage and artificial protection; that their margin of profit was always small and their scale of wages necessarily low because they were competing with an Eastern product manufactured in part by the labor of women and boys. Further, it has been demonstrated that in recent years, since the Chinese have become an inappreciable factor among operatives, and in spite of the increase of women and children, these manufactures have stood still or fallen behind.

It has been established, therefore, that such Chinese competition as there was, was slight in degree and affected only a very small number of white wage earners, chiefly Irish and German foreigners. Although the Chinese operatives constituted from 50 per cent to 90 per cent of the employes in three branches of manufacture, they were never more than a few thousand altogether in these industries; and their competition infinitesimal when compared with the whole body of 238,000 wage-earners. While it is true that at one time they constituted one-sixth of the workingmen of the state, yet fifty-eight per cent of them were at that time occupied in placer mining, domestic service, laundry work, agricultural labor, gardening and railway work—lines in which there never was any true competition with white men, and in which there was and is a chronic scarcity of labor.

Since the Chinese have become relatively very few among California wage earners, their superiority to other foreigners, and even to the inferior grades of white American labor which alone are available for the occupations in which the Chinese are chiefly engaged, has caused them to become the standard of efficiency by which other labor is measured. Their wages have steadily risen and they have almost wholly deserted the lower paid manufactures and common labor. Their efficiency, sobriety and integrity is now continually contrasted with the unsatisfactory qualities of white tramp laborers and of the variegated foreigners who have taken their places. From the facts which have been presented it must be fairly concluded that, the conditions of California industry being what they are, the question is not so much of Chinese competition with white labor but of self-preservation against the thousands of laborers of all nationalities, of all degrees of inefficiency, turbulency and instability, who are freely brought in to take their places. It must be conceded that the thrifty and capable Chinese, who come and go home again, leaving the fruits of their labor, are preferable to their successors, many of whom when they stay become a burden to the State in public institutions. The problem in California is not and never has been how to shut out Chinese competition; but rather how to obtain an adequate quantity of dependable and efficient laborers—of any race—without which her material progress must long be postponed.

CHAPTER XXI

THE CHINESE IN SAN FRANCISCO

"To all who make up the proletarian class in the Great West the Chinese is not a man but an infernal puzzle and portent."—W. M. FISHER, in "The Californians" (1876).

"They are an intellectual people and possessed of fully the average amount of shrewd common sense, intermingled with some ancient and crude superstitions which serve as a variant. With the single exception of the Emperor, their officials of all grades, from the highest to the lowest, are of and from the people themselves, and local self-government exists there to an extent not seen elsewhere. In China the people are in fact masters of the situation, and a spirit of sturdy democracy is everywhere evident. They judge men or nations much as we do, by what they do rather than what they say. Hence in any given condition or circumstances, if we infer Chinese feelings or conduct from what our own would be in the same situation, we shall not go far wrong, always, however, bearing in mind that they are more patient than we."—CHESTER HOLCOMBE.

"Sensible people will, perhaps, ask: Why do you permit the Chinese in your city to disregard the health and fire ordinances? Is it not the business of the municipal authorities to punish such infractions of the law? Must the Nation compromise its honor and disregard its Treaty obligations because the officials of your city neglect their duty?"—YAN PHOU LEE.

WITH physical and social characteristics so different from the rest of the population it was, perhaps, inevitable that the Chinaman with his flowing trousers and queue should be a conspicuous mark for race persecution in California at a time when the feeling against all foreigners was very strong. In San Francisco from the beginning the Chinese drew unfavorable attention to themselves by their clannishness and their habit of self-government. When, for political reasons, the anti-Chinese movement centered there, the stock in trade of agitators was always the horrors of Chinatown and the tyranny of the Six Companies. Newspaper reporters and tourists went through the slums of the Chinese quarter and interpreted the whole Chinese race from that experience;

lawyers and city police in close contact with Chinese criminals and prostitutes gave even a worse view of Chinese character.

The distorted and vicious image thus presented was not at all the Chinaman whom the banks, mercantile houses, express companies, insurance agents and business men knew; nor the one familiar to missionaries and teachers; but he was convenient for the politician and agreeable to the sand-lot and therefore he has become the traditional bogie for public use. It is essential to an estimate of the true value of the Chinese immigrant to know the decent Chinaman as he has been living in Chinatown through these fifty years. While highbinders, opium fiends, gamblers, prostitutes and criminals —the riff-raff of the people—have been constantly in the public eye, the average, respectable, dignified, industrious, law-abiding and reticent Chinese have come and gone without being known or appreciated.

Like all the other immigrants who came to San Francisco in the early days, the Chinese established a "quarter" in the city, partly to protect themselves, but primarily to make themselves feel at home by living close together and by organizing a society similar to that from which they came. As in China, the family tie, the clan relationship, became the basis of their colony bond. The "Four Societies," afterward enlarged to six, was the substitute for village and patriarchal association, and although purely voluntary and benevolent in their purpose, they became, because of American ignorance and prejudice, the supposed instruments of tyranny over their countrymen.[1] They were very early accused of importing coolies and prostitutes under contract; of extorting money illegally from their countrymen, of aiding criminals to evade the American courts, and diseased persons to escape the health officers; they were con-

---

[1] The Chinese word is better translated "society" than "company" but these societies are usually called "The Six Companies" in California.

fused with trade-guilds, with hatchet societies and with societies that ran gambling and brothel houses.[2] In short, whatever happened in Chinatown that was inexplicable or disreputable, was laid at their door; and to this day public men, otherwise intelligent, repeat these accusations although they rest on nothing but newspaper reiteration and tradition.

Of the four classes of social organizations most common in China, only three have been reproduced in this country. The clan organization proper does not exist here, but the trade guild, the town and district councils— in the form of the Six Societies—and the private clubs or secret societies for special objects are all found in the United States, though somewhat modified by the necessities of a new situation. The Six Societies, similar to the village councils in China, are formed in America for the control, protection and general benefit of their members. They have a company house where a register of names and addresses is kept. In the same building are lodgings and a kitchen for the use of transients. The rules of the Yeung Wo Society as it existed in 1854 in San Francisco will serve as a type of all of the early societies of this kind.[3] There was an entrance fee of ten dollars for members, payable in six months, but no fee was required of transients or invalids. The rules stipulate further:

"Disputes will not be settled by those who have not paid this fee. Members intending to return to China must make the fact known when their accounts will be examined, and measures will be taken to prevent it . . . if debts remain unpaid. In the company house there must be no concealment of stolen goods; no strangers brought to lodge; no gunpowder or other combustible

---

[2] *Alta*, May 31, 1853; *Scribner's* (o. s.) 1376, p. 862; *N. A. Rev.* v. 166, p. 230; pamphlet, *Meat v. Rice*, (Amer. Fed. of Labor) p. 5; *Sen. Doc.* 776, pt. 2, (1901), pp. 441–2, Bancroft, *Works*, p. 38, index.
[3] Article on the *Democracy of the Chinese* by Rev. Wm. Speer, in *Harper's Mo.*, v. 37 (1868); clear account of Chinese organizations in the U. S. and careful translation of the rules of the Sze Yap Society in San Francisco in 1854.

material; no gambling, no drunkenness; no cooking except in the proper quarters; no burning of sacrificial papers; no accumulation of baggage; no filth; no bathing; no filching of oil; no heaps of rags or trash; no wrangling and noise; no injury of property; no goods belonging to thieves; no slops or victuals. For the heavier of these offenses complaint shall be made to the police of the City; for the lighter, persons shall be expelled from the company. . . . Invalids that cannot labor, are poor and without relatives, may be returned to China at the expense of the company; quarrels and troubles about claims in the mines should be referred to the company . . . if any should refuse to abide by the decision of the company it will nevertheless assist the injured and defend them from violence."

The President of this Company stated that the subscriptions were devoted to buildings and repairs, assistance of immigrants, aid for the sick and burial of the poor, salaries of agents and servants and general expenses of management; that these agents were required to be men of probity who must give security; and that the Company had never employed men to work in the mines for its own profit nor purchased slaves. With variations in details, similar descriptions were given in succeeding years and the missionaries of all sects repeatedly explained that these companies were benevolent institutions and mutual aid societies whose halls answered the purpose of business exchanges and temples of worship.[4]

In 1877, the growing anti-Chinese agitation drew special attention to the Companies—by this time increased to six—and the charges that they were importers of contract coolies and prostitutes, in collusion with hatchet societies, evading American laws and governing their own people in tribunals of their own, were so often repeated that the Societies made a formal defense. The *Memorial of the Six Companies*[5] addressed to Congress

[4] *Alta*, Nov. 21, 1858, quoted from the Baptist circular. Hittell, *Resources of California*, (ed. 1861), p. 386-7; Chinese Protection Society, in Sacramento *Union*, Nov. 27, 1869.

[5] *Alta* Print, S. F., Dec. 8, 1877, pp. 29-30. In 1876 Lloyd stated the membership of the Six Societies as follows: Wing Yung 75,000; Hop Wo 34,000; Kong Chow 15,000; Yung Wo 10,200; Sam Yup 10,100; Yan Wo 4,300.

said that they were occasionally employed to collect debts due in China or in the interior of the state but that their proper character was something between a club and a benefit society; that they were originally formed of persons from the same or neighboring districts; that membership was in no way compulsory, not even by public opinion, but the convenience was so great that there was scarcely a thousand persons out of the whole number of Chinese in this country who did not belong to one of them. Again in 1886, the Consul for the Chinese defended the Six Companies from the same charges as before, in a pamphlet describing at length their origin and declaring that their functions in the United States,[6] were those of benevolent and fraternal organizations like the Odd Fellows or the New England Society in California and not in any way connected with any mercantile business.

In 1891 a number of the officers of the Six Societies testified before a Congressional committee to the same facts and their testimony was corroborated by several Americans. They all denied that the Societies arrested or tried their countrymen, or that they imported coolies and prostitutes. Some of the American witnesses said that the Six Companies had assisted the police in apprehending and prosecuting criminals.[7] Mr. Ward McAllister, Attorney, and Mr. S. C. Houghton, Master in Chancery and Commissioner, who tried about one-fourth of the *habeas corpus* cases which arose after the first restriction law, both testified to the character of the register kept by the Six Companies which was invaluable to the court in these cases. Mr. Carlton Rickards, interpreter for the Custom House, said that the Companies were not instrumental in any way in bringing in coolies or women. In 1894 Mr. Walter Fong, a native-born and well educated Chinese who lived in California,

[6] *The Other Side of the Chinese Question*, S. F. Feb. 1886.
[7] *Cong. Docs.* 1891, ser. no. 2890, H. R. 4048, see index.

wrote an account of the Six Societies which corresponds in all essential matters to the other authorities of the preceding forty years.[8] Not to multiply authorities, all the reputable Chinese and all the Americans who knew either the language or the Chinese population in the United States intimately, unite in testifying that the Six Societies are benevolent organizations, exercising extensive advisory but no coercive powers, and not to be confounded with trade guilds or secret societies of which there have been many, organized for both reputable and disreputable purposes.[9]

The second class of organizations found extensively reproduced among the Chinese in this country are the trade guilds which combine many of the features of the American trade union and the benefit society. The most important ones in San Francisco were the laundry men, the cigarmakers, shoemakers, and tailors. The cigarmakers had a president, secretary and treasurer, an interpreter and an agent in each factory, a headquarters keeper and a janitor. In this guild the position of interpreter was permanent because they worked for American employers chiefly; in other guilds they were working for Chinese employers. The admission fee was five dollars for the cigarmakers' guild and ten dollars for the washmen's guild and fines for non-attendance and collections for celebrations were customary. Before the rise of steam laundries in California the fee for washmen was thirty dollars and the guild paid dividends so that every Chinaman wanted to join; but since 1882 the number of Chinese laborers has become so much less and the competition of white laundries so serious that the washmen's guilds are much less prosperous. Formerly the

---

[8] *Overland Monthly*, 1894, v. 23, p. 526 ff.
[9] Hittell, *Resources of Cal.*, ed. 1874. Lloyd, *Lights, etc. of S. F.*; Baldwin, *Must the Chinese Go?* ed. 1890; Dixon, *The White Conquest*, 1876; Speer, Gibson, Seward, Condit, Wells, Williams, Cleveland, Kennedy, and other historians of the Chinese in the U. S. Interviews with Chinese corroborate the above.

apprentice received thirty dollars a month and board but now the boss laundrymen complain that he wants two dollars a day and there is no profit left. The laundrymen divide the territory—as, for example, the laundries must be ten doors apart—and enforce other strict rules.

The objects of the guilds are stated to be: to keep up wages, to settle disputes among themselves, to protect themselves against non-union Chinese by strikes and against Americans by suits at law. The guild headquarters serves as an employment office where members out of work report and where employers go for workers. Unemployed guild men can always have board and sometimes lodging, at any laundry. If a non-guild employer starts a washhouse, the guilds will underbid him and run him out, but their constitution forbids them to underbid each other.[10]

In addition to the Guilds and the Six Companies there are a great number of private societies organized for good and bad purposes. Of these the most conspicuous and the least understood are the so-called Highbinders,[11] more accurately named the "Hatchet men." It appears to have been an off-shoot of the Triad Society, a political organization of the period of the Tai Ping rebellion, which was brought to California about 1863. Here as the Hip Ye Tong it lost its political motive and was originally formed to protect women from slavery. But on account of the high market value of women it shortly degenerated into a society for bringing in prostitutes, and became so corrupt that the better class Chinese formed a new society—the Quong Tuck Tong—to oppose it. The agents of the latter company went to the Mail dock and when slave women were landed identified them to the immigration officials. The Quong Tucks with the

---

[10] Fong, Chinese Labor Unions in *Overland Mo.*, 1894; *Alta*, May 23, 1870; Rept. Cal. Bu. of Labor, 1887–8; Condit, *The Chinaman as We See Him*, pp. 68–70.

[11] Condit, p. 74; interview with members.

support of the merchants became very rich and after a while stopped sending the rescued women back, keeping them for themselves.[12]

The Hatchet men are generally Chinese criminals who have sneaked into this country without certificates, or young toughs corresponding to the hoodlum class among Americans.[13] They support themselves by blackmail on merchants and upon houses of prostitution, and by gambling and the assassination of obnoxious persons. If their agent who undertakes a murder is imprisoned or killed a sum of money is paid to his family; if he is arrested they agree to clear him in the courts. These societies maintain a regular band of paid fighters whose rivalries, shooting affrays and street battles are the terror of the respectable residents cf the Chinese quarters in American cities.[14] In 1902 a war in which seven men were killed occurred in San Francisco, continuing at intervals for several months. In the newspaper accounts, it was made to appear that the See Yups and the Sam Yups—two of the Six Companies—were at war.[15]

It is, perhaps, not surprising that those who are not acquainted with Chinese life should assume that the Six Companies were responsible for these outrages. Nearly every man in Chinatown belonged to one or another of the Six Companies and nearly every merchant in Chinatown was paying blackmail to the Hatchet men for immunity from annoyance. If it were known that any of them had reported the Hatchet men to the police or had assisted in their identification, their lives would have been

[12] The word "highbinder" is said to have been applied in 1860 to Irish banditti by the *Weekly Inspector*—See Masters, *Californian*, v. I, p. 62; Condit says it was first applied to a Chinaman by an Irish policeman in New York in speaking of a Chinese "tough" or "hoodlum." Before 1849 the word was used to mean a rowdy, in New York and Baltimore.

[13] See testimony of C. Rickards, Interpreter of Customs, *Cong. Docs.* 1891, s. n. 2890, H. R. 4048, p. 303 ff.; and of Jew Ah Mow, p. 536.

[14] Condit, *The Chinaman, etc.*, pp. 69–72; Masters, *Californian*, 1892, vol. I.

[15] San Francisco *Chronicle*, Nov.–Dec. 1902, Feb.–May, 1903.

in danger. Such Tong wars do not exist in China, but they thrive in San Francisco because the American police cannot speak Chinese or identify the criminals and the respectable Chinese dare not do so for fear of their vengeance.

A well-known lawyer who has had close acquaintance with the Chinese for many years, said that nearly all the crime in Chinatown was committed by these societies and almost every case of murder could be traced to quarrels over gambling and women. He was convinced that if the police would enlist the relatives of the murdered man there would be much less difficulty in identifying and convicting the criminal; and if the highbinders, when convicted, were deported instead of sent to prison, the worst criminals could easily be got rid of. The Consul-General has repeatedly proposed that they be deported, for in that case, he could procure the severest punishment for them on their arrival in China.

The ignorance of the general public, the sensational irresponsibility of the San Francisco press and the resentment of the police at being continually baffled in their pursuit of Chinese criminals and in securing testimony, have united to produce the most exaggerated and erroneous ideas of the aims and practices of the Six Companies. For many years it has been the accepted tradition that the Six Companies exercised some kind of secret control over their countrymen—acting as a private tribunal to try and punish criminals, compelling the Chinese to pay their debts, and collecting their wages. The facts already given explain in some measure how these erroneous ideas arose. In the early years the Chinese were mortally afraid of the American courts and until 1870 had no standing in them as witnesses. They were, moreover, accustomed to adjust all minor difficulties in their own country by arbitration through their village Councils. In this country they naturally took their petty disagreements which chiefly concerned claims in the mines and claims for debt, to the officers of the Six Companies, who heard and adjusted them.

Although the members were widely scattered, they came into San Francisco at New Year's, if possible, and settled their affairs. The Six Companies did not require the payment of the dues of membership until the member left for China. It was therefore the custom for each member before leaving to appear at the office of the Six Companies to pay his subscription and for him to meet his creditors there to settle with them. The Six Companies' rooms became a sort of clearing house of business for those departing to China; and in the systematic Chinese fashion the Secretary gave the departing member a paper to show that he had fulfilled all his obligations in this country. Occasionally some Chinaman would try to get away without paying his subscription or his debts; the Six Companies therefore made an agreement with the Steamship Company that he should not be allowed to purchase a ticket until he had shown a paper from them stating that he had paid his debts. In 1880 the Legislature made it a misdemeanor for the Steamship Company to exact such a statement and the Chief of Police posted a notice in Chinatown to that effect. The officers of the Six Companies resented this interference with what they considered their private affairs, and posted a notice that if departing Chinamen did not pay their debts the Six Companies would have them arrested and taken into the American courts. The Chief of Police tore down these notices and arrested the Chinese printers for conspiracy to extort money. As a result the Six Companies were compelled to give up the agreement with the Steamship Company. There was not, in this instance, nor at any other time, any evidence that the Six Companies extorted money or went farther than to make it very difficult for a man to leave the country without paying his debts.[16]

[16] *Alta*, 1881, Jan. 21. Interviews with Chinese and Americans.

Since the establishment of the Consulate many of the small matters once adjusted by the Six Companies have been attended to by the Consul and the increasing number of Christians among the Chinese who do not wish to worship in the Temple or to support it, has diminished the duties and the power of the Six Companies to a great degree. But they still arbitrate petty disputes, care for the sick, the aged and the penniless, and return the bodies of the dead to their native land.[17]

Besides the formal relations of the trade guild, the Six Companies, private Societies for various purposes, the Temple or the Church, every Chinaman is enmeshed in a thousand other relations with his fellows. As early as 1853 nearly all the Chinese in San Francisco were settled in the two blocks between Kearney and Stockton Streets, and Sacramento and Jackson Streets;[18] in 1877 the quarter had expanded considerably, and in 1906 it occupied fifteen blocks, all below Mason and South of Sacramento Street. The land and buildings were usually leased by the Chinese from white owners. Of 153 pieces of property listed in 1873 ten only belonged to the Chinese while all the rest were leased from whites— many from Frenchmen, Italians and Germans.[19] In 1904, of 316 pieces, 25 were owned by Chinese.

Just before the Kearney period there were twenty-five firms in Chinatown variously assessed at from five to twenty-five thousand dollars each, and there were several merchants reputed to be worth from two to five hundred thousand dollars. The total amount of Chinese investments in San Francisco was estimated at two millions nearly all which was in personal property.[20] At this time practically all the Chinese intended to return to

[17] Condit, p. 31-36.
[18] *Alta*, Nov. 21, 1853.
[19] Morning *Call*, 1873—May 10, Interview.
[20] In 1872, the assessment of personal property on which taxes were paid, was $421,750.00. McClellan, *Golden State* (1876) p. 473; Lloyd, *Lights, etc.*, p. 253.

China and perhaps because they felt the uncertainty of their foothold in this country, they have seldom invested in land, preferring to take long leases which they could easily sublet.[21]

Like all other pioneer towns, San Francisco was built for business, and for single men, primarily. Until a comparatively recent period, outside of the business districts, it consisted largely of hotels, lodging-houses of every grade of cheapness, respectability or disrepute, catering to single men. To this the Chinese quarter was no exception. It differed chiefly in the amount of space assigned to each man. The Chinese immigrant was unaccustomed to the extravagant expenditures of the West and since in almost every case he had come to save money to better the fortunes of his family in China, he spent as little as possible for lodging and for food. As the number of the Chinese increased late in the sixties, the enterprising white landlords cut up the buildings into smaller and smaller compartments; or, they leased their buildings to Chinese sub-landlords who in turn, cut the space into smaller and smaller rooms.[22]

On account of the strong anti-Chinese prejudice, no other lodgings would take in Chinese and there came to be blocks and blocks of buildings, subdivided like the cliff dwellings into tiny rooms six by ten or twelve feet, containing nothing except bunks, and each accommodating from two to ten men. In each of these buildings there was an assembly room where the men lounged and smoked or gambled and a kitchen with bathing arrangements, for common use.

Much energy has been expended in describing the horrors of over-crowding and the lack of ventilation in these lodging houses; they were, however, seldom full except in midwinter for a few weeks, and were quite

---

[21] D. Cleveland, (1868) *Cong. Docs.* 1868, ser. no. p. 541. Opinion of real estate men.
[22] Cal. State Legisl. 1876–7, Gibson, p. 94. See *Globe Hotel* in index.

The Chinese in San Francisco

as well ventilated and not more crowded than the cells of the city police station or the cheapest lodgings frequented by other poor foreigners in San Francisco.

The unsanitary condition of Chinatown—for many years the horror of the press and the thunder of the politician—was after all a mere matter of profit for the landlord. Chinatown property, like the property formerly leased to immigrants on the East Side in New York, was let with the stipulation that the tenant must make all repairs. The primary tenants were transient men; the lessees were Chinese lodging-house keepers who like other landlords wished to make their stake and go home; the white agents charged all the lessee would bear; and the white owner discreetly avoided the premises. The Chinese who lived permanently in the quarter came, most of them, from regions where plumbing and a city sewage system were unknown, and were inert when their cellars and cesspools became saturated with filth. With every change of Health Officers the new appointees made the motions of cleaning up Chinatown, which consisted in a squad of men arriving in the quarter to whitewash and fumigate. But the Chinese soon learned that " only those were cleaned up who didn't pay up,"—in other words they paid the police to be let alone.

In all the years during which these spasms occurred the white landlords were never compelled to put the property in order, as landlords were obliged to do in other parts of the city. Not until 1904 when the Bubonic Plague threatened the city and the Merchants' Association took the matter out of the hands of an inefficient Board of Health, were the landlords compelled to do anything. At this time, the agents of the Merchants' Association, in killing off the rats which it was feared would spread infection, discovered the unsanitary condition of the basements. In one house a great pool of filth was found; the building was condemned and was being torn down when the white owner got out an injunction. The officers simply compelled him to visit the premises and he withdrew the injunction. The fact that at this time many buildings were not only cleaned but sewered for the first time, is a sufficient commentary upon the Health Administration of the City.

Meanwhile, after the exclusion laws were passed, the number of immigrants decreased gradually and the resident Chinese spread to other states, leaving not more than half as many residents in Chinatown as there had been in 1880. The thirty-three acres of ground covered in 1902 was therefore not nearly so crowded as formerly, although with every year the old brick buildings became less habitable. Rents began to fall and property to depreciate in value; and finally the Banks refused to lend money on Chinatown property because of the hazards of quarantine and graft, and the departure of the rich merchants and their customers.[23]

The anomaly presented by the unsanitary condition of Chinatown and the low mortality and absence of epidemic diseases among the Chinese population has often been noted.[24] During the local political campaign of 1885 the Board of Supervisors investigated the quarter and made a horrifying report of its filth, but they were at the same time puzzled by the Chinese immunity from filth diseases and attributed it to opium smoking. The San Francisco *News Letter* remarked that it was a wonder that gambling was not lauded as a means of warding off disease and added:

"Either the facts are misrepresented or the inferences are false and delusive. But if the health of the Chinese does, indeed, compare in any respect whatever more than favorably with that of other citizens, it is clearly because the sanitary condition of the city is worse than that of Chinatown. . . . Nor do the personal habits of the Chinese favor the production of filth diseases. The

[23] Interviews with Health Officers and real estate men. A desirable lot occupied by merchants rented for $820 in 1884, $520 in 1894, and $450 in 1904; another property which was bringing 8% on $25,000, sold in 1903 for only $12,500.
[24] Lloyd, p. 239; Bancroft, v. 38, p. 283.

reporters only show their ignorance in stating that the Chinese are badly fed and clothed. They live abstemiously for their work is not laborious, and they are cleanly in their persons. It may be doubted if the opium habit is more destructive than the alcohol abuse. The great bane of the Chinese is undoubtedly over-crowding both in the workshops and in the sleeping rooms. The constant inhalation of bad air both day and night, is very productive of diseases, and it is certain that the mortality from consumption between the ages of 25 and 40 years is very largely in excess of what if ought to be."[25]

In the pioneer period there were occasional epidemics of small-pox in California, and in 1877 there were 1378 deaths in San Francisco alone, due, the Health Officer reported, to the wretched sanitary system of the city and to filthy habits. More than one-half of those who died were foreigners, but the death-rate in Chinatown between 1876 and 1878 decreased six per thousand.[26] Each of the Six Companies maintained a hospital for its members, but these appear to have been little more than bare places to die in. The Chinese Consul and the merchants raised a fund and bought a lot for a general Chinese hospital, but the city authorities would not allow them to manage it, and the project was dropped. In later years the native born and the higher class Chinese began to employ American physicians, and after the Bubonic Plague in 1904 they established an Oriental Dispensary with an American doctor in charge. At this time the municipal authorities passed an ordinance that all Chinese who died without medical attention must be taken to the morgue for an autopsy. The poorer Chinese had such a dread of this that they went to the Dispensary for examination even when they were under treatment with Chinese doctors.[27]

[25] Editorial: The Chinatown Report, Feb. 1886. The *Argus* of July 25, 1886, took the same view.
[26] Municipal *Rept.* 1877-8; *Alta*, Sept. 19, 1877.
[27] In the early days much was said about the prevalence of Leprosy among the Chinese; as the disease is not common in China and as lepers there are isolated, it is probable that these lepers in California came from the Hawaiian Islands. It appears that many of those called

416   Competition and Assimilation

The characteristic diseases of the laboring Chinese are constipation and inactive liver, tuberculosis—and among the Alaska fishermen, ulcers on the legs. These are the result of opium smoking, excessive tea-drinking, intermittent labor, lack of fresh air and the habit of bandaging cuts without antiseptic dressing.[28] They are exceptionally free from venereal diseases, partly because of their generally cleanly habits of body; and from bacterial diseases because they rarely drink unboiled water.[29] In the slack season, about Chinese New Year, the fishermen and laborers from the interior come into Chinatown and there they often remain inactive for several months laying themselves liable to the diseases of their class.

The police in this quarter formerly charged the Chinese with heartlessness because they sometimes found dying persons lying in the street. They were unaware that the common people believe that the spirit of the dead person haunts the dwelling and makes it uninhabitable and that therefore they will always carry a dying person into the open air. In recent years the custom has very nearly died out, probably from the decay of the superstition among the Americanized Chinamen; but it was one of the customs least understood and most shocking to Western sensibilities.[30]

---

lepers were in reality Syphilitics. During the anti-Chinese agitation in 1876-1886, 69 out of the 75 Chinese inmates of the Pesthouse were shipped to China at a cost of $3,300. The Health Officer said these were lepers, but Bancroft says that eight were lepers and twenty-eight syphilitics. Since that time there have been a very few lepers in the Pesthouse but no more of Chinese than of other foreign nationalities. It is generally understood that Chinese prostitutes are less diseased than white prostitutes.

[28] Interviews. Many of the better class go to American Doctors.

[29] Out of 3,500 cases treated at the Oriental Dispensary there were only three of Chancres and three of Gonorrhea. A physician in Sacramento, who is intimately acquainted with the Chinese, said their freedom from contagious and epidemic diseases was due to their careful diet and tea-drinking; and that in the fruitpicking districts the Chinese are seldom ill, while the Whites are often incapacitated by their reckless habits of eating and drinking.

[30] Testimony before Cal. Senate, 1877; pp. 191-2, 196, 198, 202, 208.

Many distorted and exaggerated ideas about the Chinese have been spread by newspaper reporters and the police. In fact the greater part of the first-hand information about the life of Chinatown, has come from men in search of a sensation or men in receipt of graft. On account of the inadequate police protection the Chinese merchants very early employed and paid a special staff as watchmen. These "specials" were better paid than the regular police and it was not long before their primary function came to be to act as go-betweens in buying off raids on brothels and gambling houses, and in protecting business houses from the demands of the regular police, the health inspectors and the hoodlums. In the time of Chinatown's greatest prosperity a beat there was understood to be worth from five hundred to a thousand dollars per month and several policemen employed there retired comfortably well off. There is good evidence that even in 1904 there was more immunity money paid to city officials than rents to landlords. The honest officers detailed there have always begged to be transferred—one said that everywhere he went in Chinatown someone handed him a twenty-dollar gold piece.[31]

If it be remembered that the Chinese were accustomed at home to the idea of the "official squeeze" it is easy to see that they would readily fall in with the American system of "graft." They did not understand English and whenever an official paper was served on them they took it to be a demand for money, to which they must accede or get into trouble with the authorities. Chinatown has long been a mine of money for subordinate city employes. In 1902 the *Chronicle* advised "improving it out of existence" in order to remove the stigma that San Francisco maintained it for profit.[32]

[31] In 1877 the Chief of Police said the Specials saved the City the cost of eight regular officers and were useful in apprehending criminals, recovering stolen property, and protecting the Chinese from the ruffianism of white men. *Alta*, Mar. 26.
[32] *Chronicle*, Dec. 7 and 14, 1902.

The social evil may be taken as an illustration of the way in which the worst class of Chinese have been abetted by corrupt local and municipal officers. As early as 1852 there were in all the mining camps numbers of German, Spanish, Chilean, French, and American prostitutes. A Chinese prostitute, Ah Ho from Hong Kong, imported large-footed, ignorant girls of the boat population and later the Hip Ye tong made it a regular business.[33] The Chinese women were brought in under a contract of body service for a specified time and in later years were worth from one thousand to three thousand dollars to their owners. If they succeeded in working out their term of service, they could always marry a common man. They were often stolen by one Chinaman from another with the assistance of deputy sheriffs and constables who were paid as much as five hundred dollars. Even Judges of the courts were bribed to issue warrants for arrest so that the officers could carry them off.[34]

In 1875 an act was passed prohibiting the importation of coolies and immoral women.[85] The Immigration Commissioner at San Francisco debarred Ah Fong and twenty-one Chinese women on the ground that they were lewd—it appears on insufficient proof, for although his ruling was sustained by the state courts it was reversed by the United States Supreme Court.[36] On several occasions the Chinese merchants tried to suppress the traffic in women, subscribing money to have them returned and sometimes, even coöperating with the missionaries; but the corruption or negligence of the American Consular office at Hong Kong, the connivance of steamship and

---

[33] Bonham to the Land and Emig. Commissioners, Eng. Parl. Rept. 1854; Condit, *The Chinaman*, etc., Ch. 13; Bancroft, *Works*, v. 38, pp. 355–6; Speer, *The Oldest Empire*, p. 472; San Francisco *Examiner*, Jan. 23, 1881.
[34] Interview with a pioneer Judge.
[85] 1 Suppl. R. S. 86, Ch. 141. Sec. 2158–63.
[36] Chy Lung v. Freeman; *In re* Ah Fong; see Lewis, *Legal Treatise*.

The Chinese in San Francisco 419

immigration employes, and the intimidation of the Hatchet Societies thwarted most of these attempts at decency.[37] Of the profits of importation at least one-fourth were known to go to white men in San Francisco.

In the earlier part of Consul Bailey's term of office the Tung Wah Hospital Committee at Hong Kong offered to investigate and vouch for the character of every Chinese woman emigrating to the United States, but about 1876 he ceased to avail himself of their services with the result that the number of women increased in the three years following. Along with his other faults it was then discovered that his office received from ten to fifteen dollars for every woman shipped to the United States. Consul Mosby in 1879 accepted the services of the Tung Wah Hospital Committee in ascertaining the character of women emigrants and was thanked for his coöperation in suppressing the export of prostitutes by the Chinese Consul-General.[38] After the passage of the exclusion law women became more valuable and with the gradual departure of the influential merchants, the increase of criminal societies and the corruption of the immigration service, the number of prostitutes again became considerable.

With this traffic in women the Six Companies, the merchants and the Christian Chinese have had no more to do than Americans of the same class have to do with similar transactions by which the white houses of ill-fame have long been supplied with women. Nor does it appear that the number of Chinese girls exceeds the number of Caucasian girls in proportion to the male population. It is well-known that Chinese married women are perfectly chaste both here and in China and that the line between respectable and lewd women is drawn quite as

---

[37] Sacramento *Union*, Sept. 21, 1878; Becker, *Humors*, etc., p. 27; San Francisco *Bulletin*, Sept 17, 1873; Evans, *A la California*, Condit. p. 149. See test. of slave girls, contracts, etc., in *Cong. Docs.* 1901, s. n, 4345, pp. 787-791.
[38] For full details see *Cong. Docs.* 1879, ser. no. 1913 Doc. 20.

rigidly by the Chinese as it is by Americans.[39] It is, moreover, an extreme breach of manners, of the most insulting character to ask a Chinese gentleman about his wife. The more respectable a Chinawoman is, therefore, the less she will be mentioned in conversation and the less she will be seen in public. It would be absolutely impossible for any employe of the city or state or any reporter to procure accurate information about the wives and daughters of decent men in Chinatown. Under these circumstances and with the general California tendency to enhance anything adverse to the Chinese, it would be inevitable that the number of lewd women would be greatly exaggerated and the number of wives underestimated. The figures given by the different writers for the same periods are indeed so wholly contradictory that no reliance can be put upon them.

The Bureau of Labor of California once undertook to make a statistical report of the number of prostitutes of all nationalities in the cities. The figures of the Chinese were given as follows: " 57 Respectable women, 761 herded indiscriminately, and 567 professional prostitutes " —the implication being that all except the 57 were disreputable.[40] If the figures had any relation to the facts at all, they could only mean that 57 were first wives, 761 married women but probably second wives, the first being left in China, and 567 lewd women.

Chinese brothels have been supplied with inmates with the assistance and connivance of white men;[41] and they pay a regular sum to the police to be allowed to run, exactly as the white brothels do. Occasionally the police raid the Chinese houses in order to divert attention from the wide-open white houses. At the time when the Bureau of Labor reported 1300 prostitutes in Chinatown

---

[39] See instance in Chinatown, S. F. Morning *Call*, Feb. 23, 1882.
[40] Cal. Bureau of Labor, 1877–8, *Legisl. Jos.* App. 5, p. 107–8.
[41] S. F *Chronicle*, Oct. 9, 1904.

The Chinese in San Francisco

—about one to every 200 or 225 men—there were in San Diego one white prostitute to every 150 of the white population and in Los Angeles one to each 200. The report does not pretend to give the number of prostitutes in San Francisco but the proportion to the whole population was without doubt higher than in either of these towns, and in 1906 was certainly higher than the proportion of Chinese women to men in Chinatown.[42]

If the environment of the Chinese in San Francisco be compared with their former surroundings in China—or even with the Chinatowns of the smaller towns and cities in the West,—it is apparent that all the conditions in San Francisco afforded encouragement to their vices rather than to their virtues. The greed and indifferences of landlords compelled them to live in unsanitary conditions even when they were intelligent enough to wish to live otherwise. A corrupt and neglectful municipal government habitually blackmailed them and then made it appear that they were an exceptionally law-breaking population. When the Chinese undertook of their own initiative to keep out prostitutes and compelled their countrymen to pay their debts they were accused of holding secret tribunals; and their efforts at decency and self-government were constantly thwarted by the prejudice and self-interest of property owners and officials.

Information concerning the conditions of Chinatown was habitually obtained from the worst classes of the Chinese while the coöperation of the respectable class was as habitually refused. Chinatown was the most picturesque quarter of San Francisco and for fifty years every traveler has been shown its theater, Temple and shops, its gambling and opium dens and its vile resorts. For half a century the Chinatown guides have exploited the vices and horrors of Chinatown and heralded them

---

[42] In 1855 the *Alta* referred scornfully to the number of white brothels as exceeding the Chinese.

to the world. Yet all the while the majority of the Chinese, reticent and self-sufficient, have kept to themselves, unknown, misunderstood, doubtless marveling at our taste for loathsome sights, yet stoically, submitting to the misrepresentation.

CHAPTER XXII.

THE MENACE OF NUMBERS AND NON-ASSIMILATION.

" Bringing with them slavery, concubinage, prostitution, the opium-vice, the disease of leprosy, the offensive and defensive organization of clans and guilds, the lowest standard of living known, and a detestation of the people with whom they live and with whom they will not even leave their bones when dead, they form a community within a community and there live the Chinese life."—GEORGE C. PERKINS, Senator from California, 1906.

" The Chinese are without home and families; patronizing neither home, school, library, church nor the theatre; lawbreakers addicted to vicious habits; indifferent to sanitary regulations and breeding disease; taking no holidays and respecting no anniversaries; but laboring incessantly and subsisting on practically nothing for food and clothes, a condition to which they have been inured for centuries, they enter the lists against men who have been brought up by our civilization to family life and civic duty."—JAMES D. PHELAN, Mayor of San Francisco, 1897-1901.

" It takes two to assimilate.—Senator GEORGE C. HOAR, 1882.

" All the reforming forces of our civilization center upon those who strike us as most foreign, and as a result they change, not we."—DOREMUS SCUDDER, 1905.

IT has been customary for those who were agitating for the exclusion of the Chinese to assume that the number in California was much larger than the Federal Census showed or than the Chinese themselves would acknowledge. There is no doubt that the Census figures of 1860 and 1870 were too low; but in 1880 and the following decades there is no reason to suppose that the error in the case of the Chinese was much greater than in the case of other foreigners.

The question of the numbers of the Chinese in the country played a considerable part in the debates in Congress. The Eastern defenders of the Orientals pointed out again and again that an immigration which amounted to only two or three per cent of the total to the United States, which was composed almost wholly of able-bodied laborers coming into a region which had only one or two persons per square mile, could scarcely be the extreme menace which the Californians claimed. The Congressmen from the Pacific Coast usually replied that the Chinese were congested in one limited area, that they were far more numerous than was generally supposed and that they were excessively vicious. In one respect they were justified to some extent, for the statistics made current by uninformed officials and sensational newspapers gave color to the assumption of dangerous numbers. Thomas Scharf, Chinese Inspector of the United States at the port of New York in 1898, seriously declared in a magazine article that there were 700,000 Chinese in the country.[1]

Unless the figures of arrivals and departures kept by the Immigration Service are extremely defective throughout a long period, it is proven in the following table that the number of the Chinese in the United States never reached 150,000 at any one time and only once rose above 110,000.

---

[1] *N. A. Rev.*, vol. 166, p. 97. The article is full of flagrant historical and statistical misstatements.

Menace of Non-Assimilation.

NUMBER OF CHINESE IN THE UNITED STATES
at each decade, condensed from detailed
table, p. 500, Appendix.*

Year	Number in Western Division U. S. (Census)	Number in California (Census)	Number in U. S.	Corrected Figures — No. in each year computed on basis of arrival and departures, minus deaths at 2% per year.		
				On Pacific Coast	In California	In U. S.
1850			*	†		
1852		25,000	7,520	7,520		
1860	34,933	34,933		25,116		
1870	62,831	49,277	63,199	46,897		47,000
1880	102,102	75,132	105,465	71,083	54,733	71,800
1882				104,991	76,850	108,200
1890†	86,844	72,472	107,488	132,300	92,600	
				98,894	73,670	109,880

This table, condensed from the detailed table in the Appendix, shows that the Federal Census of the Chinese in California was too low in 1860 by about 11,900 and in 1870 by about 5,500; but in 1880 and 1890 it could not have understated the numbers by more than 3000. In 1882 the news of the impending restriction act caused the hasty return of all the Chinese who had gone home to visit and a considerable increase of new immigrants. In that year there was a net gain of nearly 30,000. The highest net gain in any previous year was in 1852 and amounted to 18,258.

* This figure is much larger than the Custom House figures and is the largest estimate except one (10,000) made by any authority.

† The departures are not given after 1893 and therefore the computation could not be carried further.

‡ The only assumptions made in this table are the original figure, 7,520, and that those who arrived and departed at San Francisco remained for the most part on the Pacific Coast; the results in columns 4, 5, and 6 were obtained as follows: assuming the number in California at the beginning of the year 1851 to be 7,520, the death-rate of 2% a year would leave 7370; adding or subtracting the net gain or loss for the next year and subtracting the deaths at 2% a year gives the number left on the Coast in that year.

A careful examination of the fluctuations of arrivals and departures in the Appendix table shows that Chinese immigration was remarkably sensitive to supply and demand and to other local conditions affecting labor. After the completion of the transcontinental railway the Chinese began to be distributed quite rapidly throughout the West to the points where they were most needed and least molested. But several causes combined to make it appear to the casual observer that San Francisco was at times rapidly filling up with Chinamen. The rainy season in California begins in late November and drives all out-door employes from the ranches to the villages and towns. The Chinese New Year occurs shortly after the American Christmas and every Chinaman who intends to go home for a visit, if possible goes in December; while the country Chinese come into the towns and especially into San Francisco, to celebrate with their countrymen.

Before this body of transients distributed itself to the country again the new immigrants directly from China began to arrive to take advantage of the demand for labor on construction works and farms which opens in March. It has no doubt often happened that there were several thousand more Chinese in San Francisco from January to March than in midsummer. Unfortunately this is also the season at which white laborers flock to San Francisco and at which political campaigns are usually initiated. For these reasons there has sometimes been excuse for the superficial conclusion that the Chinese were arriving in unusually large numbers, and for seizing this opportunity to use the bug-a-boo of vast numbers as a campaign cry.

The unanswerable fact remains, however, that in spite of unparalleled opportunities, in spite of the allurements of steamship advertising, and the natural clan-tendency of the Chinese to follow their countrymen, the number of immigrants never rose above 20,000 a year nor

Menace of Non-Assimilation 427

averaged for any decade more than 14,000 per year during 32 years of free immigration. The Chinese "hordes" so often prophesied by the labor-politician and the alarmist, might have come, but in fact, they never did.

Before 1882 it was argued that the presence and fear of the Chinese had kept out white laborers. Yet after twenty-five years of restriction and exclusion during which California has made many and persistent efforts to induce a larger white immigration, during which railway fares have been cut in half, and great areas of land have been broken up into small tracts for the colonist; during which wages have been rising and the number of the Chinese has fallen to one-half—the white immigrants do not come in the numbers that are desired or that would have been expected, had the Chinese kept out white labor.

The rate of increase of the California population before and after restriction is given below:

INCREASE OF POPULATION IN CALIFORNIA BY DECADES

Year.	Population.	Increase. Number.	Per cent.
1900	1,485,053	276,923	22.9
1890	1,208,130	343,436	39.7
1880	864,694	304,447	54.3
1870	560,247	180,253	47.4
1860	379,994	287,397	310.3
1850	92,597		

From this table it is seen that the period of the greatest increase of the white population was also the period of the greatest increase of the Chinese. But if this were not proof enough that the Chinese did not prevent white immigration, it may be added that the counties which have had the largest number of Chinese since 1880, (see Table, Appendix) are the ones in which the white population has increased most rapidly. In short, it is probable, that, except as the Chinese have made the domestic labor problem easier in some places and so encouraged men to bring their families, their presence has had little or nothing to do with the increase or decrease of white population. The Chinese have merely followed the prosperous white element and the decline of some localities, the stagnation of others and the general dearth of common white labor has been due to quite other causes than race feeling, and Chinese competition.

At the time of the first Restriction law the Chinese were compared only with aliens from northern Europe; but since then the country has received an accession of two million Austro-Hungarians, two million Italians and a million and a half Russians—not to take into account the petty immigration of seventy-seven thousand Asiatics who were neither Chinese nor Japanese—whereas the entire Chinese immigration is estimated at 300,000. Since the immigration question has so largely altered its proportions and its racial aspect within the past twenty-five years the Chinese immigrant may now be viewed in a different light and the question of Chinese immigration fall into its proper proportion beside the greater menace of world-immigration.

Aside from the most important question of competition with American labor, already discussed in Chapter XX, there have been a number of other economic objections made to the Chinaman. It is said that he has brought no money and except for the meagerest subsistence, has sent home all that he earned; that he makes no investments here and pays no taxes; that he imports from China the greater part of what he consumes; and, worst of all, that he has a standard of living as to food, clothing and lodging, far below that of the American workingman.

As to the amount of money brought in by the Chinese during the period of free immigration there are no trustworthy figures; but it could scarcely have been less than the average of fifteen dollars per capita, brought by the four hundred thousand Hebrews and South Italians who constituted in 1906 one-third of the total immigration to the United States. Since this is an average, two hundred thousand of these later immigrants must have brought in much less than fifteen dollars, and it is conceded that many of them are less industrious and less capable of self-support than the Chinese. The Chinaman almost invariably came because he had relatives here, and by reason of the strength of the family tie and his membership in the Six Companies he was rarely in danger of becoming a pauper.

The estimates of the amount of money sent home by the Chinese vary so widely that they are scarcely entitled to serious consideration. In 1877, the *Memorial of the California Senate* to Congress said that the Chinese drained the country of one hundred and eighty millions annually, assuming the number of the Chinese in California alone at 180,000, although the Census showed less than half that number. This would be a net earning of a thousand dollars apiece above the cost of living, and each Chinaman must, therefore, have received from three to four dollars for every working day in the year.[3] This would hardly be called "cheap labor", even in California. On the other hand, a conservative estimate made by John S. Hittell went to show that the Chinese could not send home more than one-eighth of their earnings.[4]

Such figures can be nothing more than guesses. That the Chinese have sent home large sums of money is certain, but whether more or less proportionately than

---

[3] The Census of 1880 gave 75,218 Chinese in California.
[4] The S. F. *Morning Call* in 1882 estimated that 100,000 Chinese sent home forty-six millions annually, that is $468 per capita. Representative Hilborn of California in the debate on the Geary Act said that the Chinese had sent home three hundred millions. Hittell's estimate is found in *Overland Mo.*, 1886. See also Yan Phou Lee in *N. A. Rev.*, vol. 148, p. 477.

other classes of immigrants it is impossible to say. In 1906, sixty-three million dollars was sent through the United States post-office to European countries and in the ten years preceding, two hundred and eighty-eight millions were sent. As post-office orders are used chiefly by persons of small means, this must represent the contribution of foreign born citizens to their families at home.[5] To this sum must be added the larger amounts remitted through the banks and the cash carried home by the returning immigrants of whom there were 282,000 in 1906 alone, and a million eight hundred thousand in the nine years preceding.[6]

The Chinese in the United States have invested only a small part of their savings in real estate. That which was not sent to China was invested in personal property and for this reason the Californians have complained that they paid a mere fraction of the taxes which supported the state. But this peculiarity was by no means confined to the Chinese for between 1852 and 1872 personal property constituted almost one-half of the total of all assessments in California and in 1882 it was still one-quarter.

In 1862, when a committee of the California Senate made an investigation of the Chinese, the Six Companies supplied them with the following data on the expenditures of their countrymen:

EXPENDITURES OF CHINESE IN CALIFORNIA IN 1861.

Duties paid by Chinese importers at port of San Francisco	$ 500,000
Freights paid to ships from China.	180,683
Passage money paid to ships from China	382,000
Head tax	7,556
Boat hire	4,767
Rent for stores and storage	370,000
Licenses, taxes, etc., in state	2,164,273

[5] Chicago *Record-Herald*, Feb. 16, 1907, figures from the post-office department.
[6] On money sent out of the country by immigrants in general see Rept. of the Industrial Commission, 1901-2, index.

Menace of Non-Assimilation 431

EXPENDITURE OF CHINESE IN CALIFORNIA IN
1861—*Continued*.

Commission paid auctioneers and brokers	$ 20,396
Drayage in San Francisco	59,662
Teaming in the interior of the state	360,000
Paid for American products in San Francisco	1,046,613
" " " " " state	4,953,387
" " fire insurance in city.	1,925
" " marine insurance in city.	33,647
" " steamboat fare to Sacramento and Stockton	50,000
" " stage fare to and from the mines	256,000
" " steamboat up-river freights	80,000
Water rates for Chinese miners [7]	2,160,000
Mining claims bought by Chinese miners [8]	1,350,000
Total:	$13,974,909

The Senate committee verified many of these statements from independent sources, but allowing for some exaggeration in those items which were merely estimates, the sum total could scarcely be reduced to less than ten million dollars for a single year.

Certain items can be substantiated from state reports: the commutation tax levied at the port of San Francisco of which the Chinese paid at least one-half in the very early years and 85% in the later; the Foreign miner's license taxes, the police tax of 1862, and the poll tax. The following table gives the share of these taxes paid by the Chinese to the State of California:

TAXES PAID BY THE CHINESE IN CALIFORNIA,
1850–1878 (incomplete).*

Commutation tax, 1851–1878, (60% of total)	$ 260,000
Police tax, 1863-4, (unconstitutional)	12,813
Miners' License taxes, 1850–1870, (unconstitutional)	4,908,416
Poll taxes, 1851–1871, (50% of total)	1,530,185
Total paid (incomplete)	$6,711,414

[7] 20,000 miners buy water at 30 cents per day.
[8] 15,000 miners buy claims at 20 cents per man per day.

* Calculated conservatively on the basis of figures furnished by the Controller's Office. The taxes paid for business licenses by laundrymen, vegetable men and others and the taxes paid on personal property amounting to many thousands of dollars through a period of fifty years, are impossible to estimate with any degree of accuracy.

The early historians frequently spoke of the fact that the mining counties were dependent on the revenues from the Chinese, and many testified that whoever else escaped taxation, the Chinese seldom did. Lloyd wrote: "The Chinaman is ever under the vigilant eye of the tax gatherer—John seldom escapes. * * * * The Chinese are very punctual in paying taxes, licenses and all just public demands." The *Daily Alta* said: "If their consumption should cease it would create a monetary panic. * * * * For every Chinaman who leaves our shores there is one less producer and one less customer."[9]

On no one matter relating to the Chinese has there been more diversity of opinion and less information than on their standard of living in this country.[10] The California Bureau of Labor in 1888 published the following table as its contribution to the subject:

COST OF LIVING.

Lodging per year	$ 1.82	Wages	.90–$1.50 per day.
Food at 20c. per day	73.00		
Clothing per year	5.00		
Two queues	0.75	Earnings per year	$320.00
Shaving head twice per mo	3.60	Cost of living	84.92
	$84.92		$230.08

The only item that comes even near the truth is the cost of food. It is not uncommon for the poorest day gardener in California to give one day's work per month for the rent of his cabin on the place; as for clothing, five dollars would not pay for his shoes—for he wears coarse leather shoes like other workingmen—much less for the rest of his outfit. Nothing is allowed for incidentals, yet the Chinese ride on the street cars, smoke tobacco or opium, and have their trifling expenses the same as an American.

---

[9] *Alta*, Sept. 10, 1855; Sacramento *Union*, Feb. 5 and 10, 1859. Tuthill, *Hist.* of Cal. (1866) Corresp. of the *Union*, June 30, 1870—"If it were not for the Chinese we could not live (in Placer county)." *Lights, etc., of S. F.*, p. 252. *Alta*, 1859, Feb. 19.

[10] Durst in the *N. A. Rev.*, vol. 139.

Menace of Non-Assimilation 433

The truth is that the Chinese are very fond of good clothes, good eating and amusements, and so far from being penurious they spend generously for such things whenever they have the money.[11] They differ from many other laborers in this country chiefly in two ways: they spend less for lodging and they rarely spend all they have —they have an inborn thrift akin to that of the New Englander. In 1876 Lloyd estimated the expenditure of a Chinese laborer in America at $200 per year and in 1906 four Chinamen, running a small restaurant cooperatively, estimated their living expenses at about that amount per person.[12] A number of observers have pointed out that their staple article of food, rice, costs in this country, seven dollars per hundred pounds— twice as much as flour—and that they use quantities of pork and fish, besides an immense variety of vegetables. Kerr, who was intimately acquainted with their life in Chinatown, thought a Chinese laborer's expenditure not must less than other aliens. Kennedy declared that they fed themselves better than many other foreigners. Minister Seward wrote: " As a matter of fact, the Chinese in California dress better than other laborers and eat quite as good food. It follows that the Chinese, like most people, live well up to their incomes." [13]

Fortunately, on the item of food expenditure there is' recent and accurate information. Professor M. E. Jaffa, of the California Agricultural Experiment Station, in 1901 made a study of the diet of a Chinese dentist's

[11] See Sacramento *Union*, Nov. 27, 1869; *The Other Side*, etc., ed. 1886, *Lights, etc., of S. F.* (1876) p. 234-5; Kerr, *The Chinese Question*, p. 12.
[12] A Chinese waiter furnished the following estimate of the cost of living of laborers in this country: clothing, minimum estimate, $35 per year; food, $8-$10 per month; incidentals, $1.50-$2.50 per month; lodging is usually included in wages, a cabin or bunk in barracks in the country, the usual servant's room in the city; in Chinatown in San Francisco a single bunk in a room with many others, costs from $1.00 to $2.50 per month. Taking all of these at the minimum, the cost of living at lowest could not be less than $165 per year.
[13] *N. A. Rev.*, v. 134, p. 562 ff. See also *Alta*, Feb. 19, 1859.

family having student boarders (fifteen persons) in San Francisco, the diet of twelve laundrymen and the diet of twelve truck gardeners. The summary of his results is as follows:[14]

> "Of the Chinese dietaries as a whole it may be said that while many of the foods eaten were unknown to American households, they were wholesome, nutritious, and were combined to form a reasonably varied diet. . . . In addition to the peculiar Chinese foods a considerable number of articles which were common American foods—such as bread, cake, cabbage, etc.—were used. As regards cost, the sum expended (19 cents per man per day on the average) in the Chinese dietaries was doubtless below the average in American families, but not below that recorded in some instances where diet was regarded as satisfactory. For instance a teacher's family in Indiana had a reasonably varied and attractive diet at a cost of 18 cents per day. . . . The total amount purchased and not eaten was very small and bears testimony to excellent management. . . . As regards total nutrients and energy, the Chinese dietaries compare favorably with the tentative American standards. . . . As shown by the tables . . . rice was used in large amounts, but was far from being the only food eaten. On the contrary the diet was about as varied as that in ordinary American households, although many of the foods eaten were different. . . ."

Professor Jaffa finally concluded that the diet of the Chinese approached quite closely to the accepted American standard and was not lacking in animal food. Although cheap, it was neither scanty nor inferior; and rice, which constituted between one-half and one-third of the total food consumed, held much the same relation to the rest of the dietary as do bread and other cereals, starches *et cetera*, to that of an American family.

In assuming, as the early Californians appear to have done, that the Chinese were neither capable nor desirous of an education, they under-rated both the capacity and the ambition of these immigrants. Chester Holcombe says that for many centuries the practical government of China has been in the hands of those who have sprung

[14] Jaffa, *Nutrition Investigations, etc.*, 1899–1901, U. S. Dept. of Agri., Bul. No. 107.

from the common people; and while the United States has a list of poor boys who have become great men, such as Lincoln, Grant, Garfield, and others, they have a list vastly longer as their country is older. He says further that the Chinese boys sent to this country by their Government furnish a striking proof of the high average of intellectual ability possessed by their race. One hundred and twenty students, were sent here at the average age of eleven. All could read and write, but none of them knew any English and not a half dozen had spent a day at any other than the ordinary Chinese school. They all came from the middle classes. Hardly a single case of either persistent misconduct or mental inability developed in the entire number. They took hold of an entirely unfamiliar course of study with remarkable aptitude and throughout the entire course held rank among the upper half of the students in their classes. Their deportment was simply unexceptionable.[15]

In the smaller towns of California the few Chinese children have generally attended the public schools without much objection having been made by the parents of white children. In San Francisco, however, Chinese parents were obliged to support private schools of their own.[16] In 1859, at the urgency of certain Church people, a separate public day-school was organized for Chinese children but it was discontinued at the end of the year because not well attended. It appeared that of 77 pupils registered nearly all were over eighteen and having to earn a living, they were very irregular in attendance. The school was therefore re-established as a night school[17] but again discontinued either from motives of economy or because of the protests of the parents of white children. In 1877 the Chinese community peti-

[15] *The Real Chinaman*, p. 248.
[16] On the subsequent career in China of the students educated in this country see: Smith, *China in Convulsion*, p. 23; Michie, *Englishman in China*, V. II, p. 394-4; *Cong. Docs.* ser. no. 2368, p. 145 (1884).
[17] *Alta*, May 23, 1861.

tioned the Board of Education for night schools [18] but their petition was not granted, and it was not until 1885 that a separate graded day-school was located on the edge of Chinatown.

The number of Chinese children under fifteen years of age in California of whom at least 75% were in San Francisco has increased from 500 in 1867 to 4000 in 1900. The graded school already mentioned had in 1900 an average attendance of 130 pupils, mostly boys, for the Chinese prefer not to send young girls to school with boys. Pupils of high school age, of whom there were only a few, were allowed to attend the general high schools of the City. In this year, however, there was an attempt to compel them to attend the graded school in Chinatown although this school had no adequate High School course. When the Board of Education ordered the Chinese boys to leave the general high schools and attend the graded school, the Chinese daily papers threatened that the parents would take all their children from the graded schools. As this would throw the Principal and the teachers out of positions, the order was withdrawn, presumably at their request.[19]

The Chinese seldom exploit their children in premature labor but keep them in school as long as possible. The effort made by the parents is considerable for the hours of San Francisco Chinatown are those of an Oriental city—midday breakfast, afternoon dinner, supper late at night. Every mother who sends her child to the public school must rise very early to get him ready to go and must get another meal when he comes home in the after-

---

[18] *Alta*, Aug. 26, 1877.
[19] See also Sacramento *Union*, May 22, 1877; Morning *Call*, S. F., July 2, 1882; Healey, *Overland Mo.*, 1886. The daughter of Dr. Wong Him was denied admission to the white grammar school of his district by Judge Seawell, in 1902, on the ground that the city provided a separate school for her race. Dr. Wong Him argued that he did not live in the Chinese quarter and his children could not go so far, but they were excluded because the white parents complained. S. F. *Chronicle*, Nov. 30, 1902.

noon. Even in the matter of food the Chinese mothers are becoming Americanized and feed their children on much the same things as native children eat.

The teachers of the graded Oriental school, most of whom have taught at some time in other schools of the city, agree that the Chinese children are clean, comfortably dressed, well-behaved and have more money to spend for sweets than other children. They praise especially their superior mental ability and studiousness.

One of the American institutions of which the Chinese heartily approve is the Woman Physician and the Chinamen in San Francisco employ the best women doctors for their wives and children. The physicians in going to their patients in Chinatown have an opportunity to become intimately acquainted with the life there. They have much to say of the kindness and indulgence of Chinese husbands, their sympathy and consideration towards their wives in pregnancy and childbirth and their willingness to spend money for pretty clothes for them. Men of good family who can afford to do so, go back to China to get wives because they wish to marry women of their own rank. But when their small-footed wives have lived here awhile they nearly all unbind their feet and wear American shoes. Many of them purchase fashionable American clothing to wear in the street in order to avoid being conspicuous, but continue to wear Chinese clothing at home because it is so much more comfortable than that of an American woman.

The women like to live here, they say, because they have so much more freedom; they can go upon the street alone and they do not have to live with a mother-in-law. Life, too, is much easier; they cook on gas stoves, they have running water and plumbing conveniences and nearly all have telephones. They eat not only all the Chinese imported foods but like many American foods as well. Their chief discomfort is the cramped quarters in which they must live. Respectable families would much prefer to live outside of Chinatown but they cannot get quarters elsewhere at any price, no matter how wealthy they may be nor how quiet and cleanly. The tiny apartments in Chinatown bring an exorbitant rental and it is wonderful how cleanly the women manage to keep them and to keep their children. The story of the attempts of one Chinaman to find a place to live outside of Chinatown, in order that he might bring up his children as Christians and good Americans, will serve better than any abstract statement, to illustrate the difficulties produced by anti-Chinese prejudice. The writer of this story is a prominent member of a Presbyterian Church and the Editor of a Chinese Daily paper. He and his family speak excellent English, dress in American clothes and his children are being educated carefully after the manner of well-to-do Americans:

"In the summer of 1901 I proposed to bring my family from Los Angeles to San Francisco. I tried many times to find a suitable house outside of Chinatown so that my children might be properly brought up in the ways of the Americans, that in the years to come they may perform the duties of American citizenship.

"I found a good flat with five rooms and bath and the rent was within my ability to pay. The landlady was willing also to rent the house to me after having heard the explanation I made regarding myself. The rent was paid and preparation was made for moving in, but after two days the landlady came to my office and returned the money to me and explained the situation: the whole neighborhood had risen in arms against the idea of having a Chinese family in their midst, and since the landlady would not give up the house to me it was out of the question to move in, so my first attempt to find a home outside of the district where my own people live was a flat failure.

"A few weeks later I again tried my luck, and in the course of an afternoon, I found two houses which I thought would be suitable to me, since they were not far from Chinatown and rent was not exorbitant. The agents kindly made arrangements to rent the premises to me but when the landlords were apprised of the nationality of their prospective tenants all arrangements were annulled.

"After all these failures, I was not yet dismayed, I resolved, to try again and hoped for better results. Accordingly one ideal afternoon, after having gone through the rush of business, I sallied forth putting aside the memory of all previous defeats from my mind. I found a flat on Mason Street near Sacramento, which I thought was the ideal place for a home. The landlord was a good-natured Frenchman. He had no race prejudice in his mind and what he had there was only dollars and cents. So he agreed to rent the place to me provided his other tenants would not object and that he would let me know one way or the other in two days. At the end of the two days I called at his house and he told me that it was out of the question to rent me the house since the other tenants objected strenuously to renting the flat to a Chinese family. I was greatly disappointed but not the least surprised. I had the temerity to ask him what family objected to my living there, and he replied that it was a family of negroes. That was the last straw that broke the back of my buoyancy of hope. I then repeated again and again to myself saying, if negroes even object to my getting a house outside of Chinatown, how can I ever succeed in getting a place where no one objects. From that time on I never made another move. The proverbial Chinese perseverance seemed to have left me for good."

At least half of the Chinamen over twenty years old who came to this country were already married and the money sent back has been for the support of their wives and families, who continued to live with the husband's parents. Before the Scott Act in 1888 those who were prosperous here—even the laborers—went back for a visit every few years; and, if they had sons, brought them to this country when they became twelve or fourteen years old. Since the coming and going of registered laborers has become difficult even for those who had the necessary property or relatives, many of these men have not dared to leave the country for fear they could not get in again. Some of them have not seen their families for twenty or twenty-five years, and several laborers who had not visited China before the passage of the Restriction Act have remained in exile forty-five years, because they could not now earn so good a living in China. Yet some laborers do take the risk of going back for a visit and then attempt to get themselves smuggled in again across the borders.

The exclusion law has thus operated to separate from their families those who preferred to live in this country.

The registered laborers who came here when they were quite young have now become too much Americanized to be able to live happily in China, so that they are now in exile, practically without a country. If the admission of respectable women were made easy; if every woman were not liable to be detained as a prostitute and with prostitutes by the Immigration Bureau, and if registered laborers were permitted to come and go freely, many families would be re-united.

The Chinaman is above all, a lover of home and children and if married men were allowed to bring in their wives freely the conditions of life of the Chinese entitled to live in this country would become much more normal. In no one respect have the Chinese in America altered more than in their ideas about women.[20] Wives have a far greater amount of freedom in America than in China; daughters are no longer unwelcome. The Chinese have repeatedly tried to adopt white children and half-bloods of other races from the asylums, but the anti-Chinese prejudice is so strong as to make it impossible. It has often been rumored that the Chinese sell children in San Francisco. This idea probably arose from their custom of binding any bargain with a money payment. The contract of adoption is made final among them by the payment of a small sum of money.[21]

On account of the difficulty and expense of bringing in Chinese wives, there have been a number of marriages between the laboring Chinese and women of the darker foreign-blood—Indian and Mexican and even Europeans. A number of native-born Chinese have

---

[20] A young Chinese lady, daughter of wealthy parents in China, who came to enter the University of California in 1902, spoke to an audience of Chinamen in the Chinese theater about reforms for women, and was treated with great respect. S. F. *Chronicle*, Nov. 3, 1902.

[21] A lady intimate with the life of Chinatown said that she had never known of a case of parents selling a girl into slavery, i. e. a life of shame, though she had known of several cases where people who had taken a girl to work, afterward sold her.

Menace of Non-Assimilation 441

married American women,[22] and the children, so far from being the "monstrosities" predicted by early Californians, are superior, both physically and mentally.[23] In the Southwest, the offspring of marriages between Chinese and Mexican women are conspicuously superior; but the prejudice against the mixture of North-European whites and Chinese is extreme and has resulted in an amendment adding the word Mongolians, to the law prohibiting intermarriage of white persons and negroes, in several states and territories.[24]

It was assumed for many years that the Chinese were unassimilable and their clannishness, the slowness with which they adopted American dress and the English language lent color to the assumption. But a comparison of the Chinese with other aliens, particularly with the Italians, Mexicans and Greeks in San Francisco, discloses the fact that they are being Americanized quite as rapidly, and in some respects, make better citizens because of their superior intellectual capacity. At the time of the first Restriction act very few Chinese had cut their queues and adopted American clothes, and they chiefly because they were converts to Christianity; but since 1900 the movement in this direction has been very rapid. Only about one boy in six in the graded school wears a queue and there are now four barbers in Chinatown itself who advertise to do queue-cutting. Those who still wear the queue do so because they mean to return to China to live or to visit their parents. One very much Americanized Chinaman said that his aged mother in China would be so shocked to see him without it that he would not have it cut till he returned from the visit home which would probably be his last.

---

[22] McClellan, *The Golden State*, p. 474–5.
[23] The *Call* of Apr. 8, 1883, mentioned three cases of intermarriage; the *Chronicle* of Apr. 19, 1903, said there were 20 white women married to Chinese in Chinatown.
[24] Cal. *Stats.*, Civil Code, 1903, Sec. 60.

The majority of Chinese immigrants some time ago exchanged their baggy pantaloons for American trousers, but like many other foreigners they have not yet compassed the idea that the cut of them must be changed frequently to be truly in the American fashion. Nor have they yet generally adopted in place of the soft cotton or silk shirt the starched garment, nor in place of the loose linen or wadded silk tunic the conventional tailor-made vest and coat; although a considerable number of the educated Chinese now wear the conventional business man's dress; and the native-born Chinese of the second generation are extremely American in their clothing.

To an Oriental the mastery of English is necessarily much more difficult than to a European, but it may be set down that every Chinaman who has cut his queue and every Christian Chinaman, speaks English, and many others speak it a little. Some who speak badly have nevertheless learned to read the American papers. Just as in the case of other foreigners, if the Chinaman came to the United States when he was a little boy or if he has a wife and children here, he speaks English and is Americanized to a considerable degree; and the native-born boys are, almost without exception, fully Americanized in speech as well as in dress.

Among the few hundred men who have families in this country not many care to vote themselves, but all of them are proud of the fact that their sons can vote. One old Chinaman said: "I no care much about vote—my son, I *make* him vote." The older Chinese are sensitive about the denial of naturalization because it is a discrimination against their race, and the native-born are proportionately proud of the privilege. More than a hundred native-born Chinese registered in San Francisco as voters in 1904; and in that campaign the anomalous spectacle was presented of a Union-Labor candidate for

Menace of Non-Assimilation 443

Mayor making election speeches in Chinatown.[25] There is abundant evidence that the Chinese of the second generation mean to claim their citizenship. In the smaller towns of California and in some other states they show strong patriotism, marching in Fourth of July parades and even drilling and volunteering for the army.[26]

During all the earlier years the Chinese shipped the bones of their dead back to China for interment,[27] and no one minor peculiarity has been so often quoted as proof that they would never assimilate. Yet even in this they have disappointed the prophets, for it is now the exception rather than the rule for the bodies of the dead to be sent home. It must not be overlooked that the conclusion that the Chinese would not assimilate has been drawn from observations made upon single men, either transients crowded in lodging houses in San Francisco's Chinatown or solitary individuals throughout the country. These do indeed constitute the majority, but there are many small groups of Chinese living in a much more normal way in the towns of the West who have been less harassed and who in consequence, show a much greater degree of Americanization. A careful study of such communities reveals an astonishing assimilation, of American ideas, more even than of outward appearance. In a certain small city in California there was in 1904 about 200 Chinese and in the country round about 150 more of whom seven only were adult women. Their occupations are given in the following table:

---

[25] The Mayor's agent made a special effort to get all the native-born to register. See *Chronicle*, July 17, 1904.
[26] *Cong. Docs.* 1901, Sen. Doc. 776, pt. 2, p. 30. *Truth v. Fiction*, p. 80. On Quong Tow, a Chinese cook of Santa Ana, Cal., went to the Philippines as a volunteer soldier—*Chronicle*, Mar. 1904. Much the handsomest parade that has been seen on Fourth of July for years in Oakland, California, was held in 1907 by the Chinese; 48 native-born sons under 12 years of age and nearly as many little "native daughters" took part.
[27] Dennys, *Treaty Ports*, (1855) p. 70.

OCCUPATIONS OF CHINESE IN S— COUNTY, 1904.

Location	Merchant firms	Number of Partners	Capital invested	Cooks	Gardeners	Laborers	Vegetable men	Barbers	Tailors
City	22	64	$72,000	55	7	21	7	2	2
Town I				6	4	24			
Town II					38				
Remainder of County				18	12	13	—2		
S— County.......	*22	64	$72,000	79	61	58	9	2	2

Location	Interpreters	Farm-hand	Fisherman	Carpenter	Miscellaneous	No occupation	Laundrymen	Women
City	2	1	1	1	4	4	92	
Town I..........			1				5	
Town II.........								
Remainder of County........		1					15	
S—County.......	2	2	2	1	4	4	112	7

It is notable that these occupations do not compete with American labor and only very slightly with foreign-born labor, since the industries in which two-thirds of them are engaged are those in which there is the greatest dearth of labor of any kind and no native Americans at all. The Chief of Police said of them in an interview:

" They are the most peaceable class of people we have in town. They give no trouble at all. There are none of the lower element here, no prostitute slaves or highbinders; when we had trouble with the ' open cribs' of women there was not one Chinese woman so engaged, although the white women were all over the town. Of course they will play their fan-tan and sell lottery tickets but that is a harmless sort of thing and they don't quarrel and fight over it as some poker players do."

* 8 Groceries, 1 commission merchant, 1 opium joint, 2 lqtteries, the remainder general merchandise.

Menace of Non-Assimilation 445

The average age of the foreign-born Chinese in this locality was 45 years (in 1904) and of the ten native-born, 18 years. There were only seven wives and families of whom the two following are typical:

Q. came from a small place near Canton in 1881, being then fifteen years old. Came from San Francisco to this city, worked in a laundry till he learned the business, then started a little laundry himself, enlarged it, sold out and became a merchant and is now selling Chinese and Japanese goods. He has seven partners, ten thousand dollars capital and a large store on a principal street. Has a wife and three children who speak English and have English surnames, and he and his son wear short hair. He is very polite, intelligent and good-natured and well liked by white men. When asked if he was naturalized, he laughed and said, "No, I can't be—but I would like to, though." He goes back to China on visits but intends to live permanently in this country. He said that in that town the people treated Chinese very well and that he believed there had never been a case in court against a Chinaman—but that in ten years there would be no Chinamen left in California because there was too much prejudice.

Ah T——, a Chinese merchant, came from Canton in 1869 at the age of 21 and worked in coal mines and at manual labor in various places for ten years; saved money, became a merchant, has a wife and twelve children, all native-born with American names. He and his sons wear short hair and all the family, except the mother, wear American clothes. His oldest daughter has a diploma from a Commercial College and is office assistant to a physician; the eldest son is a dish-washer in a restaurant, the second daughter works for a photographer. The mother proudly showed her baby named after a President of the United States and said they had sent a picture to the President and would send one of the next baby to President Roosevelt. When asked whether his son would vote, the father said: "I don't know, may be they change the laws again. This is free country—but not for all."

In proof of non-assimilation it has sometimes been asserted that the Chinese in this country are pagans and will always remain so; but the Protestant clergy who have attempted to convert them to Christianity reply that their work has been greatly hindered by the unchristian treatment to which the Chinese have been subjected.[28]

[28] Henry Ward Beecher once said: "We have clubbed them, stoned them, burned their houses and murdered some of them; yet they refuse to be converted. I do not know any way, except to blow them up with nitro-glycerine, if we are ever to get them to Heaven."

446 Competition and Assimilation

The following table shows, nevertheless, that the missionaries in the United States have made substantial progress.[29]

SUMMARY OF MISSION WORK AMONG CHINESE
In the United States, 1900.[30]

Whole number of Chinese Christians in the U. S. 1850 ff.		4000
Number of Chinese Christians in U. S. 1900	600	
" " " " other parts of Pacific Coast	500	
" " " " in other states	500	
Evening schools in San Francisco		50
Scholars in attendance during one year		3700
in San Francisco	1000	
in other parts of Coast	1200	
in other states	1500	
Chinese Sunday-schools in U. S.		75
Scholars in attendance during one year		2500
Children in Mission and Public schools		500
Preachers converted in the U. S. who have labored here and in China		60
Ordained Chinese ministers converted in U. S.		12
Amount given by Chinese in U. S. for building of chapels and for Christian work	$30,000	

The principal hindrance to conversion lies probably in the fact that the majority of Chinese in this country are adult men. Even among Americans the number of adult men who join the Protestant Churches at maturity is very small, and it is not surprising that only a relatively small number of the Chinamen have become Christians. Wherever the missionaries have been able to reach families through the women and children and the boys in the night-schools, there seems to have been no more difficulty in drawing them into the churches than there would be in converting other nationalities that have a different faith.

[29] See Condit, *The Chinaman As We See Him*. This recent and trustworthy account of Protestant Mission work among the Chinese makes it unnecessary to treat the subject in detail here.
[30] Owing to the fire of April, 1906, in San Francisco, and the consequent departure of many Chinese, the above statement is approximately correct for 1907.

Menace of Non-Assimilation 447

But since the United States boasts of the fact that it tolerates Greek and Roman Catholics, Hebrews, Buddhists and Mohammedans, Theosophists and Mormons, and every variety of belief and unbelief, it scarcely seems necessary to single out the Chinese, even if they were less convertible than other races. In valuing the Chinese immigrant, the important fact to be noted in this connection, is, that he has been carefully trained in a system of morals only second to that inculcated by Christianity; a system which differs from that of Western nations chiefly in that it lays greater emphasis on family ties and filial duty, and less upon mercy and humanity.

During the period of the most acute anti-Chinese agitation much was said about the burden of the Orientals in hospitals, insane asylums and prisons. As to hospitals, they were rarely admitted to any except the pesthouse, although they always paid the same hospital and road taxes in each county as the other male inhabitants; and from 1851 to 1878 they paid, besides, a total commutation tax (for hospital purposes) at the port of San Francisco of not less than $260,000. As to their share in the institutional burdens of asylums and prisons, the accompanying table presents the facts taken from the reports of those institutions through a period of forty years.[31]

---

[31] The comparison of nationalities as to insanity and criminality has been made with the males over twenty years of age alone. Great injustice is ordinarily done in comparing the whole native-born with the whole foreign population of both sexes, since the foreign-born have a smaller proportion of women and children.

FOREIGN-BORN MALES OF CALIFORNIA, 20 AND OVER

of specified nationalities, in population, in insane asylums and in state prisons.

Decade	Foreign born Per cent			Irish Per cent			British Per cent			German Per cent			French Per cent			Spanish-American Per cent			Italian Per cent			Chinese Per cent		
(1)	P	I	C	P	I	C	P	I	C	P	I	C	P	I	C	P	I	C	P	I	C	P	I	C
1870	59	58	59	9	18	11	5	6	7	4	9	3	—	4	1	1	3	12	0.7	1	0.9	15	3	9
1880	58	64	47	6	19	9	5	7	6	4	12	3	0.9	3	1	1	2	5	0.7	2	0.8	20	3	15
1890	51	58	45	3	14	7	4	6	5	3	11	4	0.7	3	1	0.5	1.5	4	0.9	2	0.8	14	5.5	14
1900	42	33	38	1	10	4	3	5	4	3	10	4	0.5	2	1	0.4	1.1	5	0.9	2	0.1	9	4.4	6
Average	52	58	47	4.7	15	8	4	6	5	3	10	3.5	0.7	3	1	0.7	1.4	6	0.8	1.8	0.6	14	4.2	11

(1) "P" = population; "I" = insane; "C" = criminals.

Menace of Non-Assimilation 449

It is seen that for forty years the Irish, while averaging less than five per cent of the male adult population, have made up fifteen per cent of the male insane and eight per cent of the criminals; the Germans, averaging three per cent of the male adult population, have made up ten per cent of the male insane and slightly more than three per cent of the criminals. During the same period, while the Chinese have averaged fourteen per cent of the adult male population they have constituted only four and two-tenths per cent of the insane and eleven per cent of the criminals, and only once have they risen to as high a percentage of criminals as their proportion to the male adult population.

The population figures used as the basis of the table are taken from the Census; and, if, as has often been asserted—and as the corrected figures in Table (p. 425) seem to prove—the numbers of the Chinese were understated in 1860 and 1870 by the census, a comparison of the Chinese insane and criminals with their whole adult male population would be still more favorable to them. As it stands the table shows that the Chinese were less liable to insanity and less criminal even, proportionately, than the English, Scotch and Welsh, to say nothing of the Irish, the Germans, the Spanish-Americans and Italians.

If to these facts it be added, that of the 5,000 children in public institutions for dependents in California of whom at least two-thirds are of foreign parentage—the cost of maintenance being almost one-half million dollars annually—the Chinese have 12; that of the 4,140 paupers in state almshouses in 1903 they had 44 and that they are rarely if ever found in hospitals,—if all this be taken into account, the negative value of the Chinese as immigrants who can stay out of institutions is not inconsiderable to the state of California.

During periods of anti-Chinese agitation, preceding elections, much has been said of the expense of the arrest and conviction of the Chinese for offenses in the City of San Francisco. Chief of Police Crowley stated in 1893 that 20,000 had been arrested between 1883-1893 of whom 11 per cent had been convicted and that they were "the most persistent law-breakers known to the police."[32] The following table gives the number and per cent of the total arrests of whites and Chinese.

ARRESTS IN SAN FRANCISCO, 1879-1903.

From reports of Chief of Police.

Year beginning July 1	Total Arrests	Chinese Arrested	Chinese per cent of total	Year	Total Arrests	Chinese Arrested	Chinese per cent of total
1879-80	21063	1774	8.4	1890-91	24528	955	4.
1880-81	23011	1945	8.4	1891-92	28417	1318	4.
1881-82	25969	3460	13.0	1892-93	25987	1416	5.
1882-83	24149	3817	15.0	1893-94	25824	925	3.
1883-84	25591	2539	10.0	1894-95	25960	1172	4.
1884-85	24432	2734	11.0	1895-96	30462	2793	9.
1885-86	26587	4886	18.0	1896-97	29168	3762	12.
1886-87	20385	1656	8.0	1897-98	28013	3281	11.
1887-88	19466	1160	6.0	1898-99	27769	1915	8.
1888-89	23462	1744	7.0	1899-00	26448	2857	11.
1889-90	23549	1455	6.1	1900-01	27362	2893	11.
Average per cent 1880-1890,			10.0	Average 1890-1900,			7.6

From this table it appears that from 1879-1901 the Chinese constituted 8.8 per cent of all arrests while they were not less than 14 per cent of the total adult male population of the city according to Census figures, and according to the estimates of Californians, a much higher per cent. If the offenses be analyzed and classified, it is discovered that forty per cent of all arrests were for drunkenness and that of these the Chinese were no part

---

[32] Letter of Chief Crowley, printed in Cong. *Record*, 53d Cong. 1st ses., p. 3046, in a speech delivered by Senator George C. Perkins.

Menace of Non-Assimilation 451

at all. The larger part of their offenses have always been gambling, keeping opium dens and violation of fire and health ordinances, and the smaller part robbery, murder and assault to murder. From the petty offenses the city has reaped a rich harvest of fines and bail money and the police a richer harvest of graft money. In 1876, for instance, the Chinese were fined in large numbers for violation of the cubic air ordinance while other violators were not molested; and while waiting to be brought into Court, were confined in cells in the jail which did not meet the requirements of the law.[33] About one-half of all the arrests in San Francisco between 1879 and 1901 resulted in convictions. Chief Crowley himself reported that from 1883-1893 only eleven per cent of the Chinese were convicted.

Dr. August Drahms, the well-known criminologist who has been chaplain of the principal State prison of California for many years, writes that the Chinese "are not criministically inclined in any aggressively western sense," and that outside of the Tong feuds of the Highbinders, they commit chiefly commercial offenses. The Chief of Police of Los Angeles said that the chief crime of the Chinese was gambling and that aside from occasional tong feuds in which they cut but rarely kill each other, they are an exceptionally peaceable class of people.[34]

But even in the matter of gambling it appears that the Chinese—who are not Christians—although they gamble almost universally, gamble very mildly indeed. They play fan-tan or pie-gow as an Englishman plays a clubrubber of whist or Americans play bridge and poker. For years in San Francisco, while the Chinese gambling "dens" were periodically raided by the police, there

[33] Between June 6 and Dec. 6, 1876 after the queue-cutting ordinance went into effect 1012 Chinese were apprehended for misdemeanor and paid $9,020 into the City Treasury in fines; 110 served 5 days each in jail and lost their queues.
[34] Interview.

were many places where poker and other games were played openly by white men in which far larger sums were lost; and in several of the principal saloons pools were sold on the races and prize-fights. While Chinese were arrested for running lotteries, the sellers of Mexican and Honduras lottery tickets regularly went the rounds of the business offices in the principal buildings and sold tickets without active interference from the police. San Francisco is of all places the one where gambling can be least appropriately called an "Oriental" vice since every form of it has flourished among the white population under the sufferance of municipal authority.

It has been universally granted that the Chinese are the most industrious of peoples. It is, moreover, an impossibility for any race to be extremely industrious and at the same time highly immoral, intemperate and criminal. It has already been shown that opium-taking in moderation as ordinarily practised by them in this country, is no more disastrous than the use of tobacco among Americans;[35] and that when carried to an extreme its effects are scarcely more disastrous to society than the excessive liquor drinking which is the characteristic Caucasian vice. Gambling, when confined to the Chinese themselves, is mild in degree and relatively harmless in results. Edmund Mitchell says truthfully:

"It is only when the riff-raff of other races are allowed to take a hand and to utilize the Chinese tables, games and banks for the gratification of their own propensities, that anything like widespread mischief is wrought. A Chinaman in rare instances loses his all when gaming among his own countrymen; but if this result does happen, he goes next day contentedly back to work and is not, like most ruined gamblers of European stock, permanently incapacitated for honest toil."[36]

[35] See Ch. 18. Jew Ah Mow said: "A good many of them smoke it who have not the habit; they very often smoke as a matter of pastime. It is like taking a cigar with a white man and the best illustration is like a white man asking another to take a drink."
[36] *Nineteenth Century Mag.*, vol. 36, p. 613. Interviews with Chinese and Americans.

As to murder and assault, perpetrated generally in the heat of Tong feuds or as revenge by the Highbinders, the statistics of California prisons finally prove that the Chinese are less criminal than the Caucasian immigrant. Certainly the crusade against the Chinese immigrant cannot be consistently based on their evil habits and practices while many European foreigners who make a far less creditable showing, continue to be admitted.[37] As to their effect upon the social life of San Francisco, there has never been a time when there has not been power and prejudice enough to enforce the municipal ordinances and the general laws, if the officers of the city itself had not been criminal abettors, profiting by the toleration of Chinese law-breakers.

It is not to be denied, as Chester Holcombe has said, that some of the Chinese brought vicious habits from Asia and soon acquired others from association with other foreigners and with Americans, but the worst of them were not more objectionable additions to our population than many whom we have received from Europe. So far as vice and crime are concerned the Chinese, when judged fairly by the fact rather than by extravagant and partisan generalizations, are superior to all the continental European immigrants, and, it would almost appear, are not worse than our English-speaking kindred.

Even if there were only a few signs of assimilation in the United States instead of the many already quoted it would not be conclusive proof that they could or would not assimilate, for out in the Mid-Pacific an experiment has been made under circumstances not very different— except that they are more normal—and with quite different results. Doremus Scudder, a scholarly and competent writer, has described in detail the causes of this marked difference. He says that, although the 40,000 Chinese who emigrated to Hawaii were chiefly laborers

[37] Prof. J. R. Commons, *Rept. Ind. Com.* 1901-2, vol. Immigration, p. 28.

without special inducements to identify themselves with the country, they were treated with justice and kindness, were allowed to acquire land, were subjected to no social ostracism, enjoyed the privilege of intermarriage on the same terms as other foreigners and were permitted to become citizens. Mr. Scudder thus describes the results:

> "As a consequence, the Chinaman in Hawaii blossomed out remarkably in the role of a man of the world.... By 1901 no less than 1,115 Chinese in the Territory were paying taxes on real estate to the assessed value of $1,320,084, while 12,926 taxpayers of this race were rated as owning property to the amount of $3,287,802.... During the monarchy 752 Chinese became naturalized in Hawaii and to-day there are more than 300 voters of this race.... The national Census of 1900 showed the total Chinese population of this Territory to be 25,762, living in 3,247 homes of which 393 or 12% were owned.... The Chinese is the most law-abiding immigrant we have.... All the unsanitary crimes urged against this long-suffering people on American soil are in the last analysis chargeable to the carelessness, neglect or worse vices of our own authorities.... In Honolulu there is no Chinatown like San Francisco though there is a part of the city where Chinese lodging houses and shops congregate. They are no more clannish than any other nationality.... Outside of gambling and illegal liquor selling (another offense traceable to grafting by the authorities) the Chinaman does not figure largely in the criminal courts.... 92% of his children attend school and throughout the schools of the Territory they are ranked as the best pupils. In 1903 there were 16 Chinese or part-Chinese teachers in the public and 14 in the private schools of the Islands." [38]

In commenting on the general misunderstanding of the Chinese by foreigners, Michie says that the representatives of the powers, notably Great Britain and the United States, have been in the habit of evolving from their own consciousness a subjective Chinaman with whom they play "dummy"; when brought to book they find the real Chinaman entirely different from the intelligent automaton kept for cabinet use. Something like this has been the habit of the Californians who keep a bogy Chinaman for political purposes and who yet con-

[38] *Outlook*, 1905, pp. 985 ff. *Chinese Citizenship in Hawaii.*

Menace of Non-Assimilation 455

cede his superior industry, patience and intelligence and often—in private life—contrast his sobriety, peaceableness and reliability with the defects of laborers of their own and other races.

There are thousands of families in California who have counted Chinese tradesmen and employes as friends; there are hundreds of women on lonely ranches who have been indebted to Chinamen for their safety, their comfort, even for nursing of themselves and children when no other help was to be had; for in the country districts, the only common man with whom as a class, a woman is perfectly safe, is the Chinaman. Californians will tell, most appreciatively, stories of the generosity, kindness, devotion and integrity of individuals whom they have known, but the moment the question of exclusion is broached, they insist, without apparent consciousness of inconsistency, that the Chinaman is a dangerous creature, that he will not assimilate and that therefore, he must go! They are unaware or they ignore the fact that a few thousand Chinese have already assimilated and that the children of those who have families here are as much Americanized as the children of other foreigners who were not born to the English tongue.[39]

In the face of the facts stated in this chapter it can no longer be said that the Chinese do not assimilate. Although the number of Chinese families is proportionately very small compared with their total number and with other foreigners, whenever they settle they assimilate somewhat slowly in the first generation and very rapidly in the second. Single men who have been long in the country are often too much Americanized to be able to live in China; but whether they assimilate more or less is of relative unimportance, since the most of them

---

[39] For instance the native-born Chinese children are much superior to the native-born Italian children in speaking English and in general intelligence.

die here without descendants or finally return to their native land.

Every charge brought against the Chinaman can be brought with greater force against many of the Europeans who now constitute the bulk of immigration at the Atlantic ports. Indeed, Medhurst says:

> "If clannishness, patriotism, persistence in the habits and ideas in which one has been brought up, frugality, the desire to acquire money in order to lay it out at home, and a settled determination to lay one's bones on native soil, can be characterized as crimes, or objectionable traits, then many Englishmen, Scotchmen, Irishmen and Americans cannot afford to throw stones at the heathen Chinee."

To bring the comparison nearer home: it is perfectly well-known that the Italian quarter of San Francisco is unsanitary and immoral; that the Italians are clannish and very slow to speak English; that some of them are drunken, violent, even murderous; that only those of the better class assimilate in the first generation and that their children leave school early and are by no means always cleanly or intelligent. It is common knowledge that the Italian has a very low standard of living, that he accepts a low wage, that he is not easily "unionized" and that he pays an infinitesimal part of the state revenue. Yet no one in California proposes that the Italian should go, for two reasons: because he is a Caucasian and because he has a useful vote.

"The last immigrant is always the worst immigrant," said Mr. Ernest Bruncken, an American of German parentage; and this was the view taken fifty years ago even of our nearest of kin, the Irish immigrant. If, when the famine-stricken, penniless thousands of Ireland were pouring into the United States, Congress had passed an Irish Exclusion law on the ground that they sent all their money home, that they would become paupers and criminals, that they would underbid and supersede American laborers and debauch American poli-

Menace of Non-Assimilation 457

tics—it would have been justified. For the Irish sent home not less than seventy-five millions of dollars between 1852 and 1872 and are sending now not less than ten millions a year. In California although they have averaged only 5 to 7% of the total population, they constitute forty per cent of the almshouse inmates and nearly half of the arrests for drunkenness. Yet after sixty years, Irishmen are still welcome immigrants, for we know that with all their faults and vices, and even though they have superseded almost wholly native-born American labor, the better part of them can be made into good Americans. Such comparisons are doubtless odious to those who consider the color of the skin more important than character and capacity but they serve to reveal the true animus of Chinese exclusion and to strip it of all adventitious excuses. The Chinaman was and is shut out because he is yellow and because he is too industrious, not because he would not make a good American.

Long ago the Sand-lot framed a bogy Chinaman, endowed him with all the vices and all the industrial virtues potential in his race; stripped him of all human characters except avarice and deceit and set him up in the market-place of San Francisco. Though every Californian knows Chinamen who have no resemblance to this bogy except a queue and a yellow skin, yet for the sake of self-justification and under the obsession of the tradition, the bogy is periodically held up to the world as the real Chinaman—the menace of the Pacific Coast.

Yet this same Chinaman has done a large part of the common labor on the Pacific Coast, filled the unfillable labor gaps, paid his debts and his taxes, sent his savings home and with them presents to his friends, advertising our products and promoting our trade among his countrymen; and finally he is going home carrying American ideas and, it is said, even defending us with the charitable fiction, that it is the other foreigners, not the true Americans, who have abused him.

It does indeed, take two to assimilate; and non-assimilation is the least convincing and most inconsistent of all the arguments against Chinese immigration, in the mouths of those who have not wished them to assimilate nor given them opportunity to do so, and who do not, even now, recognize that many of them have become intelligent and patriotic Americans.

CHAPTER XXIII
THE EFFECT OF UNFRIENDLY EXCLUSION UPON CHINA

" Misappreciation and mismanagement have in fact been to a great extent if not altogether, the true source of all our troubles with Chinese immigrants."—W. H. MEDHURST.

" The American trade unionist does not object to the immigration of men of a high standard of living whether they be Turks, Russians or Chinese . . . whether they be yellow, red, brown or black. In certain cases, as in that of the Chinese, it was absolutely essential to the success of the law that it discriminate against the whole nation. . . . . Restriction, however, should be without prejudice or hatred, . . . should be democratic in character and should not exclude any man capable of earning his livelihood in America at the standard union rate of wages. It should not be directed by racial animosity or religious prejudice."— JOHN MITCHELL, President of the United Mine Workers.

" But in the effort to carry out the policy of excluding Chinese laborers, Chinese coolies, grave injustice and wrong have been done by this nation to the people of China, and therefore ultimately to this nation itself. Chinese students, business and professional men of all kinds—not only merchants, but bankers, doctors, manufacturers, professors, travelers and the like—should be encouraged to come here and treated on precisely the same footing that we treat students, business men, travelers and the like of other nations. Our laws and treaties should be framed so as to put these people in the excepted classes, and to state that we will admit all Chinese, except Chinese of the coolie classes, Chinese skilled or unskilled laborers."—THEODORE ROOSEVELT.

IT must not be assumed because the Chinese in America have been like pawns at chess—submitting to all demands, lawful or unlawful, and yielding to the aggressions of the exclusion laws—that they felt no resentment. Nor, because their protests failed of effect, would it be safe to suppose that they have forgotten their injuries and will ultimately acquiesce without retaliation. During the first twenty-five years of free immigration the Chinese had no means of making their views known except through the occasional remonstrance of some individual Chinaman or of the Six Companies in San Francisco. As early as 1852 they replied to Governor Bigler's attack and in 1853 one Lo Chum Qui, after protesting against the false accusations made against them, said that the most of those who came to this country were indeed poor men, but what they said about America would nevertheless be duly remembered.[1] Ten years later, Mr. Pun Chi voiced the remonstrance of the Chinese in America to Congress; through him they appealed to religion and to justice asserting that no other immigrants to California paid so large an amount of taxes or were more submissive to the laws. They begged for legislative interference to protect them from outrage and injustice, and from the importation of abandoned women from China; they asked to be allowed to take cognizance of the minor offenses of their own people and report them to the courts, and finally that Congress would decide whether they should go or stay.[2] In 1873 they made an appeal to the Supervisors of San Francisco in which they protested that they were peaceable and industrious, kept no whiskey saloons, and paid their rents, taxes and debts. They proposed that all treaty relations should be repealed between the two nations and that all Chinese should leave America and all Americans leave China.[3] In 1876 the Six Companies endeavored to check emigration from the port of Hong Kong by reporting the troubles in California, and in 1878 they sent a Memorial to the President of the United States in which they replied categorically to the accusations against them. They particularly resented the conditions of prostitution and said that the only remedy lay in honest administration of the Municipal Government— if officers would refuse bribes, then unprincipled Chinamen could no longer purchase immunity.[4] But the most

[1] *Alta*, June 23, 1853.
[2] Spear, *The Oldest Empire*, pp. 584–603.
[3] Reprinted in Sacramento *Union*, Apr. 3, 1876, from a pamphlet of 1873 entitled: The Chinese Question from the Chinese Standpoint.
[4] Mar. 26, republished in Healey and Chew's *Statements, etc.*

interesting and characteristic of these early protests is the manifesto printed in the San Francisco papers by the Six Companies shortly before the Kearney uprising, of which only a few sentences can be reprinted here:

" To the American Public : The United States has been open to Chinese emigration for more than twenty years. Many Chinamen have come; few have returned. Why is this? Because, among our Chinese people, a few in California have acquired a fortune and returned home with joy. A desire to obtain a competency having arisen in the heart, our people have not shrunk from toil and trouble. They have expected to come here for one or two years and make a little fortune and return. Now this honorable country is discussing the importance of prohibiting the further emigration of the Chinese. . . . But this result should be brought about in a reasonable manner. It is said that the Six Chinese Companies buy and import Chinamen into this country, How can such things be said? Our Six Companies have, year after year, sent letters discouraging our people from coming to this country, but the people have not believed us, and have continued to come. The necessary expenses of these poor newcomers is a constant drain upon the resources of those already settled here, so that the Chinese residents of this country are also opposed to this rapid Chinese emigration. But the capitalists of this honorable country are constantly calling for Chinese cheap labor. The white laboring men of this country are very angry because the Chinese obtain employment which they claim belongs to the white men alone, and so they hate the Chinamen, sometimes throw stones at them, sometimes strike them on the street, and constantly curse them. The Chinese people cannot return such treatment in the same kind, lest other nations hearing of such things should ridicule the laws of this honorable country as of no use. It cannot be said that Chinese labor impoverishes this country, and are not the Customs paid by the Chinese a benefit to the country? . . ."[5]

All of these documents without exception, were dignified, respectful, and reasonable in tone; they show a curiously simple confidence that whatever the common people might achieve against them, the President and Congress were still able and bound to protect them. Evidently, during these earlier years, they had no clear understanding of the workings of politics which not infrequently defeat the most important measures of justice.

[5] *Alta*, Apr. 5, 1876.

Competition and Assimilation

The thing which puzzled them most was the discrimination practised against them in favor of European immigrants who seemed to them, doubtless from their limited knowledge obtained in California, such undesirable citizens.[6]

While the Chinese thus put their case to the citizens of California and to the government of the United States, their home government was taking small account of them. Not even the violation of the treaty of 1880 by the restriction law and the Scott Act, could attract much attention from the Imperial Government while it was striving to hold the Empire together and save it from the rapacity of foreign powers. The immigrants in America were moreover only one four-thousandth of all her millions, for the most part poor men, and from the limited area of a few districts about Canton. As year by year a few thousands returned with gold and with tales of Western marvels, some knowledge of America spread gradually over the whole province of Kwang Tung, but there were still millions who had never heard of the Gold Mountains.

A few thousand merchants and a few officials and mandarins were aware of the unjust treatment of their countrymen but knew no way or had no power to make its importance felt, or to seek redress. Even when the Chinese government came to resent the discrimination and indignities to which their people were subjected in the United States, they could not but remember at the same time, the long standing friendship between the two nations and the several occasions on which the United States had stood between China and the other powers in such matters as the opium traffic, the indemnities and the partition of territory.[7]

[6] *N. A. Rev.*, v. 149—*The Chinese Must Stay*, p. 477.
[7] S. Wells Williams to Sec'y Seward, *Cong. Docs.* 1867, s. n. 1364, p. 514. Nevins, *China and the Chinese*, (1869), p. 434. Boulger, *Hist. of China*, vol. 3, (1884), p. 318. Sacramento *Union*, Apr. 12, 1879. Colton, *The Chinese*, (1891), p. 189.

The Effect of Exclusion Upon China

Yet the Chinaman has a long memory for injury as well as kindness and as the troubles of China increased from within and without toward the end of the nineteenth century, she expressed in the Boxer outbreak the "concentrated wrath and hate of sixty years" because of the policies of foreign governments—"outrageous and beyond excuse, scandalous diplomacy and unprovoked attacks upon the rights and possessions of China." [8] Although the exclusion indignities perpetrated by the United States undoubtedly contributed to this accumulated resentment, yet still China took no direct measures toward retaliation.

In the debate on the first restriction law it had been predicted that China would retaliate. After the Scott Act Minister Denby wrote Secretary Blaine that he took credit to himself for being able to settle the Chi-nan-fu troubles at all in view of the feeling of irritation existing in China—yet still there was no sign of retaliation. But at last in 1889 the Chinese government did more than politely remonstrate, in refusing to receive Mr. Blair as the representative of the United States, on the ground that his share in the enactment of the exclusion laws made him unfriendly and objectionable.[9] Yet even the Chinese newspapers—of which there were only three at this time—had still a tone of reproach and bitterness rather than of retaliation.[10]

Meanwhile China herself was being held to strict account for every treaty stipulation. Secretary Fish wrote to Minister Low: "You will not fail to make it distinctly understood that we will claim the full performance by the Chinese government of all the promises and obligations which it has assumed by treaty or conventions with the United States." [11] And in 1892 Minister Denby

[8] Holcombe, *The Outlook*, 1904, p. 407.
[9] *Cong. Docs.* 1889, s. n. 2830, p. 149.
[10] Pres. Harrison's *Message*, s. n. 2920, Dec., 1891. Yung Kiung Yen, *Forum*, vol. 14, p. 87–90.
[11] *Cong. Docs.* 1869, s. n. 1445, p. 303.

wrote to Secretary Blaine: "The chart that guides the foreign representative is the treaty. He has only to see that its provisions are complied with. If those provisions work injury to China, he cannot help it. China must find her own methods of relief.[12]

When in 1894, the Chinese Foreign Office attempted to require all American travelers to report themselves and show their passports to local Chinese officials, the United States Minister insisted on the literal construction of the treaty requiring them to show passports only on demand.[13] President McKinley, while urging the appointment of a commission to study commercial interests in China in order to find a market for the materials and manufactures of the United States, also urged strong measures for the protection of Americans in China and that "instant reparation" be demanded for every loss and injury suffered by them.[14]

Moreover, while the anti-Chinese party in America was demanding and securing legislation far beyond the terms of the treaty and the American Minister was holding China to account for all her obligations, Americans in China were frequently taking advantage of their privileges; using transit passes fraudulently to cover merchandise which they did not own;[15] refusing to register in fulfillment of the treaty of 1894, although demanding protection;[16] and settling in the interior where they had no treaty right to be. The attitude of the Chinese Government in suffering missionaries to settle in the interior outside of treaty protection and yet in not shirking the responsibility of protection and indemnity was reasonable, even generous. Chester Holcombe says:

[12] *Cong. Docs.* 1892, s. n. 3076, p. 92.
[13] *Cong. Docs.* 1894, s. n. 3292, p. 136.
[14] *Cong. Docs.* 1898, s. n. 3743, *Message.*
[15] *Cong. Docs.* 1884. s. n. 2276, p. 101; (1891) s. n. 2490, p. 385-9.
[16] *Cong. Docs.* 1896, s. n. 3477, p. 90. Minister Denby complained that without special compulsory legislation, Americans would not register; Secretary Olney replied that such legislation would be difficult to procure and that lists prepared by the consuls must do in fulfillment of our treaty obligations.

"It has never, within the knowledge of the writer, attempted to shirk full responsibility for the lives and property of American citizens in any part of the Empire, or to claim that missionaries, in establishing themselves in the interior ran their own risks, took their lives into their own keeping, and must themselves bear any financial losses which local opposition to their presence might entail upon them.... Can as much be said of anti-Chinese mobs in the United States?"[17]

The phrase, "the awakening of China", now so common, had scarcely been invented when the first restriction law was passed in the United States. It had long been an accepted theory that China was a stationary if not retrograding nation, incapable of progress and without national spirit. Yet during the twenty-five years since exclusion, while China has been beset by foreign foes and torn by civil uprisings, she has been at the same time making steady progress, proving that she has not only awakened but has the capacity to enter into modern life.[18]

Dr. Morrison says:

"The ancient spirit of evasion, delay and passive obstruction characteristic of Oriental dealings, has in a marked degree given place to a franker, bolder and more aggressive spirit of deliberate and organized resistance to foreign influence," and he adds, "they are, in truth, not opposed to modern improvements but they fear and hate foreign domination, aggression and spoliation."[19]

The exclusion of laborers and the mistreatment of the privileged classes by the United States has tended in the same direction, for it has stung them into a sense of the discrimination practiced against them even by a friendly nation. They would probably have tolerated exclusion of laborers simply, with equanimity, even though it were a race discrimination, had not the personal dignity of

[17] The *Outlook*, v. 98, p. 351. For discussion of exceptional privileges of missionaries see *Cong. Docs.* 1895-6, s. n. 3629, p. 60 ff; 1886, s. n. 2460, pp. 96-100.
[18] Holcombe, *Outlook*, 1904, Feb. 13. Martin, *The Chinese*, pp. 228-253. Consular Repts. v. 50, no. 184, (1895).
[19] Dr. G. E. Morrison, correspondent of the London *Times* in China, quoted by the *Outlook*, 1906, Jan. 20th. Yan Phou Lee, *N. A. Rev.*, vol. 148, p. 477.

the exempt classes been deeply offended by a handling similar to that accorded to criminals.

From the time of the Geary law the Chinese have shown an increasing sensitiveness to injustice and discourtesy. The discrimination was the more deeply felt because of the hitherto friendly relations existing between the two nations.[20] The United States had been the conspicuous friend of China and as such had received privileges peaceably which other nations had obtained by costly wars. The outrages upon China in America for which indemnities were refused, in one instance on the ground that they occurred in territory over which the government had little control, and in another because they occurred in a state over which it had no control at all, occurred unfortunately at a time when many other causes of discontent were seething in China. Minister Denby wrote in 1892; " The more intelligent among her people cite as grievances the importation of opium, the importation of foreign manufactured goods, the introduction of steamers, the loss of Burma and Annam, extraterritoriality, the presence of missionaries and many other things. The decline in the tea and silk trade aggravates the prevailing unrest and bad feeling."[21]

In proportion as the administration of the exclusion laws became more severe and unwarrantable, and the Chinese ministers resident in this country better acquainted with American politics and more indignant in their protestations, the United States was classed with other foreign powers against whom the whole of China was at last uniting. But for the liberal and just spirit in which John Hay, Secretary of State, treated China during the Boxer troubles, the relations of the two nations might have become seriously strained. Although thrown into the background by infinitely larger ques-

---

[20] *Cong. Docs.* 1897, s. n. 3629, pp. 63–5.
[21] *Cong. Docs.* 1892, s. n. 3076, p. 92.

tions, the sense of grievance aroused by the mistreatment of the Chinese in this country became one more influence to intensify their national consciousness and to drive them to protect their rights and possessions from all foreign powers.

From this time on there has appeared a stronger tendency to demand reciprocity of treaty privileges and obligations. Again and again in the earlier years the Chinese in America had reminded Congress that China had not desired a treaty or commercial relations, that she had been compelled to give up her traditional policy of exclusion by war; that the presence of Americans was as hateful to a large portion of the Chinese people, and as much friction was created by the presence of foreigners in China as by the Chinese in this country. They declared that American and English steamers on the rivers of China had thrown out of business a vast fleet of junks and an army of men; that the introduction of American machinery would take away the work of thousands; that the influx of missionaries and capitalists deranged the constitution of society in China quite as much as the presence of Chinese laborers deranged that of the United States.

In the debates in Congress on the successive exclusion laws the advocates of such legislation were accustomed to point out the contrast between the privileges of the Chinese in the United States and of Americans in China. As a matter of fact no great discrepancy existed. Not only all the recent historians of China but the diplomats of the United States in China have repeatedly called attention to the advantage which the right of extra-territoriality gives to the foreigner in China. Americans in China are subject to no court but their own and since, as Minister Denby once remarked, "they are by no means perfect in their conduct in China any more than

[22] Minister Denby to Secretary Bayard, *Cong. Docs.* 1886, s. n. 2460, p. 6. Minister Young, *N. A. Rev.*, 1892, v. 154, p. 601.

they are at home ", there was an attempt to restrict their residence to the localities where courts could be provided. But to this restriction the Americans have by no means always conformed. The Chinese have grown more and more jealous of the exercise of the right of extraterritoriality not only because it humbled them in the eyes of foreigners but because it disgraced them in the eyes of their own people.[22]

The treaty obligations and privileges of the two nations were, in short, sufficiently reciprocal in degree if not in kind, but since this very circumstance made evasion of responsibility easier on both sides, the Chinese have in recent years begun to demand strict reciprocity and it would seem that they are in justice entitled to the same right of regulating and limiting the entry of foreigners into the interior of China as has been exercised by other countries with regard to the introduction of Chinese labor.[23]

But in spite of the many just causes of resentment against the United States for its violation of treaty stipulations while it was insisting that China should fulfil hers, the Imperial Government had so many greater causes of rancor against Great Britain, France, Russia and Germany that she would not perhaps for many years have attempted any kind of retaliation except that involved in a general anti-foreign policy, but for the flagrant discourtesy shown at the time of the St. Louis Exposition. The result of this amazing piece of official discourtesy was that the United States, the only one of the great powers which had not despoiled her territory and which had never assumed an attitude of hostility towards China, was the first, nevertheless, to have its people and its commerce singled out for proscription in the boycott that followed. This was due to a popular movement arising in the middle classes, led by those who had suffered from the harsh administration of the

[23] Thompson, *China and the Powers*, p. 263.

exclusion laws and from personal indignities in the United States. At first there was an attempt in America to deny that the boycott was a result of exclusion, but the publication in Chinese newspapers of cartoons representing the outrages upon Chinese in the United States made its origin unmistakable. These cartoons pictured in detail the Chinese being driven into the "water-house" *i. e.* the detention shed, compelled to bathe, measured naked by the Bertillon system and subjected to violence and insult in the street.[24] In this relation Mr. Chester Holcombe said: "What is called the reaction in China is not fundamentally commercial; it is sentimental and we are reaping the harvest of the seed sown by shortsighted and stupid blindness during the past decades."

The immediate cause of the boycott appears to have been the impending negotiations for a renewal of the Chinese immigration treaty of 1894.[25] The treaty had been denounced in the summer of 1904 by the Chinese minister because of the mistreatment of merchants, students and travelers which had become peculiarly flagrant after 1899. Besides this the treatment of the Chinese exhibitors at the St. Louis Exposition at the hands of the Immigration department had been such that both the Chinese and the American newspapers had commented most unfavorably upon it. Through the early winter of 1905 there were rumors of extreme dissatisfaction and possible retaliation on the part of the Chinese and in May, Minister Rockhill on his arrival in China

---

[24] Some of these were reproduced in the Outlook of 1906, Mar. 24. In Canton early in July, 1905, fans were widely distributed which bore reproductions of similar indignities. See North China *Herald*, July 21; 1905.

[25] Out of abundant current material on the boycott, the following articles and documents are of primary value; *Cong. Docs.* 1905-6 (For. Rels.) s. n. 4941, China; Consular reports for 1905 and 1906; No. China *Herald, Daily News*, Shanghai *Times, Jo. of the Amer. Asiatic Assoc.*, 1905; Holcombe, Chinese Exclusion and the Boycott, *Outlook*, Dec., 1905.

470   Competition and Assimilation

to take his post, found that a boycott movement had already begun.[26]

At a meeting of the leading merchant guilds and the gentry of Shanghai held at the Chamber of Commerce it had been decided to request Chinese merchants throughout the Empire to stop ordering goods from the United States as a protest against the severe terms of the proposed new Chinese exclusion treaty. A Committee of the Chinese Chamber of Commerce sent telegrams to the Chambers of Commerce and the principal guilds of the twenty-two treaty ports requesting their coöperation. The merchant guilds of Canton and of Fu-Kien at once joined in the movement and shortly afterward those of Peking and Soochow. As the movement became known the initiators received encouragement and promise of support from a considerable number of cities and the tacit approval not only of many Chinese officials but of many Americans resident in China.[27]

The principal note of the early meetings in Shanghai and Canton was that Americans should be informed that, while recognizing the uniform friendliness of the United States toward China, the present steps were taken because there seemed no other way in which to protest against the proposed injustice towards Chinese entering the United States;[28] and Americans in China were asked to use their influence to persuade their government to be

---

[26] The appointment of Mr. W. W. Rockhill to the post in China just at this time was very fortunate. Mr. Rockhill had been second Secretary of Legation at Peking as early as 1884, had traveled extensively in China, and written on Oriental topics, and was Commissioner to China in 1900-1901.

[27] By July 7th it had been endorsed by the local gentry; merchants and school teachers of Canton, Macao, Hong Kong, Swatow, Amoy, Foochow, Wenchow, Ningpo, Hangchow, Shaosing, Chinkiang, Wanking, Auching, Kinkiang, Hanghow, Wuchang, Hanyang, Shasi, Ichang, Chungkiang, Chentu, Peking, Tientsin, Chefoo and Kaifeng. Chinese all over the world telegraphed approval. No. China *Herald*, July 7, 1905.

[28] The North China *Herald* of Aug. 4, 1905, said that it was not so much the form of the treaty that the Chinese complained of, as of the way in which it was carried out.

more liberal and just. Failing, however, in their joint efforts it was decided to pursue the following course: (1) No Chinese was to purchase or use any goods of American manufacture, machinery included; (2) Chinese merchants and shippers should not ship goods in American ships; (3) Chinese should not send their children to schools established and owned by Americans; (4) Chinese should not join any American firm, either as compradores or interpreters; (5) Chinese performing menial services of all kinds in American families should be asked to resign. The boycott was to begin on the twentieth of July.[29]

Early in June over one hundred members of the Shanghai Educational Association which represented some twenty-four institutions, met and decided to support the government in any stand it might take against any unjust clauses which the United States might add to the new exclusion treaty. In July, at the conclusion of a speech on the exclusion acts delivered by Dr. Gracey, the American Consul at Foochow, the students of the Anglo-Chinese College drew up a paper containing ten points on which they desired the laws and regulations to be amended, and requested the Consul to forward them to the Government at Washington. These resolutions show how thoroughly the young, educated Chinese understood the difference in the treatment accorded to them and to other nationalities under the " favored nation " clause and how bitterly the indignities of the administration of the law had been felt.[30]

They demanded that no discrimination should be made between Chinese and other immigrants to the United States; they protested against the Bertillon examination, the detention in the " water-house," the delays in the survey of papers, the exclusion of attorneys and friends from the hearings, the extreme limitation of the defini-

[29] No. Ch. *Herald*, May 19, p. 350.
[30] No. China *Herald*, July 7, 1905.

tion of the word laborer, and the restrictions on the movements of the merchants.

The Viceroy of the two Kwang provinces, from which most of the emigrants to America had come, strongly supported the boycott and on the twentieth of July, the day appointed for it to take effect, there was a mass meeting of fifteen hundred persons—merchants, students and even ladies—in Shanghai, at which the speeches were full of appeals to patriotism.[31] During the months of July and August the local newspapers were full of news of meetings in many parts of eastern China commending the action of the merchants and gentry in Shanghai.

The American goods especially named as subject to boycott were kerosene oil, piece goods (cotton) pig iron, hardware and metals, flour and Oregon pine lumber. The boycott was no sooner inaugurated than it became necessary to allow the sale of American goods already on hand and contracted for, in order to avoid too severe losses. Such goods could be sold but if after the date set, any member who had signed the agreement should secretly contract for American goods, the bankers' guilds agreed to strike off his name or the name of the shop from those to whom credit would be given.[32]

The movement had scarcely been set on foot and begun to be effective when several antagonistic influences operated to discourage it. Viceroy Yuan Shih K'ai, one of the most influential and enlightened officials, was wholly opposed to the agitation and prepared to take summary measures to put it down within his territory where a very large amount of American goods found a market.[33] It encountered also the opposition of the largest Chinese dealers with American firms who were threatened with great losses, even with bankruptcy, and even some of those who had signed the boycott agree-

---

[31] No. China *Herald*, July 20; Daily *News*, July 21;
[32] No. China *Herald*, Aug. 4, p. 288.
[33] *Living Age*, v. 249, p. 135, 190 ff.

ment repented when they realized the serious sacrifices they must make.

Under these reactionary influences the leadership of the movement gradually was transferred from the merchants to the students, most of whom had received a foreign education, who had less discretion than the merchants and gentry and nothing whatever to lose. Under their enthusiastic guidance the movement began to take on the aspect of a general anti-foreign agitation. Inflammatory placards posted in many cities depicted in exaggerated terms the ill-treatment suffered by the Chinese in America, while English goods were also boycotted to some extent. As soon as the interference with trade was sensibly felt by foreigners they began to protest to the Chinese Foreign Office against it. But, remembering the Boxer outbreak, foreigners were more alarmed by the dangerous anti-foreign complexion which the movement was taking than by the danger to trade interests, and even the conservative Chinese felt that the movement might get beyond control and become an excuse for uprising by the predatory and revolutionary elements of society.

In August the Viceroy of Wuhu, who had been apathetic, issued a proclamation urging all subjects to be patient and await instructions from the Foreign Office;[34] and shortly afterward an Imperial Edict pacified the people and corrected their misapprehensions.[35] It declared that the friendship with the United States was of long standing and that the American government had promised to discuss the immigration treaty on friendly terms; and—most effective of all—it announced that all viceroys and governors' would be held responsible for disorders and ordered the arrest of agitators.

From September onward the moderate party continued to gain ascendency. The Viceroy of the two Kwang

---

[34] No. Ch. *Herald*, Aug. 11, 1905; Daily *News*, Aug. 11.
[35] *Cong. Docs.* 1905–6, s. n. 4641, 225, translation.

provinces—a sympathizer with the boycott—was compelled to take active measures to suppress insulting placards during the visit of the American Secretary of State's party at Canton. He wrote to the Foreign Office that the boycott had originated among the merchants "who were righteously indignant at the precautions endured", and that the authorities could only suppress it gradually for fear of stirring up a revolution.[36] The boycott league still stood firm and sporadic efforts here and there were made to maintain the embargo;[37] but the Chinese Minister of Commerce took the opportunity to establish a new and burdensome tax on imports and although the boycott still presented a serious aspect in Canton and Shanghai, it was declining and practically dead by the end of the year.

Not the least factor in the decline of the movement, however, was the prompt action of President Roosevelt in remedying the grievances complained of on the one hand, and in demanding that the Chinese government should suppress the boycott on the other. Mr. Davidson, the U. S. Consul-General at Shanghai, arranged that Minister Rockhill, on his arrival about May 20th, should meet a committee of the representative guilds and bankers and explain to them that they had been misled and were evidently not aware of the true state of the treaty negotiations. He left with them a memorandum rehearsing the progress of the treaty negotiations and closing with the following words:[88]

"It may be categorically stated that neither by word or implication has the United States sought in any way to impede the return to the United States of Chinese laborers rightfully entitled to do so, nor to put burdensome restrictions in the way of Chinese subjects not belonging to the laboring classes who may wish to visit the United States or to reside therein for purposes of pleasure or study. On the contrary, it is the earnest desire of the President and the people of the United States to extend to this latter class of

[86] *Cong. Docs.* 1905–6, s. n. 4941, p. 228.
[87] *Cong. Docs.* 1905–6, s. n. 4941, p. 229.
[88] *Cong. Docs.* 1905–6, s. n. 4941, p. 205–6.

visitors all such courtesies and facilities as they may desire, to become better acquainted with our country, its resources, its industries, its mode of thought, its method of administration, by which knowledge better than all other means, the relations with China may become closer and even more friendly than they have ever been."[39]

Mr. Rockhill then asked Prince Ch'ing to take prompt action to stop the agitation, but as the Chinese newspapers continued to print inflammatory articles it could only be inferred that the Imperial government did not disapprove of the movement. Indeed, when Prince Ch'ing finally replied to Minister Rockhill's request and formal note, he said:

"This movement has not been inaugurated without some reason, for the restrictions against Chinese entering America are too strong and American exclusion laws have been extremely inconvenient to the Chinese, . . . but if the restrictions can be lightened and a treaty drawn up in a friendly manner, then this agitation will of its own accord die out."[40]

The American Association in China at the same time sent a formal statement to Minister Rockhill and to the American Asiatic Association in New York with the request that it be forwarded to Washington. This expression from Americans in China is important as denoting a certain sympathy with the causes of the boycott, and as reflecting most unfavorably upon the administration of the exclusion law. It said:

"While maintaining a reserved attitude as regards the proposed boycott, we, as the committee of this association, may be permitted to suggest that the power of the guilds is very strong in China, that the feeling of the Chinese is very intense on this special subject; that the hampering of business even due to rumors of a boycott might cause much damage to commercial and other interests, and that where a choice is offered of the same goods, dealt in by different nationalities, but at about the same scale of prices, the Chinese might readily turn to the commodities offered by the

[39] Mr. J. G. Lay, the American Consul-General at Canton issued a statement to the boycotters pointing out that American goods were better and cheaper than those of other countries; and that the boycott would injure American manufacturers and shippers who were friendly to China.
[40] *Cong. Docs.* 1905-6, s. n. 4941, pp. 207-8.

nationalities which were not American. Thus any or all of these results might follow a prolonged agitation of the immigration question." [41]

The Committee suggested that nothing should be done to further restrict the admission of the exempt classes; and that if the laws admitting such persons were so hedged around with restrictions and regulations as to cause them vexation, humiliation and delay, strong feeling would be excited among the Chinese. They dwelt upon the importance especially of allowing students to enter the United States freely because if the entry of students was made troublesome and humiliating they would surely be diverted to other countries to get an education with the consequent loss to America's future influence and commercial and other relations with China.

The Committee suggested further that the investigation of Chinese persons desiring to enter the United States should be transferred wholly to an American Bureau of Emigration in China where such a thorough examination of the status of applicants should be made as would guarantee that upon presentation of the passport furnished they could be permitted to land at any American port at the same time as other passengers.

The American Asiatic Association at once took up the matter and sent a delegation to President Roosevelt which represented the textile industries, one branch of the iron and steel industry, the kerosene oil trade and certain banking interests. They made a formal statement of their view of the unsatisfactory status of the relations of China and the United States, the most important sections of which read as follows:

"It must be held to be unfortunate that these laws (exclusion laws) are at variance with the treaty stipulations . . . which are in force between the two countries. We are not here to question the competency of Congress to modify the provisions of any treaty

[41] Letter of Am. Asiatic Assoc. of China, Shanghai, May 18, 1905, to Consul-General at Shanghai, reprinted *Jo. Am. As. Assoc.* July, 1905.

with a foreign power, but we do question the expediency of the government of the United States occupying an attitude in opposition to the principle which it has long maintained, that a nation cannot plead its domestic legislation as a bar to the observance of its international obligations. In the judgment of this delegation and the Association which it represents, the treatment accorded by the officers of this government to the exempt classes of Chinese visiting our country is more oppressive than either the letter or the spirit of the law requires. We believe, moreover, that the plainest principles of international justice demand that the law itself shall be made more liberal either by amendment or by the negotiation of a new treaty, or by both."

The Committee then pointed out the danger and loss to the commercial and industrial interests of the United States likely to arise from the conviction which had been growing in China, that our government desired to discourage the coming of the exempt classes.

The President cordially replied that he was in sympathy with the general thesis they presented but that he believed in the exclusion of the coolie class of Chinese. He pointed out that the courts had sustained the immigration officers in their interpretation of the law, that he himself was only a part of the treaty-making power and that if the delegation desired either the law or the treaty to be changed they must appeal to their representatives in Congress. He acknowledged, however, that there were cases "where the immigration officers had exhibited regrettable acts of discrimination" and said that he was about to send a letter on this subject to the Secretary of Commerce and Labor.

This letter had probably been precipitated by the case of the four Chinese students landing at Boston, which had been severely criticised by prominent citizens and by the newspapers about two weeks previous, and against whose discourteous treatment the manufacturers and commission merchants of Boston had protested. In this letter the President is understood to have expressed his indignation at the harsh treatment of the exempt classes and ordered a special circular sent to all immigration officers warning them to give no unnecessary annoyance to the Chinese, on pain of dismissal.[42]

About the same time the Secretary of War, William H. Taft, expressed himself publicly even more forcibly against the law and its administration. He said:

"I. it just that for the purpose of excluding or preventing perhaps 100 Chinese from slipping into the country against the law, we should subject an equal number of Chinese merchants and students of high character to an examination of such an inquisitorial, humiliating, insulting and physically uncomfortable character as to discourage altogether the coming of merchants and students? ... Ought we to throw away the advantage which we have by reason of Chinese natural friendship for us, and continue to enforce an unjustly severe law, and thus create in the Chinese mind a disposition to boycott American trade and to drive our merchants from Chinese shores, simply because we are afraid that we may for the time being lose the approval of certain unreasonable and extreme popular leaders of California and other Coast states? Does not the question answer itself? Is it not the duty of Members of Congress and of the Executive to disregard the unreasonable demands of a portion of the community deeply prejudiced upon this subject in the Far West and insist on extending justice and courtesy to a people, from whom we are deriving and are likely to derive such immense benefit in the way of international trade? We must continue to keep out the coolies, the laborers; but we should give the freest possible entry to merchants, travelers and students, and treat them all with courtesy and consideration." [43]

During the summer Minister Rockhill in China and the President in America continued to be besieged with protests and appeals from the trade interests which were jeopardized by the growing boycott: the Standard Oil Company, the cotton manufacturers and exporters, the ginseng dealers and most significant of all, the Northwestern Chambers of Commerce. The Seattle, (Washington) Chamber of Commerce used severe and very outspoken language in regard to the mal-administration of the exclusion laws; the Portland (Oregon) Chamber of Commerce went so far as to suggest that even the laws

[42] *Jo. Am. As. Assoc.*, July, 1905, reprints all these papers.
[43] *Associate Press*, address delivered at Miami University, June 15, 1905; Mr. Taft repeated these opinions in an interview, during his visit to Canton in September. No. China *Herald*, Sept. 15th.

excluding laborers might properly be modified; even the Portland Board of Trade—a much more democratic body—while adhering strongly to the necessity of excluding laborers, endorsed the stand which the President had taken. All these bodies appeared to think that although the boycott *per se* might not do much immediate injury to American trade, ultimately our treatment of the Chinese would react most unfavorably in the competition with other foreign nations for the trade of China.[44]

At the end of June, before the boycott had even taken effect, the President sent instructions through the Secretary of State to all the diplomats and consular representatives in China. He reminded them that although all Chinese laborers were prohibited from coming to the United States, it was the purpose of the government to extend the heartiest courtesy toward all other classes. He informed them that the immigration officers had been instructed that the law must be enforced without harshness or unnecessary inconvenience and that any discourtesy shown to Chinese persons by any official of the government would be cause for immediate removal from the service.[45] They had been instructed further to accept the certificate properly viséd by the American consul—"which was not to be upset unless good reason can be shown for so doing." The diplomatic and consular officers were then reminded that this visé was not to be perfunctory but was one of their most important functions and told that they would be held to rigid account for the manner in which they performed their duty.[46]

The President hoped, no doubt, by this prompt and energetic acknowledgment of the injustices committed in America, to induce the Chinese government to be

[44] Current newspapers and interviews with leading men.
[45] The circular to the immigration officers appears to have been the immediate result of the President's letter to Mr. Metcalf, Secretary of Commerce and Labor; reprinted in *Jo. Am. As. Assoc.*, July, 1905.
[46] Letter to the Acting Secretary of State issued June 24, 1905, by President Roosevelt.

480 Competition and Assimilation

equally vigorous in disapproval and suppression of the boycott. But when six weeks had passed after his notification to the consular and immigration officers, and the Foreign Office in China had yet done nothing actively to put down the agitation, the United States government took measures of quite another character.

Minister Rockhill was instructed to notify the Imperial government that under the provisions of article fifteen of the treaty of 1858 it would be held responsible for any loss sustained by American trade on account of its failure to stop the boycott. Mr. Rockhill reproached the Chinese government for its "extraordinary supineness" in the matter and demanded that Tseng Shao-Ching, the head of the Fu-Kien merchants' guild in Shanghai and chairman of the boycott committee, should be deprived of his official rank of taot'ai and otherwise punished.[47] A week later, no reply having been received from Prince Ch'ing, Mr. Rockhill notified the Foreign Office that in view of the agitation against the government and the people of the United States for the purpose of influencing the treaty negotiations, he had been instructed to cease the discussion of the treaty altogether.[48]

The Foreign Office then formally disclaimed any responsibility for the boycott and assured Mr. Rockhill that they had promptly telegraphed the provincial authorities to suppress it, and would do so again; and that shortly an Imperial edict on the subject would be proclaimed. The Imperial edict, which marked the turning of the tide, was proclaimed on the last day of August, and although the boycott continued for some time longer and although the American Minister continued to de-

[47] *Cong. Docs.* 1905–6, s. n. 4941, p. 215. Tseng Taot'ai on Aug. 18, 1905, wrote an open letter (see *No. China Herald*) describing his own part in the initiation of the boycott. He there says that when it had been agreed to send the telegram asking for the coöperation of all the guilds in the treaty ports, the other members did not want to sign it and that he thereupon signed and said he would stake his life if need be. It is said that his life was repeatedly threatened.

[48] *Cong. Docs.* 1905–6, s. n. 4941, p. 212 ff.

The Effect of Exclusion Upon China 481

mand more energetic action against it and the punishment of Tseng Taot'ai, the movement perceptibly declined—at first in the smaller cities—remaining serious in Canton and Shanghai for a while longer, but finally dying out altogether.

Its decline cannot be attributed to any one of the influences or actions either of the United States or of the Imperial government. It appears that the opposition aroused against it in China among the merchants because of the sacrifices which it entailed and among the conservative class by the excess of zeal of the student element; coincident with the friendly effort of the President of the United States to remedy such evils as could be cured by executive order; and followed by a firm expression of treaty rights, finally roused the Chinese government to take measures for suppression; while at the same time, they allayed to some extent both the enthusiasm and the grievances of the boycotters.

During the progress of the boycott there were many sensational rumors to the effect that the Central government of China was secretly abetting the movement and that the Japanese and other foreign nations represented in China were encouraging it for their own benefit.[49] These were not substantiated by any proof whatever nor by the subsequent events. The Foreign Office did express to the United States minister its opinion that the movement was not without just cause; and it was said that, at the very beginning, the Foreign Office attempted to prevent it by persuasion but that they were told that the government had nothing to do with it; that the common people had had their eyes opened by their returning countrymen on the interpretation of the American treaty; that now that the treaty had expired and been denounced, the gentry and merchants who had been the principal sufferers intended to show their feeling, and to prove that they were civilized and patriotic. They declared that

[49] Bolce, *Booklover's Mag.*, 1905, v. 6, 646; current newspapers.

the people could not be forced to buy anything they did not care for—and to this the Chinese Ministers had no reply.[50]

The accompanying table of trade with China should show the effect of the boycott; but unfortunately the

EXPORTS FROM THE UNITED STATES
I. TO CHINA.

Value in Gold Dollars.

Year	Cotton Cloths		Mineral Oils		Wheat Flour	
	Yards	Value	Gallons	Value	Barrels	Value
1903	181,741,678	$ 8,801,964	22,836,774	$2,542,481	78,999	$ 267,480
1904	248,671,197	13,911,566	70,781,295	7,302,467	61,954	228,748
1905	562,732,721	33,514,818	76,968,693	6,485,587	121,390	445,053
1906	270,799,225	16,704,823	50,477,086	3,715,804	541,599	1,846,388

II. TO HONG KONG.

1903	580,133	64,977	15,816,119	1,804,883	1,351,757	4,948,459
1904	346,235	52,832	24,203,660	2,448,356	1,247,813	4,835,448
1905	455,671	65,047	10,197,600	956,393	789,732	2,903,884
1906	568,328	75,021	7,784,461	772,617	929,618	3,460,161

IMPORTS INTO THE UNITED STATES FROM CHINA.

	Tea		Silks	
	Pounds	Value	Pounds	Value
1903	43,952,049	$6,221,545	2,649,761	$ 7,671,465
1904	46,076,303	6,161,530	3,527,377	9,972,386
1905	38,814,095	5,155,840	3,254,402	9,500,589
1906	32,954,924	4,335,536	2,769,228	8,698,076

consequences cannot be clearly seen owing to the complications arising from the Russo-Japanese war which undoubtedly checked trade in some directions and ex-

[50] No. China *Herald*, Aug. 4, p. e86.

panded it in others. As the boycott did not get under weigh till late summer, its effects would not appear in the statistics of trade for 1905 but rather in 1906. The export of cotton cloths fell to one-half and of mineral oils to two-thirds what it had been in 1905, while the export of flour quadrupled—probably chiefly on account of the war. But if it be noted that in 1904, the year before the boycott, the export of cotton cloths had been only one-half that of 1905, it may perhaps be justly concluded that it at least prevented the proportionate increase of trade which would naturally have occurred, if there had been neither boycott nor war.

The true significance of the boycott, however, does not lie in its effect as measured by statistics of trade. As the Consul at Canton said: "Any broad and general deductions as to figures of imports and exports have nothing to do with the question of national feeling." [51] It was in fact one of many signs, beginning with the cancellation of the Hankau railway concession, that China had entered consciously on a new foreign policy not only toward the United States but toward all foreigners.[52] The return of Chinese students and travelers from abroad, the spread of newspapers and information and the example of Japan, which in one generation was rising to the level of the great powers, were uniting to produce, even before 1905, an awakened national consciousness in China.[53] The boycott itself, merely developed public opinion and gave the middle classes practice in methods of organizing and directing a united popular undertaking.

A Chinese gentleman, who by no means favored the boycott as it was organized, said that nevertheless it had done one good thing for China which might have waited

[51] *Consular Repts.* July–Sept. House Doc. v. 58, no. 4990.
[52] *Cong. Docs.* 1905–6, s. n. 4941, pp. 124–135, documents on Hankau concession affair.
[53] *Rev. of Rev.*, v. 32, p. 281. (1905), v. 33, p. 424 (1906); No. Ch. *Herald*, July 28, 1905, Aug. 11, Aug. 26; *Outlook*, v. 81, p. 215 (1905).

years. It had developed a feeling of union in the hearts of the Chinese people who had hitherto been separated by distance and the lack of fellow feeling and patriotism; and on the other hand, it had shown the Imperial government and the official classes that where the honor of the country was concerned they might, with proper consideration, depend upon the united support of the nation. " The renaissance of China," he said, " has indeed begun. Members of the gentry and the merchants' associations of no less than sixteen out of eighteen provinces have participated in backing up the protest, although it is certain that not a few object to the extreme measures advanced." [54]

The effect upon the United States was also disproportioned to the apparent futility of the boycott. It might almost seem as if there were certain elements of public opinion long held in solution, which it needed only the threat of the boycott to precipitate. As the *Asiatic Journal* said, " It has served the excellent purpose of awakening both public and official sentiment to the magnitude of the interests which this country possesses in the Chinese Empire and to the supreme folly of trifling with them." [55]

It is probable that the very unanimity of the American press and public—always excepting California—and the prompt and remedial concessions made by the President, prematurely weakened the boycott movement. The British Press, openly in sympathy with the grievances of the Chinese, pointed out that the agitators had gained all that was possible until Congress should meet and that if carried too far, the movement might cause a revulsion of feeling in the United States.[56] The precipitating cause

---

[54] See Editorials and communications in *North China Herald*, 1905. July 28, Aug. 11, Aug. 26; T. W. Chang in *Rev. of Reviews*, v. 33, p. 424.
[55] Edit. *Jo. Am. As. Assoc.* July, 1905. See also address of President Roosevelt in Atlanta, Georgia, Oct. '05, in which he said: " We cannot expect China to do us justice unless we do China justice."
[56] The *Herald* of North China (July 14) said: " No doubt China has

of the boycott had been the attempt of the United States to renew the treaty on the same lines as before, without guaranteeing that the administration of the law should be in harmony with it and with the rights of the most favored nations. Not the least important of the results of the embargo was the definite ranging of public officials for and against a more liberal treaty and a just administration of the law. It came to be known that the President, Secretary of State Hay, Secretary of War Taft, and Secretary Garfield were all in favor of a more liberal treaty; and that the opposition of the Trades Unions to it was shared only by the Commissioner of Immigration, Mr. F. H. Sargent, and by Mr. Victor H. Metcalf, the Secretary of Commerce and Labor, who had been a California politician. The transfer of Mr. Metcalf to the Secretaryship of the Navy and the appointment of Mr. Oscar Straus to the vacancy was followed by immediate amelioration of the service, which is still in progress.

been shamefully treated by the United States and our sympathies are wholly with the Chinese in the present contention. But her wisdom lies in being sensible, cool and calm; not hasty and rash."

CHAPTER XXIV

CONCLUSION

THE remedies for the impolitic and unjust treatment of the Chinese by the United States are already suggested by the history of immigration detailed in the previous chapters. They are obviously, a reasonable administration of the laws in force by non-partisan officials, and the modification of the law to harmonize strictly with whatever treaty may be negotiated. Already the first step toward practical repentance has been taken in the open acknowledgment by American officials that the law, as it stands, is a violation of the treaty, and that its administration has been unwarrantably harsh.

But neither acknowledgment nor apology will serve as a remedy while the same laws, the same officers and the same methods are continued. If all the hostile traditions of the Chinese Bureau could be at once destroyed, there would yet remain a mass of contradictory laws and decisions, and a machinery for exclusion which must inevitably work injustice. To renovate, to modify, perhaps to do away with a large part of the existing bureaucratic practice, is a work for new men. It is a work for men with a knowledge of world relations broad enough to enable them to see that the period of exclusiveness is past, not merely for China but for other nations as well; or, if not wholly past, so limited in its scope that those nations that would maintain it for their own protection must give *quid pro quo*—equal value for the industrial and commercial privileges which they demand in Oriental counties.[1]

[1] Medhurst, *Nineteenth Century*, vol. 4, p. 518.

Conclusion

It is not the province of the historian to devise a technical solution for the inadequacy of either laws or methods, but rather to point out those principles which have emerged fully justified from the examination of the past fifty years and by which the men of this generation must be guided if they would not repeat its experiments, errors and injustice. Nothing is clearer than that all the evils of Chinese immigration, both real and prospective, have been greatly exaggerated; now that it is all but past it appears that the Chinese who would not or could not assimilate have gone home or are dying out in this country without descendants, leaving only the memory of their industry, their patience, their picturesque attire, and the labor without which California would have been infinitely less rich and comfortable than it is. The few hundreds who have tried to assimilate with us are living peaceably and usefully with their families, bringing up their children in American fashion with American ideas and contributing as stable and useful a factor as any foreign element in California to its cosmopolitan population.

In the light of this result there seems to be no reason whatever to debar the Chinaman any longer from naturalization when he shall have fulfilled the new law which requires five years continuous residence, a declaration of intention two years in advance, ability to speak the English language, a renunciation of allegiance to his native country, and a statement of intention to live permanently in the United States.[2]

It has been for many years the unanimous opinion of those who have made a study of the Chinese in this country that if they had been naturalized even in small numbers it would have caused their rights to be respected and would have protected them from many of the outrages which they have suffered. It is not to be expected that the illiterate European foreigner, conscious of his

[2] Naturalization Laws (pamphlet), Dept. of Com. & Labor, 1906.

own value as a potential citizen and intoxicated with the apparent license of an easy-going democracy, should respect the yellow man whom he cannot understand, of whose economic competition he is afraid, and whom the native American has considered unworthy of naturalization. The denial of naturalization can no longer be justified by the excuse that the Chinese are inferior either intellectually or industrially; or that they are anarchistic and incapable of citizenship; or that they are vicious, unstable and immoral. Fifty years of experience with them here and the disclosure of their national characteristics at home has shown that they are quite as desirable, tested by the ordinary tests of immigration, as many that we have already received and assimilated, and perhaps even more so than many that are now coming into the country.[3]

One of the most astonishing things in connection with the exclusion of the Chinese is the fact that the general immigration laws shutting out undesirable aliens—diseased, paupers, insane, criminal and the like—were not applied to the Chinese until 1903. They were constantly charged with all these defects, but the California statesmen who secured the exclusion laws never asked that the general exclusion law be applied to them. The records of prisons, asylums, hospitals and almshouses after fifty years, show why; if those laws alone had been applied to the Chinese there would have been very few shut out—too few to suit the advocates of no-competition with American-European labor.

It may as well be confessed that the sole basis of the present exclusion of Chinese laborers from the United States is their virtues, not their vices, either positive or negative. They can and have assimilated in small numbers under most adverse conditions, along with many Europeans; they can and do raise their standard of wages

---

[3] For the views of the Americanized Chinese on naturalization and citizenship see *N. A. Rev.*, v. 148, p. 477; v. 173, p. 315.

Conclusion 489

and of living to those of many European immigrants; they have a less proportion of paupers, insane, criminal and diseased persons in proportion to their numbers, than most of the foreign-born in this country. They are, in fact, industrious, thrifty, shrewd, conservative, and healthily selfish—like many Europeans.

They were excluded because they were a menace to American labor—by which is meant, a menace to the policy of monopoly of labor which is the present ideal of the American trade unionist. Yet it may be doubted whether Chinese labor is any greater menace to the growth of free, self-respecting, rational organized labor, than the less desirable of those European thousands whose low standard of living, wages and intelligence now threaten it; for these comparatively unintelligent and underfed additions to the body of labor must continually be educated, absorbed and uplifted by the partially Americanized laborers already in the field.

The Chinese, on the contrary, are already thoroughly organized, trained in the essential principles of trade unionism and the benefit society; and they afford an extraordinary opportunity for trade unionism to strengthen itself in California if race prejudice did not prevent.

It has already been pointed out that there has been a complete change of opinion as to the desirability of unrestricted immigration within the generation since the exclusion of Chinese laborers was effected. The "asylum" theory has given place to the theory of protection, with a strong tendency to exclude a larger and larger number of European immigrants, for a variety of reasons, as undesirable. Such a general exclusion law, operating horizontally to shut out the lowest stratum, appears to be justified by the experience of a century of free admission. Though operating much more severely against some nationalities than others, it still preserves a fundamental element of justice, in excluding the incapable and the vicious, rather than those whose skin is brown, yellow or black.[4]

CAUSE OF REJECTION	1904	1905	1906
Idiocy	16	38	92
Insanity	33	92	139
Pauperism	4,798	7,898	7,069
Contagious diseases	1,560	2,198	2,273
Conviction of Crime	35	39	205
Imported for prostitution	9	24	30
Contract laborers	1,501	1,164	2,314
Total	7,952	11,453	12,122

But even our present immigration laws were for the most part made sporadically, at the instance of some class or interest, and are therefore inconsistent if not unjust, in their effects. It is conceivable that in future years they might be harmonized and extended to exclude a larger amount of alien labor without doing injustice to any race or nationality. But whether the exclusion of labor as labor simply, regardless of nationality, will in the end prove advantageous; or whether it may not precipitate internal difficulties as great as those of unrestricted competition, is yet to be determined.

It is certain, however, that perpendicular exclusion, *i. e.*, by race solely, must shortly prove not only disadvantageous to the nation that practises it, but probably impracticable as well; if for no other reason than that trade and commerce, rapid transportation and communication, are knitting the interests of the whole world more closely together. Nations, even of secondary rank, are learning to demand reciprocity of advantages, while the strong nations' jealousy of each other prevents any from seizing too much.

[4] The numbers debarred in the last three years, not including Chinese, are given in this table from the Report of the Commissioner-General of Immigration, 1906:

Conclusion 491

For this reason it has happened that at last an undivided China has leisure and strength to learn foreign ways and to initiate a national instead of a sporadic antiforeign policy. If the Chinese people were stupid, lazy, extravagant and drunken, there would be small chance of her final entry into the family of the great nations on equal terms. But an awakened, intelligent, eternally patient, industrious and home-loving people, will inevitably learn, perhaps even quickly learn, to husband and exploit their own resources and to demand a full equivalent for what they are asked to give.

The boycott of American trade, small and futile as it has proved to be for the present, if it had been encouraged by the Imperial government, would have thrown a large part of the trade of China into the hands of the Europeans by whom it was fostered. The resentment felt in China because of the discrimination in the United States against her people, is now finding its way by means of multiplied newspapers to every part of the Chinese Empire; officials and students, not merely of the province of Kwang Tung but of all China, now understand what those discriminations mean;[5] and just in proportion as the reform movement, now begun and constantly gaining ground, takes possession of the ruling classes, in that degree will those discriminations be met with denial of concessions and trade privileges, and in a spirit of retaliation.

From the Chinese standpoint, nothing has been more illogical and unwarrantable in the treatment of the Chinese in the United States than the denial of our treaty obligation to protect them. The hiatus between State and Federal control in our national constitution which permits the Federal Government to refuse protection to foreigners on the ground that it cannot interfere with a state; and which allows any locality to

---

[5] In 1905, there were 157 papers, and almost every native family in the treaty ports, takes one. See *Independent*, v. 58, p. 909, April, 1905.

practice race discrimination and its criminal classes to perpetrate injuries,—protected by local sympathy from interference by state authorities and leaving no means of redress except through local courts permeated by the same sympathies—is an inexplicable weakness in the mind of a Chinaman. China may be slow to coerce or to interfere with local authorities, but she has never denied the obligation nor refused to pay ample indemnity for injuries upon Americans in China. The more aggressive nations whose emigrants have received injuries in this country have shown an intention to demand the fulfilment of such treaty obligations. President Harrison expressed the opinion that it was not only possible but desirable for Congress to make offenses against the treaty rights of foreigners domiciled in the United States cognizable in the Federal courts.[6] Recent outrages and discriminations in the case of the Japanese have again brought the question into prominence and foreign nations, including China, will be likely in the future to demand a fulfilment of such treaty promises.

But the history of Chinese immigration to the United States, however interpreted, constantly returns to two considerations: the violation of treaty stipulations by legislation; and the extension of legislation by official regulation. Both together have resulted in the loss not only of our prestige in China but of the good feeling long standing between the two nations. No dispassionate reader of the history of California can fail to realize that beside the immediate loss of trade threatened by the boycott of American products in China, the progress of California and the Coast states has been incalculably retarded by the exclusion of Chinese labor. In the attempt to replace them, there has been imported labor of a class and belonging to nationalities less useful, quite

---

[6] Apropos of the Italian riots in New Orleans for which the U. S. paid indemnity. See *Cong. Docs.* 1892, s. n. 2920, p. vii.

Conclusion 493

as unassimilative and far more menacing both to labor and to citizenship. But granting that it is the privilege of the Coast States to make a nominal whiteness of skin the test of immigration, and to lose thereby, it is not within their province to insult the non-laboring classes of any nation with whom the Federal government has established treaty relations, and thereby to injure the interest not merely of a class and a state but of the whole country.

The imperative reforms demanded in the light of the history of our treatment of Chinese immigrants is that the law should strictly conform to treaty phraseology and intent; and that the regulations necessary to enforce that law should as strictly conform to the reasonable interpretation of both treaties and legislation. To this end the immigration service must be purged of officers imbued with the anti-Chinese traditions of past administrations, from dishonest and incompetent employes; and from the overweening influence of organized labor, whose nominees cannot or do not carry out the law for the interest of the country, nor with equal justice to the Chinese, but solely in the interest of their class. Although the Chinese exclusion law was made at the demand and by the representatives of organized labor chiefly, it does not solely concern them; the propagandists of trade, religion and international friendship have an equal right to be heard. The law should therefore be a reasonable compromise to meet the demands of all the classes concerned.

The changes of the Exclusion law and administration recently proposed by the Chinese immigrants themselves both in print and in interviews, do not deal with the incompetence or the untrustworthiness of American officers but rather take the form of general propositions: one looking to an approach to reciprocity in treaty stipulations and the other to some form of exclusion which will permit the admission of a very limited number of laborers. The most interesting of these plans is one proposed by a laborer-merchant who has lived in this country forty years and become a leading man among his colony. He suggests that there should be another registration, fairly conducted, of all the Chinese in the country; then after one year, any Chinese should be allowed to return to China and bring back with him one able-bodied laborer, such trips being limited to one per year. If any laborer should die in China on one of these trips, his relatives should be allowed to take up his papers and send a member of his family over on them.

Certain well-known lawyers who have dealt with the Chinese for many years, propose that a certain number of registration papers having been issued, to laborers, they should be allowed to come and go without any identification. The number of laboring Chinese would thus remain constant and if the papers were watched to prevent forgery the administration of the law would be very simple and not liable to much abuse.

After all, the exclusion of Chinese labor, acquiesced in by many who have not approved the method, is not the immediate and vital question. It is rather, whether a bureau of officials and the consular service shall continue to jeopardize the relations of two nations by methods of administration unwarranted either by treaties or legislation or even by the selfish interests of the country. In short, whether the non-laboring Chinese shall not be treated with such courtesy as befits the people of a most favored nation. The remedy for present conditions necessarily involves special and highly trained officers of the service stationed in China; the devising of a passport which upon identification shall be final not mere *prima facie* evidence of the Chinaman's right to enter this country; and such that when here he shall be free from molestation. It involves also a new registration of all the resident Chinese and a non-partisan board

Conclusion 495

of inquiry or an immigration court, to which all debarred Chinese may appeal.

Some of these obviously imperative reforms are already bruited but they will be purely superficial in their effect unless a strict conformity of laws and regulations with the treaty is secured; for without this formal legislative expression of our intention as a nation to fulfil our obligations, the friendship with China cannot be restored nor her coöperation be obtained; and without her coöperation no immigration service established in China on the part of the United States can attain satisfactory results.

President Arthur, in vetoing the Restriction bill of 1881, said that the time might come when Chinese labor would be greatly needed in some sections of the United States and that he could not therefore, sign the bill excluding them for twenty years. It was, indeed, just twenty years from that time, and while Americans in Hawaii and the Philippines were protesting against the application of the law to their territories, that the reaction against the methods of Chinese exclusion precipitated a concerted and powerful attack upon it. Since then Hawaii has seriously suffered for want of Chinese labor, and even while these words are being written American engineers at Panama are clamoring for Chinese labor to build the Isthmian canal because there is almost no American labor to be had, and the Chinaman is the best contract laborer available.

The turning of the road along which California has led the rest of the United States, is in sight; it may be; but the laws of the universe are not changed even by repentance. Injustice in the guise of discrimination for self-protection has brought, and will not fail to bring, retribution in the degradation of those who practise it. The arrogant and narrow-minded temper bred by pioneer conditions, the monopolistic spirit and the lack of sanity and justice which finds its extreme expression in the treatment of the Chinese, is even now wreaking itself upon California. Lawlessness, class hatred, incapacity for coöperation—these have been in part the fruits of race discrimination.

APPENDIX.

CHINESE IN THE UNITED STATES, 1820–1882.
PART I.—PERIOD OF FREE IMMIGRATION.

Year.	Chinese arrived in U. S. From Rept. of Com.-Genl. of Immigration, 1905.	Chinese arrivals at San Francisco Custom House.	Departures from San Francisco Custom House.	+ or − net gain or loss.	Corrected figures: [17] no. on Pacific Coast in specified year, computed on basis of Custom House figures minus deaths at 2 p.c. per year.	Number in California estimated by American authorities.	Number in California and U. S. Figures of Chinese Six Companies.	Number in United States. U. S. Census.
1820–30	....	[1] 3	......	......	......	......	....	......
1830–40	....	8	......	......	......	......	....	......
1848	....	3	......	......	......	54	....	......
1849	....	325	......	......	......	791	....	......
1850	......	450	......	......	[2] 4018	......	....	......
1851	....	2716	......	......	7370	[3] 10000	[4] 7520	......
1852	......	[3] 20026	1768	18258	25116	[5] 25000	....	......
1853	......	4270	4421	− 151	24466	[6] 19210	....	......
1854	......	16084	2339	13745	37447	......	....	......
1855	......	3329	3473	− 144	36557	......	....	......
1856	......	4807	3028	1779	37569	......	....	......
1857	4524	5924	1932	3992	40730	[8] 45000	....	......
1858	7183	5427	2542	2885	42743	......	....	......
1859	3215	3175	2450	725	42599	......	....	......
1860	6117	7343	2088	5255	46897	......	....	34933
1861	6094	8434	3594	4840	50703	......	....	......
1862	4174	8188	2795	5393	54975	[7] 50000	....	......
1863	5280	6435	2947	3488	57294	......	....	......
1864	5240	2696	3911	−1215	54958	......	....	......
1865	3702	3097	2298	799	54642	......	....	......
1866	1872	2242	3113	− 871	52696	......	[10] U.S. 58300	......
1867	3519	4794	4999	− 205	51432	[9] 50000	....	......
1868	6707	11085	4209	6876	57142	......	U.S. 90837	......
1869	12874	14994	4896	10098	65896	......	[11] Cal. 41000	......
1870	15740	10869	4232	6637	71083	......	....	63199
1871	7135	5542	3264	2278	71894	......	....	......
1872	7788	9773	4887	4886	75245	[12] 62500	....	......
1873	20291	17075	6805	10270	83805	......	....	......
1874	13776	16085	7710	8375	90337	......	....	......
1875	16437	18021	6305	11716	100003	......	....	......
1876	22781	....	[16] 8525	14256	111971	......	[13] 60000	......
1877	10594	....	8161	2433	112116	[14] 65000	....	......
1878	8992	....	8186	806	110664	......	....	......
1879	9604	....	9220	384	108827	......	....	......
1880	5802	....	7496	−1694	104991	[15] 83600	....	105465
1881	11890	....	8926	2964	105796	......	....	......
1882	39579	....	10366	29213	132300	......	....	......

For footnotes see opposite page.

CHINESE IN THE UNITED STATES, *Continued*.

[1] An. Rept. U. S. Com. of Educ. 1870, p. 35, p. 422.
[2] Estimate used by S. Wells Williams and by Bancroft, v. 6, p. 124.
[3] Figures used by Otis Gibson and Theodore Hittell, taken from S. F. Evening *Post*, Apr. 13, 1876, and obtained from Custom House.
[4] Figures of S. E. Woodworth, Chinese Adviser, to Dec. 30, 1851, and precisely the same as those of Consul Forbes at Canton, see *Alta*, May 10, 1852, *Cong. Docs.* 1868, s. n. 734, H. Doc. 123, p. 107.
[5] Cal. State census, *Sen. Jo.* 1853, app. Doc. 14. This was an estimate rather than a census except in a few mining counties.
[6] *Prices Current* figured that there were 19,210 Chinese *male adults* in California on Dec. 30, 1853.
[7] *Alta*, Aug. 22, 1857.
[8] Rept. *Select Com.*, of Cal. Legisl. 1862.
[9] Estimate of Daniel Cleveland, July, 1868, *Cong. Docs.* 1868, s. n. 1364.
[10] *Alta*, July 7, 1866–figs. of Six Companies.
[11] Sacramento *Union*, Nov. 27, 1869, published a very full record, obtained from the Six Companies, of the number, occupations and distribution of the Chinese,
[12] *Alta*, June 8, 1873, based on C. H. figs. and allowing 3% death-rate.
[13] S. F. *Bulletin*, Apr. 20, 1876.
[14] *Alta*, Oct. 29, 1877.
[15] *Alta*, June 17, 1880. The Editor remarked that the numbers of the Chinese had always been grossly exaggerated.
[16] From 1876 to 1883 the figures of arrivals include transits and non-immigrants and the departures include all races and are only for San Francisco. Since the departure from San Francisco of immigrants of other races than Chinese averaged about ten per cent of totals in 1883–8, this ten per cent would probably balance the arrivals of transits and non-immigrants. The figures of the Chinese as printed in the reports of the Treasury Department from this time on are inconsistent and misleading.
[17] An attempt is made here to arrive at an accurate estimate of the numbers of Chinese on the Coast in each year to 1882. In it there are three assumptions: the one just mentioned in note 16; the original number in 1851; and the death-rate of two per cent per year. This latter was furnished by the Special Statistician of the U. S. Census, and stands between the death-rate of the male colored of same age and the male white of same age, i. e. 28.24 and 15.63.

CHINESE IN THE UNITED STATES.
PART II. (1882–1906)[1]
Grouped by Legislative periods of restriction and exclusion.

Year ending June 30.	Chinese arrived in United States.[1]		Chinese departed from United States.	Chinese arrived at San Francisco.	Chinese departed from San Francisco.	Net gain or loss at San Francisco.	Chinese arrived at San Francisco, by classes.		
	Immigrants.	Non-Immigrants.	All classes.	All classes.	All classes.	All classes.	With Legal Certificates.	Not intending to remain.	Immigrants.
1883	8031	2151	12159	9269	10894	−1633	644	1924	6701
1884	279	3194	14145	7985	12273	−4788	4900	2812	273
1885	22	5330	19655	11330	15185	−3855	6410	4901	19
1886	40	4809	17591	11110	16915	−5805	7704	3393.	13
1887	10	3754	12155	13718	11339	+2379	11162	2651	5
1888	26	2751	12893	14173	11786	+2387	12816	1357	
1889	118	1945	10226	10935	10169	+ 766	9062	1755	118
1890	1716	154	8056	832	5652	−4820			832
1891	2836	171	8924		8733				
1892	[2] 2728	462	6696		6168				
1893	2828	2484							
1894	4018	941	5966						
1895	975	530	4470						
1896	1441								
1897	3363								
1898	2071								
1899	1660								
1900	1247								
1901	2459								
1902	1649	480							
1903	2209								
1904	4309								
1905	2166								
1906	1544								

[1] These figures apparently do not include those arriving with legal certificates. The figures for the U. S. are found in Monthly Summary of Commerce, U. S. Treasury Dept. series 1902-3, nos. 7-12, p. 4439. The figures for San Francisco (columns 5-8) are in Sen. Exc. Doc. 1889-90, nos. 60-122, vol. 9, no. 97.

[2] The arrivals in columns 1 and 2 are the same as those given in the report of the Commissioner-General of Immigration for 1905, except in the years 1892 to 1896 inclusive, which differ widely. The amounts given in the Monthly Summary have been used, since they are the larger.

CHINESE POPULATION IN UNITED STATES, 1852-1900
By decades and geographical divisions, from U. S. Census.

	1900		1890		1880		1870		1860
United States (Continental)	89,963		107,488		105,465		63,199		34,933
Divisions	Number	Per cent.	Number	Per cent.	Number	Per cent.	Number	Per cent.	Number
North Atlantic	14693	16.	61707	5.	1628	1.	137		
South Atlantic	1791	2.	669		74		11		
North Central	3668	4.	2357	.2.	813		9		
South Central	1982	2.	1447	1.	848		211		
Western	67729	75.	96844	90.	102102	99.	62831	99.	34933
Montana	1739		2532		1765		1949		
Wyoming	461		465		914		143		
Colorado	599		1398		612		7		
New Mexico	341		361		57				
Arizona	1419		1170		1630		20		
Utah	572		806		501		445		
Nevada	1352		2833		5416		3152		
Idaho	1467		2007		3379		4274		
Washington	3629		3260		3186		234		
Oregon	10397		9540		9540		2330		
California	(1) 45753	51.	72472	67.	75132	71.	(2) 49277	77.	(2) 34933

(1) A rough Census of the Chinese taken in 1852 gives the number at 25,000. See Appendix Senate Jo. Doc. 14, 1853.

(2) It is generally conceded that the figures for 1860 and 1870 are too small. See Table of arrivals and departures.

CHINESE WOMEN IN THE UNITED STATES.

Year.	I. Free Immigration, 1835-1882.			Year.	II. Restriction and Exclusion. 1882-1904.				
	Arrivals in United States.	Number in U. S. Census.	Number in San Francisco.		Arrivals in United States.	Departures from United States.	Net gain or loss, + or −	Number in U. S. Census.	Number in San Francisco.
1835-51	16								
1852									
1853				1883	47	201	−144		
1854	673			1884	100	270	− 70		
1855	2			1885	123	279	−156		
1856	16			1886	92	3	+ 89		
1857	450			1887	89	241	−152		
1858	320			1888	80	253	−173		
1859	467			1889	68	4	+ −64		
1860	29	1784	406	1890	318	12	+306	3868	2790
Totals..	1973			Totals..	917	1163	−246		
1861	515			1891	233	5	+228		
1862	650			1892	241	5	+236		
1863	1			1893	179	—	+179		
1864	164			1894	247	—	+247		
1865	10			1895	116	2	+114		
1866	5			1896	59	—	+ 59		
1867	4			1897	29	—	+ 29		
1868	46			1898	10	—	+ 10		
1869	974			1899	2				
1870	1116	4574	3881	1900	12	—	+ 12	7996	1303
Totals..	3485			Totals..	1126	12	+1114		
1871	349			1901	42				
1872	183			1902	123				
1873	892			1903	40	[1] 172			
1874	243			1904	118	189			
1875	385								
1876	260								
1877	77								
1878	354								
1879	358								
1880	70	4779	1781						
Totals..	3171								
1881	83								
1882	136								
Grand tot'l	8848								

[1] At San Francisco only.

Appendix

CHINESE POPULATION OF CALIFORNIA BY COUNTIES
Which at any decade contained more than 1.3% of total Chinese in the State.
UNITED STATES CENSUS, 1852–1900.

	1900		1890		1880		1870		1860		State Census 1852	
	No.	%	No.	%	No.	%	No.	%	No.	%	No.	%
Alameda	2211	4.8	3311	4.6	4386	5.8	1939	3.9	193	....	....	....
Amador	153	....	324	....	1125	1.5	1627	3.3	2508	7.4	....	....
Butte	712	1.6	1530	2.1	3793	5.	2082	4.2	2177	6.2	....	....
Calaveras	148	....	326	....	1037	1.4	1441	2.9	3657	10.5	....	....
El Dorado	206	....	518	....	1484	2.	1582	3.2	4762	13.7	....	....
Fresno	1775	3.9	2736	3.8	753	1.	427	.9	309	....	....	....
Kern	906	1.9	1124	1.6	702	.9	143	....	....	....	....	....
Klamath	....	....	....	....	....	....	....	....	....	....	....	....
Los Angeles	3209	7.	4424	6.1	1169	1.6	542	1.1	533	1.5	....	....
Marin	489	1.1	915	1.25	1327	1.8	236	....	11	....	....	....
Mariposa	102	....	180	....	697	....	361	....	4	....	3886	15.5
Monterey	857	1.85	1667	2.3	372	....	1084	2.2	1843	5.3	3019	12.1
Nevada	6..	..	1053	1.5	3003	4.	230	....	6	....	804	3.2
Placer	3254	7.1	1429	2.	2190	2.9	2627	5.3	2147	6.15	....	....
Sacramento	13954	30.5	4371	6.	4892	6.5	2410	4.9	2392	6.8	....	....
San Francisco	1875	4.1	....	35.7	21745	28.9	3596	7.3	2719	5.	....	....
San Joaquin	1738	3.8	1676	2.3	1997	2.7	12030	24.4	139	7.8	....	....
Santa Clara	102	....	2723	3.8	2695	3.6	1525	3.3	22	....	....	....
Shasta	309	....	342	....	1334	1.8	574	1.2	415	....	....	....
Sierra	790	1.7	488	....	1252	1.7	810	1.6	2208	6.3	....	....
Siskiyou	903	2.	1151	1.6	1568	2.1	1440	2.9	415	....	....	....
Solano	599	1.3	1522	2.1	993	1.3	920	1.9	14	....	....	....
Sonoma	729	1.6	1145	1.6	904	1.2	473	.95	51	....	....	....
Tehama	336	....	892	1.2	774	1.	294	....	104	4.7	....	....
Trinity	158	....	554	....	1951	2.6	1099	2.2	1638	5.6	....	....
Tuolumne	719	1.6	253	....	805	1.1	1524	3.1	1962	5.1	2100	8.4
Yuba			974	1.35	2146	2.85	2337	4.7	1781			

IMMIGRATION TO THE UNITED STATES,

By decades and specified nationalities.

(Report of the Com.-General of Immigration, 1906).

	1861–70	1871–80	1881–90	1891–00	1901–05
Total immigrants — all races..................	2,377,279	2,812,191	5,246,613	3,687,564	3,833,076
	Per cent.	Per cent.	Per cent.	Per cent.	Per cent.
Austria-Hungary.........	8.33	2.6	6.7	16.	25.
German Empire..........	35.00	25.5	28.	14.	4.6
Italy (Sicily and Sardinia)............... ...	0.51	2.	5.9	18.	25.
Scandinavia.............	4.6	7.4	10.9	8.6	6.7
Russian Empire and Finland..................	0.2	1.9	4.4	14.	17.
United Kingdom........	38.	34.	27.	17.	9.
Total Europe...........	90.	80.	90.	96.5	95.
British North America..	5.8	14.	7.5	.08	.19
China ....,...........	2.7	4.4	1.2	.4	.33
Japan...................	@	@	@		
Total Asia..............	2.8	5.4	1.3	1.9	3.

@ less than one per cent.

SELECTED BIBLIOGRAPHY

On account of the impending publication of an exhaustive and scholarly bibliography of the Chinese question in the United States, prepared by Robert E. Cowan and Boutwell Dunlap, the original bibliography of this book has been reduced to the titles which are most accessible and of the greatest interest to the general student. A large number of rare, curious and interesting pamphlets and all magazine articles of minor value have been omitted; but the most important references on the collateral history of California, the history of emigration from China and the racial characteristics of the Chinese, have been retained. In the footnotes there will be found many supplementary references to material of casual and indirect interest.

The thorough student will find it necessary to use the following lists:

Cowan, Robert E, and Dunlap, Boutwell. Bibliography of the Chinese question in the United States. (475 titles.) San Francisco, Robertson, 1909. In Press.

Griffin, A. P. C. Select List of References on Chinese Immigration. Congressional Library, Washington, 1904. (Contains a list of the more important speeches in Congress on the Chinese question and of Government documents.)

Griffin, A. P. C. A List of Books (with references to periodicals) on Immigration. Third issue, Washington, 1907.

United States Document Index. Consult under the following headings: China; Chinese immigration; Chinese indemnity fund; Chinese labor troubles; foreign relations (China); immigration; treaties; diplomatic and consular service.

Windemeyer, Margaret. China and the Far East. New York State Library Bibliographies, Albany, 1901.

Cordier, H. Bibliotheca Sinica; Dictionnaire bibliographique des ouvrages relatifs à l'empire chinois. 2 vols. and supplement. 1904.

Birmingham Free Libraries Occasional Lists. No. 1, 1901. Books, pamphlets, parliamentary reports and magazine articles on China. Birmingham, Allday, Ltd. Printers. 128 Edmund Street.

Coöperative List of Periodical Literature in Libraries of Central California. University of California Publications, Berkeley, California, 1902.

Newspapers of California. Subject Indices are now accessible in the California Department of the State Library at Sacramento (and being continually enlarged) as follows:
Daily Alta California, 1849-1881 inclusive.
San Francisco Call, 1882-1887 inclusive; 1894-1904.
San Francisco Chronicle, September, 1902—February, 1905, inclusive.
Sacramento Union, 1859-1860 inclusive.
Californian, 1846-1848 inclusive.
California Star, 1847-1848 inclusive.

Andrews, E. B. History of the Last Quarter Century in the United States. 2 vols. New York, 1895.

Andrews, S. The Chinese in California. The Gods of Wo Lee. *Atlantic Mo.* V. 25, pp. 223 ff; pp. 469 ff.

Angell, J. B. Diplomatic Relations of China and the United States. *Amer. Jo. Social Science*, v. 17, pp. 24 ff.

As a Chinaman Saw Us. Passages from his letters to a friend at home. San Francisco. (Henry Grafton Pearson, May 10th, 1904.) New York, Appleton, 1906.

Auger, Edouard. Voyage en Californie, (1852-3) Paris, Hachette et Cie.

Baldwin, Esther E. Must The Chinese Go! New York, 1890. H. B. Elkins, 13 Vandewater Street. (Pamphlet, 3d ed.)

Bancroft, H. H. History of California, 6 vols., San Francisco, 1884-1890.
Popular Tribunals, 2 vols., San Francisco. 1887.
Works, v. 35; Some Chinese Episodes.
" v. 38; Mongolianism in America; Two Sides of a Vexed Question; Social Analysis.

Bates, Mrs. D. B. Four Years on the Pacific Coast. Boston, Libby and Co. 1858, 5th ed.

Bibliography

Beadle, J. H. The Undeveloped West. National Publishing Company, Philadelphia, Chicago, Cincinnati. 1873.

Bechdolt, Jack. San Francisco's Labor Problem. *Pacific Monthly*, V. II, no. 4 (1904).

Becker, S. E. W. Humors of a Congressional Investigating Committee. A Review of the Report on Chinese Immigration. 1877, San Francisco. (Pamphlet).

Bee, Fred. A. Memorial. The Other Side of the Chinese Question Testimony of California's Leading Citizens. Read and Judge. San Francisco, February, 1886. Woodward and Company, Printers. (Pamphlet.)

Bee, Fred. A. Opening Argument Before the Joint Committee of Congress on Chinese Immigration. (Pamphlet.) San Francisco, 1876. (Reprinted in Report of Joint Special Committee, s. n. 1834, *Cong. Docs.*)

Blasdale, Walter C. A Description of Some Chinese Food Materials and their Nutritive and Economic Value. U. S. Department of Agriculture, Bulletin 68. Washington, 1899.

Boalt, John H. The Chinese Question. A paper read before the Berkeley Club, August, 1877. (Reprinted in report of the California Senate Committee on Chinese Immigration.)

Boenigk, Otto von. Die Antichinesen—Bewegung in Amerika. Staatswissenschaftliche Arbeiten, 1896.

Bonner, John. The Labor Question on The Pacific Coast. *Californian Illustrated Magazine*, v. 1, p. 410. A Chinese Protest against Exclusion. *Californian Illustrated Magazine*, v. 5. pp. 603 ff.

Borthwick, J. D. Three Years in California. Blackwood, Edinburgh and London, 1857.

Boulger, D. C. History of China. London, W. H. Allen and Co., 1884. (V. II contains references to emigration.)

Bowles, Samuel. Across the Continent. S. Bowles and Company, Springfield, Mass. 1865. Reprinted in Our New West, 1869.

Bowring, Sir John. A visit to the Philippine Islands. London, 1859. (Emigration from China.)

Brace, C. L. The New West: or California in 1867–1868. New York, G. P. Putnam's Sons, 1869.

Brooks, B. S. Opening Statement before the Joint Committee of Congress on Chinese Immigration. San Francisco, 1876. (Pamphlet, 33 pp.)

Brooks, B. S. The Chinese in California. (Pamphlet) 1876. Addressed to the Committee on Foreign Relations of the U. S. Senate.

Brooks, B. S. Brief of the Legislation and Adjudication touching the Chinese Question. San Francisco, 1877. Woman's Coöperative Printing Union.

Brooks, B. S. Appendix to the opening statement and brief on the Chinese Question consisting of documentary evidence and statistics. San Francisco, 1877. Woman's Coöperative Printing Union. 160 pp. 8vo.

Brooks, B. S. The Invalidity of the Queue Ordinance of the City and County of San Francisco. Opinion of the Circuit Court of the U. S. for the District of California in Ho Ah Kow vs. Matthew Nunan. July 7, 1879; with Appendix being his cry of legislation of the City and County of San Francisco against the Chinese.

Bryce, James. The American Commonwealth. N. Y. 2 vols. (See chapter on Kearneyism and also appendix in last edition.)

Burlingame, E. L. An Asiatic Invasion. *Scribner's Mo*, v. 13 (1877), pp. 687 ff.

Bushee, F. A. Ethnic Factors in the Population of the City of Boston. Publications of the American Economic Association, May, 1903. Macmillan, N. Y.

Cailleux, Edouard. La Question Chinoise aux États-Unis et dans les possessions des puissances Européennes. Paris, Arthur Rousseau. 1898.

California. Memorial to the President and Congress for the Reenactment of the Chinese Exclusion Law. Adopted by the Chinese Exclusion Convention, November, 1901, San Francisco, Star Press.

California: Annual Reports of the Bureau of Labor, 1883 ff.

California: Blue Books or State Rosters, 1903 ff.

California: Index to Laws of—*See* Johnston, A. J; also Report of the Commissioners, *etc.*

Callahan, Our Relations with the Far East. Johns Hopkins Studies, v. 19, pp. 84 ff.

Capron, E. S. History of California. Boston, J. P. Jewett and Company, 1854.

Carson, James H. Life in California. Published at the office of the San Joaquin *Republican*. Stockton, 1852.

Bibliography

Chew, Ng P. and Healy, P. J. *see* Healy.

The China Mail. Published at Hong Kong, 1845 to 1867, weekly.

Chinese Exclusion Convention of 1901. Proceedings, list of delegates, etc. San Francisco, Star Press, 1901.

Chinese Immigration. Its Social, Moral and Political Effect. Report to the California State Senate of its Special Committee on Chinese Immigration. Sacramento, 1878. Contains also: An Address to the People of the United States upon the Evils of Chinese Immigration; a Memorial of the Senate of California to the Congress of the United States; and the Testimony taken before a committee of the Senate of the State of California, 1876, (several editions).

Chinese Question from the Chinese Standpoint. San Francisco, 1874. Signed on behalf of the Chinese by Lai Yong, Yang Kay, Ah Yup, Lai Foon, Cheung Leong. Translated by Dr. O. Gibson and read before the Board of Supervisors, San Francisco, May, 1873. (Pamphlet.)

Clapp, Mrs. L. A. C. Shirley's Letters printed in Ewer's *Pioneer*. San Francisco, 1854-1855.

Codman, John. The Round Trip. New York, Putmans, 1879.

Colquhoun, A. R. China in Transformation. New York, Harper's, 1898.

Condit, I. M. [Reverend]. The Chinaman as We See Him and Fifty Years of Work for Him. Chicago, Revell, 1900.

Conwell, R. H. Why and How: Why the Chinese Emigrate and the means they adopt for getting to America. Lee and Shepard, Boston, 1871.

Cronise, T. F. The Natural Wealth of California. Bancroft and Company, San Francisco, 1868.

Culin, Stewart. China in America: a Study in the social life of the Chinese in the Eastern cities of the United States. Philadelphia, 1887.

Curtis, W. E. The United States and Foreign Powers. New York, Scribners, 1899.

Cutler, H. R. Chinese Gambling. *Californian Illustrated Magazine*, v. 5, p. 312 ff.

Davis, W. J. History of Political Conventions in California. Sacramento, State Library, 1893.

Dawes, H. L. The Chinese Exclusion Bill. *Forum*, v. 6 (1889).

Denby, Charles. Chinese Exclusion. *Forum*, v. 34 (1902).

Dennys, N. B. (compiler and editor). The Treaty Ports of China and Japan... Guide Book and Vade Mecum. London, Trübner and Co., 1867.

Die Ausführing der Chinesen durch Europaer als Kulis nach West Indien und Süd Amerika und ihre Auswanderung nach Californien und Australien. *Ausland*, no. 37, 1858.

Dixon, W. H. The White Conquest. London, Chatto and Windus, 1876. 2 vols.

Dorland, C. P. The Chinese Massacre at Los Angeles in 1871. Historical Society of Southern California, v. 3, pp. 22 ff.

Dorney, P. S. A Prophecy Partly Verified. *Overland Monthly*, n. s. v. 7, pp. 230 ff. (Detailed account of riot in Los Angeles in 1871.)

Dunlap, B. and R. E. Cowan, *see* Cowan.

Durst, J. H. The Exclusion of the Chinese. *North American Review*, v. 139.

Eaves, Lucile. History of Labor Legislation in California. Published by the University of California, 1909.

Eitel, Ernest J. Europe in China. London, 1895.

Evans, Albert S. Á La California. San Francisco, 1873.

Evans, Elwood (and others). History of the Pacific Northwest. Crocker and Company, San Francisco, 1889.

Farwell, W. B. The Chinese at Home and Abroad. Together with the report of the Special Committee of the Board of Supervisors on the condition of the Chinese Quarter. San Francisco, 1885. (Pamphlet. Printed also in Municipal Report of 1885.)

Field, Stephen J. Opinions and Papers. 6 vols. (1859 to 1894.) San Francisco. See especially v. 3, pamphlets 16, 17 and 20.

Fisher, A. & C. Personal Narrative of Three Years' Service in China. London, Richard Bentley, 1863.

Fong, Walter. Chinese Labor Unions. *Chautauquan*, June–July, 1896.

Fong, Walter. The Chinese Six Companies. *Overland Monthly*, 1894.

Foster, John W. American Diplomacy in the Orient. Boston and New York, Houghton, Mifflin, 1903.

Bibliography

Geary, Thomas J. The Law and the Chinaman. *Californian Illustrated Magazine*, v. 4, pp. 304 ff. (Exclusion Bill of 1893.)

George, Henry. Chinese Immigration. Lalor's Encyclopaedia of Political Science, v. I., C. E. Merrill, New York, 1890.

Gibson, Otis [Reverend]. The Chinese in America. Cincinnati, 1879.

Gibson, Otis. Chinaman or White Man, Which ! Reply to Father Buchard. San Francisco, 1873, *Alta* Printing House.

Gompers, Samuel and Gutstadt, Herman. Some Reasons for Chinese Exclusion. Meat vs. Rice. American Manhood against Asiatic Coolieism, 1902. (Pamphlet published by the American Federation of Labor. Reprinted in *Cong. Docs.* s. n. 4231.)

Handbook to Monterey and Vicinity. Monterey, Walton and Curtis, 1875. (Chinese fishing colony.)

Hart, [Sir] Robert. These from the Land of Sinim. London, Chapman and Hall, 1901.

Healy, Patrick J. A Shoemaker's Contribution to the Chinese Discussion. *Overland Monthly*, n. s. v. 7, p. 414.

Healy, Patrick J. Reasons for Non-Exclusion with Comments on the Exclusion Convention. San Francisco, 1902. Printed for the author.

Healy, P. J. and Ng Poon Chew. Statement for Non-Exclusion, San Francisco, 1905.

Helper, Hilton R. Land of Gold. Baltimore, 1855. Published for the author.

Hittell, John S. Mining in the Pacific States. San Francisco, Bancroft, 1861. (Several later editions published under the title of Bancroft's Handbook of Mining.)

Hittell, John S. Resources of California. San Francisco, Bancroft, 1863. (Several later editions.)

Hittell, John S. History of the City of San Francisco and incidentally of the State of California. San Francisco, H. H. Bancroft and Company, 1878.

Hittell, John S. The Benefits of Chinese Immigration. *Overland Monthly*, v. 7 (1886).

Hittell, Theodore H. History of California. San Francisco. 4 vols. 1885-1897.

Holcombe, Chester. The Real Chinaman. New York, Dodd, Mead and Company, 1895.

Holcombe, Chester. The Real Chinese Question. New York, Dodd, Mead and Company, 1900.

Hopkins, C. T. Commonsense applied to the Immigrant question showing why the California Immigrant Union was founded, etc. San Francisco, Trumbull and Smith, 1869.

Huntley, Sir Henry Vere. California: Its Gold and Its Inhabitants. 2 vols. London, Thomas Cantley Newby, Publisher, 1856.

Ho Yow (Imperial Consul-General). Chinese Exclusion: A Benefit or a Harm. *North American Review*, v. 173 (1901).

Jaffa (Professor) M. E. Nutrition Investigations among Fruitarians and Chinese at the California Agricultural Experiment Station, 1899-1901. Washington, 1901. U. S. Department of Agriculture, Bulletin 107.

Johnston, A. J. Index to the Laws of California. 1853-1893. Sacramento, 1894. (*See also:* Report of the Commissioners, *etc.*)

Journal of the American-Asiatic Association, 1900 ff. John Foord, Publisher, 78 Beekman Street, New York City.

Jones, David S. The Surnames of the Chinese in America . . . .also the principal regulations governing the immigration and exclusion of Chinese. San Francisco, E. A. Jones, 1904. (Pamphlet.)

Kennedy, J. C. G. Argument in the Senate of the United States adverse to bill "To restrict the Immigration of the Chinese to the United States" Feb. 25, 1878. (Pamphlet.) Printed in *Cong. Docs.* 45th Congress, 2d sess. Senate Misc. Doc. 36.

Kerr, J. G. The Chinese Question Analyzed. A lecture, San Francisco, printed for the author, 1877.

King, T. Butler. Report on California. Washington, Gideon and Company, 1850.

Kirchoff, Theodor. Californische Kulturbilder. Cassel: Theodor Fischer, 1886.

Kohler, Max J. Coolies and Privileged Classes. *Journal American Asiatic Association*, March, 1906. Reprinted from the New York *Tribune* of Jan. 15th, 1906.

Kohler, Max J. Our Exclusion Policy and Trade Relations with China. *Journal American-Asiatic Association*, June, 1905.

Kwang Chang Ling (nom-de-plume). Why should the Chinese go? A pertinent inquiry from a mandarin of high authority. San

Bibliography

Francisco, Bruce's, 1878. Pamphlet reprinted from the *Argonaut* of 1878. 3d ed.

Kang Yu Wei. The Hostility of China. *World's Work*, v. 12 (1906).

Lang, Herbert O. A History of Tuolumne County, California. San Francisco, B. F. Alley, 1882.

Layres [Professor] Augustus. The Other Side of the Chinese Question. San Francisco, 1876, Taylor and Nevin. (Several editions.)

Layres, [Professor] Augustus. Both Sides of the Chinese Question or Critical Analysis of the Evidence for and against Chinese Immigration . . . . also a review of Senator Sargent's report with an Appendix concerning a widespread conspiracy against the Chinese. San Francisco, A. F. Woodbridge, Printer, 434 California Street. 1877.

Lloyd, B. E. Lights and Shades of San Francisco. San Francisco, 1876.

Lobscheid, W. The Chinese: What they are and what they are doing. San Francisco, Bancroft, 1873.

Loomis, [Reverend] A. W.
Chinese Women in California. *Overland Monthly*, O. S. V. 2.
How our Chinamen are employed.   "   "   O. S. V. 2.
The Chinese as Agriculturists. "   "   O. S. V. 4.
The Chinese Six Companies.   "   "   N. S. V. 2.

McClellan, R. Guy. The Golden State. Philadelphia, Flint. San Francisco, Hutchinson, 1876.

Martin, W. A. P. The Chinese: Their Education, Philosophy and Letters. N. Y. Harpers, 1881.

Masters, [Reverend] F. J.
Among the Highbinders. *Californian Illustrated Magazine*, v. 1.
Can a Chinaman Become a Christian.   "   "   v. 2.
Our Treaties with China.   "   "   v. 4.

Medhurst [Sir] Walter. The Chinese as Colonists, *Nineteenth Century*, v. 4 (1878).

Mitchell, Edmund. The Chinaman Abroad. *Nineteenth Century*, v. 36 (1894).

Nickerson, Stephen W. Our Chinese Treaties and Their Enforcement. *North American Review*, v. 181 (1905).

Nordhoff, Charles. California. New York, 1872.

O'Meara, James. The Chinese in Early Days. *Overland Monthly*, n. s. v. 3 (1884).

Phelan, James D. Why the Chinese should be excluded. *North American Review*, v. 173 (1901).

Plehn, Carl C. Labor in California. *Yale Review*, v. 4, 1896.

Pomeroy, J. N. Some Account of the Work of Stephen J. Field. Copyright, 1882, by S. B. Smith.

Pumpelly, Raphael. Across America and Asia. New York, Leypoldt and Holt, 187-

Poole, S. Lane. The Life of Sir Harry Parkes. 2 vols. London, Macmillan, 1894. (Emigration from China.)

Ralph, Julian. The Chinese Leak into the United States, *Harper's Magazine*, v. 82 (1890).

Ratzel, Friedrich. Die Chinesische Auswanderung; ein Beitrag zur Cultur und Handelsgeographie. Breslau, 1878.

Reed, W. B. China and the United States. (Diplomatic relations before 1857.) *North American Review*, v. 89.

Reid, Gilbert. China's view of the Geary Bill. *Forum*, v. 16.

Remarks of the Chinese Merchants of San Francisco upon Governor Bigler's Message and some common objections with some explanation of the character of the Chinese Six Companies and the laboring class in California. San Francisco, 1855. Printed at the office of the *Oriental* by Whitton, Towne and Company. Written by Lai Chun Chun, a merchant of San Francisco, and translated by the Reverend William Speer.

Reports of the Industrial Commission, v. 15 (1901), part IV. Chinese and Japanese Labor in the Mountain and Pacific States.

Report of the Commissioners for the revision and reform of the law [of California] . . . also an index to the laws from 1895 to 1901 inclusive. Sacramento, 1902.

Report of the Committee on the Governor's Special Message in relation to Asiatic Immigration, Apr. 28, 1852. California Senate *Journal*, 1852.

Report of the Royal Commission on Chinese Immigration, Ottawa, 1885. Printed by S. E. Dawson, Parl. Sessional Paper. no. 54.

Reports: San Francisco Municipal, especially for 1884-85.

Richardson, A. D. Chinese Immigration. *Atlantic Monthly*, v. 34 (1869).

Richardson, J. D. Messages and Papers of the Presidents. 10 vols. Washington, 1899.

Rohlfs, G. Chinesen in Californie. *Ausland* 38, (1876).

Royce, Josiah. The Golden State. American Commonwealth Series. Boston, 1886.

Ruhl, Karl. Californien: über Bevölkerung und gesellschaftliche Zustände. New York, 1867.

Seward, George, F. Chinese Immigration in its Social and Economic Aspects. New York, 1881.

Seward, George F. Mongolian Immigration, *North American Review*, v. 134 (1882).

Shaw, William. Golden Dreams and Waking Realities. London, Smith, Elder and Co., 1851.

Shanks W. F. G. Skilled Chinese Labor. *Scribners Monthly*, v. 2 (1871.)

Sherwin, H. Observations on the Chinese Laborer. *Overland Monthly*, n. s. v. 7 (1886.)

Shinn, Charles, H. Mining Camps. New York, Scribners, 1885.

Shinn, Charles H. The Geary Bill for the exclusion of the Chinese. *Nation*, v. 36.

Smith, Arthur H. Chinese Characteristics. London, 1899, 2d ed. Village Life in China. New York, 1899.

Smith, Richmond Mayo. Emigration and Immigration. New York, 1895.

Soule, F. (and others.) Annals of San Francisco. N. Y. 1854.

Speer, [Reverend] William. China and California: their relations past and present. San Francisco, Marvin and Hitchcock, 1853. (Pamphlet. Also printed in *Princeton Review*, January, 1853.)

Speer, William. An Humble Plea, addressed to the Legislature of California in behalf of the immigrants from China. San Francisco, published at the office of the *Oriental*, 1856.

Speer, William. An Answer to the Common Objections to Chinese Testimony. San Francisco, 1857. (Pamphlet.)

Speer, William. Democracy of the Chinese. *Harper's Magazine*, v. 37 (1868).

Speer, William. The Oldest and the Newest Empire, or China and the United States. 1870. Hartford, Scranton and Company, San Francisco, Bancroft.

Stone, W. W. The Knights of Labor on the Chinese Labor Situation. *Overland Monthly*, v. 7, n. s. (1886).

Swinton, John. The New Issue. The Chinese-American Question. New York, American News Co., 1870. (Pamphlet reprinted from New York *Tribune*.)

Townsend, L. T. The Chinese Problem. Boston, Lee and Shepard, 1876.

Trumble, A. The Heathen Chinee At Home and Abroad. Who he is, *etc.*, by an old Californian. New York, Fox, Publisher, 183 William Street.

Truth vs. Fiction. Justice *vs.* Prejudice. Meat for all and not for a few. A plain, unvarnished statement why exclusion laws should not be reënacted. (Anonymous pamphlet; a reply to "Meat *vs.* Rice" published by the American Federation of Labor in 1901–1902.)

Thwing, [President] C. T. Chinese Students in America. *Scribners Mo.* v. 20 (1880).

Tuthill, Franklin. History of California. San Francisco, 1866.

Varigny, C. de. L'Invasion Chinoise et la Socialisme aux Etats-Unis. *Revue de Deux Mondes*, October 1, 1878.

Walsh, Robert F. Chinese Fisheries. *Californian Illustrated Magazine*, v. 4 (1893).

Williams, S. Wells, LL.D. Our Relations with the Chinese Empire. San Francisco, 1877. (Pamphlet.)

Williams, S. Wells. Treaties between China and the United States. *New Englander*, v. 38 (1879).

Williams, S. Wells. Chinese Immigration. New York, Scribners, 1899. (Reprint of address before the Social Science Association, Saratoga, New York, 1879.)

Williams, S. Wells. The Perpetuity of Chinese Institutions. *North American Review*, v. 131 (1880).

Williams, S. Wells. The Middle Kingdom. New York, 1883. 2 vols.

Williams, Frederick W. Life and Letters of S. Wells Williams. New York, Putnams, 1889.

Willis, E. P. and Stockton, P. K. Debates and proceedings of the Constitutional Convention, Sacramento, 1880.

Woods, Daniel B. Sixteen Months in the Gold Diggings. New York, Harper, 1851.

Yan Phou Lee. The Chinese Must Stay. *North American Review*, v. 148 (1889).

Yung Kiung Yen. A Chinaman on Our Treatment of China. *Forum*, v. 14 (1892).

Young, John Russell. The Chinese Question Again. *North American Review*, v. 154 (1892).

INDEX.

Abalone trade, 72.
Agricultural life in China, 4.
Amador mines, Strike at, (*1871*), 267.
American and Chinese Commission of *1880*, 152; its *personnel*, purpose, and political motive, 153; answer of Chinese Commissioners, 156; draft of propositions submitted by American Commissioners, 157; various interpretations thereto by Chinese, 157; final form of treaty adopted, 160; discussion of disputed phrases, 164; *see also*. Treaty of *1880*.
American Asiatic Association and exclusion laws, 475.
American Association in China, 475.
American consular service in China, 308, 330.
American Federation of labor, *Meat v. Rice*, 375.
Americans in China, violate treaty rights, 464; cause of friction, 467; right of extra-territoriality, 467.
Angell, James B., 152, 175; *see also* Treaty of *1880*.
Anglo-Chinese College, 471.
Anti-Chinese feeling, Rise of, 30; increased by report of Committee on Mines and Mining interests, 31; and License tax, 32, 34; Gov. Bigler's attitude, 32, 55; other antiforeign prejudice, 39; increased by Know-nothing party, 58; and industrial discontent, 59; overshadowed by class feeling and question of slavery, 60; rising spirit of mob rule, 114; hostility expressed by Second Constitution of California, 119; disturbances in San Francisco (*1879*), 122; outrages (*1884*), 188; culmination in Geary law, 233; violence of feeling (*1876*-'77), 262; anti-Chinese ordinances revived and passed, 264; resentment assuming different character, 266.

Anti-Chinese labor agitations, causes, 378.
Appeal, Decisions by, and regulations concerning, 296; denial of right established, 237.
Arbitration, 7, 11.
Arthur, Chester A., Pres., vetoes Senate Bill no. *71*, 173, 175.
Article Nineteen, Second Constitution of California, adoption, provisions, 120, 125.

Bailey, D. H., Consul, 49, 106, 308, 419.
Bayard, Thomas F., Sec. of State, and the issuance of certificates, 187; proposes exclusion (*1887*), 192; indifference toward Chinese government, 193; discussion of Scott Act with Chinese Minister, 201; *also* 175, 271.
Becker, S. E. W., 104 *note*.
Belcher Bonanza mines discovered (*1872*), 351.
Bertillon system, 288, 306, 469, 472.
Bigler, John, Gov., message on immigration, 31, 67; uses question as campaign appeal (*1852*), 56; *also* 460.
Blaine, James G., Sec. of State, 137, 202, 205, 211, 221, 271, 463.
Blair, Henry W., Senator, refused as U. S. representative, 463; *also* 198, 199, 229.
Bonner, John, *Labor Question on the Pacific Coast*, 395 *note*.
Bonte, Rev. H. C., *quoted*, 89.
Booth, Newton, Gov., inaugural address, 66; *also* 134.
Boston, raid of Chinese colony (*1903*), 323.
Bowers, William W., 228.
Bowring, Dr. John, 46.
Boxer outbreak, 235, 463.
Boycott movement (*1905*), cause, rules, reactionary influences, 282, 469, 485; industries affected, 472;

519

Pres. Roosevelt's ruling, 474, 477; indifference of Chinese government, 480; Imperial edict proclaimed, 480; decline and consequences, 481.
Brace, Charles Loring, on industrial value of Chinese, 344.
British Passengers Act (*1855*), 18, 44.
Brown, Joseph E., Senator, 171, 198, 199.
Bubonic plague, 413, 415.
Burial of the dead, 443; *see also* Exhumation ordinance.
Burlingame, Anson, and coolie trade, 48; minister to China and envoy to U. S., 147; *see also* Burlingame Treaty.
Burlingame Treaty (*1868*), drafted by Sec. Seward, 148; refuses naturalization to Chinese, 77, 80, 129; modification demanded (*1876*), 111; propositions of Workingmen's party (*1878*), 120; attacked in Congress, 132; defended by President, 139; various interpretations of naturalization clause, 149; special commission appointed (*1880*), to modify Treaty, 152; final form adopted (*1880*), 160; mutual gains and losses, 162; discussion of disputed phrases, 164; abrogation demanded, 191; *see also* American and Chinese Commission of *1880*; Fifteen Passenger bill.
Butler, M. C., Senator, 199, 215, 217.
Butler, Roderick R., Senator, 198.

California, Bureau of Labor (*1877-'78*), report on prostitution, 430; (*1883*). statistics on cost of living, 362; Second Biennial report, shoe industry, 362; (*1884*), report on pauper labor, 381; (*1886*), report on laborers for fruit harvest, 382; (*1888*), statistics on cost of living, 432; (*1890*), investigation of woolen industry, 375; (*1900*), report on wages in cigar-making, 370.
California, Constitution of, First (*1849*), mining laws, 27; limited suffrage, 76; Second (*1878*), main ideas, 118; adoption of Article Nineteen, 120; a provision nullified, 125.

California Immigrant Union, report on wages, 353.
California Labor Exchange, organized (*1868*), 347; report on wages and nationalities, 348.
California Senate Address and Memorial (*1877*), *personnel* of the committee and witnesses, 84; report on prostitution, 87; criminality, 88; non-conversion, 89; competition, 90; coolie slavery, 91; part of foundation of first Exclusion law, 94; report on earnings of Chinese, 429.
California State convention (*1886*), 189.
Call, Wilkinson, Senator, 171, 198, 218.
Caminetti, Anthony, 230.
Campaign, National, (*1876*), 110, 113; (*1896-1900*), 240.
Campaign, State, (*1852*), 56; (*1867*), 64, 110; (*1869*), 65; (*1871*), 66.
Canada, coöperation in exclusion, 330.
Capitation tax, (*1852*), 70; (*1855*), 60, 71; (*1873*), 66; (*1878*), 134; *see also* Police tax.
Carlisle, John G., Sec. of the Treasury, 219.
Carpenter, Matthew H., Senator, 129.
Casserley, Eugene, Senator, 128, 147 *note*.
Caste, non-existent in China, 3, 42.
Census (*1850-'90*), corrected table of number of Chinese in U. S., 425; (*1870*), 9*th*, labor statistics, 358; (*1880*), 10*th*, scale of wages in shoe industry (*1875-'80*), 361.
Central Pacific railroad, (*1864-'65*), Chinese labor on, 63, 343, 349; completed (*1869*), 350; effect on industrial and political conditions, 64, 128; offer of work (*1878*), 380; *see also* Pacific railroads.
Certificates, required by Restriction Act of *1882*, 183; also by Henley bill, 185; difficulties in carrying out the law, 187, 189; proposals made by Tsung-li-Yamen, 192; Conference bill, 218; number invalidated by Scott Act, 280; merchant's entering certificate, 294; right of consular officers to issue certificates

Index. 521

withdrawn, 295; increasing stringency of U. S. government leads to protest by Chinese Minister, 296; issuance, record, and identification of, 298; variations of practice in handling, 298; traffic in, expired, 316; *see also* Detention station; Exempt classes; Scott Act; Section-Six certificate.

Chandler, William E., Senator, 217.

Chang Yen Hoon, and the Indemnity Treaty, 193; protest against Scott Act, 201.

Chen Lan Pin, Minister, 271.

Cheng Tsao Ju, Minister, and his claim for indemnity (*1885*), 271.

China becoming better known, by Chicago Exposition, 234; books and travel, 235; Boxer outbreak, 235; alteration in character of other immigration, 235.

Chi-nan-fu troubles, 463.

Chinatown, San Francisco, report on, by W. B. Farwell, 188; by State legislature, 191; social organization, 402; crime, 409; boundaries, 411; lodging-houses and sanitary conditions, 412; police protection, 417; comparative conditions, 421; schools, 435; family life, 437.

Chinese, Abuse of, at first sporadic, 258; later, concerted and official, 259; associated with political campaigns, 259; divided into periods, 269.

Chinese Commission, *see* American and Chinese Commission of 1880.

Chinese government, form, effect upon life and property, 5; its coöperation, needed to remedy evils of indiscriminate immigration, 151; new treaty negotiations desired after McCreary amendment, 236.

Chinese immigrant *v.* European, 20, 232, 456, 488.

Chinese in America, early social and industrial value, 20, 342, 344; contrasted with other nationalities, 20, 24; race prejudice gathering force, 25; movement from mines toward cities, 38; compared with Indian and negro, 75; not allowed to testify in courts, 75; denial of naturalization, 76; restrictive measures against, 78; value as laborers shown by report of Joint Special Committee of Congress, 103; recapitulation of early conditions, 255, 258; review of treatment before passage of Restriction law, 268; present day treatment, attitude of Chinese toward it, and its influence on their statesmen, 275; economic objections to, 428.

Chinese laborer, characteristics, 103, 384, 386, 390.

Chinese Protective Society, 260.

Chinese question, party platforms, 96; chief state campaign issue (*1876*), 110, 113; popular vote on, 123; debated in Congress during *10* years, 129, 141; thrown into background by Geary bill, 234; apparently dead, 240.

Ch'ing, Prince, 243 *note*, 475, 480.

Cholos labor, 385.

Christianity, Converts to, report of California Senate Address and Memorial (*1877*), 89; *see also* Missionaries.

Cigar industry, competition (*1870–'80*), 357; census (*1870*), statistics, 359, 365; establishment and growth, 365, 370; scale of wages, 366; investigated by Joint Special Committee of Congress (*1877*), 366; and by California Bureau of Labor (*1891*), 368; causes of decline, 368; nationality and sex of cigarmakers, 370; *see also* White Labor league.

Citizenship, denial of privileges of, as limiting immigration, 80; prompted by race antipathy, 81.

Class distinctions in China, 3, 42.

Cleveland, S. Grover, Pres., urges remedial legislation by indemnity, 190; Treaty of *1888* signed, 194; Scott Act signed, 200; Chinese appeal for protection, 224.

"Coaching," 305, 316.

Code of law, Chinese, 7.

Cole, Cornelius, Senator, 128.

Commercial life in China, 8.

Commutation tax, 431, 447.

Competition, California Senate Address and Memorial, report on (*1877*), 100; industries exempt from, 341; in manufactures, 358;

important factor in, 392; *see also* Chinese in America; Cigar industry; *Meat v. Rice*; Mining; Monopoly; Riots; Shoe industry; Woolen industry.

Comstock Lode, discovery (*1859*), 61; value declines, 113.

Conference bill (*1892*), see Geary bill.

Congress, *41st* (*1869–'70*), lack of unanimity on Chinese question, 128; debate on naturalization, 129; *44th* (*1876*), attempt to modify Burlingame Treaty, 132; *45th* (*1878–'79*), efforts renewed, 133; Fifteen Passenger bill debated and passed, 135, 150; *47th* (*1882*), Senate Bill no. 71, 169; other exclusion bills, 176; *48th* (*1884*), Henley bill passed, 185; *49th* (*1886*), Indemnity bill debated, 190; *50th* (*1888*), indemnity bills debated and Scott Act signed, 196; *52nd* (*1892*), Geary bill, 213; *53rd* (*1893*), McCreary amendments to Geary bill, 226; *57th* (*1902*), Kahn bill and other exclusion bills, 244; *58th* (*1904*), bill to reënact existing legislation passed, 251.

Congressional Committee of *1876*, see Joint Special Committee of Congress.

Consolidated Virginia mines, 109.

Consulate, Chinese, established at San Francisco, 270.

Convention of *1901*, its purpose and *personnel*, 243; memorial framed and sent to Congress, 244; debate centered about principal points, 245.

"Coolie," Definition of, 41.

Coolie bill, 31.

Coolie labor and cigar industry, 369.

Coolie trade, in *1850*, 17; to Cuba and South America, 19; cause, 43; countries engaged in, 44; voluntary emigration *v.* coolie trade, 46; report to U. S. government (*1862*), 48; Consul Bailey's reports, 50; assisted by Pacific railroads (*1868–'69*), 52; results, 54.

Coombs, Frank L., 245.

Cooper, Henry, 97.

Corbett, Henry W., Senator, 129.

Corporations forbidden to employ Chinese (*1879–'80*), 124.

Cost of living, 393, 432; *see also* Diet.

Court, Excluded from testifying in, (*1850*), 75; admitted (*1873*), 76; *also* 128.

Crime, report of California Senate Address and Memorial (*1877*), 88; *see also* Police statistics.

Cubic air ordinance in San Francisco (*1870*), 261; vetoed by Mayor Alvord, 261; becomes state law, 264.

Cutting, John T., 214.

Davidson, James W., Consul, 474.

Davis, Horace, Senator, attack on methods of exclusion (*1893*), 231; *also* 49, 216, 217.

Dawes, Henry L., Senator, 170, 177, 216-218.

Denby, Charles, Minister, 49, 192, 199, 205, 211, 463, 466, 467.

Detention station at San Francisco, its squalor and inconvenience, 299, 329.

Diet, 393, 437; *see also* Cost of living.

Dietary statistics, 433.

Diseases of Chinese in America, 416.

Doctrine of trespass, 29.

Dolph bill, 213; *also* 217, 218.

Drahms, Dr. August, on crime, 451.

Dress, 437, 442; *see also* Cost of living.

Dunn, James R., 247, 288, 292, 319.

Eastern states, attitude toward Chinese question (*1876*), 132.

Edmunds, George F., Senator, 172, 177, 200.

Education, see Schools.

Eight hour law, obtained by labor element (*1873*), 67.

Eight hour movement, causes riots (*1866–'67*), 345.

Emigration, provinces furnishing, 15, 19; modifying conditions, 16, 17; classes furnishing, 20; *see also* Coolie trade; Women.

English Passengers act, see British Passengers act.

European immigration, 64, 429, 488.

Evarts, William M., Senator, 199.

Exclusion, Cost of, 310.

Exclusion bills, before *47th* and *57th* Congress, 169, 176, 244, exclusion

Index. 523

debates in light of subsequent history, 178; litigation growing out of Exclusion law, 188; new draft of negotiations sent to Senate (*1894*), 236; *see also* Restriction Act of *1882*; Senate Bill no. *71*.
Exclusion law (*1882*), foundation of the first, 94; applied to the Philippines and to Hawaii (*1898*), 240; hardships of Chinese presented to Sec. Hay by Minister Wu Ting-Fang, 241; principles objected to by Simon Wolf and others, 246; administration controlled by Labor unions, 240; enforcement transferred to Bureau of Commerce and Labor, 279; appropriations for administration, 279 *note*; severity towards registered laborers, 280; restrictions by Sec. of Treasury (*1898*), 283; cost per head of handling Chinese, 311; recommendations concerning re-registration, 311; economic effects of enforcement; 332, 439; *see also* Boycott movement; Mitchell bill.
Exclusion Laws, Compilation of the Facts concerning the Enforcement, by the Commissioner-General of Immigration, analysis of contents, 302.
"Exempt classes," Definition of, (*1898*), 238; interpretation of Treaty of *1880*, 282; principle of limitation, 284; Boycott of *1905*, 476.
Exhumation ordinance becomes state law, 264.
Expatriation, Congress and rights of, 150.
Extra-territoriality, Right of, 466.

Fairbanks, Charles W., Senator, 249.
Falsehood, Chinese attitude toward, 9.
Family, social unit, 4, 10.
Farley, James T., Senator, 174, 177.
Farwell, W. B., Report on Chinatown, 188.
Felton, C. N., 215.
Fifteen Passenger bill, debated before *45th* Congress and passed (*1879*), 135, 150; vetoed by Pres. Hayes, 139.

Financial depression (*1876*), causes, 109, 113.
Financial status of Chinese, 428.
Fishing industry, absorbed by foreigners, 73.
Fishing license, 72.
Fong, Walter, account of Six Societies, 406.
Foraker, Joseph B., Senator, 166 *note*.
Foreign Miners' License tax (*1850*), passage and provisions, 29; repealed (*1851*), 30; renewed, 32; prohibitive measures, 34, 60; income to state, 35, 70, 431; declared void (*1870*), 36; results, 38; increase recommended by Six Companies (*1853*), 57.
Foreign Relations, Committee on, hearing on Chinese question (*1876*), 132; modification of Treaty advised, 134; amend Senate Bill no. *71*, 169; Henley bill reported, 184; Scott Act referred to, 200; Dolph bill, 213; Senate bill as substitute for Geary bill, 215; Kahn bill, 245.
Foreigners, Chinese attitude toward, 11.
Foster, John W., Sec. of State, and exclusion laws, 107, 219, 246, 250, and *note*.
Four Companies organized (*1862*), 21; *see also* Six Companies.
"Four Societies," *see* Six Companies.
Freedom of speech, 5.
Fruit harvest (*1886*), laborers for, 382.
Frye, William P., Senator, 216, 218.

"Gag-law" (*1877*), 117.
Gambling, *see* Police statistics.
Garfield, James R., Sec. of the Interior, and Boycott movement, 485.
Geary, Thomas J., 213, 218, 220, 227.
Geary law (*1892–'93*), provisions, 213; Senate bill reported as substitute, 215; certain sections plus Senate bill reported and passed, 218; pronounced unconstitutional, 219; public opinion, 219; protest of Chinese government, 221; declared constitutional by Supreme Court, 223; newspaper comments, 224; immediate modification demanded,

226; McCreary amendment debated and passed, 226; signed by President, 232; culmination of anti-Chinese agitation, 233; difficulty and expense of enforcement, 238; registration, 327.
George, James Z., Senator, 198.
German v. Chinese immigrants, 21.
Gold, Discovery of, in California, 17; on Fraser River, 35; in Australia, 59.
Gompers, Samuel, *Meat v. Rice*, 344 *note*; 373 *note*; 395 *note*.
Gorman, Arthur P., Senator, 199.
Governmental system, Chinese, 7.
Gracey, Dr. Samuel L., Consul (*1905*), 471.
Gray, George, Senator, 217.
Gresham, Walter Q., Sec. of State, *quoted*, 224.
Griggs, John W., Attorney-General, interpretation of restriction acts (*1898*), 283.
Grover, LaFayette, Senator, 136, 177.
Guadelupe Hidalgo, Treaty of, 29.

Haight, Henry H., Gov., 64, 112, *quoted*, 147.
Hamlin, Hannibal E., Senator, 136, *quoted*, 137.
Harrison, Benjamin, Pres., and treaty rights of foreigners, 492.
"Hatchet men," 408; *see also* Highbinder.
Hawaiian Islands, exclusion laws applied to, 240, 453.
Hawley, Joseph R., Senator, 171.
Hay, John, Sec. of State, his influence during Boxer outbreak, 466; *also* 166, 241, 283, 485; *see also* Treasury regulations.
Haymond, Hon. Creed, and Committee of investigation of Chinese immigrants, 84.
Henley bill (*1884*), introduced and reported favorably, 184; passed House and Senate, 185; complications arising from defects, 186.
Hermann, Binger, Senator, 214.
Highbinder Tongs and conflict with police, 260.
Hilborn, Samuel G., 228.
Hip Ye Tong, *see* "Hatchet men."
Hiscock, Frank, Senator, 218.

Hitt, Robert R., Senator, 185, 214, 218, 220, 227, 245.
Hittell, John S., 49, 258, 262, 398, 429.
Hittell, Theodore, 49, 95.
Hoar, George F., Senator, his attitude toward the Mitchell bill, 250; protest against abrogation of Burlingame Treaty, 137; Senate Bill no. 71, 170, 172; *also* 177, 199, 233, 250.
Holcombe, Chester, Joint Interpreter of American and Chinese Commissions, 153, 160; *also* 4, 6, 165, 166, 434, 453, 464, 469.
Ho Mun, 321.
Hong Kong, 17, 18, 44, 134, 187, 192, 211, 298, 321, 324, 418, 419.
Hong Sling, 298.
Hong Tuck Tong, 368.
"Hoodlums," their rise and abuse of Chinese, 259; increase of lawlessness, 265; *also* 86.
Hooker, Charles E., 197, 214, 220, 245.
Hospital tax, 32, 267; *see also* Capitation tax; Commutation tax.
Hospitals, Chinese excluded from, 70, 267, 447.
Huntley, Sir Henry, *quoted*, 24.

Immigration, limited by taxation and by denial of citizenship, 80; organized effort toward restriction by national government, 97; subject investigated by Joint Special Committee of Congress, 97; change of public opinion regarding unlimited, 150; report of Congressional Subcommittee (*1891*), and of Committee on Foreign Relations, 212; Geary bill debated, 213; and passed, 218; under control of Commissioner of Immigration, 240; Treaty of *1894* denounced by Chinese Minister, bill to reënact existing legislation becomes law, 251; later and earlier compared, 337, 352; average annual, 427; history of, in China, 492.
Immigration law of *1891*, 237.
Immigration service, cost of, 310, 332; its *personnel* responsible for much adverse criticism, 312, 319;

Index.

causes of odium traced, 312; Chinese interpreters, 314; instances of bribery in collusion with inspectors, 315, 318; examinations for trachoma, 318; illustrations of arbitrary power, 319; illegal arrest, 324.

Immigration treaty of *1894*, negotiations for renewal (*1905*), 236; cause of Boycott movement, 469.

Indemnity, difference of opinion regarding, 273; interpretation of the Treaty of *1880*, 273; redress through courts, 274; missionaries and traders receive, 274; *see also* Capitation tax; Scott Act; Treaty of *1888*.

Indemnity bill, debated, modified, and signed, 190; provisions, 194; additions, 195; ratification refused by Chinese government, 197.

Industrial conditions in California, in *1867*, 344; in *1876*, 113.

Industrial conditions in China, 4; characteristics of laborer, 12; comparison with European, 13.

Industrial value of Chinese, 12, 20, 342; opinions of experts, 344.

Infanticide, 11.

Ingalls, John J., Senator, 172, 177.

Insane asylums, foreign-born inmates, 447.

Intermarriage, 440.

Irish immigrant in American politics, 270.

Irish *v*. Chinese immigrants, 20, 457.

Irwin, William, Gov., annual message (*1877*), *quoted*, 114.

Italian *v*. Chinese immigrants, 232, 456.

Italians and the fishing industry, 74.

Jaffa, Prof. M. E., on diet of Chinese, 433.

Japanese school case, 275.

Joint Special Committee of Congress, appointed (*1876*), 97; *personnel*, 97, 104; report analyzed, 98; testimony concerning industrial competition and trades affected by Chinese labor, 100; untrustworthiness of report, 104; influence on social and economic conditions, 108; *see also* California Senate Address and Memorial; Cigar industry; Shoe industry.

Jones, David S., on Chinese names, 314.

Jones, John P., Senator, 170.

Ju Toy case, 237.

Kahn bill, before *57th* Congress, 244; Platt amendment substituted, 249.

Kearney, Dennis, 115, 122.

Kearneyism, Rise of, 67; riots (*1877*), 115; organized opposition to Chinese, 118; reaction against, 125; violence of anti-Chinese feeling, 262; political machine and working classes, 264; Chinese competition, 365; wage question (*1876–'80*), 380.

King, T. Butler, 26.

King, Capt. T. H., 51, 104.

Knights of St. Crispin, 360.

Know-nothing party, rise and purpose, 58.

Kung, Prince, leader of liberal movement (*1860*), 147; approached by Sec. Seward on subject of immigration, 151.

Labor, Classification of, by Carl C. Plehn, 340; conditions after *1869*, 352; Eastern and Western conditions, 395.

Labor, Foreign, substitute for Chinese since *1886*, 384; *see also* State Employment bureau.

Labor exchange organized (*1868*), 347; reports and statistics, 348.

Labor in California since *1886*, 384.

Labor party organized, 243.

Labor unions, increase of power, 239; administration of exclusion laws, 240; responsible for growth of anti-Chinese feeling, 242; Union labor vote becomes a party, 243; united by Eight-hour movement, 345; dates of organization, 345 *note*; Bonner, John, on, *395 note*; *see also* Knights of St. Crispin.

"Laborers," Definition of, 177, 282.

Land, Ownership of, 6.

Law, Administration of, in China, 8.

Legation, Chinese, established at Washington, 270.

Legislation, Federal, demanded by China, 460, 471; against paupers

and criminals (*1875*), 150; administration of exclusion laws transferred, 279; *see also* Congress.
Legislation, State, (*1852*), masters of vessels and a capitation tax, 70; (*1853*), Six Companies refute Gov. Bigler's charges, 57; (*1854*), report of committee on vice and immorality, 58; (*1855*), prohibitive taxation, 60; (*1858*), Chinese forbidden to land upon Pacific coast, 79; (*1862*), report of joint committee of Legislation and Chinese merchants, 62; (*1863*), allows testimony of negroes, prohibits that of Chinese, 76; (*1867-'77*), cubic air and other ordinances become laws, 264; (*1886*), Gov. demands abrogation of Burlingame Treaty, 191; (*1887*), Fishing license, 73; *see also* Mines and Mining interests, Committee on.
Lehlbach, Herman, 213.
Lei Yok, 295.
Lew Lin Gin, Story of, 321.
Local government in China, 4, 6.
Lo Chum Qui, 460.
Lodging-house ordinance, *see* Cubic air ordinance.
Loud, Eugene F. 228.
Louisiana Purchase Exposition, Chinese exhibitors, and rules regulating their departure, 290; *also* 319, 468.
Low, Frederick F., Minister to China, 49, 463.

Macao, non-treaty port, 17, 45, 94.
McArthur, Walter, 244.
McCreary amendment to Geary law, 226; debated, 227; passed, 230; ineffectual attempts to weaken, 230; signed by President, 232; beginning of reaction against methods of exclusion, 233.
McDonald, Mark, 112.
McDougal, Gen., and land grants (*1852*), 22.
McGowan, E. C., and capitation tax, 71.
McKinley, William, Pres., urges protection of Americans in China, 464.
Maguire, James G., 229.

Manufactures in California before (*1880*), 358.
Markham, Henry H., Gov., 225.
Marriage, *see* Women.
Martin, W. H., *see* California Immigrant Union.
Martinez canneries, Chinese attacked by Greek and Italian fishermen, 267.
Matthews, Stanley, Senator, 136.
Meade, Edwin R., 97, 107.
Meat v. Rice, by Samuel Gompers, 344 *note*; 375 *note*.
Memorial to Congress by California State Convention of *1886*, 189.
"Merchant," Definition of, 293.
Merchants, kind of entrance certificate needed by, 294; *30* denied landing (*1899*), 295.
Metcalf, Victor H., and Boycott movement, 485.
Military life in China, 11.
Miller, John F., Senator, and Senate Bill no. *71*, 169; *also* 177.
Mines and Mining interests, Committee on, report, 31, 33, 57, 71.
Mining in California, hostilities between Americans and foreigners, 26, 40; Foreign Miners' License tax, 29; Coolie bill, 31; value of Chinese labor, 38; fall of values and strikes, 59; placer mining in hands of Chinese (*1876*), 102; outrages against Chinese, 255; under control of corporations, 266; *see also* Riots.
Missionaries, summary of work, 446; treaty protection, 464; *also* 104.
Mitchell, John L., Senator, 132, 215, 217.
Mitchell bill, in Senate, 245; favorably reported, 248; composite sources, 248; supported by western representatives, debated and postponed, 249.
Monopoly of industries, 101, 388, 393.
Monopoly theory disproved, 389.
Moral standards of Chinese, 8.
Morals, System of, 447.
Morgan, John T., Senator, 136, 174, 176, 177, 198, 199, 215, 218.
Morrison, G. E., *quoted*, 465.
Morrow, William W., 190.

Morton, Oliver P., 51, 97, 103, 133, 138.
Mosby, John S., Consul, 51, 419.
Murietta, Joaquin, 256 *note*.
Murray, Hugh C., Judge, 76.

Naturalization, denied at Jamestown, 32; by Burlingame Treaty, 76; debated in *41st* Congress, 129; law of *1870*, 146; requirements of new law (*1906*), 487.
Nickerson, Stephen W., and exclusion laws, 247.

O'Donnell, Charles C., his testimony concerning lepers, 106.
Opium habit, its prevalence, 9.
Opium war of *1840*, 16.
Otis, Elwell S., Major-General, and exclusion laws in Philippines (*1898*), 240.
Outrages, *see* Riots.

Pacific coast states, their representation in Congress, 127; necessity of unanimity in local issues, 128; divided on Chinese question, 128; attempt to abrogate Burlingame Treaty, 128, 132; House bill to enforce right to vote, 130; end of discrimination in taxation, 131; failure of bills to pass, 131; attempt to work up anti-Chinese sentiment in the East, 132; efforts renewed in *45th* Congress, 133; passage of House bill regarding immigration, 135; vetoed by President, 139.
Pacific railroads and importation of laborers (*1868-'69*), 52; completion of work, 128.
Page, Horace F., 176.
Palmer, John M., Senator, 218.
Panics, (*1862*), 63; (*1869*), 128; (*1871*), in silver stocks, 351; (*1873*), Eastern, popular unrest and business conditions, 351, 380; (*1877*), financial distress, 113; (*1893*), closing of silver mines, 225.
Passports, 295, 316, 464, 494.
Paternalism in China, 5.
Patriarchal idea in China, 8.
Patriotism, Lack of, among Chinese, 7.

Pauper labor, Report on, (*1884*), 381.
Penrose, Charles B., Senator, 248.
People's Protective Alliance (*1873*), 263.
Perkins, George C., Senator, 52, 230; Gov., 125, 267.
Personal characteristics of Chinese, 11; value as laborers, 21.
Personal property, 430.
Phelan, J. D., 244 *note*.
Philippine Islands and exclusion laws, 240; *see also* Convention of 1901.
Piper, W. F., 97, 106.
Pixley, Frank, 104, 107, 112.
Platt, Thomas C., Senator 166 *note*; 170, 198, 216, 218.
Platt amendment to Senate Bill no. 71 offered and rejected, 216; substituted for House bill (*1902*), 250.
Plehn, Carl C., classification of labor, 340; on manufactures of California, 376; Chinese competition, 377.
Police statistics (*1879-'03*), in San Francisco, 450.
Police tax, 72, 431.
Poll tax, 431.
Population, Chinese, in America, census statistics, 423, 429; distribution, 426; comparative rates of increase by immigration, 427.
Portuguese government and the coolie trade, 45.
Powderley, T. V., Commissioner, 239, 320, 322-324, 328.
Prescott, Cyrus D., 176.
Pro-Chinese re-action (*1901*), 241.
Prohibition, *see* Restriction.
Prostitution, existing in China, 10; report of California Senate Address and Memorial (*1877*), 87, 91, 93; misrepresentations regarding, 307; carried on by Secret Societies, 418; report by California Bureau of Labor, 420.
Public spirit, Lack of, in China, 6.
Pun Chi, 460.
Pung Kwang Ju, Minister, 272.

Quartz mining, Development of, 38.
Quong Tuck Tong, 407.

Raymond, R. W., U. S. Commis-

sioner of Mining Statistics, report (*1871*), 39.
Ready, H. V., on labor question, 387.
Real estate, Chinese investments in, 430.
Reciprocity, Treaties of *1844* and *1858*, 146; Burlingame Mission sent to establish, 148; demanded by China, 467.
Registration, System of, set in operation, 233; hardships suffered by registered laborers, 280; definition of "laborers," 282; and of "students," 284; under amended Geary law, 327; system of re-registration advised, 494.
Republican party and Chinese question (*1869*), 128; (*1875*), 110; appoint special commission (*1880*), to modify treaties, 153; (*1888*), 196; oppose Senate Bill no. 71, 170.
Restriction Act of *1882*, its provisions, 183; confusions arising in regard to ambiguities, 184; Henley bill introduced and passed, 184; attacks upon Chinese taking place, 188; false rumors of evasion of law, 189; some results of administration, 191, 280, 383; date of expiration disputed, 212; limitation of classes and definition of "laborers," 283, 287; *see also* Fifteen Passenger bill; Henley bill.
Restriction law, First, treatment of Chinese before, 269.
Restriction law and retaliation, 462.
Rice, Alexander H., 185.
Right of appeal in China, 5.
Riley, B. C., Gov., and placer mining (*1849*), 27.
Riots (*1850*), at Sonora, Cal., 28; (*1866-'67, '69*), at San Francisco, 259, 345; Tong war, 260; (*1871*), at Los Angeles, 260; Amador mines, 267; Chinese attacked by Greek and Italian fishermen at Martinez, 267; (*1877*), 115, 259, 265; (*1878*), at Truckee, 266; (*1880*), at Denver, 271; *see also* Boycott movement; Hoodlums; Rock Springs massacre.
Roach, William N., Senator, 31, 132.

"*Robert Bowne,*" 47.
Rock Springs massacre (*1885*), 188, 273; indemnity demanded by Chinese Minister, 190.
Rockhill, W. W., Minister, 469, 470 *note*, 474, 475, 478, 480.
Roosevelt, Theodore, Pres., and Boycott of *1905*, 474; attitude toward exempt classes, 477; *also* 241.
Ross, Jonathan, Judge, 225.

San Francisco, center of social discontent, 59; corruption in city affairs, 61; establishment of first school for Chinese children, 78; attempt to exclude Chinese boys from High school, 79; financial panic of *1877*, 113; industrial conditions (*1868, '78*), 347, 380; *see also* Chinatown; Riots.
Sargent, A. A., Senator, 51, 97, 104, 106, 130, 132, 134, 136, 138.
Sargent, F. H., Commissioner of Immigration, 324, 330, 485.
Schools, in China, 12; Chinese excluded from American, 78; first school for Chinese in San Francisco (*1885*), 78; public schools in Chinatown (*1885*), 435.
Schurz, Carl, 129.
Scott Act, introduction into the House and debate, 197; signed by Pres. Cleveland, 200; motives producing and newspaper comment upon, 200; protest by Chinese Minister, 201; demand to repeal, 205; U. S. government fails to answer, 204; excuses for passage, 206; examples of delay in other international negotiations, 207; charges of fraud and evasion, 209; various interpretations and confusion arising therefrom, 208, 210; inadequate appropriation for enforcement, 211, 281; its expediency, 216; repealed (*1894*), 237; invalidated certificates, 280; effect on business, 280; further results to the country, 308; and to the laborer, 383.
Scudder, Doremus, on Chinese in Hawaii, 453.
Secret societies, *see* "Hatchet men;" Six Companies; Trade guilds.

Index. 529

Section-Six certificate, 290, 292, 296, 298, 303, 304, 311.
Security, Bonds. etc. accepted as, 268.
Senate Bill (exclusion) no. *71*, debated by Senator Miller and others, 169; provisions, 169; opposed by Republicans, 170; amended by Committee on Foreign Relations and passed, 172; vetoed by Pres. Arthur, 173; debate on veto, 174; political criticism of veto, 175; substituted for Geary bill, 215; and carried, 216; committee of conference appointed, 217; its report, 218; *see also* Restriction act of *1882*.
Seward, George F., Consul and Minister, overtures with Prince Kung regarding immigration, 151; removal from office, 152; *see also* 157, 163.
Seward, W. H., Sec. of State, coolie trade, 48; Burlingame Treaty, 148.
Sewing trades, Competition in, 101; census (*1870*) statistics, 359.
Shanghai Educational Association, 471.
Sherman, John, Senator, 174, 198, 199, 215, 217, 218.
Shoe industry, census (*1870*) statistics, 359; begun in California about *1866*, 360; value of product and scale of wages (*1875*), 361; investigated by Joint Special Committee of Congress (*1877*), 362; also by California Bureau of Labor (*1883*), 362; also by U. S. Bureau of Labor, 363; rank in 1870 and causes of decline, 365; *see also* Knights of St. Crispin.
Shrimp trade, 73.
Silver mines, closing of, (*1893*), resultant riots, and Geary law, 225.
Six Companies, organization, rules, scope, 402; coolie trade, 48; assistance to newly-arrived immigrants, 51; petition for protection in treaty rights (*1853*), 57; petition to police against lawless class (*1876*), 111; issue proclamation in relation to Geary bill, 219; report on murders committed, 258; supposed responsibility for crime, 405, 419; affected by establishment of Chinese consulate, 411; data on expenditures, 430; endeavor to check emigration (*1876*), 460; *see also* McCreary amendment; Prostitution.
Skinner, Charles R., 185.
Smith, Gen. P. F., 26.
Smith, Prof, Richmond Mayo-, and rights of expatriation, 149.
Social life in China, 4.
Social organizations in China reproduced in America, 403.
Sonora, Cal., mining riot (*1850*), 28.
Spaulding, Oliver L., Special Agent Treas. dept., and evasion of Restriction law, 190.
"Squeeze," *see* Taxation.
Squire, W. C., 213, 216.
Stanford, Leland, Senator, 49; Gov., 62, 63.
State Employment Bureau, Report (*1895-'96*), 389.
State Horticultural Society, White *v*. Chinese laborers for fruit harvest (*1886*), 382.
State prisons, foreign-born inmates, 448.
State *v*. Federal control, 491.
"*Stephen Baldwin*," 71.
Stewart, Charles V., 121, 128, 199, 215.
Stoneman, George, Gov., demands abrogation of Burlingame Treaty, 191.
Straus, Oscar, 287, 485.
Strikes, *see* Riots.
"Student" class, Definition of, 284, 286; outline of treatment, 285; intellectual ability, 435; Boycott of *1905*, 477; *see also* Schools.
Stump, Hermann, 213, 239.
Suffrage, Gov. Haight's opinion (*1867*), 64; limited by First Constitution of California (*1849*), 76; Burlingame Treaty (*1868*), 77, 129; debated in *41st* Congress, 130; for the second generation, 443; *see also 42nd* Congress.
Sulphur Bank Quicksilver Mining Company, 124.
Swett, John, State Superintendent of education (*1866*), provision for education of negro, Mongolian, and Indian children, 78.

Swift, John T., 153 *note*, 175.

Taft, William H., and exclusion laws, 478; Boycott movement, 485.
Tai-ping rebellion, 17.
Taxation, in China, 5; affecting various occupations, 74; motive for exclusion, 75, 80; end of discrimination in, 131; *see also* Capitation tax; Commutation tax; Fishing license; Hospital tax; Police tax; Poll tax.
Teamsters' strike (*1900*), 239, 243.
Teller, Henry M., Senator, 170, 199, 215.
Tingley, Senator, *see* Coolie bill.
Tongs, 389, 390, 392, 397; *see also* Labor unions.
Trachoma, Examinations for, 318.
Trade guilds, control of industrial conditions, 13, 406; *see also* Labor unions.
Trade unions, *see* Labor unions.
Tramp labor, 378.
Transit, Right of, under Treaty of *1880* and later, 287.
Transit regulations and statistics, 288.
Treasury regulations, exempt classes, 283; right of transit, 289; treatment of exhibitors at Louisiana Purchase Exposition, 290; increasing stringency and protest from Chinese government, 296.
Treaties of *1844*, *1858*, 146.
Treaty, Supplementary, *1894*, draft sent to Senate, 236; opposition, 236; provisions, 236; points gained by Chinese, 237; incessant protest a result, 238; denounced by Chinese Minister (*1904*), 251.
Treaty obligations demanded by U. S. government, 463; violated by U. S. government, 468.
Treaty of *1880*, negotiated by American and Chinese Commissioners, 152; final form, 160; discussion of disputed phrases, 164; interpretation regarding indemnity, 273.
Treaty of *1888*, signed by plenipotentiaries, 193; ratification refused by Chinese government, 197; Scott Act introduced and signed, 197; *see also* Burlingame Treaty.

Trescot, W. H., 153.
Triad Society, 407.
Truckee, Riot at, (*1878*), 266.
Tseng Shao-Ching, 480.
Tsiu Kwo Yin, 203, 205, 222, 224, 225.
Tsung-li-Yamen, and a treaty project (*1887*), 191; proposals made therein, 192, 194; Sec. Bayard's attitude toward Chinese government, 192; treaty signed by plenipotentiaries, 193; China refuses to ratify and Scott Act introduced into the House, 197; protest against Geary law, 222.
Tung Wah hospital committee and prostitution, 419.
Turner, Thomas F., report on cigar trade (*1900*), 369.

U. S. Commerce and Labor, Bureau of, immigration service transferred to, 279.
U. S. Immigration, Commissioner-General of, and exclusion laws, 239, 279; controls Chinese immigration, 240, 279; *see also* U. S. Commerce and Labor, Bureau of.
U. S. Labor, Bureau of, First Annual report on Shoe industry (*1893*), 363; *see also* State Horticultural Society; Wright's Bulletin.
U. S. Mining statistics, Commissioner of, (R. W. Raymond), report (*1871*), 39.

Vest, G. G. Senator, 177, 217.
Vigilance committee (*1856*), 25, 61; (*1877*), 115.

Wage scale (*1870–'90*), 354.
Wages, era of high, 339; before *1867*, 343; during *1865–'74*, 347, 352; *1876–'80*, 380; of women, 350; effect of Chinese on, 355; standard set by Eastern competition, 375; comparative, 385, 387.
Whampoa, non-treaty port, 45, 47.
White, Edward D., Senator, 231.
White Labor league, 367.
Williams, John S., Senator, 128.
Willis, A. S., 134, 135, 176.
Wilson, Ephraim K., Senator, 97, 107, 199.

Index. 531

Wolf, Simon, his convincing testimony against exclusion laws, 247.
Women, Chinese, treatment of, 10, 11, 420; part in emigration, 18; statistics of California Senate Address and Memorial concerning, 86; its statements concerning crime, 87; competition in trades, 102; wages (*1868–'69*), 348, 350; social and domestic life in America, 437, 440; operation of Exclusion law, 439; *see also* Cigar industry; Competition; Exclusion laws; Intermarriage; Prostitution; Quong Tuck Tong; Sewing trades; Shoe industry; Triad Society; Woolen industry.
Women physicians in Chinatown, 437.
Woolen industry, census (*1870*) statistics, 359; establishment and growth, 371; scale of wages, 372; investigated by California Bureau of labor (*1890*), 374; causes of decline, 375.
Workingmen's party, organized (*1877*), 115, 131; fusion ticket and reform programme, 118; organized opposition to Chinese, 119; reaction against radical measures, 122; demands abrogation of Burlingame Treaty, 150; *see also* Kearneyism.
Wright's Bulletin (*1870–'90*), 354.
Wu Ting-Fang, Minister, interpretation of Treaty of *1880*, 166; pro-Chinese reaction, 241 *note*; presents Chinese question to Sec. Hay, 241; adverse criticisms of exclusion law, 282; definition of "laboring" classes, 282; and of "student" classes, 284, 286, 287; *also* 320.

Yamen, *see* Tsung-li-Yamen.
Yee Ah Lum, 295.
Yeung Wo Society, *see* Six Companies.
Young, John Russell, Minister, 49.
Young's special report on wages (*1874*), 352, 358 *note*, 366, 372; *see also* Shoe industry; Cigar industry; Woolen industry.
Yuan Shih K'ai, 472.

www.ingramcontent.com/pod-product-compliance
Lightning Source LLC
Chambersburg PA
CBHW031424160426
43195CB00010BB/603